ENTREPRENEURSHIP AND SMALL FIRMS

3RD EDITION

ENTREPRENEURSHIP AND SMALL FIRMS

3RD EDITION

David Deakins and Mark Freel

London Boston Burr Ridge, IL Dubuque, IA Madison, WI New York San Francisco St. Louis
Bangkok Bogotá Caracas Kuala Lumpur Lisbon Madrid Mexico City Milan Montreal New Delhi
Santiago Seoul Singapore Sydney Taipei Toronto

Entrepreneurship and Small Firms Third Edition
David Deakins and Mark Freel
0-07-709993-1

Published by McGraw-Hill Education
Shoppenhangers Road
Maidenhead
Berkshire
SL6 2QL
Telephone: 44 (0) 1628 502 500
Fax: 44 (0) 1628 770 224
Website: www.mcgraw-hill.co.uk

British Library Cataloguing in Publication Data
A catalogue record for this book is available from the British Library

Library of Congress Cataloguing in Publication Data
The Library of Congress data for this book has been applied for from the Library of Congress

Acquisitions Editor: Tracey Alcock
Editorial Assistant: Nicola Wimpory
Senior Marketing Manager: Petra Skytte
Production Editor: Eleanor Hayes
New Media Developer: Doug Greenwood

Cover design by Ego Creative
Text design by InPerspective
Typeset by YHT Ltd, London
Printed and bound in the UK by Bell and Bain Ltd, Glasgow

ISBN 0-07-709993-1

BRIEF CONTENTS

DETAILED CONTENTS

PREFACE

The third edition has been completely revised to take account of new developments in entrepreneurship and small firms. For example, readers will find a new chapter on *E-business, the Small Firm and the Knowledge-based Economy* that includes a discussion of the impact of the Internet and E-business and its importance for entrepreneurship; however, reference is made to the importance of the knowledge economy and the Internet throughout the text in a number of other chapters. Similarly, the increased importance of entrepreneurship in terms of the policy agenda for economic development is reflected in the revision of Chapters 2 and 9. In particular, Chapter 9 on *Enterprise Support and Government Policy* has been rewritten and includes a discussion of the UK Government's launch of the Small Business Service (SBS) in 2001. This launch was accompanied by a document that stated:

"The Government's goal is that the UK should, by 2005, be the best place in the world to start and grow a business.[1]" (p. 6)

The importance of such a goal reflects a Government policy that recognizes that to achieve economic growth in a modern economy depends on having the environmental conditions appropriate for the encouragement of entrepreneurship and small firm development. Recent Foresight publications[2] paint a picture of the UK in 10 years' time. Such future scenarios predict a UK economy where entrepreneurship, small firm development and self-employment are increasingly important as careers and as part of the economic and social fabric. These trends have led to talk of an 'entrepreneurial revolution' in the modern economy and this is taken up in Chapter 2. The increased importance of entrepreneurship in the policy agenda filters down to other areas such as education, the media, taxation changes, trading regulations, finance, bankruptcy legislation and a number of measures that affect all of us, whether we are directly concerned with entrepreneurship or not. For example, in the same document that accompanied the launch of the SBS,[1] the Government stated that:

"The Government's direct interaction with SMEs form part of the overall picture but they are by no means the whole story. People may be put off starting a business if the environment in schools, further and higher education is discouraging and there are no effective role models available . . . Media stereotypes of business may cumulatively be discouraging." (p. 7)

Thus such concerns with the environment and with the education system has resulted in other measures or areas of policy concern; for example, with the formal commercial banking system in the UK, and the relationships between bankers and small firms,[3] and with education initiatives.[4] We take account of such developments in a number of chapters as well as dealing with the implications of recent major changes in entrepreneurship and small firms in Chapters 2, 8 and 9.

The rewriting and revision of the text has provided an opportunity to incorporate new learning and pedagogical features. Learning outcomes are given at the start of each chapter; boxed illustrations, *Entrepreneurship in Action*, are provided throughout the text and *Think Points*, serving as review and discussion questions, are also incorporated to review material, to allow the reader to reflect upon material and develop alternative concepts. Opportunities are taken to link material and concepts from different chapters that will encourage the student to integrate different concepts and material. We have retained, but also revised, the entrepreneurial case study material. Some new case material has been added, for example in Chapters 1, 8 and 11, but we have retained in-depth case studies at the end of Chapters 3, 4 and 7. New case study material is also available in the student's online learning resource material to supplement the main case study material that is within the text. Suggested assignments are set on each chapter, some of which incorporate the additional material in the student online material. Finally, the reader should find that the references have been completely updated, reflecting recent changes and the policy agenda discussed briefly above, and also that the recommended reading has been updated and included at the end of each chapter.

The *Lecturer's Manual*, although a feature of the second edition containing additional material such as additional case studies and comments on using case material, did not incorporate tutor lecture material. With the third edition, we have separated additional and supplementary case material that is now in the student's online learning material. The *Lecturer's Manual* has now been rewritten by Margaret Fletcher, an experienced teacher and course designer, with lecture slides and additional material for tutors. Some comments are also included in the *Lecturer's Manual* on using the case material.

USING THE TEXT

The text is aimed at undergraduate and postgraduate students of entrepreneurship, enterprise, small firms and business venturing. Comments on using the text are provided for students and lecturers.

Students will find that the text has been designed to be read in digestible sections. Chapters are broken up with highlights, such as the Entrepreneurship in Action features and with the Think Points at the end of each section. The Think Points contain review questions and have been placed at the end of each identifiable section where some significant concepts and material have been covered. The Think Points do not treat each of these sections in isolation; rather, they try to get you to consider some of the implications raised in the previous section's material and attempt to get you to think further and perhaps link the material to other sections of the text in a different chapter. Hints are given to enable you to do this. Suggested answers to the review questions are provided in the student's online learning material. However, these are not meant to be prescriptive, but provide an indication of the ways to think about the questions set which may be in a discussion form.

The text is designed to cover entrepreneurial and small firm theory, concepts, evidence, policy and practice. It is designed to link these areas together. For example, discussion of entrepreneurial concepts is followed by practical mini-case examples or by a more detailed full case study; discussion of theoretical issues in small firm development or growth of small firms is followed by a discussion of evidence; discussion of new developments in the economy such as E-business is followed by some of the policy implications, policy measures and practical examples. You are encouraged to link these distinct elements together through the Think Points and suggested assignments. For example, you may be asked to relate entrepreneurial concepts to a practical case study.

The detailed case studies are all from real entrepreneurial cases. They are designed to take you to a decision point in the case study, to put you in the place of the entrepreneur. This may form part of a class group discussion in which you discuss different options that the entrepreneur(s) may take and give a recommended course of action. It is important to realize that there is ambiguity in entrepreneurial decision-making. An ability to recognize different options can be as important as the actual decision made. A number of options can be equally valid courses of action; in other words, there is not necessarily one right answer. For some detailed case studies there are further sections provided in the online student learning material and further information in the *Lecturer's Manual*.

While much of the material in this text is designed to enable you to understand entrepreneurship and small firm and enterprise development, to apply concepts, to understand case studies and to understand new policy developments, Chapter 12 also provides a guide to preparing for entrepreneurship through the coverage of research, design and writing of business plans. Of course, other chapters of the book also provide an opportunity to develop skills and to prepare for entrepreneurship through the discussion of case material and practical examples; but Chapter 12 focuses specifically on sources of information, research methods and the planning process. Throughout the text, we combine a focus on *understanding* with *doing* and a combination of enterprise skills should be developed if you use the review questions, material, case studies and assignments in the book throughout your course. These enterprise skills include problem-solving, creative thinking, research and information gathering, presentation and strategic planning. The value of developing these enterprise skills is that they are *transferable*, whatever career is undertaken. Increasingly employers are seeking graduates with transferable enterprise skills, graduates that can think entrepreneurially, be creative, innovative and communicate new ideas. We believe that this book will help you to develop those skills and apply them in different problem-solving situations, whether you decide to follow an entrepreneurial career or not. More important, research indicates that most entrepreneurial students do not wish to enter entrepreneurship when they graduate; rather, they intend to enter entrepreneurship or self-employment after a period of employment,[5] but having undertaken study of entrepreneurship and small firms they are better prepared for such a change of career.

Lecturers will able to use this text for undergraduate and postgraduate courses in entrepreneurship, small firms and enterprise. As discussed above, it combines concepts and theory with practical entrepreneurial case studies and examples. It also has policy-related sections, where these are relevant, so that the material is placed in the context of recent developments in entrepreneurship and economic development. As indicated above, additional case material and suggested answers to the student review questions are available to students through the online student learning material. A feature of the third edition is a completely revised *Lecturer's Manual*, written by Margaret Fletcher. This provides additional course lecture slides and material for teaching purposes that can be used in teaching alongside this text. The *Lecturer's Manual* also contains further information on using the case material in the text. Apart from these additional features, lecturers familiar with the second edition should find that we have rewritten the text to take account of new developments, new research and new policy initiatives in this area.

As described above, lecturers should find that the text contains new features to improve accessibility and use for students. It should be more refreshing and exciting for your students without losing the academic rigour that we believe is important to study in this area.

Other users should find that they are able to use this text for a variety of purposes; for example, for training courses for new entrepreneurs, for an understanding of new developments in entrepreneurship and for an appreciation of concepts applied to practical examples. We hope that the new text will continue to appeal and be of use to a large and varied audience including potential entrepreneurs, trainers, policy-makers and other users with an interest in entrepreneurship and small firms.

CONTENTS OF CHAPTERS

The first four chapters deal with entrepreneurship, its importance in a modern economy and the start-up process. The text introduces entrepreneurship through the main entrepreneurial concepts dealt with in Chapter 1. This chapter examines the three main contributing fields of study: the economic functional concepts, psychological characteristics and social-behavioural approaches. In this chapter we include a discussion of the importance of different entrepreneurial environments and include a section on women in enterprise. Chapter 1 contains brief mini-cases such as the Eco-Wall case. Chapter 2 covers the importance of entrepreneurial activity for the UK economy and economic development, including a review of the importance of small firms. Given the increased importance of entrepreneurship on the policy agenda, we consider whether we can talk of an 'entrepreneurial revolution'. A brief case example is included on Laskarina. Chapter 3 deals with issues in the business start-up process including different paradigms for this process with technology-based firms. Chapter 3 includes the first in-depth case study, on ACE Cleaning. Chapter 4 covers ethnic minority entrepreneurship. This chapter has been brought up to date and deals with this important area for the UK by including recent research. An in-depth case study is included at the end of the chapter, the Alternative Publishing case.

The next four chapters deal with raising finance, innovation and the knowledge economy. Chapter 5 covers general issues in finance, but focuses specifically on formal sources of debt finance – the commercial banks. As is the case throughout the text, the chapter combines concepts with evidence and the practical reality of dealing with the bank manager. Chapter 6, by Mark Freel, is a new chapter on venture capital. The chapter covers the process of raising venture capital as well as the main sources, including formal venture capital companies, business angels and corporate venture capital. Chapter 7, also by Mark Freel, is a new chapter on innovation and entrepreneurship. It combines concepts with evidence and deals with the role and advantages of small firms in the innovation process. The chapter includes the Aquamotive in-depth case study. Chapter 8 continues the theme of innovation with a new chapter written by Professor Keogh and Dr Galloway. The chapter covers the development of the knowledge economy and the role in this of the entrepreneur and the small firm. A section is included on the impact of the Internet on businesses and deals with how small firms can use the Internet to their advantage. A case study of an Internet business, inyourcity.com, is included in this chapter.

The next three chapters deal with enterprise support, policy, entrepreneurial growth and international entrepreneurship. Chapter 9 covers the enterprise support network that currently exists in the UK, including national and regional differences. It discusses recent articles that have questioned the value of enterprise support and discussed recent policy initiatives in this area. Chapter 10, by Mark Freel, covers the concepts and evidence on entrepreneurial growth. Concepts introduced include life cycle theories that are compared to practical examples and evidence. Chapter 11 covers globalization and international entrepreneurship. It covers the importance of globalization trends for entrepreneurial activity and small firms. The chapter contains a brief case study on Nallatech, written for the text by Tom Farrell.

Finally, Chapter 12, as indicated before, covers the preparation for business start-up through the topics of: sources of information, including the Internet; research and survey methods; secondary data; designing the business plan, writing the business plan and implementing and using business plans.

As discussed, the chapters are integrated throughout the text. The reader, whether student, lecturer, trainer or other user, is encouraged throughout the text to integrate different sections and where this is appropriate it is indicated in the text. Although sections and chapters can be read on their own, it is hoped that the new style adopted for this text encourages you to integrate different sections. We hope you find the new features helpful and enjoy using this text.

David Deakins
April 2002

REFERENCES

1. Small Business Service (2001) *Think Small First: Supporting Smaller Businesses in the UK: a challenge for the Government*, DTI, London.

2. Foresight Financial Services Panel SME Sub-Group (2001) *Financing the Enterprise Society*, DTI, London.

3. Bank of England (2001) *Finance for Small Firms: An Eighth Report*, Bank of England, London.

4. Enterprise Insight (2001) *Enterprise Insight*, DTI, London.

5. Steele, L. and Maden, P. (2001) *Expanding Entrepreneurship in a University*, Paisley Business School working paper no. 01/1, University of Paisley.

GUIDED TOUR

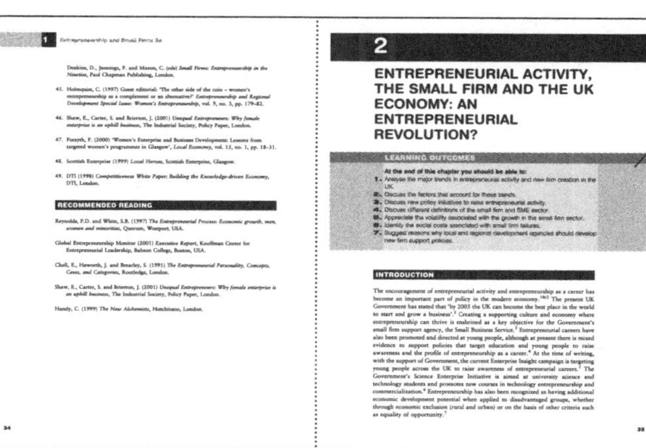

LEARNING OUTCOMES identify the abilities and skills the student should be able to demonstrate after reading the chapter.

ENTREPRENEURSHIP IN ACTION boxes provide practical examples demonstrating the application of concepts, followed by discussion questions to encourage students to analyse and discuss real world issues.

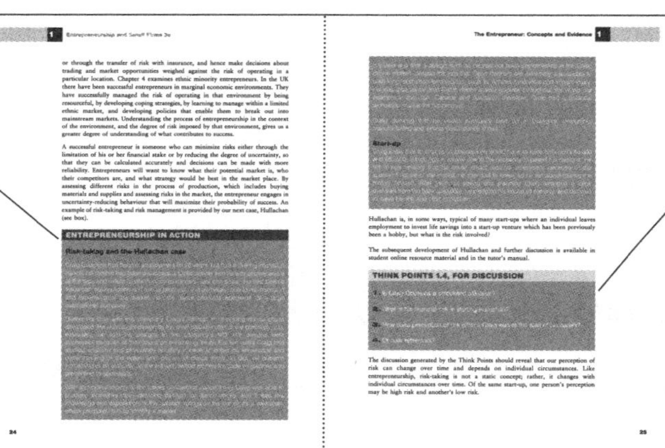

THINK POINTS are review and discussion questions placed after a significant concept or section, encouraging students to consider the topics raised and link the material to other sections. Suggested answers are included in the student's resources on the website.

CASE STUDIES provide up-to-date examples which give students the opportunity to apply what they have learnt to real life problems.

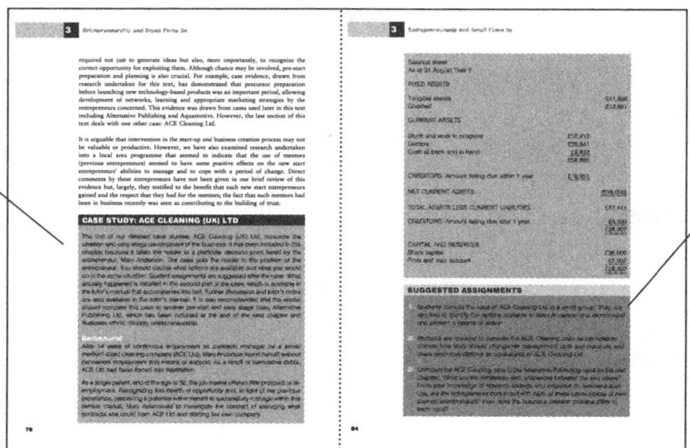

SUGGESTED ASSIGNMENTS provide tasks or discussions to reinforce the subjects covered and enable students to gain the most benefit from each chapter.

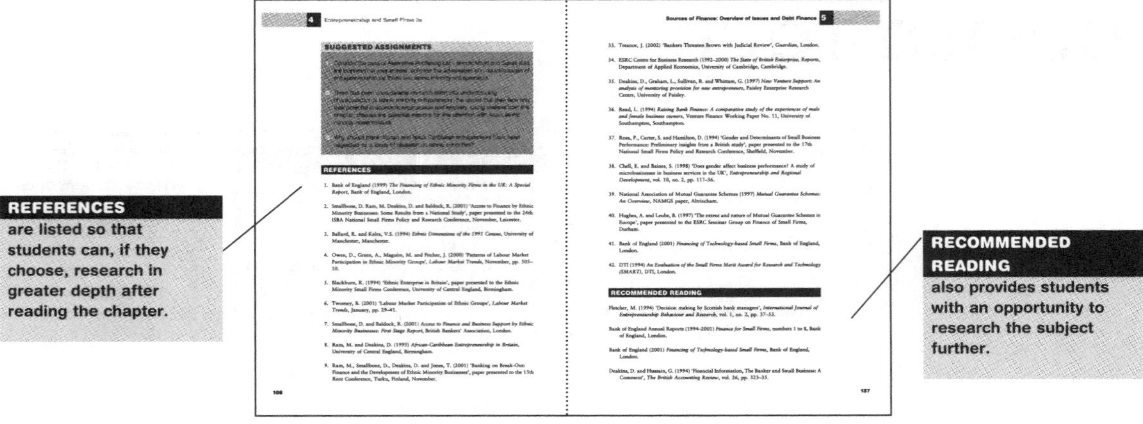

Teaching and Learning Resources

For this new edition we have updated the website which contains the following additional material free of charge.

Accessible by students

- **Chapter 11 from 2e**
- **Suggested answers to Think Points**
- **Quizzes/self-tests**
- **Additional case study material**
- **Learning outcomes**

Accessible by lecturers only

- **Instructor's manual**
- **PowerPoint slides**
- **Additional case studies**
- **Commentaries on case studies**
- **Teaching notes**

ACKNOWLEDGEMENTS

We would like to thank an anonymous reviewer for constructive comments on the first draft of the third edition. The comments have been influential in some of the features included in this text. Additional material has been included in further revisions of the text following constructive comments of other reviewers. Furthermore, we are deeply indebted to the generosity of the entrepreneurs featured in the case studies used in the text, for their time and patience while the material was being collected and, of course, we are grateful for their permission to use their experiences as case studies.

Finally, we would like to thank the following university experts who took the time and effort to take part in the market research. They have added enormously to the development of this text: David Walker, Birmingham University; Dean Patton, De Montford University, Leicester; Adrian Woods, Brunel University; Nick Theodorakopoulos, De Montford University, Leicester; Jane Mason, De Montford University, Leicester; Alistair Anderson, University of Aberdeen; Phil Morgan, Oxford Brookes University; Shaheena Janjuha Jivraj, Brunel University; Gilly Wiscarson, Oxford Brookes University; Peter Rosa, Stirling University; David Johnson, Durham University; Jan Brown, Liverpool Hope University College; Colin Souster, University of Luton; Stephen Ball, Sheffield Hallam University; Frank Martin, Stirling University; Michael Kennedy, Liverpool John Moores University; Helen Haugh, University of Aberdeen; Graham Hall, Manchester Business School.

We have endeavoured to clear all permissions for material produced in this book. However, if you are aware of any outstanding permissions please do not hesitate to contact us.

1

THE ENTREPRENEUR: CONCEPTS AND EVIDENCE

LEARNING OUTCOMES

At the end of this chapter you should be able to:

1. Describe the main theories and concepts of the entrepreneur.
2. Compare and contrast different theories and concepts of the role of the entrepreneur.
3. Discuss the application of these theories and concepts to attempts to research the personality of the entrepreneur.
4. Describe some of the problems and limitations of research into the personality of the entrepreneur.
5. Discuss some of the social and environmental factors that influence the extent of entrepreneurship.
6. Distinguish between personality of owners and the management skills of small firm owner-managers and discuss the importance of the distinction between ownership and management of a small firm.

INTRODUCTION

- **What makes an entrepreneur or small business owner?**
- **Is an entrepreneur different from other individuals or can anyone be an entrepreneur, given sufficient resources?**
- **Can anyone set up in business or do you need to have special skills and characteristics?**

These are questions that have occupied researchers and theorists for some time; indeed, theories on what makes an entrepreneur date from the early Industrial Revolution. We will attempt to answer some of these questions later when we examine factors that can encourage successful new business creation and entrepreneurial success. However, it is useful to review the contribution of the major theorists on entrepreneurship first. It is only when these have been examined that we can understand the characteristics, traits and factors that researchers have sought to find in the modern entrepreneur. Later we question much of this research effort into the characteristics of the entrepreneur; it may, for example, be better to concentrate on the management skills and competencies that are required of business owners. Developing this theme, we consider research which examines the concept of risk management and the use of insurance by entrepreneurs.

This chapter will be concerned with three approaches to entrepreneurship, which are illustrated in Figure 1.1. The three approaches are associated with the following sources:

- **from the contributions of economic writers and theorists on the role of the entrepreneur in economic development and the application of economic theory;**
- **from the psychological trait approach on personality characteristics of the entrepreneur, which is examined critically later;**
- **a social-behavioural approach, which stresses the influence of the social environment as well as personality traits.**

Each approach is considered in this chapter, and it can be claimed that all three approaches have something to contribute to our understanding of the entrepreneurship process. However, it will be seen that the value of psychological and social approaches are more controversial. Indeed, there is some dispute over whether 'entrepreneurial' characteristics can be identified at all.

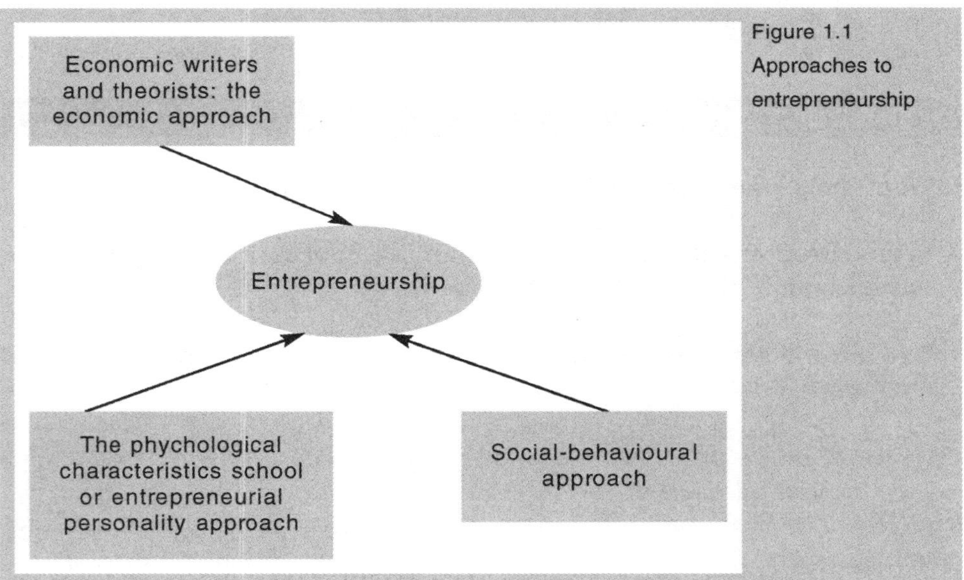

Figure 1.1 Approaches to entrepreneurship

There are many writers who have contributed to theories about the entrepreneur, but there is insufficient space here to consider more than the major contributors. For a detailed analysis of other theorists and contributors, the student is advised to consult the recommended reading at the end of this chapter.

THE ENTREPRENEUR

If we examine conventional economic theory, the term 'entrepreneur' is noticeable only by its absence. In mainstream or neoclassical economic theory, the entrepreneur can be viewed as someone who co-ordinates different factors of production, but the important distinction is that this role is viewed as a non-important one. The entrepreneur becomes merged with the capitalist employer, the owner-manager, who has the wealth to enable production to take place but otherwise does not contain any special attributes. The entrepreneur, if recognized at all, is a pure risk-taker, the reward being the ability to appropriate profits. It is a remarkable fact that the main body of conventional economic theory has developed without a place for the entrepreneur, yet there is no shortage of writers who have contributed to the development of views on the role and concept of the entrepreneur.

The idea that the entrepreneur has a significant role in economic development has been developed by writers outside mainstream economic thinking. Their contributions now have an important place, but it is only relatively recently that the importance of these contributions has been recognized. As attention has become more focused on the importance of the small and medium-sized enterprise (SME) sector for economic development and job creation, so greater attention has also been directed at theories of entrepreneurship. We examine the most important of these theories which are accepted today and they are summarized by their key insights in Table 1.1.

Writer	Key role of entrepreneur	Additional insights
Say	Organizer of factors of production	Catalyst for economic change
Cantillon	Organizer of factors of production	Catalyst for economic change
Kirzner	Ability to spot opportunity	Entrepreneur's key ability is 'creative' alertness
Schumpeter	Innovator	Entrepreneur as 'hero' figure
Knight	Risk-taker	Profit is reward for risk-taking
Casson	Organizer of resources	Key influence of the environment
Shackle	Creativity	Uncertainty creates opportunities for profit

Table 1.1 Key contributions of economic writers on the role of the entrepreneur

The term 'entrepreneur' is French in origin and a literal meaning might translate as 'one who takes between'. There are some important French writers who contributed views on the role of the entrepreneur, the most important being Cantillon and Say:

- **Cantillon was the first to recognize the crucial role of the entrepreneur in economic development, which was founded on individual property rights. Of the three classes in society recognized by Cantillon, entrepreneurs were the important class and were the central economic actors. The other two classes were landowners and workers or hirelings.**

- **Say also made the entrepreneur the pivot of the economy and a catalyst for economic change and development. The entrepreneur provided a commercial stage in three stages of production. In this way, the entrepreneur could be seen as close to the traditional mainstream view of the entrepreneur as someone willing to take the risk of bringing different factors of production together.**

Both Cantillon and Say belonged to a French school of thought known as the 'physiocrats', so called because the physical nature of the agrarian economy that dominated their thinking. It could be because of this view that developments in the concept of the entrepreneur were not seen as being relevant to the nineteenth-century industrial economy. It was much later that more modern concepts of the entrepreneur were developed. Some of these views have been developed within the 'Austrian school' of thought; however, this is such a wide-ranging term that there is not one particular view associated with this school for the entrepreneur. What is different, however, is that the entrepreneur is seen as being crucial to economic development and a catalyst for dynamic change. We turn now to these Austrian school writers who underpin many of the current theories of the entrepreneur and hence much of modern-day research into the characteristics of the entrepreneur.

Kirzner

For Kirzner, the entrepreneur is someone who is *alert* to profitable opportunities for exchange. Recognizing the possibilities for exchange enables the entrepreneur to benefit by acting as a 'middleman' who facilities the exchange. The Kirznerian entrepreneur is alert to opportunities for trade. He or she is able to identify suppliers and customers and act as the intermediary. Note that there is no necessity to own resources and that profit arises out of the intermediary function.

These possibilities for profitable exchange exist because of imperfect knowledge. The entrepreneur has some additional knowledge which is not possessed by others and this permits the entrepreneur to take advantage of profitable opportunities. The information is costless – it arises when someone notices an opportunity which may have been available all the time. It can often seem obvious after the service or product has been provided, but it still takes someone with additional knowledge to recognize and exploit the opportunity.

The role of information in the market place is important for the Kirznerian entrepreneur. Market exchange itself is an entrepreneurial process, but people can profit from exchange because of information gaps in the market. In this view, the entrepreneur may be seen as little more than a market trader, taking advantage of opportunities to trade; yet for Kirzner the entrepreneur is someone who is still creative. The possession of additional knowledge provides opportunities for creative discoveries. However, in contrast to the Schumpeterian view below, anyone could potentially possess the additional knowledge and be alert to opportunities for exchange and trade.

Schumpeter

By contrast, Schumpeter's entrepreneur is a special person. Although Schumpeter is a writer classified in the Austrian school, as shown by Table 1.1, his views on the entrepreneurial function are quite different from those of Kirzner.

The Schumpeterian entrepreneur is an *innovator*. The entrepreneur brings about change through the introduction of new technological processes or products. For Kirzner, anyone has the potential to be an entrepreneur and they operate within set production constraints. For Schumpeter, only certain extraordinary people have the ability to be entrepreneurs and they bring about extraordinary events. The Schumpeterian entrepreneur changes technological possibilities and changes convention through innovative activity, and moves production constraints. He or she develops new technology, whereas the Kirznerian entrepreneur operates on opportunities that arise out of new technology.

Although the entrepreneur is again an important catalyst for economic change, the entrepreneur is essentially temporary for Schumpeter. Schumpeter predicted the demise of the function of the entrepreneur. Technological advance and change would be carried out by teams of workers and scientists operating in large organizations. This is because, for Schumpeter, large monopolistic firms have distinct advantages over small firms in the technological process.

THE INTERNET BOOM AND THE RELEVANCE OF SCHUMPETER

The recent dotcom 'boom and bust' situation bears comparison to Schumpeter's cycles of 'creative destruction'. In 1999 and 2000 explosive growth in the use of the Internet created opportunities for many dotcom enterprises and E-entrepreneurs, among the most famous being lastminute.com, established by Martha Lane-Fox and partner. The Internet technology had made new ways of trading possible and there was a rush of money from institutions and small shareholders into such new E-entrepreneurial firms at vastly inflated prices. At the height of the boom, lastminute.com shares were issued at a price of £3.20 and briefly reached £3.80. After the dotcom bubble burst around March 2000, the shares in such companies collapsed and many cased trading (such as boo.com), although lastminute.com still survives with a more realistic share price (in February 2002) of 40p. Schumpeter predicted that such new technology waves would occur from time to time in the economy but that the life of many such new entrepreneurs would be short-lived; in order to create change it was necessary to have creative destruction – brought by new technology – but out of this, new opportunities would be available. Such dotcom entrepreneurs could be seen to be innovative – they were pioneering new ways of trading, using new technology and, in some cases, revolutionised ways of trading (such as the low-cost airlines' ticketing policies and booking through the Internet).

For a full discussion of the implications of E-commerce, see Chapter 8.

The concept that large firms are more successful than small firms in new technology-based industries is more correctly attributable to Galbraith. However, this concept has come to be associated with Schumpeter, even though he was more concerned with the advantages of monopolistic market structure than firm size. The small firm entrepreneur faces considerable disadvantages in research and development (R&D); for example, R&D is expensive, it has long development times and teams of researchers are able to benefit by feeding off one another's ideas. If the entrepreneur is an innovator then this argument suggests that he or she will find it difficult to establish new small firms. Technological change is carried out by large firms. The entrepreneur may still exist in large firms and is sometimes termed an 'intrapreneur', an individual who is capable of initiating change in large firms.

The concept that the entrepreneur is someone who is different, someone who is an innovator, is important. Some writers have carried this forward to distinguish entrepreneurs (business owners who wish to develop and expand their businesses) from other small business owners who have no ambition to expand their business or who wish to remain merely self-employed. The essential distinguishing feature for such writers is that the entrepreneur is a Schumpeterian innovator, although here the term 'innovator' would be more loosely defined to include a person who wishes to manage change or initiate change in some way. For example, Curran and Stanworth[1] state that:

"Entrepreneurship, rigorously defined, refers to the creation of a new economic entity centred on a novel product or service or, at the very least, one which differs significantly from products or services offered elsewhere in the market." (p. 12)

Knight

The commonly held view of the entrepreneur as a calculated risk-taker comes close to the view of Knight. For Knight, the entrepreneur is an individual who is prepared to undertake risk and the reward – profit – is the return for bearing uncertainty (which is an uninsurable risk).

The opportunity for profit arises out of uncertainty surrounding change. If change is perfectly predictable then no opportunity for profit exists. The entrepreneur is someone who is prepared to undertake risk in an uncertain world.

Knight made an important distinction between risk and uncertainty. Risk exists when we have uncertain outcomes, but those outcomes can be predicted with a certain degree of probability. For example, the outcome that your car will be stolen or not stolen is uncertain, but the risk that your car will be stolen can be calculated with some degree of probability and this risk can be insured against. True uncertainty arises when the probability of outcomes cannot be calculated. Thus, anyone can set up in business, but that person cannot insure against business failure because that particular outcome cannot be predicted with any degree of probability.

The entrepreneur is someone who is willing to accept the remaining risk that cannot be transferred through insurance. This important distinction established by Knight has not so far been explored in small firms research. We include some research on risk management and insurance in a later section in this chapter; however, issues such as the extent to which the entrepreneur assesses, accepts and transfers risk have yet to be properly explored in research.

This distinction helps to distinguish a small firm manager from the entrepreneur/owner. One of the characteristics of entrepreneurs (following Knight) could be considered to be the responsibility for one's own actions. If a manager assumes this then he or she is performing some entrepreneurial functions. We can also use this distinction as a criticism of some research into entrepreneurship which concentrates solely on personality traits and ignores management skills.

These distinctions are unfortunately rarely discussed in the small firms literature. However, an exception is provided by Shailer.[2] For example, Shailer considers that:

“[The] entrepreneur is now a widely used term, with considerable contemporary diversity in meaning associated with the intended interests of its users . . . Owner-managers do not necessarily fit any of the current popular definitions of 'entrepreneur'.” (p. 34)

Shailer prefers to adopt the view of entrepreneurship as a process and refers to a stage of the firm when it is in owner-management. Again we have the important concept of management of the firm, the willingness to accept risks and responsibilities. If the firm grows, it is possible to transfer this entrepreneurial function but still retain part-ownership through the issue of shares. The manager, as opposed to the owner, now takes on the function of the entrepreneur. The fact that behaviour of the previous owner-entrepreneur is likely to alter has been established (theoretically) by writers such as Jensen and Meckling[3] by applying agency theory. The concept of the importance of small business management skills is also discussed by Ray.[4] He considers that the search for the prototype has been ill-conceived and considers that 'There is no empirical evidence or conceptual base to say much, if anything, about entrepreneurs and risk taking' (p. 347).

Ray considers that we should concentrate on the development of skills and how managers acquire them. These concepts are too frequently ignored and this entrepreneurial and learning process has not been adequately researched.

We could say, then, that the Knightian entrepreneur is anyone who is prepared to undertake the risk of setting up their own business. However, equally it could be any risk-taker (and this is a source of criticism). The entrepreneur is someone who has the confidence, and is venturesome enough, to make judgements about the uncertain future, and the reward for this is profit.

Shackle

Shackle's entrepreneur is someone who is creative and imaginative. Whereas Kirzner's entrepreneur perceives opportunities, Shackle's imagines opportunities. Everyone potentially has this creative ability, which is exercised in making choices.

The role of uncertainty and imperfect information is crucial for the view of the role of the entrepreneur by Shackle. Uncertainty gives rise to opportunities for certain individuals to imagine opportunities for profit. Shackle's entrepreneur is creative and original. The act of imagination is important for identifying the potential of opportunities. This potential is compared to resources available, which can lead to the decision to produce, hence the act of entrepreneurship. Shackle's creative entrepreneur indicates that *creativity* is an important element in the entrepreneurship process. However, how this creative process occurs, and the factors which might influence it, remain areas that are only just beginning to be explored. A host of factors will influence an individual's ability to be creative, including personal background, education and attitudes; but it is likely that such influences will combine to affect the extent to which that individual is *prepared* to recognize and exploit opportunities. It is only recently that *pre-entrepreneurial* experiences (including education, employment and learning) are beginning to be recognized as important influences on nascent (pre-start) entrepreneurs; Reynolds and White.[5] In fact, the neglect of the study of important influencing factors pre-start – or the process of nascent entrepreneurship – is surprising, given its potential importance for modern economies.[6]

Casson

Casson attempts to synthesize some of these entrepreneurial attributes and concepts that have been discussed with the major writers above. Casson recognizes that the entrepreneur will have different skills from others. These skills enable the entrepreneur to make judgements, to co-ordinate scarce resources. The entrepreneur makes judgemental decisions which involve the reallocation or organization of resources.

Casson emphasizes that entrepreneurs require command over resources if they are to back their judgements and that this is likely to imply that they will have personal wealth. Lack of capital would thus be a barrier to successful entrepreneurship.

Casson's view is closer to that of Knight than other writers. The entrepreneur operates within a set of technological conditions; by making difficult judgemental decisions they are able to enjoy the reward of profit (for bearing uninsurable risk). This enables the entrepreneur to co-ordinate demand and supply under uncertainty.

In Figure 1.2 the demand curve represents the return to each entrepreneur as their numbers increase and is part of a map of such curves. The supply curve of entrepreneurs depends on access to resources and thus depends on the local economy and environment. Casson's analysis attempts to explain why in some economies entrepreneurs can flourish, yet in others there are low participation rates for people who own their own businesses. For example, in the UK, the south-east has higher participation rates of people in small business ownership than the Midlands, which in turn has higher participation rates than Scotland. The low participation rates in Scotland have been partly attributed, for example, to low home ownership, which limits the amount of equity that a nascent entrepreneur might have to invest in a start-up firm.[7] Thus, Casson's point about the access to resources would appear to be an important one. The clear implication, when we examine such participation rates, is that the environment can be a more powerful influence than any predilection among the local population for entrepreneurship.

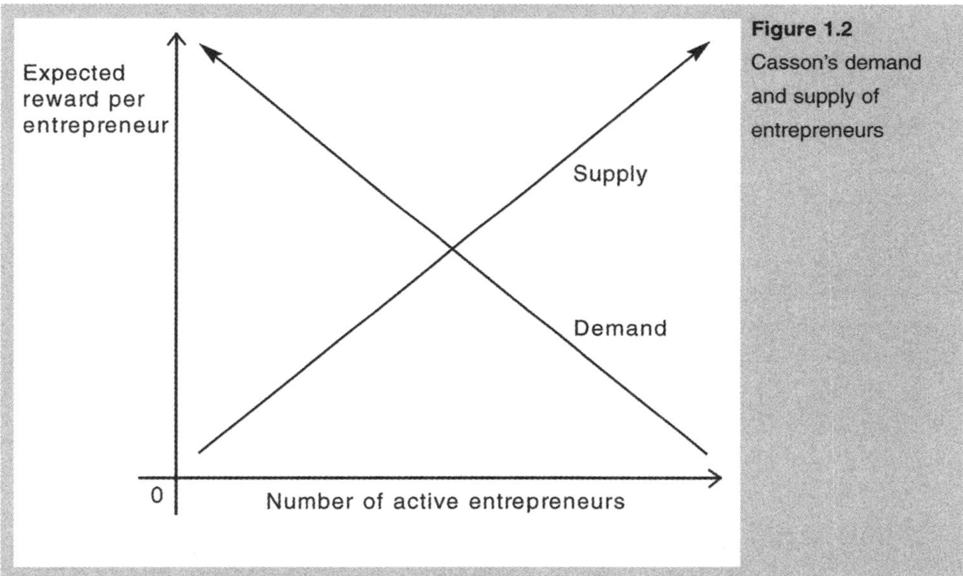

Figure 1.2 Casson's demand and supply of entrepreneurs

Casson's insight is to view change as an accompaniment to entrepreneurship. The pace of change provides opportunities and the entrepreneur chooses which one to back. Entrepreneurs can vie with each other as their numbers increase, the supply of entrepreneurs depending on their access to resources. The supply curve shown in Figure 1.2 will thus depend on the propensity of any given set of circumstances and the extent to which potential entrepreneurs have access to resources. This will depend on factors such as social mobility, and institutional factors such as the ability to access capital. An equilibrium position will result from the interaction of these factors, as shown in Figure 1.2.

A number of other economic writers and theorists have considered the development of the role of the entrepreneur. These include, for example, Thünen who could be seen as a forerunner of Knight. Thünen recognized the function of the entrepreneur as a risk-taker, involving risks that cannot be transferred through insurance, a theme which we will return to later in this chapter. For Thünen, however, the entrepreneur was also concerned with innovation and problem-solving.

It would be untrue to say that the neoclassical school of economists added little to the concept of the entrepreneur. For example, Marshall recognized a distinction between the capitalist and the entrepreneur through his 'undertaker', who was alert to opportunities but also innovative in devising new methods of production.

SUMMARY AND REVIEW

A consensus emerged that, in conditions of uncertainty and change, the entrepreneur is a key actor in the economy. The different views on the role of the entrepreneur are summarized in Table 1.1, but two major lines of thinking have developed: the Knightian approach which highlights the risk-bearing and uncertainty-reducing role of entrepreneurs; and the Schumpeterian approach in which the entrepreneur is an innovator.

Other perspectives highlight the knowledge and insight of the entrepreneur to new possibilities. This co-ordinating role has been devolped and emphasized by Casson, but in addition it is clear that there are other factors that influence participation in entrepreneurship, such as access to resources and facilities in the local environment. The entrepreneurial act of business creation is part of a process that will be the result of many historical factors as well as the opportunities arising from economic change, such as the example of the dotcom boom. As the pace of economic change increases, so opportunities increase; yet our understanding of the complete entrepreneurship process, and why participation rates (of different groups in society) are far from equitable, remains quite limited.

THINK POINTS 1.1

1. Contrast, and give examples of, the Schumpeterian view of the entrepreneur with that of Kirzner.

2. List the key contributions to our understanding of entrepreneurial abilities by each of the following:
   - Knight
   - Casson
   - Kirzner
   - Schumpeter

3. Why is the environment important to our understanding of differing participation rates in entrepreneurship?

4. How does Schumpeter help to explain the dotcom bubble of 1999–2000 and the subsequent fallout of failing dotcom entrepreneurs?

   Hint: see also Chapter 7.

We turn now to consider some of the empirical evidence on the factors that influence entrepreneurship. As we have suggested, much of research effort has gone into discovering personality traits of the entrepreneur; some of this literature is controversial, since some of it assumes that an entrepreneur must have some special ability that distinguishes him or her from other people. Unfortunately, this does not explain why there are low participation rates in entrepreneurship by women and by African-Caribbeans in the UK. As Ram[8] has pointed out, the Asian community has high rates of participation in small business ownership/entrepreneurship, yet this has more to do with negative factors of barriers to employment elsewhere than any predisposition for entrepreneurship.

Entrepreneurship: Participation Rates

The ideas and concepts surrounding the entrepreneur which have been outlined above are used as a basis by researchers for detecting traits in successful small business owners and entrepreneurs. As in any scientific method, theory can be used for developing hypotheses about the behaviour of successful entrepreneurs. These hypotheses are then tested against the observed characteristics of entrepreneurs and small business owners in the real world. However, there are a number of problems with this approach, among which is the assumption that additional factors affecting participation rates will be constant.

ENTREPRENEURIAL PARTICIPATION RATES VARY

1. Different participation rates in different regions.
2. Different participation rates by gender.
3. Active inter-firm networks vary by region.

1. Some regions are more favoured than others at establishing successful small businesses and entrepreneurs and hence their economic development is more successful. The question of whether this is due to characteristics in the population, or due to certain aspects of the environment and infrastructure which enable potential entrepreneurs to more easily exploit their skills and opportunities, remains, at this stage, an open one.

Research undertaken for Scottish Enterprise,[9] following concern with low participation rates in entrepreneurship, showed that a complex series of factors contributed to low participation rates in Scotland. For example, the historical dependence on a limited number of large employers, coupled with inward investment (North Sea oil), had produced a 'dependency culture', that is, people were used to depending on large firms for employment. Thus, the thought of going into business on their own account did not come easily to them. Other factors were found to be important as well, such as difficulties in accessing finance. Scottish Enterprise introduced a Business Birth Rate Strategy in 1993[10] with a raft of measures designed to improve access to environmental factors affecting entrepreneurship; after seven years a review of the strategy[11] concluded that a paradox existed, with improved environment and attitudes but still relatively low business birth rate figures, albeit with a slow improvement. This example shows that participation rates can vary in different geographical areas, but explanations of such spatial variations involve complex reasons.

2. Concern has been addressed at the existence of latent entrepreneurial talent. For example, why are there so few female successful entrepreneurs? In Scotland, a compilation and promotion of over 400 recent high-growth entrepreneurs (conducted by Scottish Enterprise[12] in an attempt to provide more role models that might influence possible or potential nascent entrepreneurs) contained only 16 per cent who were female entrepreneurs. Why is the participation rate of African-Caribbeans in entrepreneurship low? Again these remain open questions which appear to have no simple solution but, rather, are caused by a complex combination of social and economic reasons.

Little research has been conducted, specifically on these groups, in the UK, although a study carried out by Deakins and Ram[13] with African-Caribbean entrepreneurs suggests that motivations among this minority group, in the UK, consists of a combination of positive (pull) and negative (push) factors. Positive factors are associated with the attractions of entrepreneurship and negative factors are associated with limited opportunities in the inner-city and deprived urban environments.

3. Attention has focused on the role of networks in successful entrepreneurial development. For example, some research suggests that inter-firm networks contribute to successful entrepreneurship.

Official statistics indicate that a high proportion of new firms fail within three years of start-up. For example, in the UK, 30 per cent of new firms appear to cease trading by the third year and 50 per cent by the fifth year.[14] Official statistics need to be treated with caution and are likely to overstate the true failure rate; for example, a successful start-up firm may cease to exist when taken over by another firm; some business owners leave and re-enter self-employment, dependent on labour market conditions. However, it is accepted that there are only a small proportion of new firms that grow to employ 50 or more workers. One of the factors that might affect such limited numbers of high-growth firms is the potential loss of control faced by the entrepreneur as the firm grows. New small firms and entrepreneurs that are successful are predominantly located in the south-east in the UK, which suggests that the environment and infrastructure are at least as important as the characteristics of the entrepreneur. It is also likely that the development of inter-firm networks is more advanced in the south-east than in other regions of the UK.

The inter-organizational networks that link firms after they are established have been found to be important to the ongoing success of firms.[15] Efficient networks that foster good communications between firms contribute to entrepreneurial behaviour and success.

THE ENTREPRENEURIAL PERSONALITY

The second approach to entrepreneurship is to identify certain personality characteristics or 'traits' in individuals that appear to be possessed by successful entrepreneurs. The characteristics literature has been concerned with testing and applying some perceived characteristics in individuals. From this approach, it is possible to argue that the supply of potential entrepreneurs is limited to a finite number of people that have innate abilities, that have a set of characteristics that marks them out as special, and have particular insights not possessed by others. This has led to some controversy and, in terms of policy, it has significant implications. Obviously, if entrepreneurial characteristics are inherent then there is little to be gained from direct interventions to encourage new entrepreneurs to start new businesses, although interventions into improving the infrastructure or environment may still have an effect.

Some of these personality 'traits' are examined below, although, as will become apparent, the author does not accept the hypothesis that there is a limited supply of potential entrepreneurs. For example, many of the characteristics which are often said to be special to successful entrepreneurs are the same abilities and skills that could be applied to most successful managers and it is therefore difficult to separate out specific characteristics of entrepreneurs.

Some of this research stems from the original work carried out by McClelland,[16] who identified the historical role model influence of heroes on subsequent generations in that such influence induced a high need for achievement on the population of the subsequent generations. McClellend, however, is also associated with identifying the following key competencies of successful entrepreneurs:

PROPOSED KEY COMPETENCIES OF SUCCESSFUL ENTREPRENEURS

- Proactivity: initiative and assertiveness.
- Achievement orientation: ability to see and act on opportunities.
- Commitment to others.

Much has been made of the need for the achievement trait, as though this was the one characteristic that set potential budding entrepreneurs apart from others. An implicit assumption with this approach is that the individual bears responsibility for his or her lack of entrepreneurial activity and this proposition could be used by policy-makers, as discussed above, to divert interventions away from regions that have low rates of participation in small firm ownership.

Considering the work of writers on the entrepreneurship personality and those who might subscribe to the characteristics approach, we can identify certain key characteristics which have been identified in the literature as being important abilities of any entrepreneur.

THE ENTREPRENEURIAL PERSONALITY – KEY CHARACTERISTICS

- McClelland's need for achievement;
- calculated risk-taker;
- high internal locus of control;
- creativity;
- innovative;
- need for autonomy;
- ambiguity tolerance;
- vision.

Some writers subscribe to the view of McClelland – that the key characteristic is achievement motivation, or a high need for achievement, which can be described as a desire to excel, to achieve a goal in relation to a set of standards. High achievers are those that accept responsibility for decisions and for achieving solutions to problems, but standards will be set carefully so that they can be achieved. Satisfaction is gained from finding the solution to a problem rather than with monetary reward. Yet, partly because such a characteristic is difficult to measure, the evidence has proved to be contradictory. A high need for achievement can also be an important characteristic for success for people in many occupations, not just entrepreneurs.

Another characteristic that has been advocated is the locus of control. Individuals with a high locus of control like to be in charge of their environment and of their own destiny. Again, as with the need for achievement trait, it has not been possible to reconcile conflicting evidence with entrepreneurs with this approach to one or two important personality traits. For a critique of the characteristics literature, see Chell *et al.*[17] In a review of this approach, Delmar[18] comments that 'the [research] results have been poor and it has been difficult to attribute any specific traits to entrepreneurial behaviour' (p. 145).

A further example is provided by Meredith *et al.*[19] who give five core traits:

- **self-confidence;**
- **risk-taking activity;**
- **flexibility;**
- **need for achievement;**
- **strong desire to be independent.**

Perceived self-confidence or self-efficacy have been advocated by some writers as important concepts in entrepreneurship. High self-confidence in entrepreneurship translates into self-belief in one's capabilities to mobilize resources, motivate others and produce change (business start-up). Although there is some evidence that perceived self-efficacy is related to business performance,[18] as we have said above, researchers have been concerned with whether successful entrepreneurs display psychological traits which separate them out as individuals from others, and this approach can be criticized in a number of ways (see box).

CRITICISMS OF THE PERSONALITY CHARACTERISTICS APPROACH

- It is inappropriate to search for a significant single trait.
- It ignores environmental factors that may be more important than personality.
- It comprises an essentially static analysis approach to the dynamic process of entrepreneurship.
- It ignores the role of learning, preparation and serendipity in the process of entrepreneurship (these factors are discussed later in this chapter).

A more negative characteristic, that of the deviant (non-conformist) personality is associated with Kets de Vries.[20] The deviant personality is associated with the third approach to the entrepreneur, that of the social-behavioural school. A deviant character is associated with individuals who do not easily fit in with their existing employment, for instance someone who is out of place in a large firm. The non-conformist behaviour precipitates a desire to start their own business, rather than operate within the regulations of a large organization. However, this would seem to rule out the possibility of the dynamic employee wishing to create change in the large firm, the intrapreneur.

Writers such as Timmons[21] have attempted to summarize the personality characteristics of successful entrepreneurs and to categorize characteristics that can be acquired and those that are more innate. While Timmons does admit that many of these characteristics can be acquired, through learning or from experience, Timmons also considers that there are some attributes that cannot be acquired, which are innate, and perhaps mark out 'born entrepreneurs' from 'made entrepreneurs'.

Timmons considers that both need for achievement and locus of control can be acquired along with other leadership abilities and competencies, such as the ability to take responsibility for actions/decisions. Many of these characteristics are management skills. Entrepreneurs obviously need to be ambitious but need to be satisfied that they have achieved personal goals and ambitions.

We can assume that profit or monetary reward is not the only driving force behind entrepreneurs. There is also the need to build and achieve personally set goals, hence implying that entrepreneurs have a high need for achievement in order to establish a growing business or 'entrepreneurial' firm (this is discussed in more detail in Chapter 10). Similarly, the internal locus of control has been identified as an important characteristic of potential entrepreneurs. A high internal locus of control means that the person needs to be in control of their own environment, to be their own boss. Timmons considers that these characteristics can be acquired; many of these abilities can be taught or, at the very least, scenarios can be provided which stimulate the acquisition of these skills and abilities.

THINK POINTS 1.2

1. Suggest key personality characteristics associated with successful entrepreneurs.
2. Suggest additional key personality characteristics that may be required to be a successful entrepreneur (for example, consider the perseverance required to overcome the initial rejection of a new idea by funders).
3. Which of the personality characteristics you have listed in your answer to Question 1 could be acquired through learning?
4. Critically review the entrepreneurial personality approach with a series of bullet points.

Dealing with Failure

Timmons considers that dealing with failure can be an important attribute of entrepreneurs. However, the ability to tolerate failure depends on the culture. In the USA, failure is viewed as a learning experience and people can benefit from failure, can learn from their experience and can go on to form successful companies as a result. In Britain, the culture is less tolerant of failure and, too often, highly talented individuals have not been able to recover from failure. The culture and environment is crucial to tolerance of failure. There is little doubt that Britain has lost many potentially successful entrepreneurs because, having failed once, they have not been allowed to recover from that failure, perhaps from an inability to raise capital following bankruptcy. Failure is a very valuable learning experience, as many entrepreneurs have admitted. It is a pity that, in Britain, new entrepreneurs are often not allowed a further opportunity so that they can benefit from their experience, apply lessons learned and build a successful business.

CASE STUDY

Lack of Support in Britain: The Eco-Wall Case, by Joe Wilson

Joe Wilson was a visionary entrepreneur who risked all his personal assets to develop a new building product that he knew was revolutionary but, having failed to get overseas orders, he was unable to recover or find support to develop the product further. He takes up the story:

Eco-wall was a revolutionary building product that had taken 10 years of development, but in seeking development capital, the typical response from both banks and equity capital institutions has been that:

"The business plan is excellent, the product is excellent but head office is not interested in investing in this sector at this time. However, come back with a firm order and we will consider the proposition again."

A request had been received by a partner company, Compton Garland, to develop the product for Stena-Sealink for the requirements for a new high-speed ferry. With Eco-Wall, Compton Garland undertook twelve months of design and testing, costing in the region of £75,000 in time, materials and expenses. A finally tested panelling system that surpassed the specifications, made even tighter by Stena as time went on, was developed and produced as a prototype. Eco-Wall contracted to supply the shipyard at a price they confirmed was highly competitive. Indeed, at a pre-contract meeting in Finland the company were asked to increase their square metre price to cover for eventualities.

The new product surpassed all tests that were required. For example, a fire test, required at very short notice, known as the cone calorimeter test, carried out by Warrington Fire Research, showed the product to perform 95 per cent better than the specification from the shipyard. In the specification provided by the shipyard to the company it was stated that:

"Due to the essential requirement for the lightweight materials for this type of vessel, the insulation and lining of the hull could be considered to be carried out by types of panels of composite materials, but the weight of the solution will be the main parameter when selecting the solution."

A lightweight yet fire-retardant material was still the driving force behind these continuing negotiations. This illustrates how political decisions to use local suppliers will not necessarily work in areas where product development is led by technological advances and the feasibility of technical solutions.

At meetings with the company and Stena's naval architect and the head of interior design for the shipyard in the third quarter of 1993, it was stressed by both the client and contractor, and minuted, that the innovative solution being offered would not reflect on the choice of supplier for the contract. Both Stena and Finnyards stated that the problem that they were trying to resolve needed a technically innovative solution and that Stena, being innovators themselves, were very keen to promote such solutions.

The Outcome

After written confirmation to both the client and the shipyard that the product could be delivered 16 per cent below the specified weight and 95 per cent better than the toxicity and contribution to fire requirements and at a further reduced price, the company were informed that the contract had been awarded to a company familiar to the shipyard who had used them before but at a specification that had not been proven by testing.

The shipyard asked whether the company would be interested in providing technical solutions in small crucial areas of the vessel which their selected subcontractor was not able to meet. Eco-Wall Ltd successfully overcame technical system problems in the latter twelve-month development period and provided a commercial solution yet were defeated by a political decision

Four months after being informed that the supply contract had been awarded to a local firm, Eco-Wall were told by Stena that the local firm had not met their technical specifications and that they had informed the shipyard that a reduction in specification was not acceptable. Subsequently negotiations have reopened with the shipyard for the supply of the contract. I am assured that the publication of this case study had no bearing on the decision by Stena to insist on the local company meeting the technical specification laid down at the commencement of the bidding for the contract.

Postscript

Despite continued negotiations with Stena, Eco-Wall, as a company, was forced into liquidation by its creditors, specifically the bank. The product has since been developed for general application in the construction industry but the pioneering entrepreneur with the vision to develop the product for 10 years was forced to accept failure of his company, Eco-Wall, and as yet has received no financial benefit from the development.

THINK POINTS 1.3, FOR DISCUSSION

1. Can innovative entrepreneurs be successful with new technology in the UK?
2. The UK is a world leader in technical innovation but continues to suffer from low investment and low technology application. How can we break into the virtuous circle of high investment and high technology?
3. 'Technical innovation in the UK is both a minefield and a recipe for financial disaster for individuals and firms involved with it.' Discuss.

In practice, many of the entrepreneurial characteristics are those associated with any successful manager or indeed with any successful individual. It is therefore difficult to justify a separate set of characteristics for a successful career in entrepreneurship.

Timmons also gives additional attributes which are more innate. These are listed as:

- **high energy coupled with emotional stability;**
- **creative and innovative ability;**
- **conceptual ability;**
- **vision combined with a capacity to inspire.**

Although it may be claimed that this set of characteristics is more innate in terms of identifying people who are potential entrepreneurs, it is difficult to justify that these abilities mark people out for entrepreneurship. It also does not mean that they cannot be acquired. By the use of planning scenarios and problem-solving it is still possible to demonstrate how opportunities can be exploited, how resources can be acquired and how creative solutions can be developed.

Some institutions and writers have attempted to develop tests of potential entrepreneurial ability or enterprise. Caird, for example, has developed a measure of enterprising traits (or entrepreneurial abilities) called the General Enterprise Tendency (GET),[22] as used by the Durham Business School. It consists of a scale of different questions within the following categories:

- **12 questions which measure need for achievement;**
- **12 which assess internal locus of control;**
- **12 to determine creative tendency;**
- **12 to gauge calculated risk-taking;**

- **6 to measure need for autonomy.**

Entrepreneurial or enterprise tendency tests, however, suffer from the same limitations as the characteristics approach. Not surprisingly, these tests have been found not to be consistent in their application or selection. However, more recent work at Durham, carried out by Johnson and Suet Fan Ma,[23] with an expanded scaled test with nine dimensions, appears to claim more promising results as an enterprise tendency test.

Problems arise whenever attempts are made to measure these characteristics. For example:

- **Characteristics are not stable and change over time.**
- **In many cases they are subjective judgements that do not lend themselves to objective measurement. For example, how do we define being innovative? It can simply be the ability to deal with change and the ability to cope with new processes and solutions. How do we measure the calculated risk-taker? In many respects there are unsatisfactory definitions of these concepts, which makes their measurement difficult to justify.**
- **Concentrating on personality characteristics means that we are in danger of ignoring environmental and cultural influences which can be just as, if not more, important than any set of personality traits.**
- **Placing too much importance on an inherent set of personality characteristics reduces the role of education and training. Learning is a very valuable process that allows potential entrepreneurs to acquire skills, to develop methods of business planning. While we would agree that many people are not suited to entrepreneurship, there is still much that can be learned and acquired by potential entrepreneurs, and this process is far from understood.**

There is a danger that these approaches can influence and dominate approaches to small firm ownership and entrepreneurship, so that important influences on entrepreneurship, such as quality of the infrastructure provided in the environment, are ignored. There are a number of problems with these approaches, which have been mentioned above, and they include ignoring issues such as gender, age, social class and education, all of which can have a bearing on the propensity of an individual to enter entrepreneurship.

The Ability to Learn

Much research effort has gone into identifying entrepreneurial characteristics and it has diverted research effort away from important areas concerning the entrepreneur's ability to learn from problem solving and to gain from their business experience. We do not understand how entrepreneurs learn, yet it is accepted that there is a learning experience from merely establishing a new enterprise. The learning process that is involved in business and enterprise development is poorly understood, yet programmes have been designed and interventions are made in business development. The problem with these interventions (at least in the past) is that they were often task-oriented. They were built around particular tasks and skills in terms of business planning; for example, on bookkeeping or financial skills, on liquidity or controlling for debt. As such, they concentrated on specific tasks of running a business. A failing of such interventions is that they do little to alter the approach of the entrepreneur to solving business problems and learning from dealing with those problems. However, in recent years, in the UK, there has been evidence of the introduction of more mentoring-style assistance. Overall, though, it is not surprising that Storey and Westhead,[24] from a survey of the literature, found that there was little evidence of a link between formal training and improved performance of small firms, indicating that formal personal management development and training of the entrepreneur appears, paradoxically, to have no impact on improved performance. Gibb,[25] however, proposes that development of the entrepreneur is affected by the extent of interaction with 'stakeholders' in the small firm environment (for example, customers, bankers, creditors and supply chain relationships), thus implying that intervening to improve learning from interaction and experience should improve entrepreneurial ability and performance. According to Gibb:

“Learning better from experience implies bringing knowledge, skills, values and attitudes together to interact upon the learning process; it therefore fundamentally demands an action-learning approach.” (p. 16)

Gibb's 'stakeholder' model of entrepreneurial learning places importance on the small firm relationships with the external environment. This can be contrasted with an alternative approach based on an evolutionary theory of learning and entrepreneurial behaviour. Drawing on evolutionary theories, Costello,[26] for example, has shown that, with high-technology small firms, entrepreneurs learn to adapt behaviour into 'routines' that enable knowledge to be acquired and it is the routine (a set of rules) that enables learning to evolve. This, however, also implies that such learning becomes 'path dependent',[27] taking a critical event to change a routine.

Entrepreneurs who become task-oriented are those that are more likely to fail. Entrepreneurship involves a learning process, an ability to cope with problems and to learn from those problems. An ability to recognize why problems occur and be able to deal with them, and, more importantly, understand why they occur, will ensure that the entrepreneur will be able not only to deal with those problems, but also to learn from the experience and ensure that processes are put in place within the firm to ensure that either the problem does not occur again or that the firm can deal with the problem. As shown in Figure 1.3, this ability to learn from experiences involves the concept of double-loop learning,[28] a process which involves examining

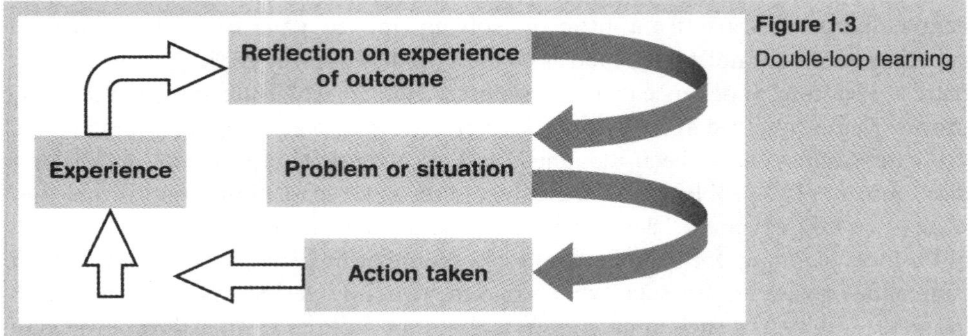

Figure 1.3
Double-loop learning

why the problem occurred and to learn from that process. It is a process of learning 'how to learn'.

Our limited knowledge and understanding of the interaction of learning and the entrepreneurship process remains one of the neglected areas of entrepreneurial research and, thus, understanding. This is surprising, given the attention that has been paid to areas such as 'the learning organization'. Case studies of the features of learning organizations have been developed in some detail,[29] yet little equivalent research has been undertaken within small firms, partly because of the lack of appropriate ethnographic and case study approaches that are capable of revealing the complex and often subtle mix of factors that will affect entrepreneurial learning. At the same time, we need developments of theories and concepts that are appropriate to entrepreneurship. Learning organization concepts are derived from large organizations; more promising are developments in evolutionary approaches to learning and the entrepreneur, as discussed above. In part, these stem from a Schumpeterian dynamics analysis of the forces of change and attempt to explain how the entrepreneur can adapt, change and thus learn from dealing with uncertainty.[30] The interaction between learning and the entrepreneurship process has been highlighted by Levinthal,[31] who stresses the adaptive role of the entrepreneur as they adjust to their environment, to their learning experience and, as a result, change behaviour. The nature of learning may follow a trial and error and discovery activity; that is, entrepreneurial behaviour becomes adapted in an evolutionary way to the discovery of information from trial and error. It is suggested that such evolutionary theories may be able to model the nature of entrepreneurial behaviour and development, although there is a need for further work in this area.

The ability of the entrepreneur, or entrepreneurial team, to learn is crucial to their behaviour and ability to succeed. To be successful, entrepreneurs must be able to learn from decisions, from mistakes, from experience and from their networks. It is a process that is characterized by significant and critical *learning events*. To be able to maximize knowledge as a result of experiencing these learning events will determine how successful their firm eventually becomes. There seems little doubt that there are methods of enhancing the learning activity, such as the careful choice of an entrepreneurial team with complementary skills. We have suggested, however, that at present there is a need for further theoretical development, which will help to guide policy-makers and, thus, interventions. Entrepreneurial behaviour is a dynamic response to a constantly changing environment. Large firm organizational theory does not capture the dynamics of learning in such an environment. Approaches that attempt to model the nature of such dynamic interaction stem from a Schumpeterian dynamic modelling of entrepreneurial response to their experience.

The author's view is that both these dichotomous approaches to entrepreneurial learning (as represented by Gibb and Costello) have something to offer in understanding the nature of entrepreneurial learning. The author has suggested that entrepreneurial learning occurs as a result of a combination of the processes involved in these two approaches.[32] The important contribution of these theories is that entrepreneurial behaviour is a dynamic process, where the entrepreneur learns to adjust decision-making, and consequently we cannot view the ability of the entrepreneur as something that is static; rather, it is continually evolving.

Risk Management

In this section we return to Knight's concepts of risk and uncertainty and of the entrepreneur as risk-taker and manager. It has sometimes been expressed that an entrepreneur is a risk-taker but 'not a gambler'; that is, that they will take calculated risks, not gambles (which are seen as uncalculated risks). However, a gambler can just as easily be described as someone who does take calculated risks – a gambler knows the odds against winning, has calculated the chances of beating those odds and hence takes a calculated risk with a financial stake. It is possible to argue that there is little difference between this approach and that of the entrepreneur who has made a calculated risk by putting up a financial stake and has worked out the odds against success. We can describe first attempts to enter business, by definition, as a form of calculated gamble. The entrepreneur can minimize those risks but there is always an element of luck, of right timing. There are always things that can go wrong – after all, the entrepreneur is dealing with uncertainty. This is the key insight of Knight, that the entrepreneur is dealing with uncertainty and takes risks that can be calculated.

It is more helpful to see the entrepreneur as a risk manager, as this identifies one of the key concepts to understanding the process of entrepreneurship. In dealing with uncertainty, the entrepreneur has to identify, assess, evaluate, manage and transfer risk. Knight saw risk as a subset of uncertainty. Events which are truly uncertain cannot be predicted with any degree of probability. However, most events are risky; their chance of occurrence can be predicted with a degree of probability. Some events have a greater degree of probability of occurrence than others. For example, insurance premiums in the inner city are high because the probability of damage to premises is higher than in other locations. A successful entrepreneur is someone who is able to identify, assess and evaluate the importance of the risk, say, of trading in the inner city. They are able to manage this risk either through preventive measures or through the transfer of risk with insurance, and hence make decisions about trading and market opportunities weighed against the risk of operating in a particular location. Chapter 4 examines ethnic minority entrepreneurs. In the UK there have been successful entrepreneurs in marginal economic environments. They have successfully managed the risk of operating in that environment by being resourceful, by developing coping strategies, by learning to manage within a limited ethnic market, and developing policies that enable them to break out into mainstream markets. Understanding the process of entrepreneurship in the context of the environment, and the degree of risk imposed by that environment, gives us a greater degree of understanding of what contributes to success.

A successful entrepreneur is someone who can minimize risks either through the limitation of his or her financial stake or by reducing the degree of uncertainty, so that they can be calculated accurately and decisions can be made with more reliability. Entrepreneurs will want to know what their potential market is, who their competitors are, and what strategy would be best in the market place. By assessing different risks in the process of production, which includes buying materials and supplies and assessing risks in the market, the entrepreneur engages in uncertainty-reducing behaviour that will maximize their probability of success. An example of risk-taking and risk management is provided by our next case, Hullachan (see box).

ENTREPRENEURSHIP IN ACTION

Risk-taking and the Hullachan case

Craig Coussins had been in employment for 20 years, but had a lifelong interest in dance; his mother had been a successful Celtic dancer and he was acutely aware of the type and extent to which injury to dancers' feet can occur. He had been a salesman, selling sports and dance products, and ultimately, due to his interest in and experience of the market, he sold dance products worldwide for a large international company.

During his time with this company Craig's interest in designing dance shoes developed. He was taught design by the chief pattern-cutter of the company and, eventually, he sold his designs to the company's MD. His designs were successful because of their focus on minimizing injury. For ten years Craig had studied anatomy and physiology privately in order to better his knowledge and understanding of the nature and causes of dance injury; in fact, he became something of an authority on the subject, writing articles for trade magazines and presenting to specialists.

With an understanding of the issues concerning dance injury Craig was able to produce innovative injury-reducing designs for dance shoes, and it was this knowledge and experience of the subject, alongside his career as a salesman, which prompted him to identify a market.

His view was that a design such as his had not been implemented in the Celtic dance market, despite the fact that Celtic dancers are extremely susceptible to both long- and short-term injuries, such as Achilles tendonitis and impact injury. He was also aware that Celtic dance is very popular throughout the world (for example in the USA, Canada and Australia); therefore, Craig had a potential worldwide market for his product.

Craig decided that he would eventually start up in business, designing, manufacturing and selling Celtic dance shoes.

Start-up

Craig knew that to start up in business he would have to raise between £40,000 and £50,000; a high figure, mainly due to the necessity to patent his designs. He felt it was unlikely that he could attract external investment because of the specialist nature of the market he intended to enter, so he set about raising the money himself. After years of saving and planning Craig arranged a large overdraft from the bank (£50,000), by pledging his house as security, and decided to leave his job and start Hullachan.

Hullachan is, in some ways, typical of many start-ups where an individual leaves employment to invest life savings into a start-up venture which has been previously been a hobby, but what is the risk involved?

The subsequent development of Hullachan and further discussion is available in student online resource material and in the tutor's manual.

THINK POINTS 1.4, FOR DISCUSSION

1. Is Craig Coussins a calculated risk-taker?
2. What is his financial risk in starting Hullachan?
3. How does perception of risk differ if Craig was at the start of his career?
4. Or near retirement?

The discussion generated by the Think Points should reveal that our perception of risk can change over time and depends on individual circumstances. Like entrepreneurship, risk-taking is not a static concept; rather, it changes with individual circumstances over time. Of the same start-up, one person's perception may be high risk and another's low risk.

Risk management and the use of insurance

Although Knight identified the importance of risk-taking, the entrepreneur needs to be able to assess which risks to accept and which risks to transfer. In this process, the entrepreneur may decide to accept some risk, reduce risk through risk management, or transfer risk through insurance. As indicated before, however, we know little of the extent to which an entrepreneur attempts to perform this function.

The availability of insurance is important because it enables the entrepreneur to transfer risk instead of accepting the full risk liability. For example, in the case of Hullachan, Craig Coussins, with a manufacturing concern, was faced with a number of risks that can prevent the business operating successfully. These included theft of stocks, fire, damage to vehicles through motor accidents, personal injury from the product and injury to employees and visitors on company premises. All of these risks can easily be transferred through insurance policies and, in some cases, such insurance is compulsory, for example employer's liability. Some risks, of course, are not transferable. The risk of making losses cannot be transferred through any insurance policy, although it is possible to transfer subsequential losses from some other risk, such as fire. In addition, the management of risk can reduce the extent of insurance needed, and risk can also be reduced by taking a number of measures that prevent the possibility of accidents. For example, special training for employees in health and safety may reduce the risk of employee accidents and hence reduce the amount of insurance premium required by the insurance company.

Some firms are faced with more risks than others. For example, Hullachan represents a case where risks are relatively high due to manufacturing a product where risks may exist in the product process (to employees and to customers); manufacturing small firms face greater risks than service sector firms. They may have product liability risks and, if their product is protected by a patent, they face the risk that another firm could copy their product, thus incurring expensive legal action to defend their patent.

The extent to which entrepreneurs undertake both risk management and the transfer of risks through insurance is largely unknown, yet the ability to manage risk (of which insurance is part) is an important subset of management skills for small firm survival. Previous research in the West Midlands and Scotland provide comparisons in the use of insurance by technology-based firms.[33] The evidence suggested that the use of more specialized insurance is low, with only 8 per cent and 9 per cent (West Midlands/Scotland) of firms taking out cover for the protection of patents and copyright. The low take-up of patent protection may reflect a low application rate of high-technology-based and innovative entrepreneurs to take out patents, which are time-consuming, relatively complicated and expensive. Follow-up research in Scotland indicated that 38 per cent of firms were concerned with acquiring patents, which would suggest that the low take-up rates of cover are due to difficulties in the insurance environment. In the case of Hullachan, it was important for Craig Coussins to lodge applications for patents for his designs, but he did not take out patent insurance.

A follow-up study by Bentley and Sparrow,[34] focusing on technology-based entrepreneurs and their perception of risks, revealed that the low take-up of some forms of insurance was due to 'cost reasons' in relation to overall risks, with high premiums for specialized insurance accounting for low take-up rates. The study by Bentley and Sparrow recommended that more attention should be given to the education of entrepreneurs in risk management, a potential area of intervention for support agencies. Clink[35] has suggested that small firms' approach to risk management can be segmented through a typology related to the proactiveness of planning and risk control within the firm, which may provide a framework for further analysis and support.

Further discussions with the insurance industry and small firm representatives, such as the Federation of Small Businesses (FSB), indicated that risk management and the use of insurance was an important topic that suffered from a low profile in research. A paper by the FSB[36] indicated that insurance was seen as a particular problem by its members, especially in the inner city, where the difficulties in obtaining adequate insurance cover were seen as a significant constraint in small firm entrepreneurship start-up and development. For example, insurance premiums in these areas are expensive, yet risk management measures were difficult to impose due to local authority restrictions on the extent of security provisions.

Women and Entrepreneurship

Although data show that the activity rates of women in business are much lower than those of men, in practice there is little doubt that participation rates are much higher because of 'hidden' entrepreneurial activity. For example, women are often supporting partners behind a spouse's business, taking critical decisions and providing advice. In the UK, self-employment data suggest that 7 per cent of women in employment are either self-employed or run their own business. In practice, actual participation rates are likely to be considerably higher. This compares to a figure of 17 per cent for men;[37] furthermore, these figures have remained remarkably consistent throughout the 1990s. However, during the 1980s, in line with other activity rates for women, the participation rates of women increased at a faster rate than that of men. The national picture is that women are catching up with the activity rates of men as some of the traditional barriers (for entering entrepreneurship) come down. Although women have higher participation rates in areas such as personal services, there are still some industrial sectors which are largely male preserves and in which women still face barriers. In other countries as well, there is evidence that women have increased participation rates in entrepreneurial activity, although the recent GEM study of entrepreneurial activity rates in 21 countries[38] stated that '[in all countries] men are much more active in start-ups than women' (p. 24). However, the same study also stated that one of the main factors in the differences of the level of entrepreneurial activity rates between countries is the rate of participation by women, with the most entrepreneurial countries having the highest female participation rates.[39]

Considerable progress has been made by women in business, but research has yet to catch up with the development of women in entrepreneurship. For example, Carter,[40] in a review of research in this area, considers that the female entrepreneur has been 'seriously neglected' (p. 179). UK research into women in entrepreneurship is still limited; Watkins and Watkins,[41] with a limited sample of 58 female and 43 male business owners, showed that some differences did exist, in particular that women had little prior experience that facilitated their entry into non-traditional areas. Goffee and Scase[42] have suggested that women in entrepreneurship are influenced by two sets of factors:

- **attachment to entrepreneurial ideals; and**
- **the extent to which they accept conventional gender roles.**

Goffee and Scase suggest a taxonomy of female entrepreneurs based on these factors, varying from a 'conventional' (a female entrepreneur who is highly committed to both entrepreneurial ideals and conventional gender roles) to 'radical' (a female entrepreneur who has a low commitment to both entrepreneurial ideals and conventional gender roles). The Goffee and Scase taxonomy has been heavily criticized and is now rather outdated.[40]

A study by Rosa *et al.*[43] showed that factors affecting women in entrepreneurship were complex and depended on environmental as well as social considerations and that the influence of different factors varied across different industrial sectors. Women were less likely to be involved in co-ownership, although, nevertheless, there were significant numbers of women in multiple business ownership. The researchers considered that women were fast catching up with male-dominated participation rates in entrepreneurship:

“If we speculate that women in business have started from a much lower tradition of achievement, then these figures are remarkable, and may indicate that they are catching up fast.” (p. 30)

In Northern Ireland a study by Borooah *et al.*[44] found that women in the province (compared to men) tended to be younger, married and better educated; but, as the authors point out, there was considerable heterogeneity within the sample of self-employed women. This point is also made in a recent editorial by Holmquist:[45]

“Another conclusion suggests that women entrepreneurs should not be treated as a homogeneous group. There are differences within the group that make all generalisations dangerous.” (p. 181)

Although it may be expected that many of the barriers to women entering entrepreneurship have been reduced, a new study of women in business in the UK for the Industrial Society by Shaw *et al.*[46] claimed that women still suffered from discrimination in enterprise, indicating that specialist entrepreneurial support programmes for women are still required.[47]

Overall, however, it is suggested that it is dangerous to make hard and fast conclusions about the existence (or the lack) of a distinctive nature for women in entrepreneurship. We have also indicated that rates of participation are probably changing rapidly as women increase their activity rates both in the economy generally and in entrepreneurship. However, as Holmquist also points out, traditionally entrepreneurship is 'gendered', that is, seen as masculine. Women are becoming increasingly important in entrepreneurship. There is evidence that increased female participation rates are associated with increased diversity, although evidence from Scotland indicates that comparatively few women in entrepreneurship have yet to be associated with recent high-growth firms.[48] It may take more time before women increase their participation as entrepreneurs associated with high-growth-performing firms.

THINK POINTS 1.5

1. Using case material in this chapter, discuss why risk management is a key attribute of the entrepreneur.
2. Review the three approaches to entrepreneurship discussed in this chapter; why do they each have something to contribute to our understanding of entrepreneurship?
3. Why is it important to treat entrepreneurship as a process?
4. What factors may still account for lower participation rates of women than men in entrepreneurship?

CONCLUSIONS

We can see that attempts to develop tests on entrepreneurial characteristics owe something to the development of theories of entrepreneurship. Shackle's creator and Schumpeter's innovator are included in the measures of creative tendency. There is Knight's calculated risk-taker. The role of co-ordinator of Casson and Kirzner is included by the need to have an internal locus of control and autonomy. These theories have been the guidelines for tests of entrepreneurial ability. Concern with the entrepreneurial personality has diverted attention away from the learning and development process in entrepreneurship and enterprise development, away from the recognition that the individual entrepreneur *acquires* skills and abilities, which are learned from the very process of entrepreneurship. Much of this learning process is not understood. There is a need to refocus research away from the investigation of the entrepreneurial personality, which is effectively a cul-de-sac, towards identifying the important factors (of which the environment might only be one) that affect the process of learning and development in entrepreneurship. Support for entrepreneurship can then be better informed to enable individuals to acquire management skills that enable them to learn from their experience, from their solution of problems.

There is little doubt, however, that the environment can be just as important as personal management skills for successful entrepreneurship. This has important implications for policy and the support of SMEs. Some of these issues will reoccur when we examine small business support later in this book. If the environment is not conducive then entrepreneurial talent will lay dormant. The importance of identifying entrepreneurial characteristics lies in encouraging potential entrepreneurs to start their own businesses. Schemes that give blanket coverage run the risk of persuading people to enter business who are not suited to the task of controlling and running their own business (however good the business idea may be) and eventually fail. There is evidence that policy has become more focused on start-ups and increasing the level of entrepreneurial activity,[49] but it is also important to ensure that policies encourage high-quality sustainable businesses.

SUGGESTED ASSIGNMENTS

1. Students undertake a small research study by interviewing small firm owner-managers about their concepts of management and entrepreneurship. For example, do they consider themselves as entrepreneurs? Small groups of students can each interview one small firm owner and discuss results in class.

2. Students have to debate the skills of entrepreneurs. Students are each given one of two briefs indicating which case they have to argue from:

   - Entrepreneurs are special and have to be born.
   - Entrepreneurship skills can be acquired and the environment that fosters entrepreneurship is important.

3. Compare risk-taking by Craig Coussins in the Hullachan case to an individual who seeks to start a business with virtually no capital. He uses a number of personal credit cards (boot-strapping) to start the business and he opens a bank account. Against his new account, on a Friday, he is able to write a cheque to acquire stock to sell at a market over the weekend, hoping that he can make enough money to cover the cheque and then pay the cash into the bank on the Monday.

   Who is taking the bigger risk?

REFERENCES

1. Curran, J. and Stanworth, J. (1989) 'Education and Training for Enterprise: Some Problems of Classification, Evaluation, Policy and Research', *International Small Business Journal*, vol. 7, no. 2, pp. 11–22.

2. Shailer, G. (1994) 'Capitalists and Entrepreneurs in Owner-managed Firms', *International Small Business Journal*, vol. 12, no. 3, pp. 33–41.

3. Jensen, M.C. and Meckling, W.H. (1976) 'Theory of the Firm: Managerial Behaviour, Agency Costs and Ownership Structure', *Journal of Financial Economics*, vol. 3, no. 2, pp. 305–60.

4. Ray, D. (1993) 'Understanding the Entrepreneur: entrepreneurial attributes, experience and skills', *Entrepreneurship and Regional Development*, vol. 5, no. 4, pp. 345–57.

5. Reynolds, P.D. and White, S.B. (1997) *The Entrepreneurial Process: Economic growth, men, women and minorities*, Quorum, Westport, USA.

6. Reynolds, P.D. and White, S.B. (1997) *The Entrepreneurial Process: Economic growth, men, women and minorities*, Quorum, Westport, USA.

7. Scottish Enterprise (1993) *Scotland's Business Birth Rate: A National Enquiry*, Scottish Enterprise, Glasgow.

8. Ram, M. (1993) *Managing to Survive: Working Lives in Small Firms*, Blackwell, Oxford.

9. Scottish Enterprise (1993) *Scotland's Business Birth Rate: A National Enquiry*, Scottish Enterprise, Glasgow.

10. Scottish Enterprise (1993) *A National Strategy for Scotland*, Scottish Enterprise, Glasgow.

11. Scottish Enterprise (2000) *Scotland's Business Birth Rate Strategy: A Review*, Scottish Enterprise, Glasgow.

12. Scottish Enterprise (1997) *Local Heroes*, Scottish Enterprise, Glasgow.

13. Ram, M. and Deakins, D. (1995) *African-Caribbean Entreprenurship in Britain*, Small Business Research Centre, University of Central England. Can be updated with EMB study reference.

14. DTI (1997) *Small Firms in Britain Report 1996*, DTI, London.

15. Butler, J.E. and Hansen, G.S. (1991) 'Network Evolution, Entrepreneurial Success and Regional Development', *Entrepreneurship and Regional Development*, vol. 3, no. 1, pp. 1–16.

16. McClelland, D.C. (1961) *The Achieving Society*, Van Nostrand, New Jersey.

17. Chell, E., Haworth, J. and Brearley, S. (1991) *The Entrepreneurial Personality, Concepts, Cases, and Categories*, Routledge, London.

18. Delmar, F. (2000) 'The Psychology of the Entrepreneur', in Carter, S. and Jones-Evans, D., *Enterprise and Small Business: Principles, Practice and Policy*, FT/Prentice Hall, London, pp. 132–54.

19. Meredith, G.G., Nelson, R.E. and Neck, P.A. (1982) *The Practice of Entrepreneurship*, International Labour Office, Geneva.

20. Kets de Vries, M. (1977) 'The Entrepreneurial Personality: A person at the crossroads', *Journal of Management Studies*, vol. 14, pp. 34–57.

21. Timmons, J.A. (1994) *New Venture Creation: Entrepreneurship for the 21st Century*, 4th edn., Irwin, Illinios.

22. Cromie, S. and O'Donoghue, J. (1992) 'Assessing Entrepreneurial Inclinations', *International Small Business Journal*, vol. 10, no. 2, pp. 66–71.

23. Johnson, D. and Suet Fan Ma, R. (1995) 'Research Note: A Method for Selecting and Training Entrants on New Business Start-up Programmes', *International Small Business Journal*, vol. 13, no. 3, pp. 80–84.

24. Storey, D.J. and Westhead, P. (1996) 'Management Training and Small Firm Performance: why is the link so weak?' *International Small Business Journal*, vol. 14, no. 4, pp. 13–24.

25. Gibb, A. (1997) 'Small Firms Training and Competitiveness. Building Upon the Small Business as a Learning Organisation', *International Small Business Journal*, vol. 15, no. 3, pp. 13–29.

26. Costello, N. (1996) 'Learning and Routines in High Tech SMEs: analysing rich case study material', *Journal of Economic Issues*, vol. 30, no. 2, pp. 591–7.

27. Freel, M. (1998) 'Evolution, Innovation and Learning: evidence from case studies', *Entrepreneurship and Regional Development*, vol. 10, no. 2, pp. 137–49.

28. Pedler, M., Burgoyne, J. and Boydell, T. (1991) *The Learning Company: A Strategy for Sustainable Development*, McGraw-Hill, New York.

29. Kline, P. and Saunders, B. (1993) *Ten Steps to a Learning Organisation*, Great Ocean, Virginia.

30. Nelson, R. and Winter, S. (1982) *An Evolutionary Theory of Economic Change*, Harvard University Press, Boston, Massachusetts.

31. Levinthal, D. (1996) 'Learning and Schumpeterian Dynamics', in Dosi, G. and Malerba, F. (eds) *Organisation and Strategy in the Evolution of Enterprise*, Macmillan, London.

32. Deakins, D. (1999) Editorial: 'Entrepreneurial Learning', *International Journal of Entrepreneurial Behaviour and Research*, vol. 5, no. 3.

33. Deakins, D., Paddison, A. and Bentley, P. (1997) 'Risk Management, Insurance and the High Technology Small Firm', *Small Business and Enterprise Development*, vol. 4, no. 1, pp. 21–30.

34. Bentley, P. and Sparrow, J. (1997) *Risk Perception and Management Responses in Small and Medium-Sized Enterprises*, Small Business Research Centre, University of Central England, Birmingham.

35. Clink, S. (2001) 'Risk Management in Small Businesses', unpublished PhD thesis, Glasgow Caledonian University, Glasgow.

36. Goodman, F. (1994) 'Insurance and Small Firms: A Small Firm Perspective', paper presented to Insurance and Small Firms Seminar, University of Central England, Birmingham, April.

37. Moralee, A. (1998) 'Self Employment in the 1990s', *Labour Market Trends*, March 1998, pp. 121–130.

38. Global Entrepreneurship Monitor (1999) *Executive Report*, Kauffman Center for Entrepreneurial Leadership, Babson College, Boston, USA.

39. Global Entrepreneurship Monitor (2000) *Executive Report*, Kauffman Center for Entrepreneurial Leadership, Babson College, Boston, USA.

40. Carter, S. (2000) 'Gender and Enterprise', in Carter, S. and Jones-Evans, D. *Enterprise and Small Business: Principles, Practice and Policy*, FT/Prentice Hall, London.

41. Watkins, D. and Watkins, J. (1984) 'The Female Entrepreneur: Her background and determinants of business choice, some British data', *International Small Business Journal*, vol. 2, no. 4, pp. 21–31.

42. Goffee, R. and Scase, R. (1987) 'Patterns of Business Proprietorship Among Women in Britain', in Goffee, R. and Scase, R., *Entrepreneurship in Europe*, Croom Helm, London, pp. 60–82.

43. Rosa, P., Hamilton, D., Carter, S. and Burns, H. (1994) 'The Impact of Gender on Small Business Management: Preliminary Findings of a British Study', *International Small Business Journal*, vol. 12, no. 3, pp. 25–32.

44. Borooah, V.K., Collins, G., Hart, M. and MacNabb, A. (1997) 'Women and Self-Employment: an analysis of constraints and opportunities in Northern Ireland', in

Deakins, D., Jennings, P. and Mason, C. (eds) *Small Firms: Entrepreneurship in the Nineties*, Paul Chapman Publishing, London.

45. Holmquist, C. (1997) Guest editorial: 'The other side of the coin – women's entrepreneurship as a complement or an alternative?' *Entrepreneurship and Regional Development Special Issue: Women's Entrepreneurship*, vol. 9, no. 3, pp. 179–82.

46. Shaw, E., Carter, S. and Brierton, J. (2001) *Unequal Entrepreneurs: Why female enterprise is an uphill business*, The Industrial Society, Policy Paper, London.

47. Forsyth, F. (2000) 'Women's Enterprise and Business Development: Lessons from targeted women's programmes in Glasgow', *Local Economy*, vol. 15, no. 1, pp. 18–31.

48. Scottish Enterprise (1999) *Local Heroes*, Scottish Enterprise, Glasgow.

49. DTI (1998) *Competitiveness White Paper: Building the Knowledge-driven Economy*, DTI, London.

RECOMMENDED READING

Reynolds, P.D. and White, S.B. (1997) *The Entrepreneurial Process: Economic growth, men, women and minorities*, Quorum, Westport, USA.

Global Entrepreneurship Monitor (2001) *Executive Report*, Kauffman Center for Entrepreneurial Leadership, Babson College, Boston, USA.

Chell, E., Haworth, J. and Brearley, S. (1991) *The Entrepreneurial Personality, Concepts, Cases, and Categories*, Routledge, London.

Shaw, E., Carter, S. and Brierton, J. (2001) *Unequal Entrepreneurs: Why female enterprise is an uphill business*, The Industrial Society, Policy Paper, London.

Handy, C. (1999) *The New Alchemists*, Hutchinson, London.

2

ENTREPRENEURIAL ACTIVITY, THE SMALL FIRM AND THE UK ECONOMY: AN ENTREPRENEURIAL REVOLUTION?

LEARNING OUTCOMES

At the end of this chapter you should be able to:

1. Analyse the major trends in entrepreneurial activity and new firm creation in the UK.
2. Discuss the factors that account for these trends.
3. Discuss new policy initiatives to raise entrepreneurial activity.
4. Discuss different definitions of the small firm and SME sector.
5. Appreciate the volatility associated with the growth in the small firm sector.
6. Identify the social costs associated with small firm failures.
7. Suggest reasons why local and regional development agencies should develop new firm support policies.

INTRODUCTION

The encouragement of entrepreneurial activity and entrepreneurship as a career has become an important part of policy in the modern economy.[1&2] The present UK Government has stated that 'by 2005 the UK can become the best place in the world to start and grow a business'.[2] Creating a supporting culture and economy where entrepreneurship can thrive is enshrined as a key objective for the Government's small firm support agency, the Small Business Service.[3] Entrepreneurial careers have also been promoted and directed at young people, although at present there is mixed evidence to support policies that target education and young people to raise awareness and the profile of entrepreneurship as a career.[4] At the time of writing, with the support of Government, the current Enterprise Insight campaign is targeting young people across the UK to raise awareness of entrepreneurial careers.[5] The Government's Science Enterprise Initiative is aimed at university science and technology students and promotes new courses in technology entrepreneurship and commercialization.[6] Entrepreneurship has also been recognized as having additional economic development potential when applied to disadvantaged groups, whether through economic exclusion (rural and urban) or on the basis of other criteria such as equality of opportunity.[7]

The result of the increased attention with entrepreneurial activity and the promotion of entrepreneurial careers has also focused attention on the role and importance of the small and medium-sized enterprise (SME) in the UK economy. The recent Global Entrepreneurship Monitor (GEM) reports claim that entrepreneurial activity (willingness and ability to create new firms) is important for vitality of the economy and for growth in GDP.[8] Therefore, a healthy and vigorous small business sector is important to the performance of the UK economy. Comparisons are sometimes made between the UK performance and that of other regions, such as areas in the USA or southern Germany that have had vibrant SME sectors. A report comparing SMEs across Europe[9] commented that, in the UK, the industrial structure of the economy is still dominated by the large firm sector.

ENTREPRENEURSHIP IN ACTION

Reasons for being high on the Government's policy agenda

- The belief that a positive relationship exists between entrepreneurship and economic development.
- To diversify declining sectors of the economy (compare to Schumpeter's creative destruction).
- To revitalize declining industrial areas such as parts of Scotland, the north-east and the north.
- To legitimize activity that might otherwise be in the black economy (to encourage people to declare self-employment as a valid and legitimate activity).
- As a policy measure to relieve economic and social exclusion.
- The modern knowledge economy requires increased levels of entrepreneurial activity to exploit opportunities (see Chapter 8).

ENTREPRENEURSHIP POLICY IN ACTION

Enterprise Insight

Targeting young school-age people, Enterprise Insight is a UK national campaign to raise awareness of entrepreneurship as a career and to change cultural attitudes to enterprise and new entrepreneurial activity. It has recruited prominent entrepreneurs, such as Richard Branson and Alan Sugar, as supporters and speakers at their events. The campaign attempts to remove any negative connotations with entrepreneurship as a career and place entrepreneurial activity in a positive light (see www.enterpriseinsight.co.uk).

Questions for discussion

- Is raising enterprise awareness in this way a valid objective of policy?
- Should raising entreprise awareness in school be left to teachers, educationlists and career officers?
- Are there any dangers with a wholly positive approach to policy promotion of entrepreneurship as a career?

DEFINITIONS AND MEASUREMENT

In the previous chapter, we saw that it can be difficult to define both the term entrepreneur and the process of entrepreneurship. Precise definitions of small firms and the small business sector are similarly elusive. Entrepreneurship does not necessarily coincide with small firm ownership, although throughout this book we will use the term entrepreneur in connection with small firms. However, the entrepreneurship concept and entrepreneurial skills can be applied to large companies. Unlike entrepreneurship, which is essentially a subjective concept, small firms lend themselves to objective definitions. For example, criteria such as turnover or numbers employed can be applied to distinguish the SME sector. The number of firms that are below certain turnovers or employee size may constitute the SME sector of the economy, although there are difficulties with comparable definitions. We might say that small firms are all those that employ less than 50 employees. However, there will be big differences in the size of firms with such a definition across different industrial sectors. For example, a clothing sector firm employing less than 50 will be much smaller than, say, an information technology firm employing less than 50 and there may well be little comparison between their respective turnovers.

DEFINITIONS OF SMALL FIRMS

After Bolton,[10] the following have been applied to define small firms:

The employee definition: Small firms can be classfied by some maximum number of employees, depending on the nature of capital intensity that varies from one industrial sector to another.

The turnover definition: Turnover definitions have the advantage of being comparable across different sectors.

The characteristics definition: That a small firm is characterized by:

- having a small share of the market;
- management by its owners or part-owners in a personalized way;
- operating independently.

The three definitions combined (see box) were meant to be used in different circumstances. Turnover might be used in some sectors where there was some consistency in the turnover levels of firms. However, the characteristics definition can be incompatible with some small firms that may have a formal management structure and do not necessarily have a small share of the market.

The multiplicity of criteria of Bolton has been replaced in most circumstances by a European Union (EU) definition of the small and medium-sized enterprise as an enterprise employing less than 250 employees, as revised by the European Commission in 1996.[11] As we will see later in this chapter, this definition covers 99 per cent of all the enterprises in the UK. It is now generally accepted that there is a need to identify different sizes of firms within the SME sector. In particular, it has been recognized that very small firms are important to the economy; these are referred to as micro-enterprises to distinguish them from other small firms.

DEFINITION OF SMALL FIRMS

The EU definition

The three EU definitions use the criterion of number of employees as the distinguishing factor of size according to the following:

Number of employees	Size of enterprise
0–9	micro
10–49	small
50–249	medium

DEFINITIONS OF SMALL FIRMS

Why are they important?

- Policy measures may depend on small firm definitions, for example, the Government agency the Small Business Service works only with small businesses.
- Small firms may qualify for additional funding and assistance, so it is important to have appropriate definitions.

- Some EU structural funds only apply to the SME sector.
- For research purpose, it is important to have consistent and acceptable definitions of small firms.

Table 2.1 shows that the EU definition of SMEs covers 99 per cent of all firms in the UK. Even if we reduce the definition to include only those firms that employ 20 or less, we would still capture 98 per cent of all the firms in the UK. If we are to use a small firm definition based on number of employees, the evidence in terms of firm size distribution, as shown in Table 2.1, would suggest that we restrict our analysis to firms employing less than 20 employees. Table 2.1 illustrates the importance and growth of the micro-sized firm in the UK. The dramatic growth in the numbers of small firms is shown more graphically by Figure 2.1. Comparing the UK's SME sector to other European countries seems to show that the UK still has less micro-sized firms than the EU average, as shown in Table 2.2.

	1979		1989		1999	
Firm size	No. (000)	Share of employment	No. (000)	Share of employment	No. (000)	Share of employment
0–9	1597	19.2%	2802	28.6%	3490	30.2%
10–19	109	7.6%	92	6.0%	109	7.0%
20–49	46	6.9%	57	7.6%	47	6.7%
50–99	16	5.3%	18	5.8%	15	4.6%
100–199	15	10.2%	9	7.2%	8	5.2%
200–499	5	8.1%	6	10.6%	5	6.8%
500 +	4	42.8%	3	34.2%	4	39.4%
Totals	1791*	100%*	2988*	100%*	3677*	100%*

Note: * Totals may be different due to rounding.

Source: Employment Gazette, Labour Market Trends (modified) February 1992 and other editions; Small Business Service, *Small and Medium-sized Enterprise Statistics for the UK, 1999*, September 2000.

Table 2.1 Firm size and share of employment UK, 1979–99

It is worth noting that the methodology behind the calculation of the numbers of small firms in the UK economy has improved in recent years. The latest figures available by size distribution, as shown by Table 2.1, now include more accurate estimates for the 'zero-employment' firm, including the self-employed. The numbers of small firms are now calculated from the Inter-Departmental Business Register (IDBR). This includes all businesses operating PAYE and registered for VAT, but with an allowance made for very small zero-employment businesses.[12]

It is not surprising that some researchers have turned to alternative definitions to operationalize studies with small firms. For example, a previous study[13] of service

Number of employees	EU average by percentage share of employment	UK average by percentage share of employment
1–9	33.8%	30.2%
10–49	18.8%	13.7%
50–249	13.1%	11.5%
250 +	34.1%	44.6%
Totals	100%*	100%*

Note: * Totals affected by rounding.

Source: Small Business Service, *Small and Medium-sized Enterprise Statistics for the UK, 1999*, September 2000; The European Observatory for SMEs, *Executive Summary, Sixth Report*, July 2000.

Table 2.2 EU v. UK by size of enterprise and share of employment, 1999

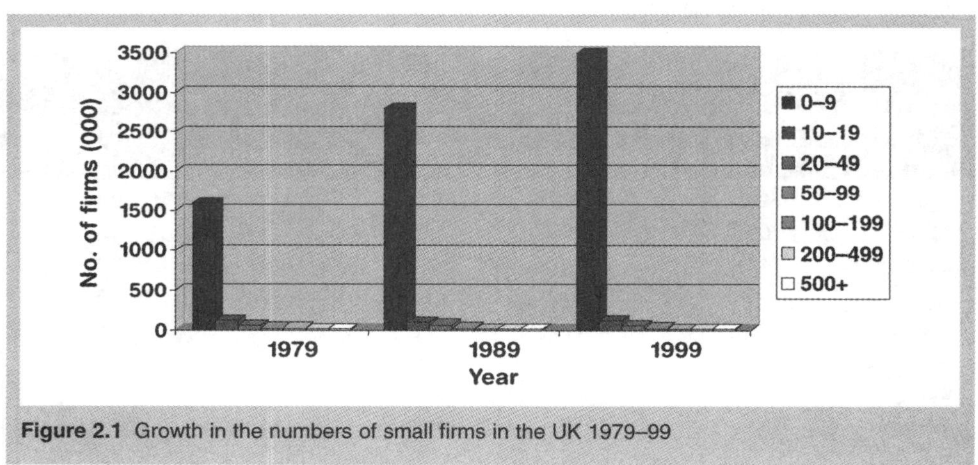

Figure 2.1 Growth in the numbers of small firms in the UK 1979–99

sector firms operationalized definitions with a 'grounded' definition of size adapted for the different services covered. The researchers considered what the small firm owner and representatives of the sector considered to be small in relation to the economic activities in which they were involved.

It may not be possible to define statistically the small firm or the small firm sector. As we will see from the evidence given in the tables, there is no doubt that entrepreneurial activity and the small firm has become more important in the last 20 years. One of the reasons for the increased importance of the small firm is its ability to respond quickly to change. As the pace of technological change has increased in society, so the ability of the small firm to respond quickly to change has given it an advantage over the large firm. This characteristic of small firms has been called 'flexible specialization' and reflects the ability of the small firm to be both specialized and responsive to change. As the demands of society change, it may be that the growth in the importance of the small firm merely reflects those changed demands. In the same way that the UK labour market has changed dramatically, with employment no longer based on long-term careers with large firms in one occupation, and in favour of a more 'flexible' labour force, so the structure of the economy has changed in favour of the small, flexible and specialized firm.

In such circumstances, and in the face of the increasing pace of change, it may be folly to attempt to define the small firm, because the notion of what is small is changing anyway, as is the type of small firm considered to be important. We turn now to examine the evidence concerning the importance of small firms in the economy.

The Importance of the Small Firm Sector in the UK

Table 2.1 shows the trends in the numbers and importance of small firms for share of total employment in the 1980s and 1990s. One striking trend is the increased numbers and growth in importance of the very small or micro-firm that employs less than 10 staff. The numbers of such firms have nearly doubled in the 1980s, and continued to increase strongly in the 1990s, as did their share of employment. It is also noticeable that the number of firms that employ more than 10 staff has remained virtually static during the same period. Thus most of the growth in the importance of small firms has come from the micro-businesses.

Why there should have been this concentration of growth in micro-firms is less clear. There are reasons associated with the restructuring of the economy. Large numbers of workers were made redundant in the early 1980s; workers who often had substantial redundancy payments and little prospect of retraining. Faced with a lack of opportunity, it is not surprising that many people were tempted into starting their own (micro-)businesses. However, this factor alone cannot account for the growth in the importance of such businesses in the share of employment. Also, the numbers of micro-enterprises may be under-reported. Although adjustments are made by the Office for National Statistics (ONS) to allow for very small, zero-employment businesses, figures are still based on VAT registrations and PAYE data, as discussed above. Some very small businesses, however, may still not enter official calculations. The explanation of the growth of these micro-firms is more complex than simple push factors from high unemployment rates and is probably tied to underlying structural changes in the economy, as discussed above – structural changes that had been in place for some time.

Across the EU as well, there has been a significant growth in small firms that employ less than 100. According to a European study,[9] between 1988 and 1993 these firms were responsible for creating 3 million jobs whereas other firms were net losers of jobs, suggesting that there are significant structural changes in all European countries in favour of small firms and entrepreneurs that employ less than 100 people.

AN ENTREPRENEURIAL REVOLUTION?

Reasons for growth in the small firm sector

1. Structural changes including growth of the service sector and knowledge-based firms, where a smaller size of firm is more 'optimal'.

2. The ability to the smaller firm to be more flexible and respond to 'market opportunities'; the ability to be both specialized and flexible.

3. Changes in government policy to raise awareness of entrepreneurship, as discussed in the introduction.

4. Changes in macro-economic policy in favour of small firms, e.g. changes in corporation tax to ensure a fairer treatment of small firms and the introduction of tax incentives for self-employment.

5. A more important role for the small firm in local authority policy, e.g. some economic development units have launched initiatives to help smaller firms. Contracting out of public sector services has also encouraged the growth of the small firm entrepreneur.

The data shown in Table 2.1 is reinforced when we examine turnover levels for small firms. Table 2.3 gives the size distribution of firms with turnover figures for the period 1994 to 1999. Some of the micro-sized firms will have very low turnovers, many less than the VAT threshold of £52,000. This gives further weight to the importance of the micro-firm. It also makes one wonder at the nature of operation of many small firms. It will become clear that, far from being prosperous, many of these micro-firms spend much of their time trying to survive from day to day (one reason why there is little forward planning in small firms). As we will see below, being in business for many small firm owners can only be a part-time occupation, generating very small turnover levels.

ENTREPRENEURSHIP IN ACTION

Using small size to advantage – Laskarina

An example of how a small firm can use its flexibility and small size to advantage in niche markets is provided by the story of Laskarina, a travel company specializing in holidays for UK customers in unspoilt Greek islands. Laskarina was started by Kate Murdoch, together with her husband Keith, back in 1976 when travel to Greece was dominated by the big package holiday operators. Kate recognized an opportunity to cater for people desiring to holiday in the 'real Greece' and started with holidays in just one Greek island, Spetes. Kate took the name of Laskarina from that of a heroine and a native of the island of Spetes, Laskarina Bouboulina. So important did the company become for the island that the people of Spetes gave Kate Murdoch a special award for helping the island's tourism industry. The company has also brought some wealth and tourism to a number of other less popular Greek islands, which would otherwise have remained relatively backward. The company has been highly successful, winning best company travel awards from the *Observer* for an amazing six years on the run, from 1996 to 2001, and it also won the 2001 Holiday Which? Award for the best tour operator; yet the company has remained small. It eschews marketing through travel agents and instead markets its holidays direct from a small office in Wirksworth, Derbyshire. It focuses on a specialized niche market by supplying good-quality accommodation and ensuring that customers are well looked after while they are in Greece. It is a formula that has been highly successful, illustrating that a small firm can use its flexible and specialized nature to advantage against much larger operators. It is also a formula that has been copied by many other small travel operators specializing in niche holiday markets, a sector that contains many examples of the small firm entrepreneurial revolution.

Even by 2002 the Murdochs still described themselves as 'a very small family company employing thirteen UK staff – and fifteen British representatives in Greece.'

	1994			1999		
Firm size	**No. (000)**	**Turnover (£m ex VAT)**	**Share of turnover**	**No. (000)**	**Turnover (£m ex VAT)**	**Share of turnover**
0–9	3380	283,123	18.4%	3490	419,877	19.4%
10–19	107	109,378	7.1%	109	146,069	6.7%
20–49	59	117,222	7.6%	47	142,989	6.6%
50–99	19	103,372	6.7%	15	103,069	4.8%
100–199	9	138,144	9.0%	8	112,700	5.2%
200–499	5	158,320	10.3%	5	336,326	15.5%
500 +	3	626,466	40.8%	4	902,979	41.7%
Totals	3581*	1,536,026	100%*	3677*	2,164,009	100%

Note: * Totals affected by rounding.
Source: Small Business Service, *SME Statistics for the UK, 1999*, September 2000.

Table 2.3 Number of businesses and turnover, 1994–99 (current prices)

THINK POINTS 2.1

1. What factors account for the increased policy attention given to entrepreneurial activity and the small firm sector?

2. What are the accepted definitions of:
- micro-firms?
- small firms?
- medium-sized firms?

3. Account for the growth in entrepreneurial activity in the last 20 years; discuss whether, in your view, this constitutes an entrepreneurial revolution.

Small Firm Volatility

Table 2.1 may show a net growth in small firm formation, but the table also hides high volatility due to both high birth rates and high death rates in the 1990s. Births and deaths of firms are illustrated in Table 2.4 for the period 1994–99 and it shows that small and micro-firm death rates (de-registrations) are in some years higher than birth rates (registrations), that is, during recessions.

	1994	1995	1996	1997	1998	1999
Registrations (births)	168,240	163,960	168,200	182,570	186,250	178,460
De-registrations (deaths)	188,170	173,240	165,065	164,455	155,930	171,970
Difference (net loss)	(19,930)	(9,280)	3,135	18,115	30,320	6,490

Source: Research and Evaluation Unit, Small Business Service, October 2000.

Table 2.4 Business start-ups and closures, 1994–99

Not surprisingly, official figures show low survival rates for new firm formation. Official figures show that less than 55 per cent of new VAT registrations survive for longer than three years, and less than 40 per cent survive for longer than five years.[14] Cressy and Storey,[15] using an independent database, claimed that less than 30 per cent of new firms survived longer than six years. Gibb, however, has argued that high death rates of small firms is a myth,[16] partly because VAT registration survival rates may not be indicative of true survival rates; a de-registration may not indicate business closures as such, just a decision to leave the VAT register but continue trading. Gibb claims that *stability* rather than *volatility* is truer picture of the small firm sector.

Whatever the reality of small firm volatility or stability, the failure rates of new firms, which are the result of increased entrepreneurial activity rates, are too often ignored by the Government and policy-makers. The social costs associated with a drive to improve start-up rates may be high. For example, high bankruptcy rates among small firm owners and entrepreneurs, who have often pledged much of their wealth and personal assets into the business, leave many people who have lost more than they put into the business. Although plans to change bankruptcy laws have recently been announced,[17] they will still require secured creditors to be paid first, with the result that small firm creditors are often the last to be paid. During a recession, this situation can lead to a domino effect as one business failure forces other small firms to cease trading.

The problem of small firm survival rates has been illustrated by Westhead and Birley.[18] They show that VAT de-registrations have been highest in the older industrial areas and conurbations, leading to high net losses of firms even during the boom period of 1987–90. They comment that:

> ***"This aggregate macro-level analysis reinforces the micro-level evidence that the majority of new firms are doomed to death in their formative years. De-registration rates were found to be markedly lower in rural environments and significantly higher in urban areas." (pp. 56–7)***

High business birth rates may look impressive, but they hide the fact that some of the new starts will not survive beyond the first year of operation and many will not survive the first three years. In the past, policy-makers have been too preoccupied with quantifiable numbers of new firm starts and have shown insufficient concern with the quality of business start-ups. However, recently that there has been more attention given to the quality of new firm start-ups.[19] As we comment below, greater focus on the potential of surviving and growing new firms has led to changes in policy away from blanket coverage and incentives for all new starts.

GROWTH FIRMS AND JOB CREATION

The gradual realization that we should be more concerned about the quality of new small firm start-ups has led to greater focus on small firm start-ups that have the potential to grow – the so-called 'fast track' new firms with the potential for job creation. There has been some controversy surrounding the job creation of small firms. Numbers of small firm starts do not give an indication of job creation, nor do we have a picture of whether new firm starts can replace the job losses of larger firms that have continued to rationalize and cut jobs in the 1990s.

The claim for the role of small firms in creating employment stems from a paper by Birch, which stated that, in the USA between 1969 and 1976, 66 per cent of net new jobs were created by firms employing less than 20 workers.[20] However, the assumptions and conclusions of Birch have been criticized by subsequent writers. In the UK, Fothergill and Gudgin have claimed that firms employing fewer than 25 people only accounted for 0.8 per cent of the growth in total manufacturing output in the period 1968 to 1975.[21] A study by Daly *et al.* claims that small firms employing less than 20 people were equally important (to large firms) in the UK in job creation between 1987 to 1989.[22]

THE ENTREPRENEURIAL REVOLUTION

Quantity v. quality – should we encourage more new firms?

- Studies on small firm job creation are usually based on VAT registrations that exclude some of the very small firms (due to the VAT turnover threshold) and do not give a complete picture. (Although adjustments are usually made, it is difficult to allow for non-registrations and de-registrations that are not deaths.) The VAT turnover threshold also increases over time; at 1 April 2000 it was £52,000.

- Some small firm creation can lead of job replacement rather than job creation. For example, if an individual starts in business under a public sector-provided grant scheme, they may force another individual out of business (because they are subsidized).

- We have hinted that job creation may be low quality in small firms. Employees are often non-unionized. The evidence on industrial relations is mixed and Ram and Holiday, for example, show that in small family-run firms relations are not as harmonious as might appear and consist of a form of 'negotiated paternalism'.[23]

It has been suggested that net job generation is only accounted for by a very small proportion of new small firms. For example, only a small minority of firms will grow to employ 50 people. Storey claims that out of every 100 new firm starts only a handful, perhaps 3 or 4, will turn out to be major job creators and high-growth potential firms.[24] Using data from manufacturing firms in the north of England for the period 1965–78, Storey shows that out of 774 firms surviving to 1978, only 5 per cent had more than 50 employees and only 1 per cent had more than 100 employees.

It is not surprising that only a minority of firms will grow to any size, given that national data such as that shown in Table 2.1 indicates that 98 per cent of all firms employ less than 20 people. More important, however, is the contention that a very small number of firms will create the major proportion of new jobs. For example, Storey calculates that 'over a decade, 4% of those businesses which start would be expected to create 50% of employment generated' (p. 115).

A study by Gallagher and Miller supports the contention that a majority of jobs will be created by a small minority of firms.[25] From a study of 2000 new firms in Scotland and 20 000 in the south-east, they found that, in Scotland, 11 per cent of firms created 68 per cent of the jobs and, in the south-east, 18 per cent of firms created 92 per cent of jobs. However, Daly *et al.*, using national data, claim that the growth of employment is more dispersed and slower than the evidence given above might suggest.[22] They claim that over 50 per cent of net job generation was accounted for by firms moving from less than five employees to less than ten employees, that is, the existence of fast track new firms or 'high flyers' is less important than has been claimed for job generation.

THINK POINTS 2.2

1. Should policy-makers focus merely on encouraging more entrepreneurial activity and new firm start-ups?
2. Why should an emphasis of policy on quality start-ups (rather than blanket support) be worthwhile?
3. Should under-represented groups (e.g. women) in the entrepreneurial revolution be targeted by policy-makers?
4. Why might reported high death rates of new firm creation be considered to be a myth?
5. What factors might account for small firm volatility or stability?

REGIONAL VARIATIONS

Using VAT data, Keeble and Walker show that there are significant regional variations in the growth of new and small businesses.[26] The data reveal a north–south divide in new firm formation during the last 20 years. Table 2.5 shows that the south-east, south-west and East Anglia have much higher enterprise formation rates than the north, Scotland and Northern Ireland. These regional differences in new firm formation rates add weight to our argument in Chapter 1 that the environment is a powerful factor in entrepreneurship. Keeble and Walker model a series of factors that affect firm formation, growth and death. Significant factors for both formation and growth were local population growth, capital availability, and professional and managerial expertise. They also found that support from enterprise agencies does help to reduce the death rates. Self-employment rates for 1999 are also shown in Table 2.5 and also reflect similar regional variations.

However, a study by Barkham *et al.* on differences in regional performance and growth rates of small firms found that high-growth performing firms in Northern Ireland outperformed equivalent firms from comparative regions in England.[27] In a four-region comparative study, rather surprisingly, their results show that the best-performing region was Northern Ireland and the poorest-performing region was Hertfordshire. They compare permutations of 'pairs' of regions, but the most striking comparison is between Hertfordshire and Northern Ireland. In a discussion of the possible reasons for the disparities between these two regions, the authors suggest that contributing factors include differences in operating cost, such as wages and rent. The authors do not pursue the intriguing possibility that the performance

Region	Number of new firms 1980–99 (000)	Formation rate 1980–99[1]	Formation rate 1999[2]	Self-employment rate 1999
South-east	850	100.3	66	13.5%
South-west	190	99.7	38	14.0%
East Anglia	79	95.8	n/a	13.1%
East Midlands	140	79.3	34	11.4%
Wales	93	77.5	26	11.5%
West Midlands	180	72.1	34	10.4%
Yorks and Humberside	158	70.3	29	9.8%
North-west	207	68.7	33	10.6%
Northern Ireland	39	61.1	28	13.0%
Scotland	134	55.4	28	9.3%
North-east	77	55.3	21	8.8%
UK	2,147	81.4	38	11.7%

Notes: [1] Per 1,000 civilian labour force, 1981.
[2] Per 10,000 resident adults, 1998.

Source: Keeble, D. and Walker, S. (1993) 'New Firms, Small Firms and Dead Firms: Spatial Patterns and Determinants in the UK', *Regional Studies*, vol. 28, no. 4, pp. 411–27; and *Labour Market Trends*, November 2000.

Table 2.5 Regional variation in new firm formation rates and self-employment rate, 1980–99

of firms in Northern Ireland may have been influenced by the Local Enterprise Development Unit (LEDU). The regional differences are assigned to 'one of the swings of fortune' (p. 137) and the authors do not subscribe to the possibility that public sector intervention can overcome the constraints imposed by limited markets in a peripheral region.

As mentioned in Chapter 1, following their own research into new firm formation in Scotland, Scottish Enterprise launched their own strategy for improving the business birth rate in Scotland.[28] This has recently been revised following extensive reviews,[29&30] but the Business Birth Rate Strategy remains in place, albeit with considerable revision. The analysis of Keeble and Walker would suggest that the low population growth in Scotland and lack of home-ownership will continue to limit new firm formation in Scotland. Research by the author with high-technology small firms in the West Midlands and Scotland illustrated that the gap between the two regions (which the strategy of Scottish Enterprise was trying to close) in new firm formation rates for new high-technology small firms was quite daunting with a very much smaller proportion of high-technology small firms in Scotland formed in the five years 1990–95 than in the West Midlands.[31] This is supported by a recent review by Scottish Enterprise, after seven years of the strategy found that new firm formation rates remained stubbornly low despite a claimed 'paradox' of improvements in the environment brought about by policy.[29] An independent review after eight years of the strategy concluded that 'the estimated effect from the strategy is small, amounting to an increase ... of around 3% or 2124 businesses by 1999.'[30] This suggests that the Barkham *et al.*'s conclusion above may be accurate. The Scottish Enterprise Strategy has developed a 'Personal Enterprise Campaign', which targets potential new start entrepreneurs in conjunction with local, innovative mentoring programmes of support for new firm formation. There is some qualitative evidence on the effect of this continuing strategy that suggests that policy interventions can have an effect on performance and survival rates[32] (this is discussed in more detail in Chapter 3). However, combining evidence from both Scotland and Northern Ireland suggests that co-ordinated intervention can make a small but significant difference to the formation rates of high-quality growth firms.

The significance of home-ownership as a means of providing collateral and equity is a theme that we will return to in Chapter 5. Home-ownership can reduce the liquidity constraints that face entrepreneurs and influence the propensity to enter entrepreneurship.[33,34] It is a constraint that has been identified as significant by Scottish Enterprise in its enterprise strategy.

Self-Employment Rates

Although not as marked as regional variations in new firm formation rates, Table 2.5 also shows some regional variation in self-employment rates. This table, however, masks larger variations within regions. For example, although Scotland has one of the lowest rates, within Scotland rates vary with rural areas, such as Dumfries and Galloway in south-west Scotland having rates of 15 per cent. In general, self-employment as a contributor to GDP will be more important for rural areas than urban areas, with the result that the importance of self-employment is often underplayed in rural areas. For example, a study of the importance of self-employment in south-west Scotland found that it accounted for over 20 per cent of the area's GDP during the period 1994 to 1998.[35]

The self-employed are often portrayed in a stylized fashion, as owning low-value 'lifestyle' businesses with zero-levels of employment and limited ambitions for their business. However, the evidence from the study suggests that this stylized view is too simplistic; in practice the self-employed demonstrated growth ambitions, with average employment levels of 1.5 FTEs creating a significant number of jobs in a rural economy. A report for the DTI's Foresight Panel has predicted that self-employment will become more popular, with the professional self-employed becoming a typical lifestyle pattern for young individuals by 2010.[36]

THINK POINTS 2.3

1. What evidence from the UK economy migh support the contention of an entrepreneurial revolution in the last decade?

2. Why is new entrepreneurial activity important to the health of a nation's econonmy?

3. What policy measures have been used to target young people to raise enterprise awareness?

4. Why are different views held on the volatility or otherwise of the small firm formation and failure rates?

5. Which regions in the UK have relatively low rates of new firm formation and entrepreneurial activity rates?

6. Why is it important to establish consistent definitions of small firms?

CONCLUSIONS

We have concentrated on the importance of small firms in the UK economy. Historically, the UK's small firm sector, however defined, has been less important than other developed nations that have enjoyed better economic performance and growth. A recent GEM report places the UK in the middle ranking of 29 industrial countries for the level of entrepreneurial activity.[37] In the last 20 years greater attention has been paid to the small business sector for its potential in generating jobs and providing the engine for new economic growth. The result is that it is now received Government policy that the small firm sector will provide the main vehicle for economic growth and development and will be the main provider of jobs into the twenty-first century.

Close examination of small firm statistics in the UK, however, reveals that the vast majority of small firms are not major job creators and 98 per cent will probably never employ more than 20 people. Much of the balance of evidence suggests that high-growth small firms are rare, perhaps only 3 or 4 for every 100 new firm start-ups. While the number of small firms has increased, especially in micro-firms employing less than 10 people, this pattern is very uneven throughout the UK, with large regional (and sectoral) variations.

The last two decades may, in the future, be called a period of sustained growth of small firms in the UK, but whether it can constitute an entrepreneurial revolution is open to debate. An entrepreneurial revolution would need to encompass a change in attitudes to entrepreneurship and here the evidence is very subjective. It is often forgotten that it has been a period of high volatility in the small firm sector; high business birth rates were accompanied by high business death rates. Many people have been encouraged to start their own business who did not have the management skills to survive. The social costs were high, due to the personal tragedies that lie behind the bland statistics. In addition, the quality of many of the jobs created was questionable, often low-paid, part-time and insecure. Secondary labour markets have expanded in line with the growth of small firms in the 1980s and 1990s.

Although successive governments have claimed that they have fostered the successful growth of the small firms sector during the last 20 years, there are a number of factors that suggest that the growth would have occurred to some extent anyway, since small firms are better equipped to meet the rapidly changing demands of the late twentieth and early twenty-first centuries.

There are signs that we have learned some lessons from the 1980s decade of small firm growth. The emphasis in policy has switched to quality rather than quantity. Supportive policies in new firm formation, such as those in Scotland, Wales and Northern Ireland, are still selective, targeted at firms that have the potential to survive and grow. Policy is now focusing on quality, although we will see later that, as yet, few criteria have been developed to target fast-growth firms.

SUGGESTED ASSIGNMENTS

1. Students are allocated to small working groups and are required to present and contrast the growth in the numbers of small firms in the UK compared to large firms. Student groups are required to discuss their adopted definition of a small firm and account for the differences shown.

2. Students discuss reasons for differences in small firm formation rates in different regions in the UK, as shown in Table 2.5. Why should the south perform better than the north?

3. Students are allocated to groups to discuss factors that have contributed to the growth in the numbers of small firms. Their required task is to suggest why small business ownership has become an attractive alternative career for many people compared to large firm employment in the modern labour market.

REFERENCES

1. DTI (1998) *Competitiveness White Paper: The knowledge-driven economy*, DTI, London.

2. DTI (2001) *Think Small First: Supporting smaller businesses in the UK*, DTI, London.

3. Small Business Service (2001) *SBS Strategy Document*, SBS, DTI, London.

4. Sundes, O. (2001) *The State, the University and the Development of Enterprise*, unpublished PhD thesis, Worcester College, Oxford University.

5. Enterprise Insight (2001) *Enterprise Insight*, DTI, London.

6. Science Enterprise Challenge (2001) Office for Science and Technology, London.

7. Bank of England (2000) *Finance for Small Businesses in Deprived Communities*, Bank of England, London.

8. Global Entrepreneurship Monitor (2002) *The UK 2001 Report*, GEM, London Business School, London.

9. The European Observatory for SMEs (1994) *Second Annual Report*, EIM Small Business Research and Consultancy, Netherlands.

10. HM Government (1971) *Report of The Committee of Inquiry on Small Firms (Bolton Report)*, HMSO, London.

11. European Commission (1996), *Journal of the European Communities*, no. 107/6, Brussels.

12. Small Business Service (2000) *Small and Medium Enterprise Statistics for the UK, 1999*, Research and Evaluation Unit, SBS, September.

13. Curran, J., Blackburn, R.A. and Woods, A. (1992) 'Profiles of the Small Enterprise in the Service Sector', paper presented to the 14th National Small Firms Policy and Research Conference, Blackpool, November.

14. DTI (1997) *Small Firms in Britain*, DTI, London.

15. Cressy, R. and Storey, D.J. (1996) *New Firms and Their Bank*, Centre for SMEs, University of Warwick, Coventry.

16. Gibb, A.A. (2000) 'SME policy, academic research and the growth of ignorance, mythical concepts, myths and assumptions', *International Small Business Journal*, vol. 18, no. 3, pp. 13–35.

17. HM Government (2001) *Budget Statement*, March.

18. Westhead, P. and Birley, S. (1994) 'Environments for Business De-registrations in the UK, 1987–90', *Entrepreneurship and Regional Development*, vol. 6, no. 1, pp. 29–62.

19. Fraser of Allander Institute (2001) *Promoting Business Start-ups: A New Strategic Formula, Stage 1 Final Report*, Scottish Enterprise, Glasgow.

20. Birch, D.L. (1979) 'The job generation process' *MIT study on neighbourhood and regional change*, MIT, Massachusetts, USA.

21. Fothergill, S. and Gudgin, G. (1979) *The job generation process in Britain*, Centre for Environmental Studies, University of Leicester, Leicester.

22. Daly, M., Campbell, M., Robson, G. and Gallagher, C. (1991) 'Job-creation 1987–89: the contributions of small and large firms', *Employment Gazette*, November, pp. 589–94.

23. Ram, M. and Holiday, R. (1993) 'Keeping it in the Family: Small Firms and Familial Culture', in Chittenden, F., Robertson, M. and Watkins, D. (eds) *Small Firms: Recession and Recovery*, Paul Chapman, London.

24. Storey, D.J. (1994) *Understanding the Small Business Sector*, Routledge, London.

25. Gallagher,C. and Miller, P. (1991) 'New Fast Growing Companies Create Jobs', *Long Range Planning*, vol. 24, no. 1, pp. 96–101.

26. Keeble, D. and Walker, S. (1993) 'New Firms, Small Firms and Dead Firms: Spatial Patterns and Determinants in the UK', *Regional Studies*, vol. 28, no. 4, pp. 411–27.

27. Barkham, R., Gudgin, G., Hart, M. and Hanvey, E. (1996) *The Determinants of Small Firm Growth: An Inter-regional Study in the UK 1986–90*, Jessica Kingsley Publishers, London, and Regional Studies Association, London.

28. Scottish Enterprise (1993) *Improving the Business Birth Rate: A Strategy for Scotland*, Scottish Enterprise, Glasgow.

29. Scottish Enterprise (2000) *Review 2000 The Business Birth Rate Strategy*, Scottish Enterprise, Glasgow.

30. Fraser of Allander Institute (2001) *Promoting Business Start-ups: A New Strategic Formula, Stage 1 Final Report*, Scottish Enterprise, Glasgow.

31. Deakins, D. and Paddison, A. (1995) *Risk Management and the Use of Insurance by High Technology-Based Entrepreneurs*, Paisley Enterprise Research Centre, University of Paisley.

32. Deakins, D., Graham, L., Sullivan, R. and Whittam, G. (1997) *New Venture Support: An Evaluation of Mentoring Support for New Entrepreneurs*, Paisley Enterprise Research Centre, University of Paisley.

33. Evans D. and Jovanivic, B. (1989) 'An estimated model of Entrepreneurial Choice under Liquidity Constraints', *Journal of Political Economy*, vol. 97, no. 4, pp. 808–27.

34. Batstone, S. and Mansfield, E. (1992) 'Births, Deaths and Turbulence in England and Wales', in Robertson, M., Chell, E. and Mason, C. (eds) *Towards the Twenty-first Century: the Challenge for Small Business*, Nadamal Books, Macclesfield, pp. 179–208.

35. PERC (2000) *Self-Employment in Dumfries and Galloway 1994–98; Final Report*, PERC, University of Paisley, unpublished research report.

36. Foresight (2000) *Report of the Financial Services Panel*, Foresight, DTI, London.

37. Global Entrepreneurship Monitor (2001) *Executive Summary 2001*, Babson College, Boston, USA.

RECOMMENDED READING

Gibb, A.A. (2000) 'SME policy, academic research and the growth of ignorance, mythical concepts, myths and assumptions', *International Small Business Journal*, vol. 18, no. 3, pp. 13–35.

Barkham, R., Gudgin, G., Hart, M. and Hanvey, E. (1996) *The Determinants of Small Firm Growth: An Inter-regional Study in the UK 1986–90*, Jessica Kingsley Publishers, London, and Regional Studies Association, London.

Global Entrepreneurship Monitor (2001) *Executive Summary 2001*, Babson College, Boston, USA.

Fraser of Allander Institute (2001) *Promoting Business Start-ups: A New Strategic Formula, Stage 1 Final Report*, Scottish Enterprise, Glasgow.

Websites

www.enterpriseinsight.org.uk
www.scotent.co.uk
www.newbusiness.org.uk
www.sbs.gov.uk

3

ISSUES IN BUSINESS START-UP

LEARNING OUTCOMES

At the end of this chapter you should be able to:

1. Discuss the importance of different factors that affect the business creation process.
2. Analyse the role and importance of education in creativity.
3. Identify factors that inhibit or block creativity and ideas formulation.
4. Describe the importance of developing, modifying and refining ideas over time.
5. Discuss the different paradigms involved with the start-up process in different types of new ventures.
6. Evaluate the provision of start-up support programmes with previous entrepreneurs as mentors.
7. Argue the case for and against state intervention in the start-up process.

INTRODUCTION

In previous chapters we have reviewed the greater attention with entrepreneurship and entrepreneurial activity; we focus again on the process of entrepreneurship by exploring in greater detail some of the start-up issues. It is worth bearing in mind that this start-up and development process can occur over a considerable period of time. Initial business ideas take time to formulate, research, raise funding, find partners and may be considerably refined before the launch of the business. Every business start-up is a unique event; circumstances that contribute to success are intangible and may be different for each individual entrepreneur. Thus we need to be careful about recommending 'paths to success'; what may work for one entrepreneur may not for another. However, we suggest that intervention and support still has a role in the start-up process. Later in this chapter, we examine research with start-up entrepreneurs on the impact of the provision of mentoring support and suggest that such intervention and support can achieve an impact on survival and performance of new business start-ups.

The business start-up process can be broken down into a number of stages:

STAGES IN THE START-UP PROCESS

- the formation of the idea;
- opportunity recognition;
- pre-start planning and preparation including pilot testing;
- entry into entrepreneurship;
- launch and subsequent development.

Each of these stages will have a number of factors that will impinge on the process. These may either encourage further development or have a negative influence, perhaps causing the individual nascent entrepreneur to terminate the process. These factors will include the nature of the local environment, culture, access to finance, local support networks, role models and enterprise support and encouragement. A representation and suggested paradigm of this process is illustrated in Figure 3.1. For the sake of simplicity the representation abstracts from reality. In practice a host of factors may affect each stage, for example, the psychology of the individual entrepreneur, mental processes and personal characteristics such as tenacity and perseverance in overcoming obstacles and barriers. Some of these factors will be brought out in the case study that is included in this chapter (and other cases in other chapters of this book), but for this part of the chapter we discuss some of the more 'external' factors that can impinge upon the different stages. Again we don't attempt to capture all of these but some of the most important are represented in Figure 3.1 and discussed below.

IDEA FORMULATION

The formation of business ideas will be affected by a nascent entrepreneur's past experience, training, education and skill development. This accumulation of knowledge, skills and experience is termed human capital, a concept used particularly in the context of labour markets by economists following pioneering work of Gary Becker.[1] Formulation of business ideas may be influenced by work experience, by individual training and recognition that a particular product or process 'could be done better'. Recognizing that a process or product could be done in a superior way has been the spur behind many new businesses. Later in this book we discuss the case of Aquamotive – a case study concerned with innovation. The entrepreneurs in this case developed an innovative new product after identifying a problem and realizing that they could provide a better solution. The majority of new business ventures are known to be in sectors or industries where the new business owners have had previous experience. For example, Cressy has argued that human capital is an important determining factor in new business creation.[2] The importance of human capital tends to be reinforced by external financial institutions, since

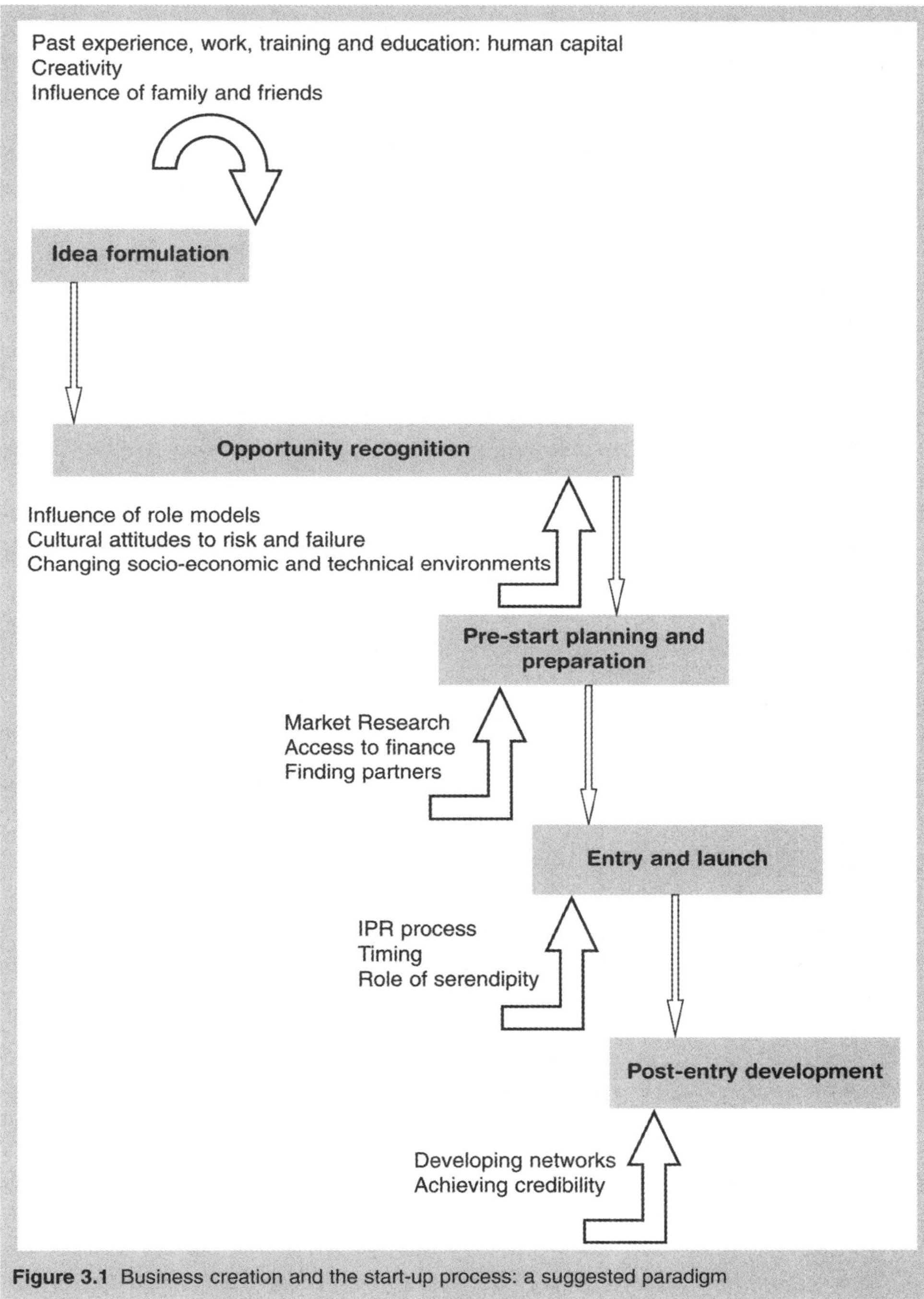

Figure 3.1 Business creation and the start-up process: a suggested paradigm

research has shown that bank managers rate previous experience as an important factor in lending to new venture entrepreneurs.[3]

For younger entrepreneurs, who will have limited human capital, it can be argued that education can have an important role in providing a conducive environment for idea formulation. It has been suggested that younger entrepreneurs (below 30) are under-represented in entrepreneurship because of limited personal capital and limited access to finance.[4] The limited experience (or human capital) that potential entrepreneurs in this age range can draw upon will limit the scope of opportunities for developing ideas. Youth, however, can also be an advantage. Young entrepreneurs may be more willing to test different ideas and bring a different perspective to trading opportunities. Idea formulation here will be affected by educational experience and early training. It is arguable that education should provide scenarios that encourage creativity, lateral thinking and problem-solving. However, there can be a conflict in providing sufficient scope within a curriculum for the development of such transferable and 'core' skills. There are indications that greater importance is being placed on 'enterprise' abilities including problem-solving, group work and ideas generation. The Enterprise Insight initiative[5] has been mentioned in the previous chapter and, in Scotland, as part of a Business Birth Rate Strategy (mentioned in Chapter 1), a programme geared at all levels of education, 'P1 to plc' has been introduced into schools with some success.[6] Other examples of attempts to widen the curriculum, such as Young Enterprise, can, unfortunately, be 'add-ons' rather than developments that are embedded in the curriculum.[7]

ENTERPRISE EDUCATION INITIATIVES

Summary of examples

Young Enterprise: a programme encouraging young pople to form a trading company.

Enterprise Insight: a campaign to raise awareness of entrepreneurship and encourage positive attitudes.

P1 to plc: a Scottish programme aimed at introducing enterprise in the curriculum to all primary and secondary school children.

Science Enterprise: a programme aimed at science and technology students in universities to encourage commercialization of student business ideas.

Education systems are important in the development of creativity and idea formulation; for example, Timmons[8] comments:

> ***"The notion that creativity can be learned or enhanced holds important implications for entrepreneurs who need to be creative in their thinking." (p. 43)***

Thus, education is an important conditioning experience. Creative thinking can be enhanced or constrained by the education system and this will affect the way we view opportunities, not just in our formative years but later in life as well.

Creativity

Figure 3.1 indicates that creativity will affect idea formulation. The process of creative thinking is now recognized as an important element in management. It has spawned a literature in its own right,[9] so we can only recognize and comment on its importance here. Such literature suggests that obtaining the right environment and the right team of individuals is important for creative thinking and hence idea formulation.[10] According to Clegg, creativity is the ability to connect previously unrelated things or ideas.[11] A creative individual will think laterally rather than vertically (defining a problem in one way), perceive many possible divergent options rather than focus on a unique convergence and use imagination rather than apply logic. The alternative to creative thinking is analytical and logical reasoning; these different ways of thinking are appropriate in different circumstances, but creative thinking is a necessary but not sufficient condition for idea formulation. Providing sufficient conditions implies providing the appropriate circumstances and environment for creativity. There are known techniques which can be employed to improve creative thinking and hence idea formulation, such as 'brainstorming' techniques, but equally important can be the removal of blockages.

BARRIERS TO CREATIVE THINKING

- vertical thinking: defining a problem in only one way;
- stereotyping situations and compartmentalism;
- compressing information;
- complacency and non-inquisitiveness.

Reacting and conforming to 'norms' often limits creative options. To encourage individuals to think creatively, it may be necessary to change the environment or employ different techniques. John Kao's 'Idea Factory' is one example of an attempt to provide an environment as an incubator of new business ideas and to nuture creativity, being designed to provide an environment that is safe, casual and liberating.[12]

Finally, it should be realized that idea formulation can take considerable time. The sudden breakthrough is comparatively rare. Ideas take time to refine; they benefit from discussion with others, from research, from information gathering and from feedback. Thus, being creative is only part of the process. Additional skills must be developed that can take basic ideas, then modify and refine them – perhaps involving considerable research – before ideas become viable business start-up ventures.

THINK POINTS 3.1

Thinking creatively

1. Why is the environment important for creativity?
2. List barriers to creativity in your organisation/university.
3. How can group dynamics affect creativity?
4. Give an example of an entreprise education intiative; why might an emphasis on creativity be an important part of such an initiative?

OPPORTUNITY RECOGNITION

Converting an idea into a business opportunity is the key element of the process of business creation. Moving from the idea stage to the exploitation of the opportunity requires many elements to be in place. The economic environment has to be conducive, the culture must be appropriate for risk-taking and the nascent entrepreneur must have the confidence to take an idea suggested by opportunities through to fulfilment. Opportunities are generated by change. Change may be political, economic, social, demographic or technical. For example, economic change may be characterized by a period of economic growth and expanding demand, which may create opportunities for new business ideas that take advantage of increased affluence, leisure time and spending power of the population. The growth in the leisure industry has spawned many new developments and opened niche markets in areas such as sports, holidays and travel. The increased pace of technical change has created the opportunities for new business ventures in new technologies, in new developments in information technology, such as the Internet, and in new applications in biotechnology. Social and demographic change may provide opportunities through changing attitudes or through creation of new markets in ageing population structures.

These factors are the engines of change, but harnessing such change to create new business ventures requires entrepreneurs to formulate ideas and fit them to the opportunity. It is this combination that is important. The idea has to be right for the opportunity. For example, in the Aquamotive case (which is examined later) the entrepreneur recognized an opportunity to develop a new fish farming application service, but the market required considerable development. The market was not ready or receptive to the new technology. Thus the correct timing of the idea with the opportunity, created by forces of change, is important.

Cultural attitudes to risk and failure can also impinge at this stage. For example, it has been suggested that in the UK we have lower tolerance levels of failure than other nations such as the USA and different attitudes to risk-taking.[13] Cultural factors are obviously intangible and difficult to gauge, but they help to determine whether the entrepreneur that has a business idea – has recognized an opportunity – will be encouraged or discouraged from attempting to exploit that opportunity. If failure is heavily punished, as we have suggested it is in the UK, then fear of failure may act as a significant constraint on this process.[14] We suggest that the existence (or otherwise) of role models will also affect such a process. In Scotland a deliberate attempt has been made to provide more role models of new and recently successful entrepreneurs through the publication of *Local Heroes*, which promotes them as such.[15] Other developments to provide more role models and 'surface' examples of under-represented groups have also been made in the UK, for instance with successful black female entrepreneurs.[16] Role models remove one of the stumbling blocks in the process of new business creation – they help to identify with success and encourage the next step of developing the business idea and identifying the right opportunity. Such role models should not be too successful, as potential nascent entrepreneurs need to be able to identify with them, where they came from and how they were successful, and more publications that help to identify entrepreneurs from many different ethnic and cultural backgrounds are needed as source material.[17]

Habitual and Portfolio Entrepreneurs

The phenomenon of habitual entrepreneurs – entrepreneurs who repeatedly start new businesses through the development of new ideas and exploitation of opportunity – has been identified by several writers.[17,18] The recognition of opportunity does not have to come from new entrepreneurs; existing entrepreneurs will be in a position to recognize new opportunities, buy other businesses and use previous success to develop new ideas. New opportunities will arise just from being in business. These may be exploited by setting up additional businesses (portfolio entrepreneurs); or perhaps through selling an existing business, perhaps to a large firm competitor, and using the harvested capital to launch another (new) business, a process that may be repeated several times by the same entrepreneur (habitual entrepreneurship). Richard Branson and Stelios Haji-Ioannou (see Entrepreneurship in Action box) are classic examples of the former. Examples of the latter, which are more common but less well known, include Sir Clive Sinclair (ZX Computers) and Tom Hunter (Sports Division).

ENTREPRENEURSHIP IN ACTION

Stelios Haji-Ioannou and the easyGroup

The son of a Greek-Cypriot shipping tycoon, Stelios Haji-Ioannou is well known as the entrepreneur responsbile for starting easyJet, yet he has also started other ventures including easyCar, easyInternetcafe and easyCinema. These qualify him as a porfolio or, as he describes himself, a 'serial entrepreneur'. He founded easyJet in 1995 with a £5m loan from his father. The company has achieved spectacular growth in seven years by exploiting a successful model from the USA of a low-cost airline, South-West Airlines. By 2001 it was carrying 8.25 million passengers on 40 routes. Far from being affected by the events of 11 September 2001, easyJet has continued to expand, thrive and increase profits, while the major airlines have, of course, struggled to survive, with famous names such as Sabena in bankruptcy. Adopting an aggressive price-cutting strategy using Internet bookings and ticket distribution, easyJet seeks to fill seats at the lowest cost. As a result, in 2002 easyJet is continuing to expand and handling more passengers. The airline illustrates how a successful and high-profile entrepreneur has achieved success by copying a business model from elsewhere.

In April 2002, however, after floating easyJet on the London Stock Exchange, Stelios Haji-Ioannou found himself up against City institutional shareholders concerned about corporate governance practices and was forced to resign as chairman of the company. He was quoted as saying his skills lay in 'starting new ventures, taking risks and being a serial entrepreneur', and he was turning his attention to launching yet more new ventures. The case illustrates how some portfolio entrepreneurs may be (more) suited to starting and early stage development of ventures rather than their subsequent development.

The reader should also consider this example alongside the entrepreneurial growth theories discussed in Chapter 10.

PRE-START PLANNING AND PREPARATION

A further combination of factors will be important to the eventual success of new business creation. Among the most important are research, obtaining information (to determine entry strategy) and raising sufficient finance. For obvious reasons, little research has been done on new business ventures that subsequently fail, but it is commonly asserted that one of the main reasons for the noted high failure rates (see Chapter 2) of such new ventures is under-capitalization.[19] Researching the market and the competition is dealt with in more detail in Chapter 12, but additional search activity will be required in raising finance.

The length and time of the search activity will depend on the opportunity and the characteristics of the new venture. If formal venture capital is required, raising such finance may take some time because of due diligence procedures (12 months), as well as research and preparation. However, for certain businesses, such as Internet start-ups, such time periods may be compressed into a matter of weeks or even days. Recent research undertaken by the author with entrepreneurs using non-executive directors produced a number of cases where the entrepreneurs had spent some time researching opportunities in preparation for a management buy-in (MBI).[20] In these cases the entrepreneurs had researched a large number of potential candidate companies (up to 100) as a target for an MBI. If informal, or business angel, finance is sought, this will still involve a search and matching process by the entrepreneur before a suitable investor may be found.[21] Even raising bank finance can involve a search procedure and time to find sufficient bank finance and the best terms and conditions.[22]

Preparation means finding the right management team with complementary skills. Evidence on team starts suggests that they have advantages over individual entrepreneurs because of the match of skills brought together within the team.[23] However, the evidence is far from conclusive. Oakey concluded that, with new technology small firms, the best performers were those with a single founder.[24] Teams starts have been the focus of policy 'best practice',[25] but it must be remembered that it is important to get the right 'mix' of skills in the proposed entrepreneurial team. Involving a friend who has been privy to the development of a new business idea may not work unless each person involved is able to bring knowledge or skill that is required in the business. Our research with entrepreneurs that had appointed non-executive directors demonstrated that the matching process was crucial to the success of the relationship and impact on the growth and performance of the firm.[26]

Chapter 12 discusses in more detail the process of business planning, focusing on designing, writing and implementing business plans. Therefore, we do not go into the planning process in detail in this chapter but, as indicated in Chapter 12, pre-start prepartion through market research, competitor analysis and careful planning of entry strategy cannot be underestimated for determining the success of the business start-up process.

THINK POINTS 3.2

1. What are the start-up stages we have covered so far before the market entry and launch?
2. Why should creativity be encouraged in young people with potential business ideas?
3. Discuss, either individually or in a group, whether the traditional education system encourages creativity.
4. Why does change affect the formation of business ideas? Can this explain the minor explosion of dotcom business ideas with the growth of Internet use and trading?
5. What are the research and search procedures necessary in the pre-start and planning stage?

ENTRY AND LAUNCH

As suggested above, the timing of entry is important. While advantages exist to first movers, moving too early can result in insufficient customers to make heavy investment worth while. The issue of timing becomes crucial if the protection of intellectual property rights (IPR) is involved. This is covered in more detail in Chapter 7, but the entrepreneur with a new product or process needs to decide whether and when to patent. Patents are expensive and time consuming but they may be a necessary prerequisite for formal or informal venture capital. Developing the entry strategy is an important part of the launch of the new business; attention will need to be paid to marketing, a factor that is sometimes neglected by a technology-based entrepreneur.[27] The important relationship between marketing and entrepreneurship has been noted by a number of writers,[28] but the concept of the development of the idea and formulating strategies has been explored only by a few writers. The issue of developing entry and early stage strategy is illustrated with a number of cases in this book and, later in this chapter, we also suggest an alternative paradigm for high technology-based firms based on some of our case study evidence.

The role of serendipity is often an underplayed factor in the business creation process. To the casual observer, the entrepreneurial and marketing strategies developed in the case study firms may appear to contain a strong element of chance, yet precursor developments can be highly important as preparation for exploitation of the business opportunity. With high technology-based cases, non-high technology development beforehand, in different cases, was an important preparation for the development of entrepreneurial and marketing strategies concerned with the technology-based ventures. The role of serendipity has scarcely been acknowledged, let alone researched, in entrepreneurial development and strategies,[29] yet our evidence demonstrates that chance is only one element; the entrepreneur must be prepared to exploit opportunities, recognize and take advantage of them. The role of the non-technology phase of development lies in learning with customers, and with suppliers and with bank managers, and in gaining general business experience.

POST-ENTRY DEVELOPMENT

Early stage development is a crucial phase for the novice entrepreneur. The entrepreneur is naive and must learn quickly to understand customers, suppliers, cash flow and dealing with other stakeholders in the new business, which may include the bank manager or other financiers. For businesses in a team start, it is only the post-entry stage which leads to the testing of relationships between individuals, confirmation of their role and the value that each of them can bring. One of the most important issues that a new business faces is credibility. Being new, especially if markets are competitive, means that customers have to take quality on trust, that suppliers will be unwilling to give trade credit and that banks will unwilling to extend significant credit facilities. One strategy that can overcome this lack of credibility is to include an experienced entrepreneur as a part-time director in early stage development. From our research with small companies that employed non-executive directors, we isolated a sub-sample of start-up companies only; in this sub-sample the most important reason for employing a non-executive director was to achieve credibility.[30] Alternatively, the use of an experienced entrepreneur as a mentor may also lead to introductions to key customers, to achieving credibility with suppliers, and to bringing invaluable experience that overcomes the relative naivety of the start-up entrepreneur. A discussion of the value of mentoring support is given later in this chapter.

In addition to achieving credibility, the establishment of early stage networks can be important in the development of new ventures. Part of the reason for bringing in experienced entrepreneurs will be to access their extensive networks of contacts. Where this is not possible, new entrepreneurs need to establish their own network of contacts that may help them to break into new markets during the crucial early stage development of the new business. There is now an extensive literature on networks; as an example, Shaw has provided evidence of the importance of networks in a competitive sector.[31]

MARKETING

A neglected function in post-entry development?

Early stage entrepreneurs may suffer from a form of myopia through too much focus on the product or service, rather than attention to entry and subsequent marketing strategy. This may be particularly true with new technology-based entrepreneurs, and we discuss their situation as a special case below. However, any entrepreneur may take a mere reactive approach to customers, rather than a proactive marketing strategy.

In marketing terms, products or services may be seen to have an efficiency dimension. Customers will buy products and services because they perform what they are meant to do and often entrepreneurs will focus on ensuring that their product or service is as good or better than their competitors', or that it provides something that is different. However, this is not the only explanation for purchase. Customers may also buy products because of 'reputation effects' or 'symbolic effects'.

During early stage development new entrepreneurs may have to compete with established firms that have established reputations and find ways of attracting and retaining customers. This may mean that the early stage entrepreneur has to find novel ways of delivering the service or product. Two examples are given from material in the text:

1. Adopting a direct marketing strategy, as was the case with Laskarina in Chapter 2. Although Laskarina focused on ensuring that the service was of high value, they also adopted a direct marketing strategy to maintain value.

2. In the case of ACE Cleaning, given at the end of this chapter, the entrepreneur purchases an existing contracts list to 'buy-out' a previous owner. In a competitive industry such a move saves an initial expensive marketing campaign to attract customers and, instead, the focus can be on retaining customers rather than winning new customers. Although such a strategy may appear expensive, in reality this was less expensive than establishing a new company and trying to win new customers.

There are a number of factors in the post-entry development stage that new start-up entrepreneurs may not prepare for, or may underestimate in importance. Through naivety, inadequate approaches may be taken to cash flow, dealing with late payers, payment of VAT, cost and stock control and putting in place employment contracts for staff – to name just some examples of common areas that may be neglected by early stage entrepreneurs. The ACE Cleaning case study at the end of this chapter provides one example of how the entrepreneur dealt with such issues in early stage development.

NEW TECHNOLOGY-BASED ENTREPRENEURS: A SPECIAL CASE?

It is generally accepted that start-up for a technology-based entrepreneur may not involve a product on the market during the post-entry and early stage development stage. For example, such entrepreneurs can decide to start trading while still undertaking R&D, or still developing a prototype, perhaps funded by grant aid to overcome negative cash flow. A standard paradigm for such a start-up is shown in Figure 3.2, where the technology-based entrepreneur comes from one of two sources: a public sector research institution or the R&D department of a larger private sector firm. For such entrepreneurs, obtaining patents (to secure markets and funding) may be more important than achieving credibility. Also, because the market may still have to be developed such entrepreneurs are generally seen to face special marketing problems.[32]

New Technology-Based Entrepreneurs: An Alternative Paradigm

Figure 3.3 presents an alternative paradigm for early stage development of such entrepreneurs. Drawn from case study evidence, it suggests that high-technology development can occur after an initial non-technical start-up. The non-technical start-up provides an important preparation for the entrepreneur through the learning experience, providing the basis for the development of more advanced strategies

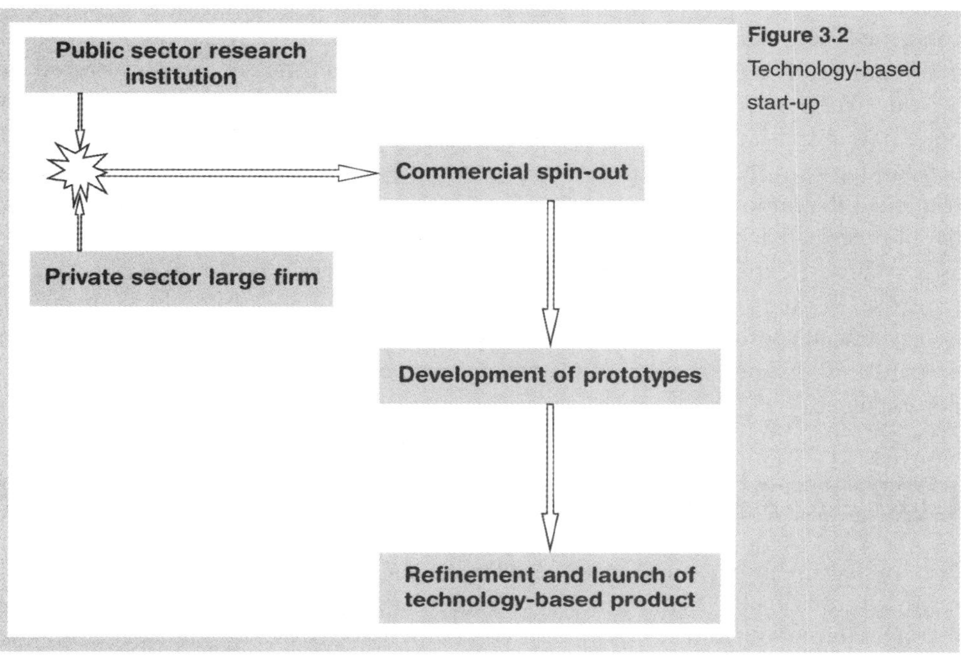

Figure 3.2 Technology-based start-up

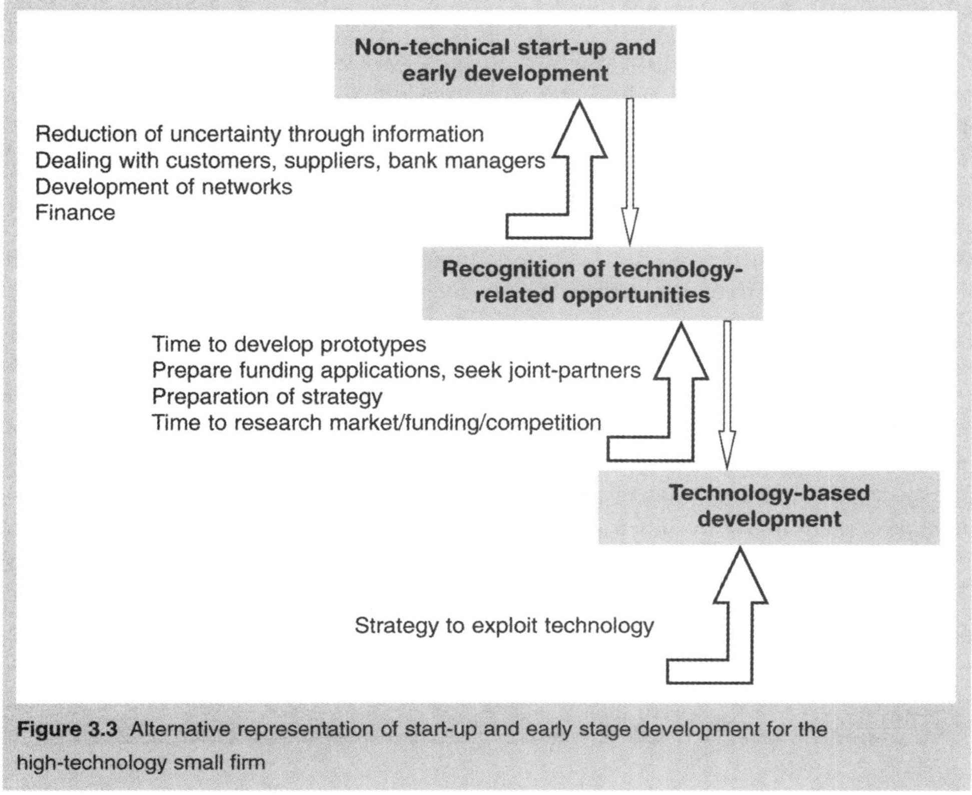

Figure 3.3 Alternative representation of start-up and early stage development for the high-technology small firm

concerned with marketing, finance and risk management for the technology-based development. The importance of this preparation should not be underestimated. It provides the novice entrepreneur with a valuable window of development when potential mistakes can be overcome, lessons can be learned, and contacts and networking can be developed. During this period the entrepreneur learns to recognize the importance of marketing strategies, while moving away from ad hoc developments. The traditional view normally sees the technology-based entrepreneur as a technical expert, in a high-technology environment, and lacking commercial expertise. We suggest that an alternative paradigm can be presented; that a precursor non-technical period of development can be valuable and necessary in the preparation of entrepreneurial strategies appropriate for the technology-related development.

MANAGEMENT BUY-OUTS AND MANAGEMENT BUY-INS

Both management buy-outs (MBOs) and management buy-ins (MBIs) have not been regarded traditionally as examples of entrepreneurship and business creation. MBOs involve the buy-out of the equity of a company by the existing management team, often funded by a venture capital institution. Although this can lead to changes in management style and strategy, it can be argued that little new is created. MBIs involve an outside entrepreneur or management team buying into the equity of an existing company, again often funded by a venture capital institution. As stated before, our research with small companies that employed non-executive directors revealed MBIs where single outside entrepreneurs were involved in the processes of new business creation, thus entailing considerable pre-MBI planning, research and search activity.

MBOs, by their nature, do not lead to new business creation per se and have been regarded as very different from new start business creation. This may well be the case where an existing management team are given an opportunity to 'buy-out' the equity of previous owners, a situation which does not lead to new business creation. However, some MBOs can be much closer to entrepreneurship, where either a team or an individual can virtually transform an old company and its associated way of doing business. In addition, where an MBO is undertaken by an individual, rather than, say, the previous management team, this can be virtually equivalent to new business creation. The ACE Cleaning case study considered later in this chapter is an example of this type of transformation and 'new' business creation. Although it is not strictly a case of 'new business' creation, it does illustrate some of the management issues in early stage development and a management 'crisis'.

FRANCHISING

Another entry route, again not always associated with entrepreneurship, is to take on, or take over, a franchise. Franchising still involves new business creation and also, therefore, all the aspects of the process that have been identified in this chapter. The difference, of course, is that the franchisor, rather than the franchisee, undertakes much of this process, including idea formulation, opportunity recognition, pre-start planning and market research. Franchising has become a growth industry in its own right, with 50 per cent of franchise systems less than five years old[33] and, according to one estimate, one new franchise opening every eight minutes.[34] Although the large franchises are well known and are present on almost every high street, the vast majority of franchises are much smaller, with 43 per cent having less than ten outlets.[35]

Buying a franchise, rather than undertaking *de novo* entrepreneurship, can have advantages as well as disadvantages for the individual. The main advantages and disadvantages are illustrated in Table 3.1.

Advantages	Disadvantages
The franchise is usually based on a proven and tried-and-tested recipe for business success	Proven track records have their price – successful franchise systems require very large investments by the franchisee
The franchisee can benefit from economies of scale, e.g. in marketing, advertising and buying supplies	Although you can sell on to someone taking over your role as franchisee, this may be less than could be achieved with *de novo* entrepreneurship
Market research may be undertaken by the franchisor	Trading is limited by geographical area and location, hence growth of the business will be finite and limited
Training is provided by the franchisor	Problems may exist in the relationship with the franchisor, leading to financial disputes
The franchisor may act as a business mentor, providing early stage advice	Innovation may be limited because the franchise operates to strict formula for production, sales and marketing
Stationery and other business systems may be provided as part of the franchise package	
Benefits from the strong brand name	
Franchise systems are often favoured by banks due to established track record	

Table 3.1 The main advantges and disadvantages of buying a franchise as a means of business start-up

Despite the considerable disadvantages shown in Table 3.1, arising from the loss of control in a franchise, their popularity has mirrored the importance and growth of small firms in the economy, as discussed in the previous chapter. The appeal of the reduced risk, while still retaining elements of entrepreneurship, has obviously been a powerful motivating factor for many people, and the growth of franchising seems likely to continue unabated in the new millennium.

SUPPORTING BUSINESS CREATION

In this section we examine some research undertaken with clients on a local area start-up programme that used experienced entrepreneurs as mentors for new venture client entrepreneurs. The support programme was local to the west of Scotland. The significant difference in this support programme was that it used 'mentors' rather than professional 'advisers' to provide help and advice. To recruit the mentors, advertisements were placed with local media and previous or existing entrepreneurs interviewed and recruited.

We have discussed in Chapter 2 the high turbulence associated with business start-up and creation, a feature which tends to militate against intervention. For example, Storey[36] has compared the provision of start-up support to 'a lottery in which the odds of winning are not good' (p. 16). The basis for this view has been that the blanket coverage of start-up support programmes, such as the Enterprise Allowance Scheme (EAS), have not resulted in a noticeable impact on the quality of firm starts and may have encouraged low-quality firm start-ups, even though Storey considered the EAS to be one of the 'better schemes'. The vast majority of new firm starts are known to be poor job creators.[37] Thus, it has been argued that the opportunity cost of such start-up support is high. The careful targeting of public funds, in the form of enterprise support, at the small number of high-performing growth firms that are new starters should result in a more cost-effective way of supporting new venture development.

The research into the local area programme was conducted on an interview-basis with a sample of 45 new venture entrepreneurs who had been allocated a mentor as an adviser during the 18-month early stage development period. Profile data for these new entrepreneurs are shown in Tables 3.2 to 3.6. More important, and central to the present discussion, however, was the value of the intervention of the mentor. Table 3.7 indicates the perceived value by the new entrepreneurs of the adviser/mentor's advice in the light of other sources of advice used.

The importance of the adviser/mentor was significantly higher than that of other sources of advice and demonstrates the importance of the mentor for short-term and general business advice. For more specific and specialized advice, the role of the business adviser/mentor was less important. For example, when asked who they would turn to for help in financial matters, 36 per cent of the entrepreneurs stated

Criteria		
Gender	male = 80%	female = 20%
Average age	male = 41 years	female = 49 years
Prior employment status	80% employed	9% unemployed

Table 3.2 Personal profiles of the new start entrepreneurs

Business Sector	Number
Business services	19 (42%)
Domestic/personal services	15 (33%)
Domestic and business services	4 (9%)
Retail/wholesale	3 (7%)
Manufacturing	2 (4.4%)
Financial services	1 (2.2%)
Forestry	1 (2.2%)
Total	45 (100%)

Table 3.3 Business profiles

Legal form	Number
Sole trader	23 (51%)
Partnership	6 (13%)
Ltd company	16 (36%)
Totals	45

Table 3.4 Legal status

	Average	Standard deviation
Turnover	£118,655	£179,526
Employment (FTEs)	3.6	8.94

Table 3.5 Average projected turnover and employment

Source of finance*	Mean score	Standard deviation
Personal sources, e.g. savings, redundancy, etc.	4.16	1.38
EAS (First Business Grant)	2.91	2.13
Local authority grant	2.13	2.16
Trade credit	1.71	2.06
Bank overdraft	1.53	2.01
Other public sector source	1.24	1.97
Family/friends	1.07	1.91
Bank loan	0.93	1.76
Venture capital or business angel	0.24	0.96
Other specified source	0.24	0.98

Notes: Likert scale 0–5: n = 60.

* At start-up.

Table 3.6 Sources of finance

Source of advice	Mean score	Standard deviation
Business adviser/mentor	3.78	1.2
Accountant	2.47	1.8
Family	2.33	1.8
Bank manager	1.98	1.7
Friends	1.49	1.8
Other	1.36	2.0

Note: Likert scale 0–5: n = 60.

Table 3.7 Importance of sources of advice

Advice	Percentage of clients
Basic start-up including producing a business plan	44%
General advice on running a small business	24%
Strategic advice	27%
Marketing strategy	13%
Planning for growth	11%
Other categories	2%

Note: Sample size, n = 45.

Table 3.8 Advice received

they would turn to the bank, 14 per cent to their accountant and only 22 per cent to the business adviser. However, in terms of other or more general business advice, 62 per cent said the adviser, with only 4 per cent turning to either the bank manager or accountant.

The type of advice received, as expected, focused on general business start-up and construction and implementation of a business plan. Table 3.8 illustrates that a much smaller number of clients received advice that had a more strategic focus; the table confirms that for other categories of advice the clients turned to more specialized providers.

Table 3.9 illustrates one of the key findings on the value and significance of the intervention and the key value of the mentoring support provision. When clients were asked to rank various criteria according to their significance, the softer and subjective criteria, such as the ability to cope with problems and even the ability to learn, rated more highly than differences made to 'hard' measures such as turnover, employment and profit. In terms of achieving objectives, 43 per cent reported that the mentoring relationship had made a substantial difference to their ability with this criterion. These objectives were concerned with short-term ability to cope with

Difference to	Rank order	Score
Achieve objectives	1	47
Ability to cope with problems	2	32
Ability to learn	3	31
Ability to manage	4	27
Ability to cope with change	5	26
Turnover	6	24
Profitability	7	19
Employment	8	17

Note: Based on Likert scale, no difference to substantial difference (0 to 2).

Table 3.9 Significance of intervention: rank order

problems and general management. The abilities represented by Table 3.9 were relatively generic.

This study concluded that the most positive result was in terms of the value of intervention and the type of support. The support provided was highly valued by the new venture client entrepreneurs and, encouragingly, had more effect on managerial abilities and the ability of the new entrepreneurs to cope with change than with short-term outcomes. In principle, mentoring support, using previous entrepreneurs, should be effective in overcoming the crucial early stage learning period when new entrepreneurs have to learn how to handle change, crises and make strategic decisions. However, there is a balance: such support should not be too interventionist and the findings indicated that training and case work by the team of mentors seemed to be encouraging the right balance. We suggested that this balance could easily be lost as the team of mentors grew (ironically) partly because of the success of the programme.

THE ENVIRONMENT AND BUSINESS CREATION

Chapter 4 examines ethnic minority entrepreneurs who have created new ventures in inner-city environments; by operating in ethnic enclaves, such entrepreneurs have achieved remarkable success in a difficult environment. Similarly, it is arguable that rural environments provide environmental problems associated with limited access and limited (or peripheral) markets and should be treated as a special case.

Business creation in a rural context

Clearly enterprise does not exist in a vacuum. Environments affect organizations through the process of making available or withholding resources and organizations can be ranked in terms of their efficacy in obtaining resources. The creation of new enterprise occurs within the context of an environment; the more supportive this environment, the greater the likelihood for micro-enterprise. However, the efficacy and ability of the entrepreneur to draw on this environment may play an important role in new venture creation. The nature of the environment may even affect the type of new ventures and the reasons for their creation. For example, the expansion of information technology creates a rich opportunity for new software businesses. The environment can therefore affect motivation. It also impacts upon venture survival and growth, so that the environmental resources which a firm controls play a key role in its success.[38]

Environments are described as being abundant (i.e. munificent) or lacking (i.e. lean) in terms of critical resources associated with business creation.[39] These resources have been argued to consist of a well-developed infrastructure: human activity, power, influence, reputation, money and knowledge.[40] Environments are dissimilar, each possessing distinct advantages and disadvantages, and the entrepreneur has to engage with their environment to survive and prosper. This environmental dissimilarity is another reason why there is a wide variation in the kinds of new ventures. Since environments vary, different kinds of entrepreneurs exist and many influences may interact to cause a particular individual to form a particular business at any particular time and place.[41] Two specific factors have been highlighted as determining the level of new business creation.[42] First, the perception of environmental munificence; that is, the extent to which the entrepreneur perceives the availability of critical resources. Second, resource acquisition self-efficacy; where the small business owner's ability to mobilize and gather the required resources from their environment becomes vital.

The rural environment is perceived as being disadvantaged, but it also offers the ideal circumstances in which to study business creation. First, rural areas, by most definitions, are less concentrated in terms of business activity than urban areas and this means it is easier to trace patterns of activities. Second, rural areas are viewed as being lean in terms of those resources associated with business start-up. They are portrayed as being distanced from main markets and main centres of business activity, have a lower and more dispersed population, a 'weaker' infrastructure, local markets are limited due to lower population, the cost of both obtaining and having raw materials delivered is higher due to the remoteness of location, and there may be shortages of skills within the local labour market. It is perceived to be scarce in terms of environmental munificence and the critical resources associated with the entrepreneurial process. Consequently, examining the process within the context of rurality is interesting, since it enables us to see how entrepreneurs overcome what could be viewed as being potential difficulties and hindrances to growth and development. The associated discussion in the student's resource uses the rural context to investigate what entrepreneurs do and develops this into a working definition and description of entrepreneurial actions.

Despite the apparent difficulties in starting up and running a rural business, the number of rural businesses has grown. In the example of the Scottish Highlands, an increase of 24 per cent occurred in self-employment between 1981 and 1991.[43] By

1997, the south-west of England, a predominantly rural area, relied on micro-sized firms to provide 40 per cent of all employment.[44]

This level of growth has been attributed, at least partially, to the attraction of the quality of life which the countryside was perceived to provide, drawing people to rural areas who have set about providing their own jobs.[45] These were often lifestyle businesses. It has also been suggested that the flexibility associated with rurality, the need to be more innovative and competitive, has meant that the more dynamic expansionist firms have tended to be concentrated in smaller towns and rural areas.[46]

Further discussion of the impact of rural environments is given in the student's resource, which also includes two case studies of business creation in a rural environment. Despite the problems of peripherality and limited local markets, these examples demonstrate that entrepreneurship associated with business creation in rural areas can be very successful. This supports some evidence that rural firms are more profitable and enjoy greater business growth (in certain size ranges) than their urban counterparts, possibly because rural environments have compensating factors such as a high-quality and loyal labour force.[47] Thus, although the environment may be a limiting factor, in practice, if sufficient pre-start preparation, planning and research is undertaken, an opportunity for business creation can still be exploited successfully.

THINK POINTS 3.3

1. Suggest ways in which new start entrepreneurs can overcome the credibility problem.
2. What is the difference between an MBO and an MBI? Could you consider MBOs and MBIs as valid entrepreneurial activity?
3. Why can timing be crucial to the business entry decision?
4. Describe why a rural or urban environment can affect the business creation process.
5. How might mentors/business advisers help new start-up entrepreneurs?
6. What assistance is provided in your locality for new start-up entrepreneurs?

CONCLUSIONS

This chapter has considered the process of business creation, often regarded as the distinguishing feature of entrepreneurship. We have seen that the entrepreneur is required not just to generate ideas but also, more importantly, to recognize the correct opportunity for exploiting them. Although chance may be involved, pre-start preparation and planning is also crucial. For example, case evidence, drawn from research undertaken for this text, has demonstrated that precursor preparation before launching new technology-based products was an important period, allowing development of networks, learning and appropriate marketing strategies by the entrepreneurs concerned. This evidence was drawn from cases used later in this text including Alternative Publishing and Aquamotive. However, the last section of this chapter deals with one other case: ACE Cleaning Ltd.

It is arguable that intervention in the start-up and business creation process may not be valuable or productive. However, we have also examined research undertaken into a local area programme that seemed to indicate that the use of mentors (previous entrepreneurs) seemed to have some positive effects on the new start entrepreneurs' abilities to manage and to cope with a period of change. Direct comments by these entrepreneurs have not been given in our brief review of this evidence but, largely, they testified to the benefit that such new start entrepreneurs gained and the respect that they had for the mentors; the fact that such mentors had been in business recently was seen as contributing to the building of trust.

CASE STUDY: ACE CLEANING (UK) LTD

The first of our detailed case studies, ACE Cleaning (UK) Ltd, concerns the creation and early stage development of the business. It has been included in this chapter because it takes the reader to a particular decision point faced by the entrepreneur, Mary Anderson. The case puts the reader in the position of the entrepreneur. You should decide what options are available and what you would do in the same situation. Student assignments are suggested after the case. What actually happened is detailed in the second part of the case, which is available in the tutor's manual that accompanies this text. Further discussion and tutor's notes are also available in the tutor's manual. It is also recommended that the reader should compare this case to another pre-start and early stage case, Alternative Publishing Ltd, which has been included at the end of the next chapter and illustrates ethnic minority entrepreneurship.

Background

After 14 years of continuous employment as contracts manager for a small/medium-sized cleaning company (ACE Ltd), Mary Anderson found herself without permanent employment and means of support. As a result of cumulative debts, ACE Ltd had been forced into liquidation.

As a single parent, and at the age of 52, the job market offered little prospect of re-employment. Recognizing this dearth of opportunity and, in light of her previous experience, perceiving a potential within herself to successfully manage within this familiar market, Mary determined to investigate the concept of salvaging what contracts she could from ACE Ltd and starting her own company.

Start-up

The original ACE Ltd had gone into receivership with debts in excess of £80k. Mary, in acquiring their contracts list and goodwill, was required to take on board this debt. Although the debt referred specifically to leasing and purchasing agreements for equipment and stock, the low capital intensive and high labour intensive nature of the contract cleaning industry is such that a company's value can be measured to a greater extent by its contracts list and customer goodwill. Thus, such contract lists have a certain sale value. By taking responsibility for the £80k debt accrued by her previous employers, Mary ostensibly purchased the plant and equipment required to run the company.

In addition to the £80k that it had cost to 'purchase' the contracts list from her previous employers, the new company required working capital for wages and stock. The industry's staff are paid on a weekly basis, while invoice turnover and customer payment has a minimum cycle of 30 days. In addition, turnover on stocks has a lag period of between 4 and 8 months. As a result, though Mary required little finance for the purchase of capital equipment, the endeavour she proposed was not self-financing in the immediate term.

Financing

In effect, a nominal funding package in excess of £100k was required to finance the launch of ACE Cleaning (UK) Ltd. This figure was greater than any personal savings held by Mary. However, she was able to negotiate the phased payment of accrued debts by offering a 'director's guarantee' of future reimbursement. Thus, the outstanding £80k debt was to be repaid from monthly turnover over a period of 2–3 years.

By offering this director's guarantee to creditors, Mary was also able to ensure the continuation of previous leasing and supply agreements. However, there still remained the requirement for operating capital in the region of £30–40k. On approaching the bank to request the provision of an overdraft facility for this purpose, Mary met with some initial resistance. Although she was in the position to invest £5k from private means, the shortfall she had hoped that the bank would provide in the form of an overdraft (£25k) would result in the company being relatively highly geared. By means of collateral, to compensate in some manner for the adverse gearing ratio, Mary was able to offer her house. The bank, in turn, would accept the collateral, valuing the house equity at £25k. However, there remained difficulties to obtaining the funding. ACE Cleaning (UK) Ltd was heavily in debt, had little or no tangible fixed assets/capital in the conventional manner and, while the contracts list inherited from the former ACE virtually amounted to guaranteed orders, the bank required assurances regarding cash flow and customer payment. Thus Mary was informed that provision of the overdraft facility would be contingent on the company securing an agreement for the factoring of its invoices.

Mary initially had difficulties in securing the factoring agreement. Many of the leading factoring companies were not prepared to accept the risk. An agreement was eventually reached with a factoring company whereby 100 per cent of her invoices would be factored at a cost of 4% of total invoice value. Consequently the bank settled on the provision of a £25k overdraft facility. ACE Cleaning (UK) Ltd was now in a position to begin trading.

Premises

The company had little scope when choosing premises at start-up and Mary chose to continue with the occupation of premises leased by the former ACE Cleaning. Although these were far from ideal, necessity dictated that they would suffice for initial trading purposes and they had the additional benefit of association. Since ACE Cleaning (UK) Ltd hoped to gain a majority of the custom enjoyed by the original ACE, the benefits of continued occupation, and hence visibility and ease of approach for previous ACE customers, were obvious.

Marketing and Client Acquisition

Although Mary was unable to secure the custom of all those firms with whom she had previously worked during her time as contracts manager at the original ACE, at start-up she had succeeded in regaining sufficient custom to expect turnover on these contracts alone to be in the region of £200k (75 per cent of which would be expended on the associated wage bill). This custom had been gained primarily through going 'cap-in-hand' to former clients, offering security through perceived continuity. Further, as a result of her employment with ACE, Mary had been able to establish a considerable network of personal contacts within industry and client groups and her standing and visibility were high within the geographical confines of her immediate market.

No specific activities were undertaken with regards to the direct marketing of the company and its product. It was felt that, since it was extremely difficult to compete on non-price factors (quality being the exception, but not demonstrable prior to sales), given the low profit margins involved, making price competition more subtle, and appreciating the limitations of budget, a sophisticated marketing campaign would not prove to be either cost effective or, indeed, viable. This being the case, Mary continued to use direct, personal approaches. As Mary was made aware of the existence of a potential customer through industry contacts, or public information boards (e.g. newspapers, television, local authority contracts, bulletins, etc.), she made direct speculative enquiries, offering free quotations to ensure that initial contact was gained.

A further operational practice, which can be viewed in some way as an extension of the marketing activities of ACE Cleaning (UK) Ltd was the decision to undertake the contract cleaning of private dwellings. Profit margins in these cases were even lower than those for commercial cleaning contracts. Yet Mary chose to pursue this type of work, utilizing it in a similar manner as 'loss leaders' are used by supermarkets. Carrying out this work increased the visibility of the company. Its vans could be seen out and about, and it could hope for the benefits of word-of-mouth and referral business, since those individuals who could afford the services of a contract cleaner were often in a position of relative authority within commerce.

As a result of these activities, shortly after commencing trading ACE Cleaning (UK) Ltd gained its first significant contract independent of the goodwill and contracts list associated with the original ACE. This contract, the Hilton Hotel at a major UK airport, represented £45k and provided the young company with a broader foundation from which to develop for the future.

With regards to customer maintenance, or the securing of repeat custom, Mary appreciated that her business, in common with all service sector endeavours, required a strong customer orientation. From the outset, customer care, quality and thoroughness were viewed as essential to success. She personally visited each individual corporate client to allow them to identify the managing force behind ACE Cleaning (UK) Ltd and make any complaints, or offer any suggestions, directly to the top.

At the end of the first year the company's turnover had risen to over £350k and, through the activities described above, the company was beginning to enjoy the benefits of referral business.

Management Structure and Style

At start-up ACE Cleaning (UK) Ltd employed in the region of 70 staff. This figure was split into office staff (three, including Mary) and field staff (the number was growing steadily in line with client acquisition). The office staff, excluding Mary, were primarily concerned with administrative and clerical tasks and had no management responsibility per se. Of the field staff, there were two supervisors while the rest of the company's relatively large staff were cleaners. Low profit margins, profits per capita, made it difficult for the company to employ essentially non-productive members of staff, in the form of supervisory or management positions.

The effect of this organizational structure, borne of Mary's desire to maintain a high degree of direct, personal and regular intercourse with clients and the company's concern with customer orientation, resulted in a managerial style that was in some manner dictatorial or autocratic. The structure did not lend itself to the devolution of responsibility. There was no middle-management with which to insulate or separate Mary from the line managers and in-field employees. Any empowerment which was exercised was limited to low-level, on-site tasks. As a result, Mary's time was concerned almost exclusively with the daily operational issues of her company, leaving little scope for strategic questions. Although business planning was undertaken, this was more often a mental activity on the part of Mary, with little time available to establish a formal planning process.

Early Stage Growth

During the first two years trading ACE Cleaning enjoyed steady, if unspectacular, growth. Turnover rose from £354,565 for the first year to £380,772 for the second trading year. However, net profit fell from £12,925 to a loss of £4,495 in the same period. During this period the personal drawings of Mary Anderson followed no formal path and were dependent on the capital needs of the company – when there arose a requirement for the purchase or maintenance of plant and machinery this affected Mary's salary. In effect she was paid, directly, what the company was able to afford.

This relative success over the first two years was the result of increasing the client base from the approximate £200k turnover represented by clients salvaged from the original ACE. Although no formal marketing activities were undertaken to achieve this success, Mary felt that, in the absence of product differentiation capabilities, the vigour and determination of their direct approaches to potential customers played a significant role in gaining additional custom. Everything she owned was on the line and, as such, her motivation to succeed was strong.

This initial growth was further reflected in the relocation of ACE Cleaning to new premises towards the end of the second financial year.

Relocation

Mary was made aware of the availability of alternative premises. These new premises were of a considerably superior quality to those inhabited from start-up, and at a significantly reduced rate (the first three months of occupancy being rent free with the following three months at half rent). A further benefit gained through this move was the establishment of foundations for a working relationship with the local Enterprise Agency, which was acting as agent in the leasing of the industrial estate.

The VAT Dilemma

After two years' trading with relative success, the company may have reasonably expected to have gained a degree of security. However, at the end of the second year ACE Cleaning were suddenly faced with closure. As discussed, they had been trading and trading well; however, they had been trading in the VAT. That is to say, the company had been charging clients the requisite 17½ per cent and, through naivety, had been failing to transfer this revenue to the appropriate government body. In Mary's words the company had been over-trading. Mary had been under the mistaken impression that she would be able to pay the VAT owed by the company late and had been using all incoming revenue for prompt, and even early, payment of suppliers. As a result, the company found themselves with a demand for £18,000 from HM Customs and Excise and one week with which to pay in full. Although from a turnover in excess of £380k this may seem a small sum, the fact remained that, due to the nature of business costs, the money was not available. Furthermore, no assets existed with which to raise the necessary finance and Mary Anderson stood to lose everything.

In retrospect, Mary believes that this situation forced her to 'face up to some home truths'. Until then she had been 'the Boss', enjoying the power without the responsibility. The shock of this crisis brought her to the realization that her role as managing director was to manage and to direct the business, not 'to boss'. She had responsibilities to those who worked for her, to her creditors, and to her customers. After consideration she came to the conclusion that her business and those involved in it constituted an excellent venture which had suffered from *her* poor management, and she determined not to let others endure the consequences of her failings. Mary stood to lose everything but, more importantly to her, her staff (now in excess of 200) stood to lose their jobs.

Included in this case study are the profit and loss accounts and the balance sheets from the first two years of trading.

Financial accounts of ACE Cleaning (UK) Ltd

Profit and loss accounts

For the year ended 31 August Year 1

Turnover		£354,565
Cost of Sales		£269,730
GROSS PROFIT		£84,835
Administrative expenses		
Staff costs	£15,813	
Depreciation	£9,437	
Other operating changes	£46,660	
		71,910
NET OPERATING PROFIT		£12,925
Interest payable		£1,603
PROFIT ON ORDINARY ACTIVITIES BEFORE TAX		£11,322
Tax on ordinary activities		£1,912
PROFIT ON ORDINARY ACTIVITIES AFTER TAX		£9,410

STATEMENT OF RETAINED EARNINGS

Retained profit for the year		£9,410
RETAINED PROFIT CARRIED FORWARD		£9,410

Balance sheet
As at 31 August Year 1

FIXED ASSETS		
Tangible assets		£43,007
CURRENT ASSETS		
Stock and work progress	£10,090	
Debtors	£31,286	
Cash at bank and in hand	£783	
	£42,159	
CREDITORS: Amount falling due within 1 year	£60,165	
NET CURRENT ASSETS		(£18,006)
TOTAL ASSETS LESS CURRENT LIABILITIES		£25,001
CREDITORS: Amoung falling due after 1 year		£4,841
		£20,160
CAPITAL AND RESERVES		
Share capital		£10,750
Profit and loss account		£9,410
		£20,160

Profit and loss accounts
For the year ended 31 August Year 2

TURNOVER		£380,772
Cost of sales		£292,369
GROSS PROFIT		£88,403
ADMINISTRATIVE EXPENSES		
Staff costs	£20,346	
Depreciation	£8,836	
Other operating charges	£63,716	
		£92,898
NET OPERATING PROFIT		(£4,495)
Interest payable		£3,925
PROFIT ON ORDINARY ACTIVITIES BEFORE TAX		(£8,420)
Tax on ordinary activities		(£1,192)
PROFIT ON ORDINARY ACTIVITIES AFTER TAX		(£6,508)
STATEMENT OF RETAINED EARNINGS		
Retained profit for the year		£9,410
RETAINED PROFIT CARRIED FORWARD		£2,902

Balance sheet
As at 31 August Year 2

FIXED ASSETS		
Tangible assets		£41,886
Goodwill		£13,591
CURRENT ASSETS		
Stock and work in progress	£10,412	
Debtors	£39,641	
Cash at bank and in hand	£8,832	
	£58,885	
CREDITORS: Amount falling due within 1 year	£76,951	
NET CURRENT ASSETS		(£18,006)
TOTAL ASSETS LESS CURRENT LIABILITIES		£37,411
CREDITORS: Amount falling due after 1 year		£8,509
		£28,902
CAPITAL AND RESERVES		
Share capital		£26,000
Profit and loss account		£2,902
		£28,902

SUGGESTED ASSIGNMENTS

1. Students discuss the case of ACE Cleaning Ltd in a small group. They are required to identify the options available to Mary Anderson and recommend and present a course of action.

2. Students are required to consider the ACE Cleaning case as consultants; discuss how Mary should change her management style and practices and make recommendations as consultants to ACE Cleaning Ltd.

3. Compare the ACE Cleaning case to the Alternative Publishing case (in the next chapter). What are the similarities and differences between the two cases? From your knowledge of research findings and evidence on business start-ups, are the entrepreneurs concerned with each of these cases typical of new start-up entrepreneurs? How does the business creation process differ in each case?

4. Argue the case for and against intervention in the start-up process by public sector enterprise development agencies.

5. Why might the use of previous entrepreneurs as mentors to new start entrepreneurs be beneficial in terms of impact and development of such new start businesses?

REFERENCES

1. Becker, G.S. (1962) 'Investment in Human Capital', *Journal of Political Economy*, vol. 70, pp. 9–49.

2. Cressy, R. (1996) *Small Business Failure: Failure to Fund or Failure to Learn*? Centre for SMEs, University of Warwick, Coventry.

3. Deakins, D. and Hussain, G. (1994) 'Risk Assessment with Asymmetric Information', *International Journal of Bank Marketing*, vol. 12, no. 1, pp. 24–31.

4. Scottish Enterprise (1993) *Scotland's Business Birth Rate: A National Enquiry*, Scottish Enterprise, Glasgow.

5. Enterprise Insight (2001) *Enterprise Insight*, DTI, London.

6. Scottish Enterprise (2000) *P1 to plc*, Scottish Enterprise, Glasgow.

7. Gavron, R., Cowling, M., Holtham, G. and Westall, A. (1998) *The Entrepreneurial Society*, IPPR, London.

8. Timmons, J.A. (1994) *New Venture Creation: Entrepreneurship for the 21st Century*, Fourth Edition, Irwin, Illinois.

9. Goodman, M. (1995) *Creative Management*, Prentice Hall, London.

10. Proctor, T. (1998) *Creative Problem Solving for Managers*, Routledge, London.

11. Clegg, B. (1999) *Creativity and Innovation for Managers*, Butterworth-Heinemann, Oxford.

12. Kao, J.J. (1997) *Jamming: The Art and Discipline of Business Creativity*, HarperCollins, London.

13. Birley, S. and Macmillan, I. (eds) (1995) *International Entrepreneurship*, Routledge, London.

14. Reynolds, P. and White, S. (1997) *The Entrepreneurial Process: Economic Growth, Men, Women and Minorities*, Quorum, Westport, USA.

15. Scottish Enterprise (1997) *Local Heroes*, Scottish Enterprise, Glasgow.

16. Wanogho, E. (1997) *Black Women Taking Charge*, E.W. International, London.

17. Westhead, P. and Wright, M. (1999) 'Contributions of novice, portfolio and serial founders located in rural and urban areas', *Regional Studies*, vol. 33, no. 2. pp. 157–74.

18. Carter, S. (1999) 'The economic potential of portfolio entrepreneurship: enterprise and employment contributions of multiple business ownership', *Journal of Small Business and Enterprise Development*, vol. 5, no. 4, pp. 297–306.

19. Cressy, R. (1996) *Small Business Failure: Failure to Fund or Failure to Learn*? Centre for SMEs, University of Warwick, Coventry.

20. Deakins, D., Mileham, P. and O'Neill, E. (1998) 'The Role and Influence of Non-Executive Directors in Growing Small Firms', paper presented to Babson Entrepreneurship Research Conference, Ghent, Belgium.

21. Mason, C.M. and Harrison, R.T. (1995) 'Informal Venture Capital and the Financing of Small and Medium Sized Enterprises', *Small Enterprise Research*, vol. 3, no. 1, pp. 33–56.

22. Deakins, D. and Hussain, G. (1991) *Risk Assessment by Bank Managers*, Small Business Research Centre, University of Central England, Birmingham.

23. Vyakarnaram, S., Jacobs, R. and Handleberg, J. (1997) 'The Formation and Development of Entrepreneurial Teams in Rapid Growth Businesses', paper presented to Babson Entrepreneurship Research Conference, Babson College, Boston.

24. Oakey, R.P. (1995) *High Technology New Firms: Variable Barriers to Growth*, Paul Chapman Publishing, London.

25. DTI (1996) *Small Firms in Britain Report, 1996*, DTI, London.

26. Deakins, D., Mileham, P. and O'Neill, E. (1998) 'The Role and Influence of Non-Executive Directors in Growing Small Firms', ACCA research report, ACCA, London.

27. Oakey, R.P. (1995) *High Technology New Firms: Variable Barriers to Growth*, Paul Chapman Publishing, London.

28. For example, Carson, D., Cromie, S., McGowan, P. and Hill, J. (1995) *Marketing and Entrepreneurship in SMEs: An Innovative Approach*, Prentice Hall, London.

29. Martello, W.E. (1994) 'Developing Creative Business Insights: Serendipity and its Potential', *Entrepreneurship and Regional Development*, vol. 6, no. 2, pp. 239–58.

30. Deakins, D., Mileham, P. and O'Neill, E. (1998) 'The Role and Influence of Non-Executive Directors in Growing Small Firms', ACCA research report, ACCA, London.

31. Shaw, E. (1997) 'The Real Networks of Small Firms', in Deakins, D., Jennings, P. and Mason, C. (eds) *Small Firms: Entrepreneurship in the Nineties*, Paul Chapman Publishing, London, pp. 7–17.

32. Jones-Evans, D. (1997) 'Technology Entrepreneurship, Experience and the Management of Small Technology-Based Firms – exploratory evidence from the UK', *Entrepreneurship and Regional Development*, vol. 9, no. 1, pp. 65–90.

33. Tikoo, S. (1996) 'Assessing the Franchise Option', *Business Horizons*, vol. 9, no. 3, p. 78.

34. International Franchising Association (1997) *Franchising Industry Report*, IFA, USA.

35. Dickie, S. (1993) *Franchising in America: the development of a business method*, The University of North Carolina Press, North Carolina.

36. Storey, D.J. (1993) 'Should We Abandon Support to Start-up Businesses', in Chittenden, F. and Robertson, M. (eds) *Small Firms: Recession and Recovery*, Paul Chapman Publishing, London, pp. 1–26.

37. Storey, D.J. (1994) *Understanding the Small Business Sector*, Routledge, London.

38. Chandler, G.N. and Hanks, S.H. (1994) 'Market Attractiveness, Resource-Based Capabilities, Venture Strategies and Venture Performance', *Journal of Business Venturing*, vol. 9, no. 4, pp. 331–47.

39. Judge, W.Q. and Krishnan, H. (1994) 'An Empirical Investigation of the Scope of a Firm's Enterprise Strategy', *Business and Society*, vol. 33, no. 2, pp. 167–90.

40. Aldrich, H.E. (1979) *Organisations and Environments*, Prentice Hall, Englewood Cliffs, NJ.

41. Cooper, A.C. and Dunkelberg, W.C. (1981) 'A New Look at Business Entry: Experiences of 1805 Entrepreneurs', in Vesper, K.H. *Frontiers of Entrepreneurship Research*, Babson College, Boston, Massachusetts.

42. Brown, T.E. and Kirchoff, B.A. (1997) 'The Effects of Resource Availability and Entrepreneurial Orientation on Firm Growth', paper presented at the 17th Babson Entrepreneurship Research Conference, Wellesley, Massachusetts, April.

43. Anderson, A.R. (1997) 'Entrepreneurial Marketing Patterns in a Rural Environment', paper presented at the Special Interest Group Symposium on the Marketing and Entrepreneurship Interface, Dublin, January.

44. DTI (1998) *Small and Medium Enterprise Statistics for the UK, 1997*, SME Statistics Unit, DTI, Sheffield.

45. Curran, J. and Storey, D. (1993) 'The Location of Small and Medium Enterprises: Are there Urban-Rural Differences?' in Curran, J. and Storey, D. (eds) *Small Firms in Urban and Rural Locations*, London, Routledge.

46. Anderson, A.R. (1995) *The Arcadian Enterprise: An Enquiry into the Nature and Conditions of Rural Small Business*, unpublished PhD thesis, University of Stirling.

47. Smallbone, D., North, D. and Kalantardis, C. (1996) 'The survival and growth of manufacturing SMEs in remote rural areas in the 1990s', paper presented to the 19th ISBA National Small Firms Policy and Research Conference, Birmingham.

RECOMMENDED READING

Kao, J.J. (1997) *Jamming: The Art and Discipline of Business Creativity*, HarperCollins, London.

Kao, J.J. (1991) *Managing Creativity*, Prentice Hall, London.

Reynolds, P.D. and White, S.B. (1997) *The Entrepreneurial Process: Economic Growth, Men, Women and Minorities*, Quorom, Wesport, USA.

Martello, W.E. (1994) 'Developing Creative Business Insights: Serendipity and its Potential', *Entrepreneurship and Regional Development*, vol. 6, no. 2, pp. 239–58.

Shaw, E. (1997) 'The Real Networks of Small Firms', in Deakins, D., Jennings, P. and Mason, C. (eds) *Small Firms: Entrepreneurship in the Nineties*, Paul Chapman Publishing, London, pp. 7–17.

Timmons, J.A. (1998) *New Venture Creation: Entrepreneurship for the 21st Century*, Fifth Edition, Irwin, Illinois.

4

ETHNIC MINORITY ENTREPRENEURSHIP

LEARNING OUTCOMES

At the end of this chapter you should be able to:

1. Describe the importance of ethnic minority entrepreneurs for the continued local economic development in the UK, especially the inner-city areas.
2. Discuss and account for the importance of Asian and African-Caribbean entrepreneurs.
3. Describe the untapped potential of development that still exists with black entrepreneurs.
4. Explain why ethnic minority entrepreneurs are dependent on bank finance.
5. Discuss why the issue of 'break-out' has become an important concern for the future development of ethnic minority entrepreneurs.
6. Describe policy measures that could be taken to encourage 'break-out' by ethnic minority businesses in their future development.

INTRODUCTION

The predominance of ethnic minority entrepreneurship in some areas of Britain has led to attempts to explain this phenomenon. For example, writers have sought to explain the motivations of such entrepreneurs and the issues they face, particularly the inherent characteristics of ethnic minority small firms and entrepreneurs who are often 'stereotyped' as concentrated in particular industrial sectors. The most notable stereotyping has been applied to Asian entrepreneurs who are often typecast as 'corner shop' retailers and seen as concentrated in the retailing, catering and clothing sectors. As we will see, this stylized view of the Asian entrepreneur is outdated. Rather more important is the diversity of ethnic minority entrepreneurs with business success in emergent industrial sectors as well as the traditional industrial sectors.

Although Asian entrepreneurs are the most often described and discussed, there are of course many ethnic minority groups in the UK with their own entrepreneurial characteristics. The most important ethnic minority groups in the UK that have been the subject of studies regarding their entrepreneurial activity are Indians, Pakistanis, Bangladeshis, Chinese and black African and black Caribbeans, although the intensity of such entrepreneurial activity varies between these groups.[1] The participation rates for the main ethnic minority groups in self-employment are illustrated in Figure 4.1. This shows that blacks (Africans, Caribbeans and other blacks) have much lower rates of entrepreneurial activity than other ethnic groups.

Not only is business ownership and participation lowest with black African and black Caribbeans in the UK, but they also appear to have the greater difficulties in accessing finance.[2] After a brief review, this chapter examines some of the issues that concern ethnic minority entrepreneurs and uses research evidence to discuss successful entrepreneurial strategies adopted by them. It concludes with a case study of a start-up business drawn from this research.

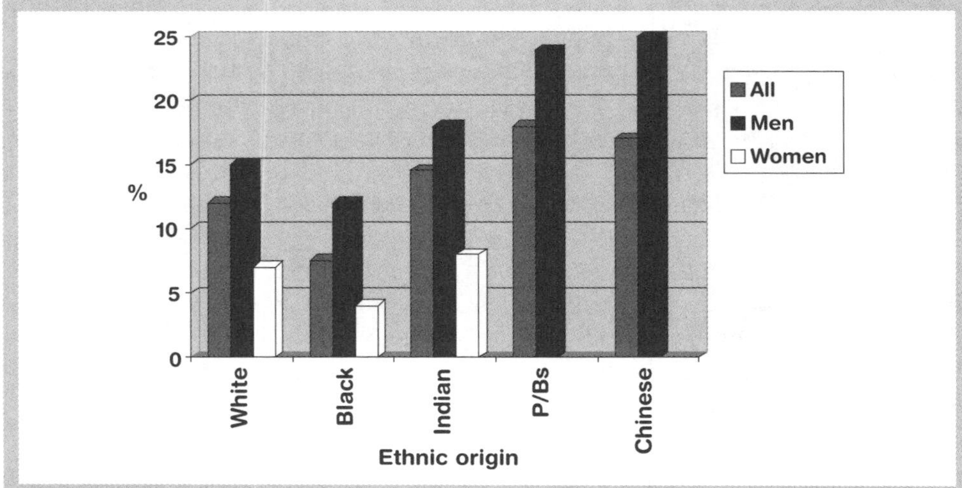

Figure 4.1 Self-employment as a percentage of all employment by sex and ethnic origin, summer 1999 to spring 2000, Great Britain (not seasonally adjusted).

Notes: P/Bs = Pakistanis and Bangladeshis. All refers to all persons. The proportion of women for Pakistanis, Bangladeshis and Chinese is not shown because the sample is too small to be representative.

Source: *Labour Market Trends*, January 2001.

In Britain's history, ethnic immigrants have traditionally been of crucial importance to economic development, a tradition that goes back to groups such as the Huguenots. These ethnic groups have been willing to accept new practices or bring new skills that facilitate significant economic developments. The tradition continues to be significant in the modern economy where Asian entrepreneurs were the first to open retail outlets on Sundays, pre-dating a modern movement towards Sunday opening in most retail sectors. Ethnic entrepreneurs have also been willing to develop in areas that are shunned by 'mainstream' or white entrepreneurs, for example, economically marginal inner-city areas. The location in these inner-city areas has significant implications for ethnic minority entrepreneurs. Not only does the location often limit the available market to the ethnic enclave, but it also makes the acquisition and availability of resources, especially finance and insurance, difficult or (in the case of insurance) expensive.

The potential of ethnic minorities in economic development has been highlighted by statistical analysis of 1991 census data by Ballard and Kalra, who show that one of the demographic features of ethnic minorities is their considerably younger age profile.[3] For example, 33 per cent of the ethnic population were under 16 years of age compared to 19.3 per cent of the white population. At the time of writing detailed analysis from the 2001 census data is still to emerge but Owen *et al.* have indicated that the changing demographic profile and entrepreneurial potential of ethnic minority groups is crucial to the future economic development of Britain.[4]

THE PATTERN OF ETHNIC MINORITY ENTERPRISE IN BRITAIN

As Blackburn has pointed out, entry into self-employment is uneven between ethnic minority groups.[5] Self-employment rates are among the highest in Pakistani, Bangladeshi and Chinese groups and lowest in black (Caribbean and African) groups, with self-employment rates of 25 per cent for men in the former groups, compared to 12 per cent for men in the latter.[6] Recent research has also confirmed that the firms owned by black African and Caribbeans are more likely to be micro-sized firms than those owned by other ethnic minority groups.[7] This recent research confirms earlier findings from our study of black African and Caribbean entrepreneurs.[8] We found that such businesses were typically small (average employment created was only three full-time employees and average turnover was only £25,000) and young (the average age of the business being only four years). However, it should be noted that, given the young age of such black African and Caribbean entrepreneurs and the location of the majority in the inner-city, they have made significant progress and contain high-growth and high-performing firms, although they appear to have more problems accessing finance.[9] Wanogho has also demonstrated that black women entrepreneurs can achieve successful growth businesses in such inner-city environments.[10]

The potential contribution of ethnic minority entrepreneurs to the regeneration of inner-city areas is confirmed by national data that illustrate the concentration of ethnic minorities in the traditional conurbations. Ram and Jones have reviewed the literature on ethnic minorities in business and confirm their dependency on ethnic communities.[11] The economic wealth and high unemployment of such communities often limits ethnic minority entrepreneurs in terms of enterprise development.

ISSUES IN ETHNIC MINORITY ENTREPRENEURSHIP

The literature on ethnic minority enterprise development has focused on three main issues: *accessing resources*, notably finance and labour; *accessing markets* and *motivation*. Earlier literature focused on the cultural and additional forces that led early stage immigrant labour into self-employment and high rates of participation in entrepreneurship. For example, Light stressed the importance of cultural minority status that produced a strong sense of social solidarity in immigrant and ethnic enterprise in North America.[12] Bonacich *et al.*'s study of Koreans in Los Angeles identified access to resources and informal support networks as two of the key factors that accounted for the success of this ethnic minority group in entrepreneurship.[13] Some writers have pointed to the success of ethnic groups despite difficult trading conditions, with survival achieved through piecing together a living from semi-legal activities.[14,15] Light identified particularly the difficulties of black entrepreneurs in North America due to limited access to resources.[12] Models of such ethnic enterprise development (for example those of Waldinger and Waldinger *et al.*)[16,17] reflect these issues and focus on how the entrepreneurial attributes of different ethnic groups determine the ability to access resources and markets to achieve entrepreneurial success.[18,19]

Accessing Resources

The first of the three issues has concerned the ability of ethnic minority entrepreneurs to generate or access resources. In some cases, writers have claimed that advantages of informal networks have given ethnic minorities in business an advantage due to the access to informal sources of finance and family labour.[20,21,22] Waldinger also pointed to the importance of informal networks as a key factor in successful entrepreneurial development of ethnic immigrants in New York.[16] More recently, ethnic minority entrepreneurs' relationship with banks has attracted research. Curran and Blackburn's study of Bangladeshis, Greek-Cypriots and black African and Caribbeans in the UK highlighted the problems of the last group in accessing bank finance, which they considered was due to poorly prepared business plans.[23]

Curran and Blackburn confirm much of the author's previous research carried out with ethnic minority entrepreneurs,[8,26] which shows that small firms owned by ethnic minority entrepreneurs are no different from white-owned small firms in being heavily dependent on the banks for external finance. However, they find that reliance on bank finance was much less significant for black African and Caribbeans; a finding also confirmed by the author's research.[8] As Curran and Blackburn suggest, this could be due to either a reluctance to approach bank institutions through perceived discrimination or differences in approach by the banks to different minority groups. Curran and Blackburn suggest that variations between the ethnic groups in the use of bank finance can be accounted for by different business problems (rather than different treatment by the financial institutions).

The Bank of England Report[1] indicated that there was a perception by ethnic minority entrepreneurs of prejudice by the banks but perceived problems by ethnic minority entrepreneurs may be due to sectoral concentration of ethnic groups rather than any discrimination and called for more systematic research. For example, the report commented:

"There are a number of possible explanations as to why ethnic minority businesses encounter difficulties, including risk aversion behaviour by lenders, sectoral concentration of ethnic businesses, failure rates and lack of business planning." (p. 7)

As a result of this report action has been taken to set in place the sort of systematic and longitudinal research that the Bank called for. The author has been involved with an ongoing systematic study led by Ram involving a demand-side baseline survey of the five main ethnic groups with a white control group, longitudinal case studies and an extensive programme of supply-side interviews with bank managers and support agencies.[24] This study is continuing but, as indicated earlier, the demand-side research has confirmed particular problems of access to finance for black African and Caribbeans.[8] The supply-side findings reflect variety in practice in bank managers' dealings with ethnic minority applications, despite proactive policies towards ethnic minority entrepreneurs by all the banks.[25] This confirms our earlier research with Asian entrepreneurs in the West Midlands and commercial banks that revealed much variety in practice in the importance of financial constraints.[26] For example, in some cases, good practice by bank managers had led to involvement in the Asian community and improved ability of Asian entrepreneurs to access bank loans. This practice, however, was very uneven and was often disrupted by the tendency for bank managers to move from one branch to another, and by changing strategies and staffing policies. Thus, generalizations about accessing resources cannot easily be made, even across one ethnic minority community. Research with black African and Caribbean entrepreneurs[8] revealed that this ethnic group was disadvantaged by its low profile in some cities and had distinct problems that could not be attributed to all ethnic minority entrepreneurs.

THINK POINTS 4.1

Accessing resources by ethnic minority entrepreneurs

1. Commercial banks and mainstream support agencies may be seen by ethnic minority entrepreneurs as 'white' institutions. This can be overlain by perceptions of prejudice in such institutions against them. What could the banks do to reduce such perceptions in order to improve the access to formal bank finance? Similarly, what could support agencies do?
2. Why are ethnic minority entrepreneurs important to Britain's future prosperity in the twenty-first century?
3. What are the five main ethnic minority groups in the UK?
4. Which group appears to be the most under-represented in entrepreneurship? What factors might account for this?

The importance to ethnic businesses of the use of family and co-ethnic labour has been highlighted by studies such as Wilson and Portes, whose research of Cubans in Miami pointed to the importance of ethnic preferences in hiring labour, which allowed this ethnic group to thrive where native whites did not; even where the native population had superior access to resources.[27]

Accessing Markets

The second issue has stressed the reliance of ethnic minorities in business on co-ethnic markets.[28,29] While this may be a deliberate strategy,[17] Light has argued that, in the case of black Americans, their concentration in ethnic enclaves traps them in a potentially disadvantaged cycle from which it is difficult to break into the mainstream of officially registered businesses.[12] UK studies have stressed the importance of the need for successful break-out into mainstream white-dominated markets,[30,31] an issue that we would expect to be more important where markets are limited and peripheral. The related issue of location and the geographical characteristic of concentration of ethnic businesses in inner-city areas has further highlighted problems of break-out.

In the UK, the success of ethnic minority entrepreneurs has been officially recognized in the past, for example with the reports from the Ethnic Minority Business Initiative (EMBI),[32] but the constraints that such entrepreneurs have overcome have not always received the same recognition. Their success has been achieved in marginal economic environments of the inner city and with limited access to either resources or mainstream markets. Debate on developing the need for break-out, following the EMBI Report, led to the view that ethnic minority businesses can only be secured through the development of more diversification into different sectors with discussion about the best way to secure strategies to move away from dependence on ethnic market niches.[23,31] The ability of ethnic firms to achieve successful break-out has been shown to depend on successful integration of a holistic strategy involving marketing, finance, human resources and 'key' contacts with mainstream markets.[33]

Motivation

Attempts in the literature to explain the importance of ethnic minority entrepreneurs concentrate on the relative primacy of 'negative' or 'positive' factors in the motivations and development of ethnic minority small firm owners; for example, Ward and Jenkins.[18] The debate surrounds whether or not the discrimination faced by ethnic minorities in the labour market was the predominant motivating factor in business ownership and entrepreneurship or whether positive factors, such as a group's background experience of business ownership, were more important in the motivation decision. Although Curran and Blackburn[23] have indicated that motivational factors such as 'independence' were significant in entry to entrepreneurship, there is little doubt that a history of disadvantage and discrimination has led to the concentration of ethnic minority firms and entrepreneurs in marginal areas of economic activity.

Curran and Blackburn surveyed 76 ethnic minority entrepreneurs from three minority groups in three different localities. As indicated before, the three groups were black African and Caribbeans, Bangladeshis and Greek-Cypriots and were selected from London, Sheffield and Leeds. On motivation, perhaps surprisingly, they found that positive factors associated with the desire to be independent were higher than expected and they claim that this was on similar levels to white-owned businesses. To some extent, the strong motivational factors were confirmed by our research with black African and Caribbean entrepreneurs in UK cities and with Asian entrepreneurs in Scotland.[8,34,35] Over 80 per cent of black African-Caribbean and Asian entrepreneurs agreed with positive statements concerning ambition and control of their environment. Yet, for a significant minority, negative factors associated with the lack of opportunity elsewhere were also important. Over 40 per cent (for both these groups) agreed that they had faced discrimination in previous employment. In such circumstances, discrimination and the lack of opportunities in the labour market are significant 'push' factors. Evidence from these studies showed that such entrepreneurs were often more highly qualified than equivalent white entrepreneurs. Analysis on motivation factors with black African and Caribbean entrepreneurs showed that a 'mix' of positive and negative factors were important in start-up and motivation. Negative factors included the lack of employment opportunities (although this may also be a significant factor for white entrepreneurs) and the lack of career opportunities when in employment. It may be that black African and Caribbean entrepreneurs have the characteristics that we would expect for white entrepreneurs. However, evidence of discrimination and frustrated career ambitions was found to be a factor with some of the black African and Caribbean entrepreneurs.

Although a number of issues remain unresolved in motivation, such as the low participation rate of black African and Caribbeans in entrepreneurship, attention has shifted from start-up to enterprise development issues. For example, ethnic minority entrepreneurs are perceived to be located in ethnic niche markets, such as Asian clothing firms supplying the needs of the Asian community or black Caribbean hairdressers supplying a service that meets the needs of their community. The issue of 'break-out' from this reliance upon ethnic niche markets has come to the fore and has been recognized as a policy issue for ethnic minority entrepreneurs.

The next section concentrates on the development of successful entrepreneurial strategies, drawing on in-depth case study work and the experience of ethnic minority entrepreneurs in Scotland.[36] Such experience can of course be applied in other areas of the UK, and to other groups of entrepreneurs, but it is also possible to argue that ethnic minority entrepreneurs faced special issues and problems that have been discussed above.

THINK POINTS 4.2

Motivations of ethnic minority entrepreneurship

1. Give examples of factors that would be regarded as positive and negative motivations for ethnic minority entrepreneurs.
2. How would you expect motivations to differ between new start business owners in different ethnic minority groups?
3. In the past, problems of accessing resources may have caused some ethnic minority entrepreneurs to enter sectors that have low barriers to entry; for example, clothing manufacture, retailing and wholesaling. How is increased competition in these sectors likely to affect such ethnic minority businesses today?

SUCCESSFUL ENTREPRENEURIAL STRATEGIES

For this section we combine research undertaken with ethnic minority businesses over a sustained period, involving upwards of 100 business owners in interviews to develop insights on successful 'break-out' strategies and separate case material. One of these cases, Alternative Publishing Ltd, has been developed and discussed at the end of this chapter. 'Break-out' requires successful diversification and breaking into close-knit and mainstream markets. Selected ethnic minority entrepreneurial firms had achieved success 'despite the odds' of their limited access to finance, problems in accessing markets and successfully diversifying, and being trapped in sectors that had declining market shares. Ethnic minorities in business, throughout many areas of the UK, have previously been successful in traditional sectors such as retailing, wholesaling and clothing manufacturing, yet they are increasingly facing declining market share and need to achieve successful diversification and break-out from ethnic market niches if they are to continue to be successful in the future. We examine some of the key success factors involved in the study firms and draw lessons that can be applied in other areas of the UK. These factors are identified under five headings: *accessing markets, accessing finance, networking, diversification strategies* and *empowering the community through entrepreneurship.*

Accessing Markets

One of the key success factors was marketing strategy. Although we found a high proportion of sales to white customers (63 per cent), it is likely that successful future development will be in market niches that depend on high quality of service and product, where the entrepreneurs concerned can use their abilities to react quickly to changes. For example, the owner of a specialized computing and software supplier commented, 'For us it was important to be focused in a certain area, to have a niche product and to control credit and product development.'

In common with other entrepreneurs that had successfully diversified, gaining the initial break was seen by a previous retailer, who had successfully diversified into manufacturing, as important: '[Important issues were] initially gaining premises, machinery, staffing and trying to get into the big boys, the large chain shops, breaking into the market.' For any small firm, breaking into new markets is crucial. For ethnic minority entrepreneurs, overcoming this hurdle was seen as particularly daunting since barriers were overlain and reinforced by issues of race. These factors need to be dealt with sympathetically by support agencies, perhaps through the use of specialists and intermediaries.

A majority of the entrepreneurs recognized the need to innovate, to manage change and to respond quickly to market conditions. It was generally accepted that part of successful development lay in the need to break into new markets. However, barriers were identified that prevented successful exploitation of niche markets. For example, a food manufacturer, when trying to break into a new market, commented on difficulty experienced in the following terms:

> ***" We think it is our colour. We have tried to knock on the door of these supermarkets to no avail. We think that discrimination plays a part, but also, we don't offer anything new. They chop and change suppliers regularly but they are not giving us a chance at all. "***

Dealing with racial bias requires a strategy; it requires persistence, resources and emphasis on quality. As illustrated by our case study publishing firm, diversification may mean pioneering activity in sectors or areas that have no previous ethnic minority firms and, as a consequence, such activity encounters inherent bias. One entrepreneur commented, 'We overcame this [prejudice] by sheer perseverance.'

Accessing Finance

As discussed before, Asian entrepreneurs have been identified with a competitive advantage arising from their ability to finance business start-up and development from informal sources within their own community.[18] While this was still significant in some cases (a characteristic which might lead to less reliance on bank finance), in general we have found that access to bank finance was not seen as an important issue. As Chapter 5 will demonstrate, some banks have made attempts to improve relationships with the ethnic minority community, recognizing the potential of increased business; yet practice is variable between different banks and between different bank managers. There were one or two important points concerning how ethnic minority entrepreneurs can be helped to realize their potential.

We have mentioned that banks require well-presented information through carefully prepared business plans, and points were made which supported further development work with entrepreneurs to improve presentation skills. In addition, for business development, a majority of entrepreneurs said that they would consider equity investments from business angels. Business angels are individuals who are prepared to invest long-term risk capital, but who have individual preferences for certain sectors or firms (see also Chapter 6). More could be done to develop this source of capital, perhaps placing informal networking and finance on a more formal footing, such as the establishment of a 'capital matching agency' by support agencies.

Small Firms' Loan Guarantee Scheme (SFLGS)

The potential role of the SFLGS has been a 'thorny' issue, since the inner-city location of much ethnic minority enterprise would lead us to expect that take-up rates of the SFLGS would be significant. However, we know that take-up rates generally on this scheme, and particularly in Scotland, have been variable (see also Chapter 5).[37] Only a small percentage of businesses were involved with the SFLGS. Its potential needs to be harnessed much more successfully in the inner-city areas, where take-up should be higher. As with other studies, we found that the problem lies in one of *engagement*. Awareness rates are often high, as with other inner-city schemes, but with ethnic minority entrepreneurs there are also relevance problems to be overcome. Achieving relevance means working with banks and ethnic communities to ensure that appropriate communication is used and that bank managers are working with appropriate people in the community.

Networking

One of the keys to successful marketing strategies lies in establishing effective networks of contacts. The case study of the publishing firm illustrates the importance of networks. The two founding entrepreneurs brought in a third director to help with their marketing strategy, but as one of the entrepreneurs commented:

> ***"We brought in [. . .] because of his contacts; he had a network of contacts in the industry. The [desktop publishing] industry is close-knit and you have to fight hard to establish your reputation."***

A network of contacts was often the key to market entry in sectors, particularly when the firm is relatively new. The case study firm was able to solve the problem of successful entry by bringing in an established person with existing contacts. There may be a potential role for similar 'brokers', who may be able to provide market access, or broker resources such as finance. Successful enterprise development strategies may depend upon the identification of 'brokers' who can bring the right contacts to the firm.

Networking must be with the full business community, not just within the ethnic community. As a result, it can involve a bilateral strategy, one strand connecting to the full business community and the second strand concentrated on building and gaining advantage from the existing ethnic network of business contacts. One way to develop effective networking with the wider community is through the development of business/enterprise forums that involve the full enterprise community.

Business and Enterprise Forums

The establishment of business forums can enhance the effectiveness of networks. To be effective they must be relevant to the ethnic community, but they must also involve mainstream entrepreneurs and communities. A comment from a well-respected leader of the Asian community recognized the need to involve all groups to make the forum effective:

“We have taken the first step . . . and it has taken us a long time to persuade all the different ethnic minority groups [Sikhs, Muslims, Hindus] to come together because they all want to form their own business club . . . and it will be open to everyone.”

Diversification Strategies

Diversification strategies are closely tied into marketing and may be addressed as part of an overall marketing strategy. Successful diversification requires careful research, perhaps through a feasibility exercise. First, it requires recognition that there is a need to change, and then a focused strategy for development. This process had been successfully carried out by one entrepreneur who had broken into the marketing of flowers. He comments on the process as follows:

“It is very hard to break away from the traditional wholesaler or importer; we had to do something different, something unique. We tried to get products in that nobody else had. Because of the nature of the market we had to constantly innovate. A fairly big obstacle for us was people's reluctance to buy from a coloured person. I wouldn't call it discrimination, more bias.”

And in developing a strategy: ‘We had to hire a consultant who was here for about six months.’

The need for diversification is exemplified by the rapidly changing nature of the retail trade. A large cash and carry wholesaler predicted:

“In December 1993 the independent sector had 9 per cent via the corner shop; I predicted in the year 2000 they are only going to be left with 6 per cent – we are going to lose 40 per cent of the business from that sector.”

Of course, translating the need for diversification into a workable strategy requires considerable thought and planning. It also requires education and training of shop owners if economic decline for the Asian community is to be avoided. As one entrepreneur commented:

“There is scepticism, there still is, and independent shopkeepers – they do tend to put the cart before the horse really – [they need to] accept that they need to change [and] accept that there has been a lack of planning.”

Empowering the Community through Entrepreneurship

Empowerment was found to be an important factor in motivation and enterprise development in the case study at the end of this chapter. It concerned a publishing bureau started by two young Asian entrepreneurs. As an example of a start-up it was atypical. Both entrepreneurs were young (under 25), highly qualified, had professional careers and their decision to enter entrepreneurship represented a high opportunity cost. One of them had been working as a doctor and could look forward to a career leading to a position as a consultant. Motivation for him lay with empowering himself to achieve his goal of working in and helping his local community. Commenting on the reasons for starting the business, he stated:

“I had a decision to empower myself. Working as a doctor, you do not have time to commit yourself to working in the community. You are working at the cutting edge of a caring profession – you think you are in a position to help them (socially), but you cannot simply because of your position.”

Although the entrepreneurs had different backgrounds, their uniting objective was to work in and help their community. They identified entrepreneurship merely as a means to achieving this objective. This was carried forward to the establishment of a fund at some future date that could channel profits (from their business) to help the community. As one of them said, 'We would like to set up a charitable fund at some point in the future to spin-off some of the profits.' The business was operated virtually as a community enterprise. Where possible they brought in workers from the community. They commented: 'We would help by having people working with us from time to time as well.' The two entrepreneurs took the entry decision knowing that this was going to adversely affect their standing in the Asian community. Again they commented, 'Our status within the community changed drastically when we gave up our professional career.'

This particular case study, along with others, illustrated how successful enterprise development was achieved from the specialization in expanding niche markets. Innovation was achieved through the introduction of either a new service or a new product. Two of the cases represented niche software firms, but in both cases a strong desire to achieve was reinforced by the empowerment principle.

CONCLUSIONS

This chapter has examined issues in ethnic minority enterprise development. The literature is now well established and has indicated, in North America and in the UK, the potential importance of ethnic minority entrepreneurs for the revitalization of the inner-city. More recent literature has studied the maintenance of successful ethnic minority entrepreneurship through accessing mainstream markets. Constraints in the past have been perceived to be concerned with accessing resources, especially finance, and with accessing new markets. However, apart from highlighting these issues and problems that characterize ethnic minority enterprise development, there has been little in the way of positive suggestions for overcoming these constraints and developing successful entrepreneurial strategies.

Our research with ethnic minority entrepreneurs in Scotland confirmed the importance of accessing finance and the crucial need to develop diversification strategies that tackle the reality of the business environment in which they operate. Successful strategies hinged upon the development of effective marketing and networks, appropriate support when required and the availability of financing instruments that met the need of the community. The diversity of ethnic minority enterprise development emerged from the research, a point that has been made by other writers.[38] Yet initiatives designed to help ethnic minority entrepreneurs overcome the constraints associated with the inner-city environment and limited access to capital are often generic and ignore the diversity of such enterprise and entrepreneurial activity.

Issues, constraints and barriers have long been recognized, yet the take-up of initiatives designed to overcome these barriers has been woefully low. Ethnic enterprise development has succeeded largely outside mainstream support and largely without access to special support. In Scotland, success has been achieved through entrepreneurs and other community leaders taking individual action and setting up their own initiatives, using ethnic literature to ensure that firms and entrepreneurs are engaged. As one Asian entrepreneur commented:

“One thing that the agencies have got to start doing is to market effectively to ethnic minority businesses, for example, Scottish Power . . . wanted to reach the black and ethnic communities – they designed a leaflet in different ethnic languages and then took their message to the temples and mosques, and they had a lot of success.”

The diversity of ethnic minority enterprise is increasing. Generational issues have not been explored in this chapter, yet new young Asian and other ethnic minority entrepreneurs are entering entrepreneurship from very different backgrounds from their parents and grandparents. While the family experience and tradition is still important in the Asian community, many of these new young ethnic minority entrepreneurs may have a family background that does not have the tradition of business ownership. It is these new entrepreneurs that are forging the future of ethnic minority enterprise development in the UK. They have different expectations, are often highly educated and enter entrepreneurship against a background of high family expectations not to follow a career in self-employment. Policies continue to defy this experience.

This diversity of enterprise development needs to be addressed through policies that are more flexible and responsive to the needs of individual ethnic minority entrepreneurs and their firms. In Scotland, enterprise forums have been established by individual Asian community leaders, who have recognized the need to widen the business contacts of the Asian (and other) business communities and to develop them with mainstream businesses and agencies. These initiatives, from within ethnic minority communities themselves, need encouragement and support. Best practice means working with the infrastructure and community links that already exist. Developing completely new policies is not only wasteful of resources, but it is also likely to be demoralizing to community leaders who have already invested considerable effort and resources to establish links.

One way forward should be through the establishment of more flexible 'expert' team arrangements, such as a *task force*. The principle involves the establishment of a team that may consist of ethnic community leaders, business and marketing expertise and be capable of drawing on additional expertise in response to the individual needs of ethnic minority firms. This type of support has a number of advantages which include: flexibility, relevance to the ethnic community, responsiveness to changing needs of firms and entrepreneurs, and the ability to use appropriate advertising and other media that will be recognized as relevant by ethnic minority entrepreneurs and small firm owners. In should also overcome, in a flexible and cost-effective way, the problems of low engagement in support that have been discussed in this chapter.

Accessing finance remains a crucial constraint for ethnic minority entrepreneurs. Policies to overcome this constraint have focused on special funding and incentives geared to the needs of firms in the inner city, for example through special incentives for take-up, as exist with the SFLGS. Inner-city Glasgow appears to be little different from other inner-city areas, with low participation rates on such schemes. More such schemes are *not* required; rather, what are needed are mechanisms to achieve greater take-up. Developing effective forums/networks that can promote these funding schemes can be the challenge to the team-based task force. It is a challenge that has to be met if successful future enterprise development in the inner city is to be achieved.

THINK POINTS 4.3

Ethnic minority entrepreneurship

1. Why is the study of ethnic minority entrepreneurship important in the UK?
2. What are the main locations (cities) of ethnic minority entrepreneurship in the UK?
3. What advantages and disadvantages can you point to from the location of ethnic minority entrepreneurs in the inner city in such locations?
4. Why has ethnic minority entrepreneurship attracted the attention of policy-makers?

CASE STUDY: ALTERNATIVE PUBLISHING LTD (PART A)

This chapter concludes with the discussion of the start-up part of a case study of a firm started by two young Asian entrepreneurs, Alternative Publishing Ltd. The tutor's manual provides additional material on the subsequent business development of the case, which illustrates some of the strategies of ethnic minority entrepreneurs discussed in this chapter. It can also be used to illustrate some of the issues in start-up for any business (see Chapter 3). The purpose is to provide the student with a pre-entry and start-up situation and the associated decision-making.

Background

Alternative Publishing Ltd (AP Ltd) was started by two young entrepreneurs, Majid Anwar and Suhail Rehman. The firm focused on business services in desktop publishing and associated computer services such as software development. It was established in a UK city centre.

Both entrepreneurs were in their early twenties when the idea of starting in business was first conceived. They were British born but of Asian background. Apart from this characteristic they both have very different histories. Majid was from a medical family and had himself followed this career after leaving school. Suhail was the same age but had studied avionics at university and his position differed in that his family had a predominantly business background.

They met through one of their extra-curricular activities – community work – to which they both allotted significant amounts of time. This afforded an opportunity to put something of human value back into the community that they had been brought up in and so help young people from an inner-city environment. Both had a desire to help their ethnic community.

After leaving university they found professional jobs with strong career structures. Majid started work as a junior doctor, working in various hospitals, while Suhail started work as a software engineer with GEC Ferranti.

Motivating Factors leading to Business Start-Up

Putting Profits into Community Projects

The entrepreneurs' main motivating factor was the wish to put something back into their ethnic community. They had also devoted a lot of time to voluntary work. The plan was to skim off, in the future, some of the profits and put them into a charitable fund which would benefit others within the ethnic community to realize their aims (and also enter business).

The Desire to Empower Themselves

Majid had a strong desire to be able to empower himself. Starting a business was one way in which he could take his own decisions about every aspect of his life.

This wish to empower himself was not an easy option. He wanted to be able to influence the decisions regarding the course of his life and had to justify them to himself, his family and members of his ethnic community that had supported his career.

Family Background

For Suhail, the reasons for going into business were broadly similar, though his family involvement in business gave him an additional motivation to take this course. He had always had an inclination to go into business from an early age, though he felt that due to a lack of work experience it would have been unwise to do it straight from leaving university. Thus he had followed the plan that he had set himself of going to work for a few years for a large company.

Barriers To Entry

The Influence of the Ethnic Community

They experienced much cumulative pressure to continue with a professional career. In the Asian community a lot of emphasis is placed upon the younger generation achieving a professional career in contrast to their parents, who may not have had the same educational and career opportunities. Therefore, they faced much opposition from members of the ethnic community, who were not able to appreciate why they were motivated to start a business. Also, because of the value placed upon a professional career, to leave their jobs meant a consequent loss in status, which in addition resulted in a narrowing of their marriage prospects.

Loss of Professional Status

The other factor which might be seen to militate against a business start-up was that their professional careers offered them relative security with the prospect of high salaries in the future.

Planning and Implementing the Business Start Up

The Choice of Business

Both of the founders possessed a strong interest in publishing and printing from their days of voluntary work, where knowledge of publishing had been acquired. They were both interested in computing from their extra-curricular activities and, in Suhail's case, from his previous job as a software engineer.

Finally, both partners recognized that future technological changes were going to make computing skills and knowledge even more crucial for a publishing career and their interests fitted this trend. From the outset both of them knew there was a gap in the market which had yet to be satisfied and initial market research had established the feasibility of business entry.

Planning and Initial Phase

Even though they had identified publishing as a route to take, both founders were only in the early stages of planning. They realized that market research had to be done before any business could be started. In the initial phase they had to do a lot of the marketing themselves. They discovered that the building that they were located in was actually the hub of the printing industry in the city centre. This was a feature that had not been known, but it proved fortunate since it provided plenty of opportunities for networking. As a result, both Majid and Suhail were able to use the location as the basis for forging contacts and creating a network of links within the sector.

The marketing skills required for desktop publishing were different from more traditional printing. The importance of networking soon become apparent, as well as the need to forge contacts. Therefore, they decided to bring in another partner and recruited Imran as a third director. Imran was older than the other two founders. They reckoned that his greater experience relative to them would be useful in making contacts.

In terms of director responsibilities, it was decided that Majid should be responsible for the design and artwork, while Suhail would deal with sales, marketing and administrative duties.

Customers and Competition

They had to make various decisions about how to deal with customers and elicit business. The path taken was to listen to the requirements and specifications of the customer for the job. From this the directors would then go back to them with a price for the job and a sample.

Majid and Suhail estimated that that the public sector was the chief market that they wanted to develop. They recognized that there were many projects emanating from these authorities which would require new skills and expertise. In the initial phase they encountered two features of this sector: first, that the culture was generally less competitive and demanding; second, that the sector was generally difficult to break into or, as Majid put it, 'business tends to go round in circles'.

By contrast, the competitive market was variable. For example, in some areas, such as traditional printing, trading patterns were vertical with some competition, whereas in new areas there was little or no competition. In these new areas of desktop publishing and 'printing with technology' it was possible to set their price. This was where they were offering specialized services and in these cases it was possible to dictate price. In areas where there was a lot of competition there was little customer loyalty and they were compelled to negotiate prices each time. As a result, both directors felt that to get themselves established in such a market took a lot longer than for some of their more specialized niche markets.

Included with this part of the case are financial extracts and forecasts from the business plan for the first year.

Financial projections for AP Ltd Year 1

Expenditure	
Insurence, electricity, rent & rates	£6,000
Wages	£4,800
Telephone/postage	£1,500
Subscriptions (journals, etc)	£100
Consumables	£1,500
Legal & professional fees	£500
Advertising/publicity	£2,000
Equipment	£5,500
TOTAL	£21,900
Income	
TOTAL from directions/investors	£15,600
Sales	
Turnover for first year	£25,000
Assets	
As equipment less 20% depreciation	
Liabilities	
VAT	
Directors' loans	
TOTAL EXPENDITURE	£21,900
TOTAL income	£40,600
NET profit before tax	£18,700
NET profit margin	43%

AP Ltd cash flow forecast

	Oct M1	Nov M2	Dec M3	Jan M4	Feb M5	Mar M6	Apr M7	May M8	Jun M9	Jul M10	Aug M11	Sep M12	TOTALS
Expenditure													
Insurance, electricity, rent & rates	1500	0	0	500	500	500	500	500	500	500	500	500	£6000
Wages	400	400	400	400	400	400	400	400	400	400	400	400	£4800
Telephone/postage			375			375			375			375	£1500
	75			25									£100
Subscriptions (journals, etc)													
Consumables	100	20	20	50	150	160	160	160	160	170	170	180	£1500
Legal & professional fees		500											£500
Advertising/publicity	400	150	150	300	125	125	125	125	125	125	125	125	£2000
Equipment	700	200	200	4000			400						£5500
TOTAL expenditure	3175	1270	1145	5275	1175	1560	1585	1185	1560	1195	1195	1580	**£21900**
Income													
Directors/investors	12300	300	300	300	300	300	300	300	300	300	300	300	£15600
Sales		500	1000	1000	1500	2000	2000	3000	3000	3000	4000	4000	£25000
TOTAL income	12300	800	1300	1300	1800	2300	2300	3300	3300	3300	4300	4300	£40600
Cash flow	9125	(470)	155	(3975)	625	740	715	2115	1740	2105	3105	2720	£18700
Opening Balance	12300	9125	8655	8810	4835	5640	6200	6915	9030	10770	12875	15980	
Closing Balance	9125	8655	8810	4835	5640	6200	6915	9030	10770	12875	15980	18700	

SUGGESTED ASSIGNMENTS

1. Consider the case of Alternative Publishing Ltd – should Majid and Suhail start the business? In your answer, consider the advantages and disadvantages of entrepreneurship for these two ethnic minority entrepreneurs.

2. There has been considerable research effort into understanding characteristics of ethnic minority entrepreneurs, the issues that they face and their potential in economic regeneration and recovery. Using material from this chapter, discuss the potential reasons for this attention with Asian ethnic minority entrepreneurs.

3. Why should black African and black Caribbean entrepreneurs have been neglected as a focus of research on ethnic minorities?

REFERENCES

1. Bank of England (1999) *The Financing of Ethnic Minority Firms in the UK: A Special Report*, Bank of England, London.

2. Smallbone, D. Ram, M. Deakins, D. and Baldock, R. (2001) 'Access to Finance by Ethnic Minority Businesses: Some Results from a National Study', paper presented to the 24th ISBA National Small Firms Policy and Research Conference, November, Leicester.

3. Ballard, R. and Kalra, V.S. (1994) *Ethnic Dimensions of the 1991 Census*, University of Manchester, Manchester.

4. Owen, D., Green, A., Maguire, M. and Pitcher, J. (2000) 'Patterns of Labour Market Participation in Ethnic Minority Groups', *Labour Market Trends*, November, pp. 505–10.

5. Blackburn, R. (1994) 'Ethnic Enterprise in Britain', paper presented to the Ethnic Minority Small Firms Conference, University of Central England, Birmingham.

6. Twomey, B. (2001) 'Labour Market Participation of Ethnic Groups', *Labour Market Trends*, January, pp. 29–41.

7. Smallbone, D. and Baldock, R. (2001) *Access to Finance and Business Support by Ethnic Minority Businesses: First Stage Report*, British Bankers' Association, London.

8. Ram, M. and Deakins, D. (1995) *African-Caribbean Entrepreneurship in Britain*, University of Central England, Birmingham.

9. Ram, M., Smallbone, D., Deakins, D. and Jones, T. (2001) 'Banking on Break-Out: Finance and the Development of Ethnic Minority Businesses', paper presented to the 15th Rent Conference, Turku, Finland, November.

10. Wanogho E. (1997) *Black Women Taking Charge*, EW Publishing, London.

11. Ram, M. and Jones, T. (1998) *Ethnic Minorities in Business*, Small Business Research Trust, Milton Keynes.

12. Light, I. (1984) 'Immigrants and Ethnic Enterprise in North America', *Immigrants and Ethnic Enterprise in North America*, vol. 7, no. 2.

13. Bonacich, E., Light, I. and Wong, C. (1977) 'Koreans in Business', *Society*, vol. 14, pp. 54–9.

14. Light, I. (1980) 'Asian Enterprise in America', in Cummings, S. (ed.) *Self-Help in Urban America*, Kennikat Press, New York, pp. 33–57.

15. Glasgow, D. (1980) *The Black Underclass*, Josey-Bass, San Francisco.

16. Waldinger, R. (1988) 'The Ethnic Division of Labour Transformed: Native Minorities and New Immigrants in Post-industrial New York', *New Community*, vol. 14, no. 3.

17. Waldinger, R., Aldrich, H., Ward, R. and Associates (eds) (1990) *Ethnic Entrepreneurs*, Sage, London.

18. Ward, R. and Jenkins, R. (eds) (1984) *Ethnic Communities in Business*, Cambridge, London.

19. Waldinger, R., Aldrich, H., Ward, R. and Associates (1989) *Ethnic Entrepreneurs*, Sage, London.

20. Light, I. and Bonacich, E. (1988) *Immigrant Entrepreneurs*, California University Press, Berkley.

21. Werbner, P. (1990) 'Renewing an Industrial Past: British Pakistani Entrepreneurship in Manchester', *Migration*, vol. 8, pp. 7–41.

22. Ward, R. (1991) 'Economic Development and Ethnic Business', in Curran, J. and Blackburn, R. (eds) *Paths of Enterprise*, Routledge, London.

23. Curran, J. and Blackburn, R. (1993) *Ethnic Enterprise and the High St Bank*, Kingston Small Business Research Centre, Kingston University.

24. British Bankers' Association (2001) *Ethnic Minority Businesses: Access to Finance and Business Support*, Press Release, BBA, London.

25. Deakins, D., Ram M., Smallbone, D. and Fletcher M. (2002) 'Decision-making and the Development of Relationships with Ethnic Minority Entrepreneurs by UK Bankers', paper presented to the 2002 Babson Entrepreneurship Research Conference, Boulder, Colorado, June.

26. Deakins, D., Hussain, G. and Ram, M. (1993) *The Finance of Ethnic Minority Entrepreneurs*, University of Central England, Birmingham.

27. Wilson, K.L. and Portes, A. (1980) 'Immigrant Enclaves: An analysis of the labour market experiences of Cubans in Miami', *American Journal of Sociology*, vol. 86, pp. 295–319.

28. Reeves, F. and Ward, R. (1984) 'West Indian Business in Britain', in Ward, R. and Jenkins, R. (eds) *Ethnic Communities in Business*, Cambridge, London.

29. Jones, T., McEvoy, D. and Barrett, J. (1992) 'Raising Capital for the Ethnic Minority Small Business', paper presented for the ESRC Small Business Research Initiative, University of Warwick, September.

30. Ram, M. (1993) *Managing to Survive: Working Lives in Small Firms*, Routledge, London.

31. Ram, M. and Hillin, G. (1994) 'Achieving Break-Out: Developing a Strategy for the Ethnic Minority Firm in the Inner-City', paper presented to the Ethnic Minority Small Firms Seminar, UCE, Birmingham, March.

32. Ethnic Minority Business Development Initiative (EMBI) (1991) *Final Report*, Home Office, London.

33. Ram, M. and Hillin, G. (1994) 'Achieving Break-Out: Developing Mainstream Ethnic Minority Businesses', *Small Business and Enterprise Development*, vol. 1, no. 2, pp. 15–21.

34. Deakins, D., Majmudar, M. and Paddison, A. (1995) *Ethnic Minority Enterprise in the West of Scotland*, Paisley Enterprise Research Centre, University of Paisley.

35. Deakins, D., Hussain, G. and Ram, M. (1994) *Ethnic Entrepreneurs and the Commercial Banks: Untapped Potential*, University of Central England, Birmingham.

36. Deakins, D., Majmudar, M. and Paddison, A. (1997) 'Developing Success Strategies for Ethnic Minorities in Business: Evidence from Scotland', *New Community*, vol. 23, no. 3, pp. 325–42.

37. Scottish Enterprise (1993) *Scotland's Business Birth Rate: A National Enquiry*, Scottish Enterprise, Glasgow.

38. Ram, M. and Sparrow, J. (1993) 'Minority Firms, Racism and Economic Development', *Local Economy*, vol. 8, no. 3, pp. 117–29.

RECOMMENDED READING

Ram, M. and Jones, T. (1998) *Ethnic Minorities in Business*, Small Business Research Trust, Milton Keynes.

Bank of England (1999) *The Financing of Ethnic Minority Firms in the UK: A Special Report*, Bank of England, London.

Smallbone, D. and Baldock, R. (2001) *Access to Finance and Business Support by Ethnic Minority Businesses: First Stage Report*, British Bankers' Association, London.

Twomey, B. (2001) 'Labour Market Participation of Ethnic Groups', *Labour Market Trends*, January, pp. 29–41.

5

SOURCES OF FINANCE: OVERVIEW OF ISSUES AND DEBT FINANCE

LEARNING OUTCOMES

At the end of this chapter you should be able to:

1. Discuss the importance of alternative sources of finance for entrepreneurs and small and medium-sized enterprises.
2. Describe why entrepreneurs and SMES are at a disadvantage compared with large firms in financial markets.
3. Appreciate some of the problems that face the providers of finance to the SME sector.
4. Compare survey results and known national characteristics on the importance of sources of finance for start-up entrepreneurs and existing ventures.
5. Describe research findings comparing risk assessment practices of English and Scottish bank managers and be able to indicate the main differences in these practices.
6. Appreciate and account for the importance of bank finance as a source of external finance for entrepreneurs and small firm owners.

The following additional learning outcomes are applicable if the Peters' case study, available in the students' online resources, is also used in conjunction with this chapter. You should be able to:

7. Discuss how this case differs from the majority of small firms and typical start-ups as shown by Chapters 3 and 4.
8. Describe the roles and main functions of the three entrepreneurs and discuss how these match the concepts of entrepreneurs discussed in Chapter 1.
9. Understand some of the financial constraints involved in a non-standard start-up.
10. Be able to answer questions from bank managers on any start-up proposition for a new firm, including that of your own business.
11. Describe the advantages of a 'team start' as opposed to an individual start-up.

INTRODUCTION

This chapter is concerned predominantly with sources of finance for entrepreneurs and small firm and medium-sized enterprises (SMEs), taking definitions of SMEs as given in Chapter 2. Thus for many small firms certain sources of finance are not available due to entry barriers. For example, many entrepreneurs and SMEs are automatically excluded from some financial sources, such as the Stock Exchange, and face difficulties raising types of finance such as long-term loans, because of the automatically higher risk associated with firms that have little equity in the form of share capital. In the majority of cases the only equity is that of the proprietors. This chapter will give an overview of the sources of finance, but the focus is on debt finance. The following chapter will examine sources of equity finance. Some time will be spent examining theoretical issues that provide the foundation for an examination of this important area. The students' online learning resources contain a case study, Peters and Co., which is linked to this chapter to give a practical example of a start-up proposition that is seeking finance.

It is worth making a distinction between the theoretical basis of entrepreneurs' and SMEs' finance and what we know about the sources of finance that they actually use. It is easy to hypothesize, from what has been said above, about the difficulties facing entrepreneurs and small firms; that they are likely to rely heavily on personal savings and equity for long-term finance, and perhaps trade credit for short-term finance. However, these hypotheses need to be balanced about what actually happens (i.e. the empirical evidence). We will consider each in turn.

There are a variety of sources of finance available to the entrepreneur and the small and medium-sized firm. A simple way of classifying these sources is shown in Figure 5.1. This figure shows sources of finance classified as internal and external.

Internal sources of finance include the personal equity of the entrepreneur, usually in the form of savings, remortgages, or perhaps money raised from family and friends. After the initial start-up of the firm, retained profits and earnings provide internal capital. Usually within an SME it is normal for internal sources to provide the major proportion of the firm's capital and financial structure. External finance can be drawn from a number of sources. As shown by Figure 5.1, the principal sources for the entrepreneur are advances from banks, equity from venture capitalists and informal investors and short-term trade credit. Other external sources may include leasing, hire-purchase and factoring. In the UK the small firm entrepreneur may qualify for grants or 'soft loans' from government bodies such as the DTI (e.g. Regional Selective Assistance, RSA) or qualify for other schemes such as the Small Firms' Loan Guarantee Scheme (SFLGS). Local government may also provide loans and grants, and there are a number of agencies that have attempted to set up their own financing schemes for small firms. These may include venture capital and loans from enterprise agencies, Business Links, Regional Development Agencies (RDAs) or, in Scotland, the Local Enterprise Companies (LECs) and other development agencies.

Whether entrepreneurs face real difficulties in raising external finance can be disputed; but the concern with this area by policy-makers has given rise to a range of assistance that is now available to small firms and entrepreneurs. In particular small-scale community-based funds have been the subject of recent initiatives through funds established via the Small Business Service, notably the Pheonix Fund and the

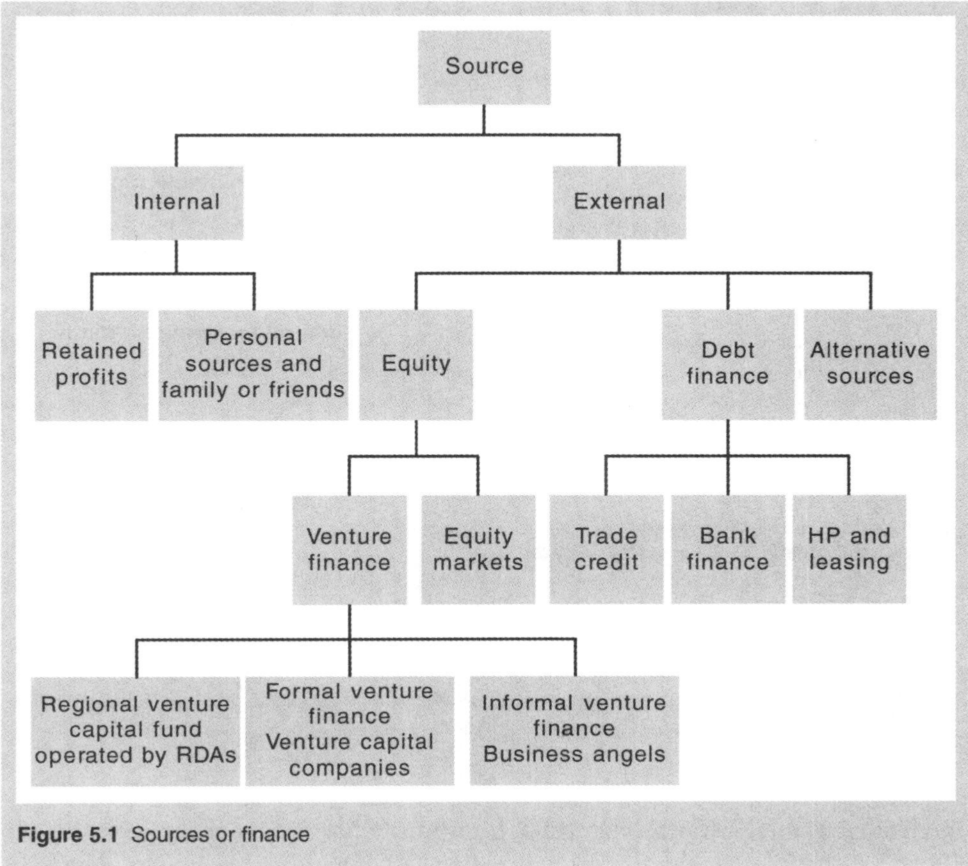

Figure 5.1 Sources or finance

Early Growth Fund.[1] Whether these schemes are effective is an issue which we touch upon later, but they have arisen at least in part because of theoretical concerns that small firm entrepreneurs will be at a disadvantage in raising finance compared to large firms. In particular, concern has centred on whether entrepreneurs face finance gaps, because the supply of relatively small amounts of finance that small firms require, less than £200,000, can be uneconomic to provide and subsequently monitor by financial institutions (especially when considering sources of equity capital). We turn to consider these issues in more detail.

ISSUES FOR SMEs AND ENTREPRENEURS

1. Finance Gaps

If gaps arise they do so because of mismatches between supply and demand. The existence of a finance gap will arise because demand from small firms is greater than the willingness of financial institutions to supply the finance at current market conditions. For finance such as bank loans, these gaps may be termed credit rationing. A gap may exist such as that illustrated by Figure 5.2, where demand exceeds the available supply at current market rates of interest.

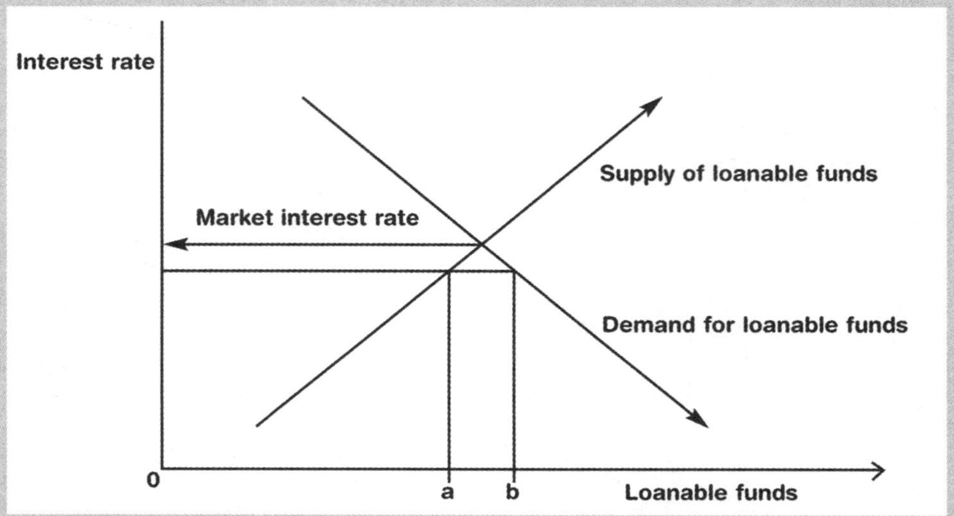

Figure 5.2 Demand and supply for bank credit

Notes

i) The market interest rate is likely to be established below the equilibrium level due to state and Bank of England regulation.

ii) The demand for loanable funds is assumed to consist of homogeneous and 'good' propositions seeking bank finance, implying a 'gap' which could be met by rationing.

In Figure 5.2, total advances that small firms would like to take up are given by ob. However, the amount that banks are willing to supply is given by oa. Hence the existence of a debt gap given by the distance ab. Governments can attempt to close this gap by shifting the supply curve of (debt) finance to the right by the introduction of schemes such as the Small Firms' Loan Guarantee Scheme (SFLGS).

The discussion so far is an over-simplification of the market for small firm entrepreneurs' finance. For example, we are assuming that all propositions from small firms that banks receive are homogeneous. This will patently not be the case and we would expect some propositions to treated more favourably than others. An equally important point arises about whether the 'good' propositions receive finance and whether the 'poor' propositions do not. This is the problem of adverse selection that is discussed in more detail below.

Finance gaps, however, have been recognized for over 60 years. They were first highlighted by the Macmillan Report of 1931[2] and subsequently termed the 'Macmillan gap'. Macmillan found, at the time, that small businesses and entrepreneurs would find it difficult to raise amounts of less than £200,000, equivalent to £4 million today. The Stock Exchange required a minimum figure of this amount to allow the trading of equity capital in a firm. There is little doubt that this gap has been substantially narrowed with the development of the venture capital industry in the UK. However, various official reports and other researchers have pointed to the continued existence of an equity gap in the UK.[3] There is general consensus that there is still a gap for raising equity of amounts below £250,000, although, as discussed in the next chapter, there have been important recent developments in the promotion of sources of informal venture capital. This equity gap for SMEs and entrepreneurs still exists because of the factors discussed below.

Reasons for the continued existence of equity gaps

1. It is not economic to issue shares for relatively small amounts of equity on the Stock Exchange (e.g. commission costs are high for small issues of less than £1m).

2. Difficulties can exist in getting a listing on the Stock Exchange. This did become easier with the development of the Unlisted Securities Market (USM) and the Third and Over The Counter (OTC) markets, but the need for a trading record of at least three years is a barrier to many small firms. The demise of the USM in 1993 was a testimony both to the problems of entrepreneurs and small firms in the raising of equity and to the problems of providers in the administration of markets for relatively small amounts of equity capital. The launch of an Alternative Investment Market (AIM) has been more successful, however, and has provided a successful alternative stock market to the London Stock Exchange.

3. It is not economic for venture capitalists to provide relatively small amounts of equity capital. The reasons for this are that venture capital companies will want to monitor the performance of the company closely, because they supply equity – not debt – capital and are consequently not guaranteed a return. Furthermore, the costs of arranging the finance and the appraisal of propositions are generally fixed costs.[4] A full discussion of venture capital is given in the next chapter.

4. Venture capitalists require high rates of return because they are assuming higher risks than the banks. Only certain high-performing entrepreneurs and firms, the high-growth firms, will be able to achieve the high rates of return required by venture capitalists who have in turn to satisfy the requirements of the shareholders in the venture capital fund. As a consequence of this, venture capitalists tend to concentrate on certain sectors of the economy only, or on certain types of finance, such as management buy-outs (MBOs) (see Chapter 6). Recent figures on the formal venture capital industry show that the majority of the sector's funds are invested in MBOs and management buy-ins (MBIs),[5] so that the importance of this sector for the finance of SMEs and entrepreneurs is limited.

5. Venture capitalists will apply a 'due diligence' procedure to any proposition that is being considered for investment. This will take a considerable period of time and only a small proportion of applications for formal venture capital eventually receive funding after the due diligence procedure. Less than 5 per cent of applications for such formal venture capital will receive funding from this sector. It is worth noting that for a time due diligence was short-circuited during the

Internet 'bubble' of 1999–2000, with the need to secure venture finance in 'days' rather than 'months'. Well-publicized Internet companies' problems since then have seen such short-circuit mechanisms largely decline, for example the demise of First Tuesday, a networking market mechanism for Internet entrepreneurs and venture capitalists that was popular in terms of attendance during the Internet company boom.[6]

6. Venture capitalists will also require an exit route for the sale of their shareholding after a period of time with their investment in the entrepreneurial concern. The normal method of seeking an exit route for such a holding will be to seek an initial public offering (IPO) on the Stock Exchange or AIM. Thus, venture capitalists will seek high-growth entrepreneurial concerns that can be turned within a short period (say five years) into public companies and provide an IPO as an exit route for their holding and their funds.

7. Venture capitalists will also seek to take an active part in the management of the company to safeguard their investment. They will seek to add value to their investment through an active role in the management and use their networking capabilities to open up additional opportunities for the growth of the entrepreneurial concern. The extent to which venture capitalists can add value to the management of investee companies has been one of the concerns in the venture capital sector.

Informal venture capital, which has seen important developments in recent years, has considerable potential to reduce equity gaps for small firms and is discussed in more detail, together with a full discussion of the formal venture capital industry, in the next chapter. For the rest of this chapter we focus on the banks as a source of entrepreneurial finance.

2. Finance and the Banks

For the entrepreneur, banks are easily accessible (through high-street branches) and provide short-term debt finance that in theory is attractive; the entrepreneur does not give up control and debt may be provided at times to suit the entrepreneur. However, banks, theoretically, face issues in assessing propositions from entrepreneurs. These issues arise in any investment situation where providers and borrowers have different sets of information. However, for banks we get two problems – adverse selection and moral hazard.

ADVERSE SELECTION

Adverse selection occurs when either the bank provides finance for a venture that subsequently fails or the bank refuses finance for a venture that would have been successful. It may occur because the bank does not have all the available information or the information is imperfect. The difficulty here is that the information required by the bank to assess perfectly the risk of the proposition is not costless to obtain. However, it can be argued that banks should reduce the mistakes they make, since they should have the skills and resources necessary to increase the frequency of correct decisions.

MORAL HAZARD

Moral hazard is more difficult for the bank to control. Once an entrepreneur has raised the bank loan, there is no guarantee that they will act in the best interests of the bank. Therefore, moral hazard is a monitoring problem for the bank and, for relatively small amounts of finance, it is not economic for banks to monitor performance closely. For this reason banks will usually require security, yet this contributes to the problems facing entrepreneurs. Those entrepreneurs without substantial equity and insufficient security will fall into the debt gap.

Bank assessments of small firm applications for loan finance are examples of decision-making under uncertainty, incorporating asymmetric information for the provider and the client. The foundations of analysis of possible mismatches between supply and demand that can occur under these conditions have been laid down by Akerlof's seminal 1970 paper.[7] Writers have developed the significance of these conditions for finance theory using a principal–agent framework.[8,9,10] The relevance of these insights is limited when considering the finance of entrepreneurs and small firms that have restricted access to financial markets. Concepts of moral hazard and adverse selection, however, are still important and have been further refined by later writers.[11,12,13]

Stiglitz and Weiss have shown that the problems of moral hazard and adverse selection are likely to produce credit rationing, insufficient credit available for all sound propositions.[14] It is possible to argue that these problems can lead to a credit glut[15] and at least one report has suggested that growing firms who wished to expand with sound propositions were able to raise finance when they needed to.[16] However, surveys for the Forum of Private Businesses and the Federation of Small Businesses[17,18] suggest that there are still mismatches between providers (the commercial banks) and entrepreneurial business owners.

THINK POINTS 5.1

Raising entrepreneurial finance

1. What difficulties do entrepreneurs face in raising equity finance? How do you expect this to differ with start-ups and with established firms?
2. List the main sources of debt and equity finance for entrepreneurs.
3. Taking the bank manager–entrepreneur relationship:
   (a) What flows of information might exist between the bank manager and entrepreneur?
   (b) Why might adverse selection and moral hazard exist for bankers as a result of the nature of such flows of information?

Research by the author has revealed that adverse selection certainly occurs in the UK and that risk assessment practices of UK bank managers are considerably different from their counterparts in Germany and Holland.[19,20] Criteria used in Germany and Holland for risk assessment are different and less likely to lead to adverse selection.

RESEARCH WITH BANK MANGERS

What we did

Using a real business plan, the author has previously taken the role of entrepreneurs seeking a funding proposition from 30 bank officers in the UK for a new venture. We expected bank officers to place more importance on the abilities and experience of the entrepreneur, since financial information which might appear as financial projections of income and costs in the cash flow forecast will be subject to uncertainty and treated with caution. Of course, with new propositions there is no financial track record of profitability and other criteria which may be used to assess existing propositions such as liquidity, sales growth, debtors and other measures of financial performance.

If the new entrepreneurship involves an application of new technology, we have the added factor of technological uncertainty. For these propositions, we expected the banks to develop networking methods with outside institutions that can provide information on the assessment of the technology and the technical abilities of the entrepreneur that would help to reduce the more acute problem of asymmetric information.

What we found

We found that, of the 30 bank officers, 50 percent would have backed the proposition and 50 per cent would not, but that there was also considerable variation in the approach of different officers. We also found that there was a bias in approach to financial criteria, whereas important management criteria were discounted. Table 5.1 illustrates the importance of different information sought by bank managers on the proposition. We can see from this table that only 10 per cent of managers considered small business experience and enterprise ability to be important. Further research by the author revealed that, in Germany, much greater importance is placed on managerial information.[20]

The research was extended by Fletcher with 38 Scottish bank managers.[21] Taking the same proposition but with modifications to allow for slightly different economic conditions and the Scottish environment, Fletcher found a number of significant differences between the Scottish bank managers and the findings of the author's study. A greater proportion of Scottish bank mangers (68 per cent) were prepared to back the proposition and some Scottish bank officers were prepared to back the proposition without security, despite the relative high gearing of the proposition.

Information[a]	Percentage of managers[b]
Gearing	83%
Entrepreneurs' personal financial position	73%
Forecasted balance sheet and P & L account	66%
Entrepreneurs' drawings	63%
Entrepreneurs' contacts in industry	60%
Timing of income payments	60%
Contingency plans	57%
Entrepreneurs' personal collateral	50%
Market research	50%
Entrepreneurs' qualifications and careers	43%
Cash flow assumptions	40%
Entrepreneurs' starting separately[c]	37%
Role of I.T. consultant	33%
I.T. development costs	27%
Business/managerial strategy	13%
Enterprise and small business experience	10%

Notes:

[a] These are selective criteria.

[b] $n = 30$.

[c] Applied in this case because results are based on a team-start proposition.

Source: Deakins, D. and Hussain, G. (1991) *Risk Assessment by Bank Managers*, Birmingham Polytechnic Business School, Birmingham.

Table 5.1 Criteria used or sought on the entrepreneurial proposition

Some of the differences are illustrated in Table 5.2. Fletcher attempts to account for them by reference to the different banking structure and relationships in Scotland. The three Scottish banks, the Royal Bank of Scotland, the Bank of Scotland and the Clydesdale Bank, operate with closer relationships to their business customers than the main English clearing banks. This, coupled with the different environment (e.g. there is less owner-occupied housing in Scotland), might account for some of the differences found in practice between English and Scottish bank managers, with Scottish bank managers closer to the German approach, where greater emphasis was placed on the entrepreneurs' abilities and managerial experience.

3. The Role of Security

We can also suggest that bank officers will stipulate requirements on the entrepreneur that may involve frequent monitoring of information to reduce moral hazard. However, a cost minimization approach will also include using methods that ensure commitment on the part of the entrepreneur. We would expect collateral (assets that may be pledged as security) to have an important role because it can ensure commitment and also provides a fail-safe method for the bank to recover losses in the case of the form of adverse selection that involves selecting a business

Score out of 10*	Number of officers	
	English	Scottish
0	1	1
1	4	3
2	4	1
3	3	2
4	3	5
5	1	1
6	3	4
7	10	13
8	1	7
9	0	1
10	0	0
Total	30	38

Note: *The score (out of 10) was applied arbitrarily by the authors to the 'favourability' of bank managers' decisions on the case example proposition. A score of 5 and above was positive; below 5, the proposition was rejected by the bank manager.

Source: Deakins, D. and Hussain, G. (1991) *Risk Assessment by Bank Managers*, Birmingham Polytechnic Business School, Birmingham; Fletcher, M. (1994) 'Decision making by Scottish bank managers', *International Journal of Entrepreneurship Behaviour and Research*, vol. 1, no. 2.

Table 5.2 English v. Scottish bank managers' decisions

failure. In conditions of uncertainty, signalling is obviously important, and following Spence,[22] a number of writers have developed theoretical implications of the importance of signalling.[23,24,25] The importance of signalling commitment has also been recognized.[26] Thus liquidity constraints and uncertainty combine to encourage the provider of finance to require security when this is available. Also Chan and Kannatas have pointed out that the type of security provided by the entrepreneur can supply information for the provider.[27]

Collateral, however, is not without costs and its own problems; for example, there are valuation problems, there might be depreciation to consider, and it might be necessary to revalue collateral at intervals. The taking of collateral, then, needs to be balanced against the costs of management for the bank. Also, the taking of collateral does nothing to reduce adverse selection; it merely provides a method for the bank to recover (some) potential losses where it considers risks to be high. However, if we assume that bank mangers are risk-averse, we can expect that collateral will be required where risks are perceived to be high, for example with new technology entrepreneurs or with propositions which have high gearing. Table 5.3 illustrates the importance of general criteria from our study with English bank managers. While security requirements do not appear to be of high importance, in practice they will often be critical requirements where risk is perceived to be high, such as the

Criteria	Rank order	Mean score
Trading experience	1	4.43
Projected income	2	4.37
Existing profitability	3	4.30
Equity stake	4	4.18
Repayment of previous loans	5	4.12
Gearing	6	3.82
Client an existing customer	7	3.78
Net profit to sales	8	3.75
Previous loans	=9	3.73
Personal guarantees	=9	3.73
CVs of clients	11	3.70
Trade debtors	12	3.65
Liquidity ratios	=13	3.62
Gross profit to sales	=13	3.62
Trade creditors	15	3.57
Charge on personal assets	16	3.55
Fixed charge on business assets	17	3.52
Floating charge	18	3.00

Note: 6-point scale used from 0 to 5.

Table 5.3 Importance of criteria used to assess lending propositions

proposition that was involved in our research. For example, of those that would have backed the proposition, all required security. The importance generally of gearing (the ratio of debt to equity) as a criterion is reflected in Table 5.3, which reinforces the view that financial information such as the gearing level are critical factors for bank managers in the UK.

Theoretically, adverse selection should not occur if the bank has perfect information and can rely with certainty on cash flow predictions. Following Altman,[28] we have argued that it is necessary to define two different categories of adverse selection. First, the bank could approve a proposition that turns out to be a business failure. Second, the bank could refuse to accept a proposition that turns out to be a business success. As illustrated in Figure 5.3, we define these categories as Type II and Type I errors respectively.

Outcome	Funded	Not funded
Proposition successful	Correct decision	**Type I error**
Proposition fails	**Type II error**	Correct decision

Figure 5.3 Potential outcomes from decision-making on a proposition

Note: The reader may like to note that this classification of potential errors reverses the original Altman classification.

As can be seen in Figure 5.3, it is more likely that bank officers would be concerned with avoiding Type II errors (partly because Type I errors will not be discovered) and, in our study, we concluded that this contributed to adverse selection.[29]

Systems that control for Type II errors may minimize risk, but they also miss profitable opportunities associated with business propositions that might contain higher risk but provide profitable opportunities for growth in the business of the bank. These hypotheses provide theoretical explanations of why bank officers may turn away small firm propositions that have high potential for growth and profitability.

THINK POINTS 5.2

Raising entrepreneurial finance

1. What factors might account for the variation of decisions by bank managers in our research using a real business plan for a start-up proposition?

   Hint: consider the earlier discussion on the role of information and adverse selection and your answers in Think Points 5.1.

2. Taking this further, why should some bank managers ask for security and others not?

3. What is the role of security in bank loans? Why might some entrepreneurs be disadvantaged with security requirements of the banks?

4. You are a senior strategy manager with a commercial bank. You are given the results from our study, as reported in Tables 5.1 to 5.3. What action might you take to improve the consistency of decision-making in the bank?

RAISING ENTREPRENEURIAL FINANCE: THE ROLE OF SECURITY AND THE SMALL FIRMS' LOAN GUARANTEE SCHEME

Most modern economies have a state-sponsored loan guarantee scheme with the main objective being to assist entrepreneurs with little security to raise bank finance. The state accepts that bankers will require security (although the importance of this is changing for bankers; see section on credit-scoring below).

In the UK, the Small Firms' Loan Guarantee Scheme (SFLGS) provides a vehicle for entrepreneurs with little security with the Government guaranteeing up to 80 per cent the loan. In the UK, take-up rates have improved on this scheme but the evidence seems to suggest that the use and promotion of the SFLGS by bankers has been variable.[30] To qualify for the Scheme, propositions have to be put forward to the DTI by bankers, and it requires additional paperwork to be undertaken by bankers. Under the early operation of the scheme, in the 1990s, default rates were high but in more recent years these have improved.

The Scheme is intended to be self-financing and the entrepreneurs who qualify pay a premium interest rate of 0.5 to 1.5 per cent. The amount borrowed under the Scheme can be up to a maximum of £250,000 over a period of seven years.

4. Credit-Scoring

The advent of computerized credit-scoring for personal customer loan applications has been mirrored with the recent introduction by some banks of credit analysis systems of applications for credit by business customers; or a form of credit-scoring. Credit-scoring relies upon the application of predictable variables for an individual's credit rating, such as occupation, post code from home address, family commitments and previous payment record. Scores are attached to each of the criteria, which will lead to an automatic acceptance/rejection decision issued by the computer, effectively disenfranchising the bank officer of any responsibility to make subjective judgements about individual applications. When such systems are applied to business applications, in theory the potential for variation in bank manager decisions (as discussed with our research above) should be reduced to a minimum. However, it also means that individual bank manager discretion to use local knowledge and local information about the entrepreneur is removed, perhaps leading to automatic rejections that, before the advent of credit-scoring, would have been carefully considered by the banks.

At present in the UK, each of the main commercial banks (Bank of Scotland (now HBOS), Barclays, HSBC, Lloyds/TSB, Nat West and the Royal Bank of Scotland) operate different systems for credit applications from entrepreneurs. Three of the banks have adopted a centralized system where the role of the bank manager has become a purely relationship role with credit applications referred to a central credit risk unit.[31] The manager still has a role in preparing the application, but has no discretionary powers in decision-making on the application, which is credit-scored by the central risk unit. The other three commercial banks have adopted a form of credit-scoring for business applications, but have retained local discretion in decision-making.

Credit-scoring has brought costs and benefits for banks and entrepreneurs. It may automatically rule out some applications (which would otherwise be successful) because of the credit history of the entrepreneur or because of previous credit judgements (for example a county court judgement, which will automatically result in a reject decision) but it has also meant that bank manager discretion can be increased and it has reduced the extent of security levels required.[31]

Credit-scoring, however, at the time of writing, cannot be used with start-up applications, which implies that there will still be considerable variety in banks' decision-making for start-up applications, as indicated by our previous research.

ARE THE COMMERICAL BANKS A COMPLEX MONOPOLY?

It can be claimed that the UK banking system could be classed as a complex monopoly (particularly since the RBS has taken over Nat West and the Bank of Scotland has now taken over the Halifax bank and is operating as HBOS). In addition, 80 per cent of the small business banking market is controlled by only two of the main commercial banks. In the UK a complex monopoly is not automatically a violation of anti-trust laws, as it might be in the USA for example; however, such a complex monopoly is grounds for investigation by the Competition Commission. The Commission reported to the DTI in 2001 and has recently been made public.[32] The report ruled that the four largest commercial banks were making excessive profits from the small business sector and the UK Government have subsequently announced new requirements on the trading practice of the main commercial banks with their small business customers.[33] These measures, however, are not targeted at the processes of decision-making.

5. Some Empirical Evidence

In terms of empirical research, it is known from various sources that entrepreneurs and small firms are highly dependent on internal sources of finance, as might be expected to follow from our earlier discussion in this chapter. Research by Cambridge University's Centre for Business Research (CBR) 1992–2000 has indicated that bank finance is by far the most important source of finance for entrepreneurs and SMEs.[34] Figure 5.4 gives their figures for sources of finance received in the period 1995–7. In 1998, the CBR study found that 41 per cent of their sample of 1,520 SMEs and entrepreneurs had attempted to raise finance from external sources in the previous three years.

From research undertaken as part of a project on the financing needs of ethnic minority entrepreneurs, published data on the percentage accessing finance is shown in Table 5.4.[35] This shows that 39 per cent had attempted to raise finance in the previous year.

It is likely that internal sources and the entrepreneur's equity will be very important for start-up finance. For comparative purposes, using our study of start-up small firms discussed in Chapter 3,[35] we report the results in terms of importance for sources of finance in Table 5.5. Although it shows that a high proportion of start-ups do use bank finance, a more significant feature is the comparative importance of personal savings, which are rated significantly higher than bank finance in importance, as a source of finance.

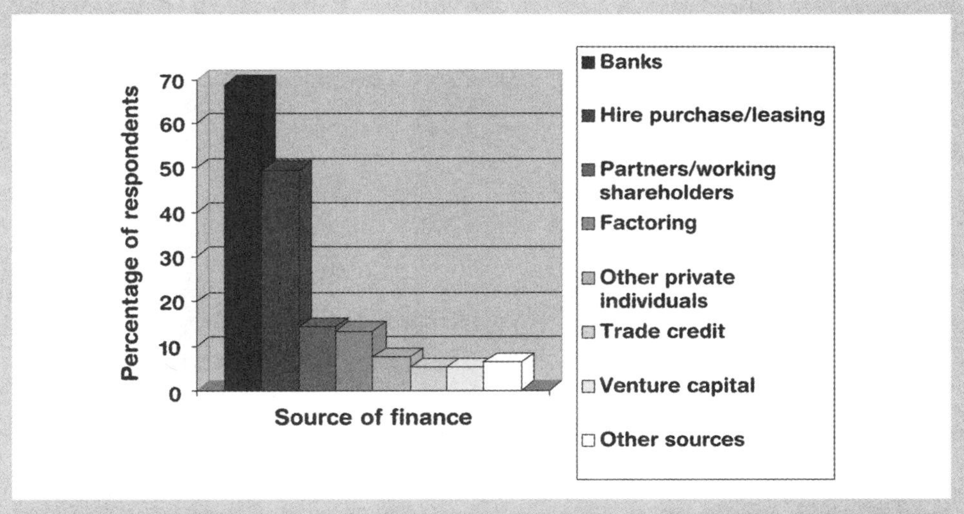

Figure 5.4 External sources of finance from a sample of 2,520 small firms, 1995–7

Source: ESRC Centre for Business Research (1992–2000) *The State of British Enterprise, Reports*, Department of Applied Economics, University of Cambridge, Cambridge.

Ethnic group	Proportion of business owners seeking source of finance
African-Caribbean	31%
Pakistani	35%
Indian	41%
Bangladeshi	34%
Chinese	51%
All ethnic businesses	39%

Source: Smallbone, D., Ram, M., Deakins, D. and Baldock, R. (2001) 'Access to Finance by Ethnic Minority Businesses: Some results from a national study', paper presented to the 24th ISBA National Small Firms Policy and Research Conference.

Table 5.4 External finance sought by ethnic minority business owners at start-up

QUESTION FOR DISCUSSION

Do female entrepreneurs face disadvantages when raising finance compared to male entrepreneurs?

Source	Percentage of respondents	Importance (mean score)
Personal sources	80%	4.20
Enterprise Allowance Scheme*	66%	2.90
Local govt grant	50%	2.10
Trade credit	44%	1.70
Bank overdraft	37%	1.50
Other public sector	29%	1.20
Family and friends	20%	1.10
Bank loan	22%	0.90
Venture capital	7%	0.20
PSYBT**	12%	4.86
Other source	7%	0.20

Note: * The importance of the EAS is accounted for by the large majority of respondents which were trading for less than one year.
** Prince's Scottish Youth Business Trust (applies to young entrepreneurs only; less than 26 years old).
Source: Deakins, D. *et al.* (1997) *New Venture Support: An analysis of mentoring provision for new entrepreneurs*, Paisley Enterprise Research Centre, University of Paisley.

Table 5.5 Start-up finance for a sample of 60 start-up entrepreneurs in Scotland

It has been suggested that if entrepreneurs and small firms face problems in raising finance and are faced by finance gaps, then female entrepreneurs and small business owners face more acute problems since their propositions may not be taken (as) seriously by funders or they may face disadvantages through lack of equity, security and possibly support from their spouse. It is only recently that systematic and careful research has been carried out on this topic. Three studies have adopted careful research methodology which overcomes some of the limitations of previous (more ad hoc) attempts to research this issue.

First, Read has examined the question of whether bank managers have any preference for lending to men rather than women.[36] She examined matched samples of 40 pairs of male and female entrepreneurs and found 'more similarities than differences' in their relationships with the bank and their use of overdrafts and loans. However, she did find some evidence of patronizing treatment of a minority of the female entrepreneurs by the bank and some differences in the relationship suggesting that women adopt a different strategy when dealing with the bank manager.

Second, Rosa *et al.* have also made a careful study of the differences between male and female entrepreneurs.[37] They found that differences in terms of capitalization and economic performance between male and female entrepreneurs were complex, but women were likely to have significantly lower levels of capitalization and hence levels of external finance. However, as they comment, given that female entrepreneurs have started from a much lower base, they conclude that the performance of female-owned businesses has been quite remarkable and that they are 'catching up fast' with male-owned businesses.

Third, Chell and Baines have examined the differences between male and female business owners in their study of micro-firms in the business services sector.[38] In terms of financial performance they found 'no significant differences'. Although, unfortunately, they do not include data on external finance, they conclude that we should treat stereotypical views of either male- or female-owned businesses with extreme caution. This perhaps indicates that if women do face disadvantages in raising finance, these are likely to be quite subtle; for example anecdotal evidence suggests that women may be asked different questions by potential funders compared to men with similar propositions.

RELATIONSHIPS BETWEEN ENTREPRENEURS/SMALL FIRMS AND THE BANKS

Work on the relationship between the entrepreneur/small business owner and their bank has been carried out in the comprehensive surveys by Binks *et al.* on behalf of the Forum of Private Business.[17] Bank charges, although frequently cited in the press, may not be the most important concern to small business owners and entrepreneurs; but Binks *et al.* did find that only 26 per cent of respondents thought that bank charges were good value for money. There have been improvements by the banks, particularly in staff training and developing specific posts such as 'Enterprise Managers', but entrepreneurs do have genuine grievances if charges are not itemized and the bank operates a hands-off policy. This is something that the banks have tried to correct with their Small Business Charters. However, Binks *et al.* considered that 'Bank charges, interest rates and the banks' demand for collateral remain important constraints on small firms'.

Over time, the relationships between entrepreneurs and the banks seem to have improved, although the surveys carried out for the FPB indicate that the extent of this improvement varies between the different commercial banks.[17] For example, there has been an overall improvement in the relationships, but individual commercial banks have made efforts to improve their relationships with small business customers. The authors comment: 'The overall improvement in bank performance may reflect more positive trading conditions for businesses and banks but also genuine substantive improvements in bank service quality' (p. 1152).

BANKS AND ENTREPRENEURS: MUTUAL GUARANTEE SCHEMES: UNTAPPED POTENTIAL?

Mutual Guarantee Schemes (MGSs) are popular in European countries, notably Spain, France and Germany, but, at the time of writing, they exist only as small pilot schemes in the UK.[39] Figure 5.5 illustrates the principles of an MGS. It operates through a 'club' of member firms that establish an MGS fund with a commercial bank. They are able to borrow at below normal market rates from the bank. In return, members provide mutual guarantees. Banks have the attraction or reduced risk of lending as a result of the guarantee and, hence, should have no need for additional security.

It is claimed that MGSs have additional advantages for member small firms through the improvement of management competencies and encouragement of members to participate in training schemes.[39]

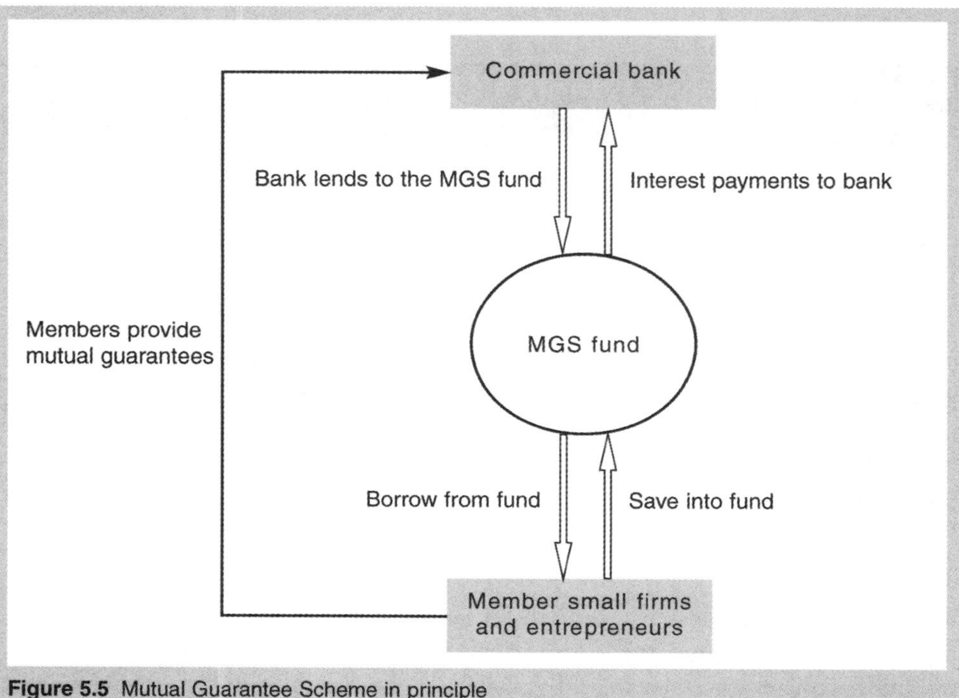

Figure 5.5 Mutual Guarantee Scheme in principle

BANKS AND ENTREPRENEURS: MUTUAL GUARANTEE SCHEMES: UNTAPPED POTENTIAL?

In the UK, MGSs have not been part of policy promotion and have only recently been established. Establishing an MGS presents considerable legal barriers as well as difficulties achieving co-operation and networking of member small firms. However, eight pilot schemes have been established with the assistance of the National Association of Mutual Guarantee Schemes (NAMGS), which all differ in their practice and membership.

In theory the co-operative principles of MGSs should heighten awareness of members to support and advice and provide self-help. Evidence in Europe, however, suggests that problems can arise with the administration of individual societies and with ensuring the agreement of members.[40]

Despite the potential of MGSs to encourage beneficial networking between small firm entrepreneurs, in the UK they will remain of only minor importance while they are not part of a policy promotion.

THINK POINTS 5.3

Raising entrepreneurial finance

1. The empirical evidence in this chapter suggests that entrepreneurs have a preference for finance in a distinct order: personal sources, debt from banks, and then venture capital sources. This result has been called the Pecking Order Hypothesis; that entrepreneurs will seek finance in this order of preference.

   What factors would account for such a 'pecking order' of preference by entrepreneurs?

   Hint: consider obligations of entrepreneurs to debt and equity funders.

2. What is the main purpose of the Government-sponsored Small Firms' Loan Guarantee Scheme? Do you consider that there is still a need for such a scheme?

3. What do you understand by credit-scoring?

4. What implications for entrepreneurs might exist from the advent of credit-scoring applied by the commercial banks to business applications?

5. What benefits might a Mutual Guarantee Scheme provide to its member small firms and entrepreneurs?

CONCLUSIONS

In this chapter, we have taken an overview of the important issues in the finance of SMEs and entrepreneurs. Much of this discussion has centred on finance gaps and their implications for entrepreneurs and small firms. We have tried to show, theoretically, why these gaps might emerge, given problems of uncertainty and asymmetric information.

We have shown that entrepreneurs and SMEs continue to be dependent on banks for external finance, despite schemes that attempt to improve the availability of equity capital. We have shown that entrepreneurs also face problems in raising bank finance and that UK bank practices of risk assessment can be variable and that adverse selection (where potentially viable projects are not receiving finance) is higher than it needs to be.

By now you should be able to discuss the advantages and disadvantages of the most important of these sources. You should also have an understanding of why small firms and entrepreneurs are at a disadvantage compared to larger firms in financial markets and also have an appreciation of the problems that face providers of finance.

This chapter has focused on debt finance; the following chapter will examine in more detail the sources of equity finance (including formal and informal venture finance) and some of the issues in raising equity.

Before the next chapter, however, a mini-case study provides the bank manager questions that were asked on our case study of Peters and Co.; we also discuss the case of technology-based entrepreneurial start-ups that can be seen as a special case. The full version of the Peters and Co. case study is available in the students' online resource material and further discussion is also given in the tutor's manual; it can be seen as a technology-related start-up, although the case does not involve the full elements of a technology-based firm.

CASE STUDY: RAISING BANK FINANCE

The case study of Peters and Co. involved a business plan for a team-start but with limited equity investment by the three co-directors. Each of the three committed £10,000 equity and required a bank loan of £60,000 to cover the forecast deficit on the cash flow. This meant a debt to equity ratio or gearing ratio of 2:1, whereas bankers' preferred gearing ratios are 1:1. Typical bankers' comments on this proposition were:

"We like to see the entrepreneurs match the bank to show commitment."

"You will be using the bank's money without matching it yourself."

A typical interview by a bank manager focused on the following issues:

1. *What are your assumptions behind the income shown in the cash flow statement?*

2. *How many orders do you expect to achieve per month*?

3. *When will your income be paid*?

4. *What customers have indicated that they will deal with you*?

5. *Why do you need an office premises with high rents in a town centre*?

6. *What role will each of the entrepreneurs take in the business*?

7. *What can you do that is better than your competitors*?

Being prepared for such questions meant that the interview could be handled confidently; among the answers given at the time were:

1. The cash flow is based on extensive experience of the three co-directors and represents a conservative estimate of income with a small number of orders in the first months rising to 12–15 at the end of the first year.

2. We will be building to achieving 20 per month after the first year.

3. It is fee-based income paid in instalments for each job.

4. We had guaranteed orders from exclusive clients we had known for 15 years or more.

5. Prestigious offices are necessary for the type of clientele.

6. Roles were clearly defined with tasks such as marketing/finance split between different directors.

7. Our competitive edge is based on the application of the latest CAD techniques to quantity surveying. This gave us a technology-related advantage over our competitors, allowing a full cost-based service from design to build.

RAISING ENTREPRENEURIAL FINANCE: TECHNOLOGY-BASED START-UPS A SPECIAL CASE?

Technology-based start-ups can be seen as a special case[41] with distinct financing needs due to:

1. Extensive R&D periods for product development (see the Eco-Wall case in Chapter 1). This necessitates raising finance for R&D and prototypes known as *seed capital*.

2. Although patents can be used to protect new products/processes, they are intangible assets and banks are unwilling to accept them as security.

3. Developing cash flow forecasts for the business plan can be problematic since, with new products, existing markets do not exist. Consequently banks are unwilling to lend against forecasts.

4. The new technology will need a technology appraisal to determine the viability and banks are not equipped to undertake such approaches.

The financing of technology-based start-ups is seen as a special case by the Government with recognized potential market failure to provide debt and equity finance.[41] The Government scheme to assist technology-based start-ups in the UK is the Small Firms Merit Award for Research and Technology (SMART).

SMART provides grants to help new start technology-based entrepreneurs research and develop new innovative products. Grants very from £25,000 to £150,000; they are awarded on a competitive basis and assist with developing prototypes and market testing.

The problem with SMART for many entrepreneurs is that grant-funding is only for research and developpment of prototypes; it does not provide funding for the often lengthy time required to achieve full commercialization.[42]

SUGGESTED ASSIGNMENTS

1. Using the Peters and Co. case study available in the students' online learning resource material, students are required to:
   - Familiarize yourself with information on the venture.
   - Prepare for a role-play exercise by taking the role of one of the entrepreneurs.
   - Research additional information on sources of finance and risk assessment.
   - Carry out a role-play exercise by arranging an interview with a bank manager (tutor).

2. Complete a report on the issues in the finance of start-up entrepreneurs.

3. Collect material on lending and services to small firms and entrepreneurs from the local high-street banks including charges:
   (a) Compare the services and discuss whether there are any differences in services or charges.
   (b) Do you agree with the recent Competition Commission Report[32] that the UK commercial banks are uncompetitive and over-charge their small business customers?

REFERENCES

1. Small Business Service (2001) *Phoenix Fund and Early Growth Fund*, Small Business Service, DTI, London.

2. HM Government (1931) *Report of The Committee on Finance and Industry* (Macmillan Report), CMND.3897, HMSO.

3. For example, Bank of England (1994–2001) *Finance for Small Firms Annual reports*, Bank of England, London.

4. Harrison, R. and Mason, C. (1991) 'Informal Investment Networks: A Case Study from the UK', *Entrepreneurship and Regional Development*, vol. 3, no. 2, pp. 269–79.

5. BVCA (2000) *Venture Capital in the UK: Annual Report*, British Venture Capital Association, London.

6. Bank of England (2001) *Finance for Small Firms – An Eighth Report*, Bank of England, London.

7. Akerlof, G. (1970) 'The Market for Lemons: qualitative uncertainty and the market mechanism', *Quarterly Journal of Economics*, vol. 89, pp. 488–500.

8. Mirrlees, J.A. (1974) 'Notes on Welfare Economics, Information and Uncertainty', in Balch, M., McFadden, D. and Wu, S. (eds) *Essays in Economic Behaviour Under Uncertainty*, North Holland.

9. Mirrlees, J.A. (1975) *The Theory of Moral Hazard and Unobservable Behaviour*, Nuffield College, Oxford.

10. Jensen, M.C. and Meckling, W.H. (1976) 'Theory of the Firm: Managerial Behaviour, Agency Costs and Ownership Structure', *Journal of Financial Economics*, vol. 3, pp. 305–60.

11. Harris, M. and Townsend, R.M. (1981) 'Resource allocation under asymmetric information', *Econometrica*, vol. 49, pp. 33–64.

12. Hellwig, M. (1987) 'Some recent developments in the theory of competition in markets with adverse selection', *European Economic Review*, vol. 31, pp. 319–25.

13. Magill, M. and Shafer, W. (1991) 'Incomplete markets,' in Hildenbrand, W. and Sonneschein, H. (eds) *The Handbook of Mathematical Economics*, vol. IV, North Holland.

14. Stiglitz, J. and Weiss, A. (1981) 'Credit rationing in markets with imperfect information', *American Economic Review*, vol. 71, pp. 393–410.

15. De Meza, D. and Webb, D. (1987) 'Too much investment: a problem of asymmetric information', *Quarterly Journal of Economics* vol. 102, pp. 281–92.

16. Aston Business School, (1991) *Constraints on the Growth of Small Firms*, DTI, HMSO.

17. Forum of Private Business (1998 and 2000) *Small Businesses and Their Banks*, FPB, Knutsford.

18. Federation of Small Business (2000) *Barriers to Survival and Growth in UK Small Firms*, FSB, London.

19. Deakins, D. and Hussain, G. (1991) *Risk Assessment By Bank Managers*, Birmingham Polytechnic Business School, Birmingham.

20. Deakins, D. and Philpott, T. (1993) *Comparative European Practices in the Finance of Small Firms: UK, Germany and Holland*, University of Central England Business School, Birmingham.

21. Fletcher, M. (1994) 'Decision making by Scottish bank managers', *International Journal of Entrepreneurship Behaviour and Research*, vol. 1, no. 2, pp. 37–53.

22. Spence, A.M. (1974) *Market Signalling*, Harvard University Press.

23. Crawford, V. and Sobell, J. (1982) 'Strategic information transmission', *Econometrica*, vol. 50, pp. 1431–51.

24. Quinzii, M. and Rochet, J.C. (1985) 'Multidimensional signalling', *Journal of Mathematical Economics*, vol. 14, pp. 261–84.

25. Cho I-K. and Kreps, D. (1987) 'Signalling games and stable equilibria', *Quarterly Journal of Economics*, vol. 102, pp. 179–221.

26. Milgrom, P. and Roberts, J. (1982) 'Limit pricing and entry under incomplete information: an equilibrium analysis', *Econometrica*, vol. 50, pp. 443–59.

27. Chan, Y. and Kannatas, G. (1985) 'Asymmetric valuations and the role of collateral in loan agreements', *Journal of Money, Credit and Banking*, vol. 17, no. 1, pp. 84–95.

28. Altman, E.I. (1971) *Corporate Bankruptcy in America*, Heath Lexington.

29. Deakins, D. and Hussain, G. (1994) 'Financial Information, The Banker and Small Business: A Comment', *The British Accounting Review* vol. 26, pp. 323–35.

30. Deakins, D., Ram M., Smallbone, D. and Fletcher M. (2002) 'Decision-making and the Development of Relationships with Ethnic Minority Entrepreneurs by UK Bankers', paper presented to the 2002 Babson Entrepreneurship Research Conference, Boulder, Colorado, June.

31. Deakins, D. and Fletcher, M. (2002) Reports on the Supply of Bank Finance to Ethnic Minority Businesses to the British Bankers' Association, London (forthcoming).

32. Competition Commission (2002) *The Supply of Banking Services by Clearing Banks to Small and Medium-Sized Enterprises*, DTI, London.

33. Treanor, J. (2002) 'Bankers Threaten Brown with Judicial Review', *Guardian*, London.

34. ESRC Centre for Business Research (1992–2000) *The State of British Enterprise, Reports*, Department of Applied Economics, University of Cambridge, Cambridge.

35. Deakins, D., Graham, L., Sullivan, R. and Whittam, G. (1997) *New Venture Support: An analysis of mentoring provision for new entrepreneurs*, Paisley Enterprise Research Centre, University of Paisley.

36. Read, L. (1994) *Raising Bank Finance: A comparative study of the experiences of male and female business owners*, Venture Finance Working Paper No. 11, University of Southampton, Southampton.

37. Rosa, P., Carter, S. and Hamilton, D. (1994) 'Gender and Determinants of Small Business Performance: Preliminary insights from a British study', paper presented to the 17th National Small Firms Policy and Research Conference, Sheffield, November.

38. Chell, E. and Baines, S. (1998) 'Does gender affect business performance? A study of microbusinesses in business services in the UK', *Entrepreneurship and Regional Development*, vol. 10, no. 2, pp. 117–36.

39. National Association of Mutual Guarantee Schemes (1997) *Mutual Guarantee Schemes: An Overview*, NAMGS paper, Altrincham.

40. Hughes, A. and Leube, B. (1997) 'The extent and nature of Mutual Guarantee Schemes in Europe', paper presented to the ESRC Seminar Group on Finance of Small Firms, Durham.

41. Bank of England (2001) *Financing of Technology-based Small Firms*, Bank of England, London.

42. DTI (1994) *An Evaluation of the Small Firms Merit Award for Research and Technology (SMART)*, DTI, London.

RECOMMENDED READING

Fletcher, M. (1994) 'Decision making by Scottish bank managers', *International Journal of Entrepreneurship Behaviour and Research*, vol. 1, no. 2, pp. 37–53.

Bank of England Annual Reports (1994–2001) *Finance for Small Firms*, numbers 1 to 8, Bank of England, London.

Bank of England (2001) *Financing of Technology-based Small Firms*, Bank of England, London.

Deakins, D. and Hussain, G. (1994) 'Financial Information, The Banker and Small Business: A Comment', *The British Accounting Review*, vol. 26, pp. 323–35.

6

SOURCES OF VENTURE FINANCE

LEARNING OUTCOMES

At the end of this chapter you will be able to:

1. Discuss the nature of the equity gap for small firms' finance.
2. Describe the differences between formal and informal venture capital.
3. Discuss the nature of the formal venture capital industry.
4. Discuss the potential of business angels for closing the equity gap for small firms' finance.
5. Describe the process of a venture finance investment.
6. Advise an entrepreneur on requirements of venture capital companies, if seeking venture finance.

INTRODUCTION

As the previous chapter makes clear, the bulk of academic and policy discussions regarding small firm finance has tended to concentrate on the firm's ability to access bank debt; or, to rephrase, the extent to which small firms are 'debt rationed'.[1] This is as it should be. Studies invariably conclude that, where such funding is sought, banks are significantly the most important source of external finance for the SME sector.[2] The most recent Cambridge University survey, for instance, reported that 84.2 per cent of sample firms approached banks for finance during the period 1997–9 (of which over 90 per cent were successful in accessing at least some funds), while, in contrast, only 6.8 per cent of firms sought access to venture capital over the same period (of which a remarkable 67 per cent were, at least partially, successful).[3]

However, notwithstanding the dominance of banks as a potential source of finance – indeed, in many respects, as a result of it – there has been growing concern over the shortage of long-term risk capital, or equity, within the financial structure of many small firms.[4] Reliance on bank debt to fund start-up or growth and development may give rise to a number of problems. Among the most obvious of these is the imposed short-termism. Debt capital is not patient capital, and term loans rarely exceed 3–5 years. However, perhaps more importantly, debt capital is seldom committed capital. As discussed in the previous chapter, debt may be secured (against either the business' or the owners' assets) and requires periodic repayment of interest and ultimate payment of the principal. This places the firm in an extremely exposed position in the event of a slump in sales or other pressures on profitability and, crucially, cash flow. In situations where firms default on debt repayments, and as a last resort, banks may either repossess assets or force the company into receivership (after Government, banks have 'first call' on the assets of insolvent firms). Accordingly, and at least for those firms with significant growth potential, commentators argue that patient and committed risk capital, the returns to which will be contingent upon the success of the business, is more appropriately required.

The idea that there exists an 'equity gap', or deficiency in the provision of smaller amounts of risk capital, is not new. The inability of UK small firms to access small-scale risk capital for either start-up or business development has been widely accepted since at least the 1931 *Macmillan Report*[5] and, thereafter, in government terms, the 1971 *Bolton Report*,[6] the 1979 *Wilson Report*[7] and the 1989 *Williams Report*.[8] This gap has traditionally been thought to fall somewhere between the resources which may realistically be provided by private individuals (such as the entrepreneur, family, friends and associates) and the capital required for stock market flotation (though this is clearly very wide, and a 'new equity gap' of between £50,000 and £500,000 is now more commonly recognized). Accordingly, it is with reference to the amelioration of equity gaps that the current chapter seeks to outline the potential and actual role played by venture capital.

THE NATURE OF VENTURE CAPITAL

So, what is venture capital? As the name suggests, it is capital that clearly involves a degree of risk. However, more specifically, venture capital may be defined, generically, as financial investment in *unquoted* companies, which have significant growth potential, with a view to yielding substantial capital gains in line with the additional risk and illiquidity of an investment, which cannot be freely traded during the lifetime of the investor's commitment to the business. Moreover, venture capital is thought to provide the bridge between the levels of capital which may be provided by the founder, family and friends (the 3 Fs) and private investors – which is often exhausted at the prototype or 'proof-of-concept' and start-up stages (if a technology-based entrepreneur) – and the significant amounts required for a stock market listing and to attract large-scale institutional investments (Figure 6.1).

Classic venture capital assists young and growing firms with the potential for significant future growth, and is frequently a complement to debt finance. However, venture capital is fundamentally equity oriented. As Mason and Harrison[9] note:

> ***"The objective [of venture capital] is to achieve a* high return *on the investment in the form of* capital gain *through an* exit, *achieved by the sale of the equity stake rather than through [interest or] dividend income. Exit is normally achieved either through an initial public offering (IPO), involving the flotation of the company on a stock market where its shares are traded freely, or through a trade sale in which the venture capital fund, normally along with all the other shareholders in the company, sell out to another company."* (p. 15)**

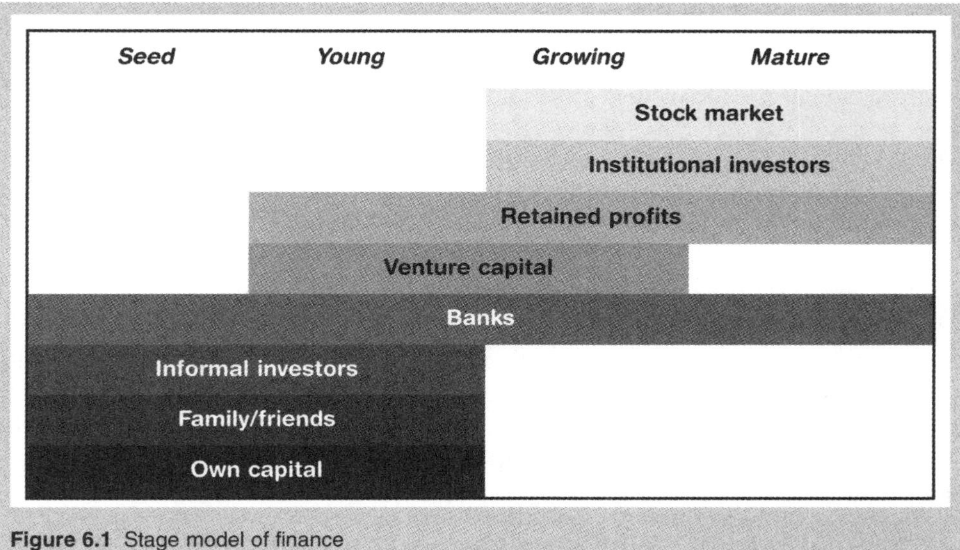

Figure 6.1 Stage model of finance

Within this broad framework a number of 'types' of venture capital are commonly identified:

Institutional venture capital (or formal venture capital) – investments in entrepreneurial ventures by firms of full-time professionals who raise finance from pension funds, banks, insurance companies and other financial institutions.

Informal venture capital (or business angel finance) – investments by wealthy private individuals who are prepared to use their financial resources to make risk investments based upon their experience and interests. Business angels are often retired senior executives of large companies, or entrepreneurs who have sold their companies and now wish to use the money.

Corporate venture capital (or corporate venturing) – minority investments made by large companies in smaller enterprises for a principally strategic (such as gaining a window on new technologies) rather than an exclusively financial motive. As McNally[10] notes: '[t]he combination of a small firm's know-how, inventive efficiency and flexibility and a larger firm's financial, production, marketing and distribution resources can provide opportunities for synergies that can contribute to both firms' competitive advantage' (p. 16).

Public sector venture capital – while government plays a role in encouraging private sector venture capital (through policy instruments such as the Enterprise Investment Scheme or offering [primarily, capital gains] tax incentives), it may, more occasionally, act more directly as a provider of venture finance. The most visible examples of such direct public sector activities, during the 1970s and 1980s, included the investment arms of the Scottish and Welsh Development Agencies.[11] However, the trend is emphatically towards hybrid public–private partnerships.[12] In such cases (e.g. the new Regional Venture Capital Funds, to which the English Regional Development Associations contribute), private and public sector capital is pooled, though fund management is undertaken along private sector (institutional) lines and follows a largely commercial imperative, rather than being bound by exclusively social or welfare considerations. Nonetheless, such funds aim at filling 'gaps', or alleviating deficiencies, in mainstream venture capital provision, by ensuring a more even spatial distribution of activity, or by directing a larger proportion of the fund towards higher risk, early stage and high-technology investments.

However, notwithstanding the growth in public sector and corporate venturing, these 'types' of venture capital still account for a relatively small proportion of private sector equity investments. The bulk of investment activity remains the province of institutional venture capitalists and business angels. Accordingly, these latter two form the basis of the current chapter.

Clearly, to the extent that it involves equity investment in smaller firms with a view to capital gain, venture capital is not a new phenomenon. Throughout history, wealthy private individuals have frequently invested in smaller enterprises or ventures, sharing part of the risk, in return for a share in the outcome. However, in its formal, institutional guise, venture capital is largely a contemporary phenomenon, dating from the post-Second World War period.[13,14] In the United States, the genesis of the institutional venture capital industry is typically traced to the founding of American Research and Development Corporation (ARD) in 1946 and, in the UK, the founding of Industrial and Commercial Finance Corporation (ICFC – now renamed 3i plc) by the Bank of England, and the major clearing banks, in 1945. In both instances, these were probably the first firms, as opposed to individuals, dedicated to providing risk capital to new and potentially super-growth firms, principally in manufacturing or technology-based sectors. However, contrary to popular mythology, neither the US industry nor, as is generally accepted, the UK industry experienced much growth until considerably later. As Timmons[15] observes, 'the [US] venture capital industry did not experience a growth spurt until the 1980s, when the industry "went ballistic" – rising from approximately $0.5 billion, in 1977, to just over $4 billion in 1987' (pp. 441–3). Similarly, in the UK, venture capital investments rose from £66 million, in 163 companies, to £1.65 billion, in 1,569 companies, over the period 1981–9.[16] However, notwithstanding the lag in activity, these early progenitors effectively established the 'rules of the game', which have served to determine the 'shape' of independent venture capital firms on both sides of the Atlantic. That is, in common with many of the more successful early venture capital firms, the dominant contemporary legal form is of a limited partnership.[a] Specifically, venture capital funds usually comprise a management company (whose directors are the general partners), which raises risk capital from financial

[a] Though, as a matter of historical interest, ARD, as a result of institutional investor reluctance, was structured as a publicly traded, closed-end fund and marketed mostly to individuals (Lerner, J., 2000, *Venture Capital and Private Equity: A Casebook*, John Wiley).

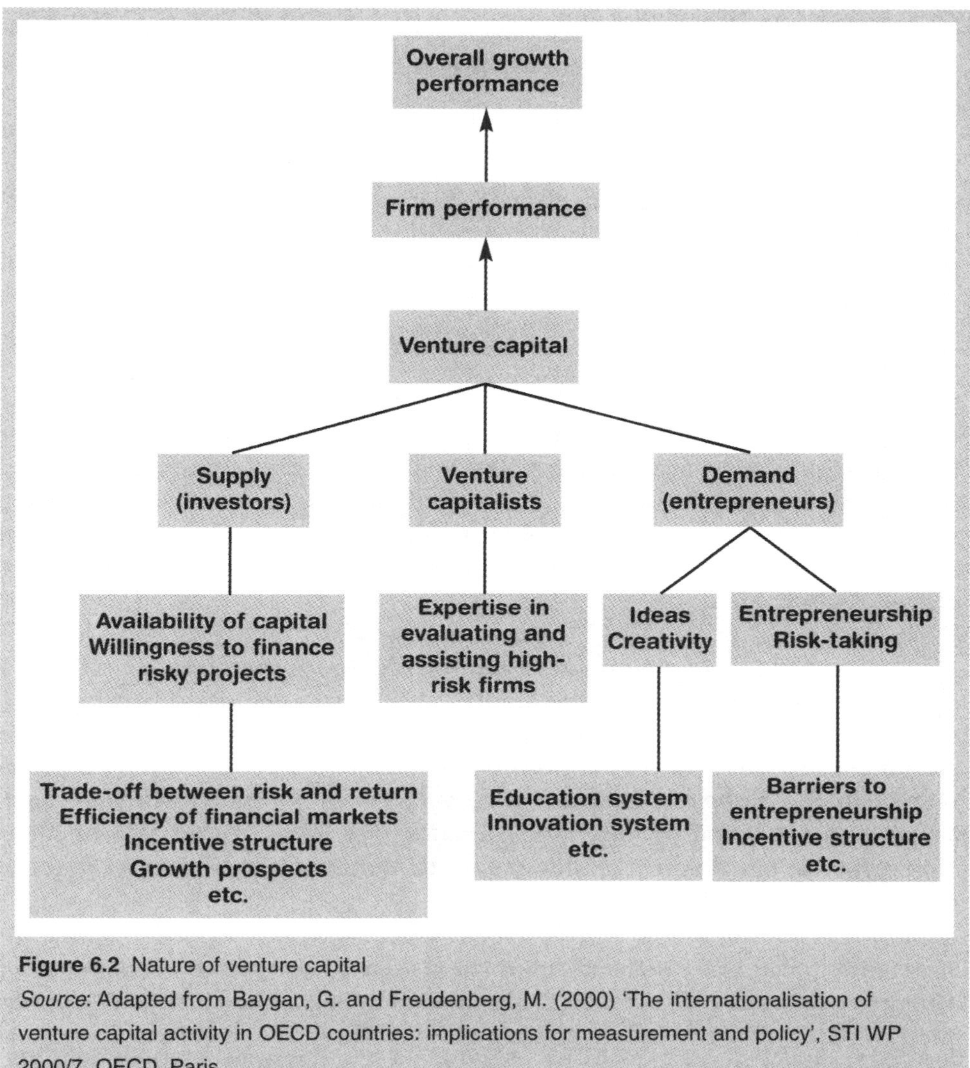

Figure 6.2 Nature of venture capital
Source: Adapted from Baygan, G. and Freudenberg, M. (2000) 'The internationalisation of venture capital activity in OECD countries: implications for measurement and policy', STI WP 2000/7, OECD, Paris.

institutions (the limited partners). The key issue here, however, is that venture capital firms are essentially intermediaries in the venture capital process (Figure 6.2).

As Figure 6.2 makes clear, the use and economic impact of venture capital is likely to be a function of a number of underlying supply- and demand-side framework conditions. On the demand side, it is clear that the flow of good entrepreneurial projects, allied to a willingness to share equity, is a necessary element of a successful venture capital system. This in turn is likely to be a function of the education and innovation systems and of the prevailing culture in society and will be facilitated, or hindered, by institutional framework conditions, such as the nature and level of taxation, legislation and regulation. On the supply side, the flow of venture capital funds will be determined by, among other things, the efficiency of financial markets and the availability of alternative investment opportunities, investor attitudes towards risk and return, the taxation system and the growth prospects of the economy as a whole. It is worth noting, however, that the relative efficacy of demand and supply mechanisms are not independent. It is surely no coincidence, that those economies with comparatively low institutional barriers to entrepreneurship tend also to have relatively more active venture capital industries and vice versa.[17] Countries with high-level venture capital activity and low barriers to entrepreneurship include the USA, UK, Canada and Sweden. By contrast, countries such as France, Italy, Austria and Switzerland tend to have lower levels of venture capital activity and relatively higher barriers to entrepreneurship.

Notwithstanding the potential negative association between venture capital activity and barriers to entrepreneurship, the role of venture capitalists, per se, remains the same. That is, as intermediaries. In this model of the system, venture capitalists bring expertise in evaluating, assisting and monitoring high-risk firms. Entrepreneurs are in want of capital, and investors are in want of expertise and knowledge. Venture capital firms encourage the former and provide the latter. In particular, their *raison d'être* concerns the ability to reduce the costs of information asymmetries (see below). As Amit *et al.*[18] note:

> ***“Venture capitalists operate in environments where their relative efficiency in selecting and monitoring investments gives them a comparative advantage over other investors ... [accordingly] ... Venture capitalists should be prominent in industries where informational concerns are important, such as biotechnology, computer software, etc., rather than in 'routine' start-ups such as restaurants, retail outlets, etc. The latter are risky, in that returns show high variance, but they are relatively easy to monitor by conventional financial intermediaries.” (p. 441)***

So venture capital firms attenuate information asymmetries (i.e. reduce the costs of incomplete information), providing, as a minimum, finance and assistance to firms and expertise to investors. But, to what end? As Figure 6.2 intimates, the general supposition holds that the involvement of venture capitalists will lead to the superior performance of investee firms and, ultimately, to growth in the economy as a whole. Indeed, studies undertaken on behalf of the venture capital associations in the USA and Europe have noted that VC-backed companies outperform Fortune 500/FT-Excel 500 companies in terms of employment growth, exports and investment.[19,20] It should be noted, however, that since only firms with demonstrable growth potential are likely to received VC backing, this finding is perhaps less remarkable than at first glance. Nevertheless, the European Venture Capital Association[9] describes venture capital supported companies as 'engines for our economies' (p. 2).

THINK POINTS 6.1

Raising entrepreneurial finance

1. Review your understanding of the difference between venture finance and debt finance; what is classic venture capital?

2. Why are venture capitalists seen as financial intermediaries?

3. What factors might account for the explosive growth in the venture capital industry in the 1980s and 1990s?

4. How do venture capitalists reduce the costs of information asymmetries?

THE SCALE AND SCOPE OF VENTURE CAPITAL

Now that we understand a little about the nature of venture capital, the next questions one might ask are: How much is there? Where does it come from? and, Where does it go? That is, what is the scale and scope of venture capital activity?

	1995	1996	1997	1998	1999
United Kingdom	3,442	3,773	5,018	7,947	12,256
United States	5,457	11,178	17,406	21,687	59,531
Canada	487	802	1,316	1,116	1,831
France	1,112	1,077	1,414	1,988	3,002
Germany	870	908	1,502	2,179	3,366
Netherlands	611	753	861	1,184	1,823
Italy	331	641	684	1,043	1,896
Sweden	112	533	398	227	1,361

Source: Baygan, G. and Freudenberg, M. (2000) 'The internationalisation of venture capital activity in OECD countries: implications for measurement and policy', STI WP 2000/7, OECD, Paris.

Table 6.1 Total private equity/venture capital investment (US$ million)

Table 6.1 provides a partial answer to the first of these questions for a number of Western industrialized nations. In all the countries shown, venture capital/private equity investments grew substantially over the closing years of the last decade. Moreover, as the table makes clear, in absolute terms, the United States dominates global venture capital activity, followed, at some distance, by the United Kingdom. Given the historical make-up of the financial systems within these countries, this is not surprising. Tylecote, for instance, distinguishes between different capital market regimes.[21] In historically 'stock exchange-based' economies (such as the USA and the UK), larger firms look to the stock market as a major source of equity and investment. Accordingly, banks play only a limited role in providing risk capital 'since their lending is *transactional* rather than relational' (p. 262). Each loan is considered a one-off, secured against collateral or against the scrap value of the firm's assets. In these economies, venture capital is viewed as an alternative source of risk for those firms that cannot bear the transaction costs associated with a market listing. By contrast, in 'bank-based' economies (e.g. Germany and Japan), comparatively few firms are 'listed' on the stock exchange and the market is not considered a major source of funds. Rather, firms rely on private (or occasionally state) banks as the principal source of external finance. Loans are no longer of a one-off nature and lending is relational rather than transactional,[21] 'seen as part of a long-term relationship in which the firm is bound to inform the bank fully as to its position and prospects and the bank is committed to support the firm through bad times, in return for influence over its policy and personnel' (p. 262).[b] In such instances, banks become adept at managing or alleviating information asymmetries and the opportunities for venture capitalists are limited.

However, this historical distinction between stock exchange- and bank-based financial systems has become somewhat blurred. For instance, many economies, formerly classed as 'bank-based' (such as Germany), have begun a drift towards occupying some middle ground between bank- and stock exchange-based systems (as evidenced by the failed merger talks between the Frankfurt and London exchanges, the merger of the Dutch, Belgian and French exchanges – now called Euronext – and the growth in venture capital activity throughout Continental Europe),[9] while UK banks, for instance, would undoubtedly argue that they have made a shift towards relationship- rather than transaction-based lending. However, notwithstanding this trend, the figures still point to more vigorous venture capital activity in the UK and the USA. Indeed, this holds even when one controls for the size of the respective economies (Figure 6.3), though, in this case, the relative positions of the UK and the USA are reversed. Moreover, by adjusting for the size of national economies, the gap between the top two performers and the rest is significantly reduced. In particular, venture capital investment, as a proportion of GDP, in the northern European economies of Sweden and the Netherlands does not lag far behind the United States.

Notwithstanding international comparisons, the figures paint a picture of a fairly buoyant venture capital market in the UK. But where does the capital come from? As Figure 6.4 indicates, the bulk of 'tracked' private equity, or formal venture capital, is raised from large institutional investors – primarily pension funds and insurance companies. Typically, venture capital represents only a small proportion of the portfolio of investments held by these funds and is, in this sense, a peripheral activity. Provided that these investors are holding diversified portfolios they will not be worried about the idiosyncratic risks of a single project, but only how the risk of the project contributes to the risk of their overall portfolio. Accordingly, the promise of very high returns offered by VC-backed companies may prove to be an attractive investment opportunity, for a limited proportion of the total fund, set against the

[b] This argument is given *in extremis*.

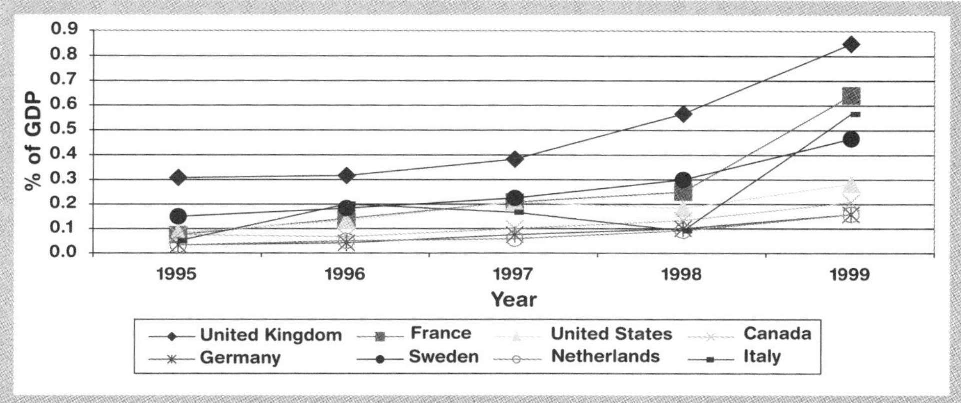

Figure 6.3 Private equity and venture capital investment as a percentage of GDP

Source: Baygan, G. and Freudenberg, M. (2000) 'The internationalisation of venture capital activity in OECD countries: implications for measurement and policy', STI WP 2000/7, OECD, Paris.

risk-return profile of their other investments. Murray notes that, even during the boom years of the late 1980s, the amounts invested in venture capital was consistently less than 1 per cent of annual institutional investment in the UK.[4] Moreover, he argues, '[t]his plausibly explains why most institutional investors are prepared to allow independent venture capital companies to manage their limited exposure to this specialist activity rather than bringing the investment responsibility in-house' (p. 139).

In contrast to institutional investors, academic institutions, government and capital markets make a limited contribution to 'visible', or formal, venture capital activity,

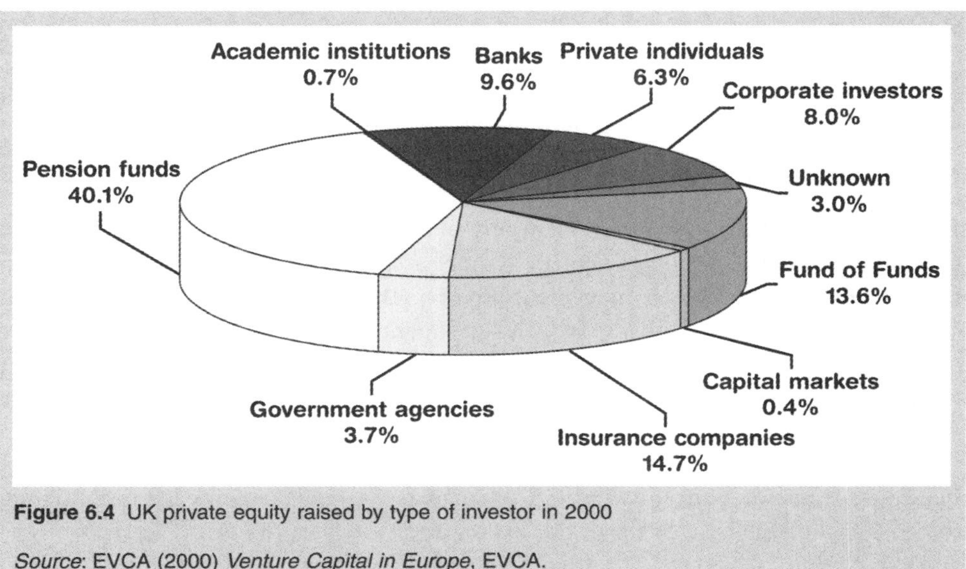

Figure 6.4 UK private equity raised by type of investor in 2000

Source: EVCA (2000) *Venture Capital in Europe*, EVCA.

though, in the case of corporate investors and private individuals, the data in Figure 6.4 undoubtedly under-represents their contribution. Corporate investors, for instance, often invest directly, while the greater proportion of investments by private individuals is 'informal', and indeed invisible, and so not covered by the methodology of the EVCA.

Finally, in this section, we turn to the destination of venture capital finance or, more specifically, the types of investments that are made. Typically, five broad types, or stages, of investment are distinguished:[22]

Seed financing – Aims at facilitating pre-market development of a business concept. It is an investment made very early in the business development cycle and is frequently concerned with research and development, the manufacture of prototypes or business planning and market research activities, prior to bringing a product to the market and commencing large-scale production. This is often called 'proof-of-concept' funding.

Start-up financing – Investment in those firms who have made few, if any, commercial sales. However, product development and market research activities are complete and funding is required to support initial production and marketing activities.

Expansion finance – Capital provided to support the growth and development of an established company. Occasionally commentators discern a further three sub-stages within the broad heading of expansion finance: *first stage*, when a firm has begun trading but requires further capital to materially increase production; *second stage*, when additional finance is required to increase production capacity and expand into new markets; and, *mezzanine finance*, which seeks to provide further expansion or working capital with a view to an initial public offering.

Replacement capital – The provision of finance 'to allow existing non-venture capital investors to buy back or redeem part, or all, of another investor's shareholding' (p. 18).

Buy-in/buy-out finance – Management buy-out (MBO) finance is provided to enable the current operating management to acquire a significant shareholding in the firm they manage. By contrast, management buy-in (MBI) finance enables managers from outside the company to buy into it. A less frequent occurrence in this category is the curiously named buy-in management buy-out (BIMBO), which allows the incumbent management to purchase the business they manage with the assistance of some incoming management.

Figure 6.5 illustrates the distribution of investment funds and investments among these stages for the UK. As the graph makes clear, the vast majority (77 per cent) of venture capital is directed towards later stage financing. Giving that information asymmetries, associated costs and risks are likely to be reduced in situations where

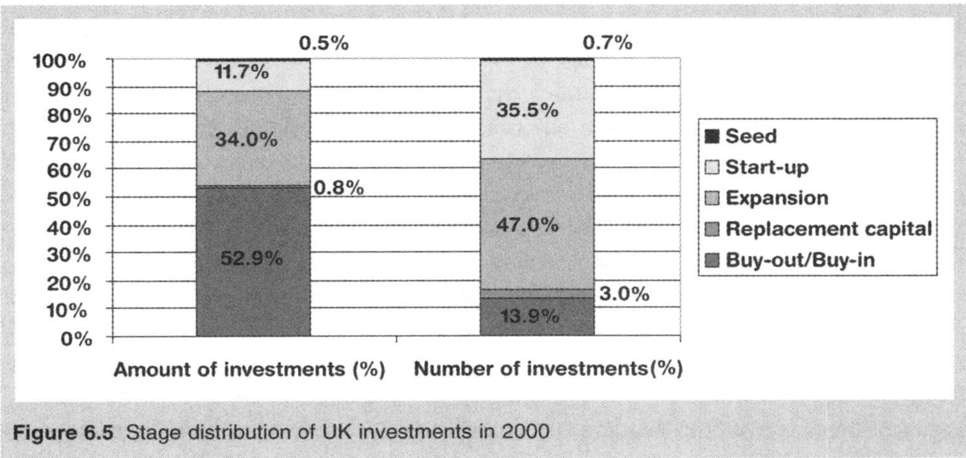

Figure 6.5 Stage distribution of UK investments in 2000

firms have an established track record, this is unsurprising. Moreover, and notwithstanding our belief in the ability of venture capitalists to more efficiently manage information asymmetries, one would anticipate that:[18]

> ***"... they will still prefer projects where monitoring and selection costs are relatively low or where the costs of information asymmetries are less severe. Thus, within a given industry where venture capitalists would be expected to focus, we would expect venture capitalists to favour firms with some track records over pure start-ups." (p. 441)***

Furthermore, it is known that the transaction costs of venture investments are proportionately higher for smaller projects.[23] Thus, we would expect a higher proportion of funds and of deals to be directed to larger-scale expansion or buy-out projects. Yet, despite the logic of these trends, a number of concerns are rightly raised. In particular, a number of recent publications have highlighted the special problems faced by small high and new technology-based firms in accessing appropriate venture finance.[24,25,26] The general consensus holds that.'[25]

> ***"The distinctive requirement of technology-based firms at seed, start-up and early stage is for genuine*** **risk capital.** ***Amounts required may be relatively small, but investment horizons may be long ...*** **Classic venture capital** ***should provide part of the answer, but the industry in the United Kingdom has tended to focus less on early stage investments (especially in technology) and more on development capital and MBOs/MBIs." (p. 6)***

Another concern, hinted at in the second line of the above quote, relates to the typical size of VC investments. In general, due to the disproportionate burden of transaction costs, very few venture capitalists are willing to invest less than £500,000, while the average investment is in excess of £1 million.[27] Clearly, a predilection for investments of this scale necessarily excludes many promising small and early stage entrepreneurial firms. From a supply-side perspective, this is believed to be the basis of the new equity gap discussed earlier.

One proffered solution to these observed deficiencies in institutional venture capital provision saw the launch, in the 1995 Finance Act, of Venture Capital Trusts (VCTs). VCTs are quoted companies that aim to encourage investment in smaller unlisted (unquoted and AIM-quoted companies) UK companies by offering private investors tax incentives, on funds up to £100,000, in return for a five-year investment commitment. Certain types of activities, or 'qualifying firms', are ineligible for investment under the scheme. Generally, these activities are similar to those excluded under the Enterprise Investment Scheme (EIS) and, most notably, include land and property development. However, it is not yet clear to what extent VCTs may address the bias towards expansion and buy-in/buy-out finance. One other potential solution may be provided by the informal venture capital market. That is, as commentators have increasingly suggested, business angels may, in this context, be effective 'gap funders'.[28] Accordingly, we return to the role of informal investors later in this chapter.

THINK POINTS 6.2

Raising entrepreneurial finance

1. What amounts of finance can be considered within the size of the equity gap for entrepreneurial small firms seeking to raise venture finance?
2. From the discussion given in the chapter, why do you think that this equity gap arises?
3. What are the main sources of venture finance funds in the UK?
4. Why is the apparent gap between the UK and the USA for venture finance funds not as large at is might appear?

Asymmetric Information, Adverse Selection, Moral Hazard and Venture Capital

Although we have discussed the nature and implications of asymmetric information, adverse selection and moral hazard in relation to bank finance in the previous chapter (for a discussion in relation to debt finance see Chapter 5), there are additional implications for venture finance. We have already noted a general belief in the function of venture capitalists as managers or attenuators of information asymmetries. Indeed, this viewpoint is fairly well established in the academic literature.[18,29,30] Accordingly, it is worth briefly outlining what we mean by information asymmetry and its implications for the venture capital investment process. This can be compared with our discussion on the implications for bankers in the previous chapter.

In the economics literature, the classic exposition of the effects of information asymmetry on market efficiencies probably dates from Akerlof's example of the market for used cars.[31] In this illustration, sellers of used cars have private information about the quality of the cars they are selling, which is not available, *ex ante*, to potential buyers. Accordingly, as a result of the opportunistic behaviour of some sellers, poor-quality cars (or lemons, as Akerlof terms them) dominate, and the market selects 'adversely'. In other words, buyers demonstrate a preference for potentially not buying a good car rather than potentially buying a lemon. In this situation, the market collapses and few deals are done.

Adverse selection problems of this kind are likely to arise in most real-world contracting situations and, in the current context, it is generally held that 'without such financial intermediaries [i.e. specialist venture capital firms], the market would tend to fail.' This is because relatively poorly informed investors who were drawn into bad projects ('lemons') would subsequently cease to provide venture capital finance.[30] In venture capital contracting relations, the investee firm is liable to have information not readily available to the potential investors. Moreover, firms have a clear incentive to 'talk up', or provide an optimistic view of their business history, current position or project potential.[32] On the other hand, investors may find it prohibitively costly to determine the true nature of these. This is often characterized as a problem of 'hidden information' and, it is suggested, venture capital firms are sufficiently experienced and specialized in such high-risk investments to be able to cope with, or reduce, information asymmetries of this type. However, this is by no means to suggest that venture capitalists eliminate the potential for adverse selection. Indeed, since the proportionate costs of 'due diligence' (i.e. gathering the requisite information about a potential investee firm) are generally believed to be inversely related to firm size and age, adverse selection may still persist in the market for seed, start-up and early stage investments. This, in turn, may partly explain the observed preference for later stage, and larger scale, expansion and buy-out/buy-in financing. Nonetheless, the key issue is that venture capitalist serve to reduce the *ex ante* information asymmetries which lead to adverse selection and ameliorate the problems of 'hidden information', which may deter institutional investors from direct involvement in venture capital activity.

As discussed in Chapter 5, information asymmetries also commonly occur *ex post*. Here, the general idea is that the (partial) separation of ownership and control creates scope for moral hazard. A firm that is insured, in part, against the risk of failure, through the sale of equity, may alter its behaviour in such a way as to act to the detriment of investors. To use the jargon of economics, the firm (agent) will seek to maximize its own utility irrespective of whether or not this coincides with the maximization of the investor's (principal's) utility. This, in turn, leads to higher agency costs, as the investor firm is required to supervise and monitor the activities of the investee firm. On this point, agency problems (and the requisite agency costs) are thought to be highest; when the level of *ex ante* information asymmetry is high (as noted above), when the agent has the incentive and ability to affect the distribution of income streams, and when partial ownership permits agents to consume firm resources/assets at a lower cost than their value to the firm and/or the investor.[33] Such a situation commonly marks the small firm–investor relationship. While the notion of adverse selection is fairly unproblematic (associated with problems of 'hidden information'), we may more clearly term moral hazard an 'asymmetry of interests', associating it with problems of 'hidden actions'.[34,35] Moreover, high agency costs inevitably lead to higher direct and indirect funding costs for the innovative small firm. That is, institutional investors are likely to require a greater equity holding, from small firms than from large, for a proportionately similar investment. One commonly suggested means to mitigating moral hazard, or minimizing agency costs, is through staged investment, which creates the option to abandon the project and provides an incentive for the entrepreneurial firm to act 'appropriately'. In addition, syndication (i.e. co-ordinated investment by two or more venture capitalists) may be a further means to reducing the problems caused by information asymmetries.[36] Nonetheless, the most common means of reducing moral hazard is through tightly specified contracts, though clearly these are costly to enforce. Again, however, the key issue is that venture capitalists are better placed to manage *ex post* information asymmetries than the institutional investors they represent.

THE INVESTMENT PROCESS

Before outlining a 'typical' investment process, to the extent that such a thing exists, it is worth reiterating the low levels of venture capital use in the small firm sector generally (studies invariably put the figure at between 2 and 4 per cent of firms). This, in itself, is hardly remarkable. Since we know that very few firms enjoy significant growth,[2] only a small number of firms will, in turn, represent sufficiently attractive investment opportunities to venture capitalists. Moreover, research suggests that venture capital firms[9] 'are seeking companies that can provide an internal rate of return of at least 30% in the case of established companies, rising to 60% or more for seed and start-up investments' (p. 15). Accordingly, it is likely that many of the best projects will eschew venture capital as too costly, choosing instead to leverage longer-term debt. For instance, it is suggested that, in addition to allowing individual entrepreneurs to maintain control, the acceptance of debt may act as a positive market signal.[34,37,38,39] That is,[34] 'high-quality managers [of high-quality projects] will signal their quality by choosing a capital structure involving a large percentage of debt, that will not be copied by the low-quality manager' (p. 321). This debt cannot be assumed without a high degree of confidence in the profitability of the project and the ability of the firm to make periodic repayments. Further, acceptance of debt may also signal the entrepreneur's unwillingness to share in the expected gains from any investment. In part, the extent to which the requirement for returns in excess of 30 per cent acts as a disincentive to seek venture capital may point to an additional asymmetry to those discussed above – an 'asymmetry of expectations'. Indeed, this 'asymmetry of expectations' may go to the heart of the debate regarding the extent to which 'equity gaps' are demand- or supply-side phenomena. As Moore and Garnsey note,[35] there exists a clearly established 'expectations gap between the owners of firms and venture capitalists, in terms of the scale of returns required and the size of the equity stake demanded' (p. 509).

However, notwithstanding the relative peripherality of venture capital, a growing number of (high-growth potential) firms are thought to be seeking it. Yet, of these firms, a very small proportion of applications which are assessed, ever gain access to capital and this does not include the great many applications which are not given more than the most cursory screening. For instance, a recent study of the Midlands Enterprise Fund noted that, of 206 applications assessed, only 3 investments were made – i.e. an investment ration of 1.46 per cent.[40] While this fund was particularly specialized, in having both economic development and commercial imperatives, investment ratios of this magnitude are fairly standard. Accordingly, it is important that we have an appreciation of the process by which venture capitalists decide upon which projects to fund and which to discard.

To this end, a number of studies have sought to delineate the investment cycle, invariably describing it as a sequential process of between 5 and 10 steps.[41,42,43] However, at the risk of oversimplifying, these have largely served to extend Tybejee and Bruno's[44] early work, and have been broadly faithful to its essence. Tybejee and Bruno outline an ordered process, comprising five key steps: deal origination; screening; evaluation; deal structuring; and monitoring or post-investment activities, as illustrated in Figure 6.6.

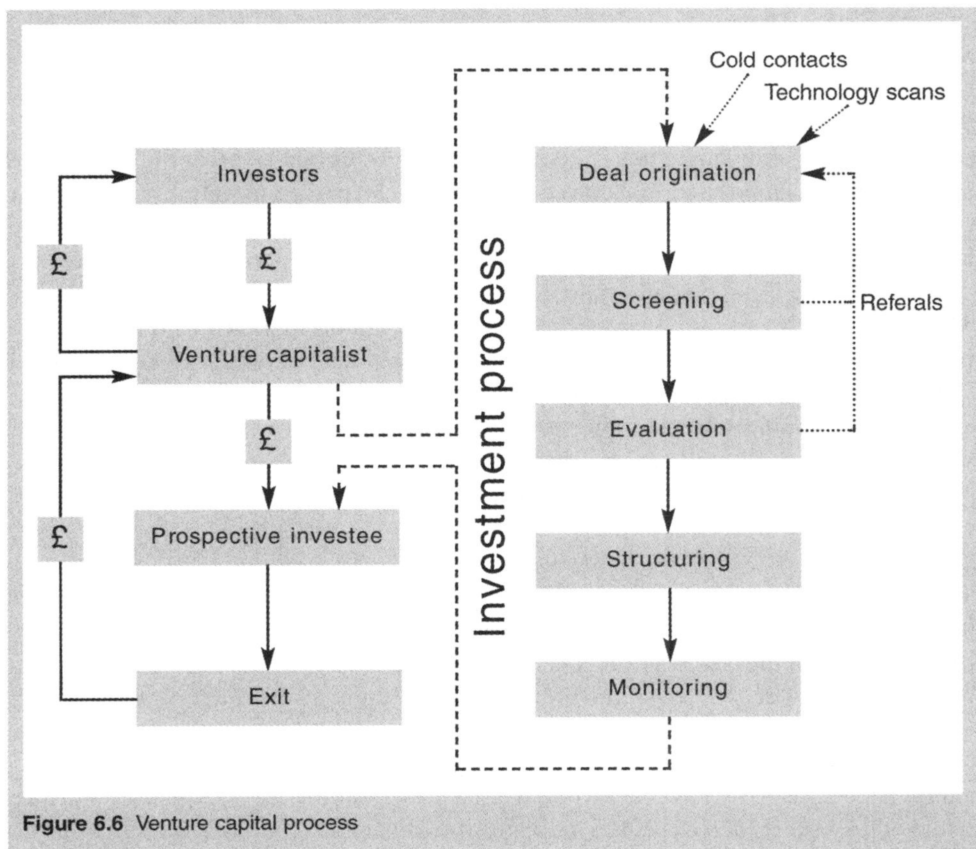

Figure 6.6 Venture capital process

In detail, these steps are:

Deal origination Prospective investments may come from a number of sources including unsolicited applications and technology scans. However, the most common means are either through an intermediary or by referral from another financial institution.

Screening It is common to further sub-divide this step, for example into venture capital specific and generic screening.[43] However, the essence is much the same. Screening consists of an examination of the business plan in an attempt to identify features that warrant further investigation. Rather worryingly, UK studies have suggested that the average first reading time for an application is between 10 and 15 minutes.[45]

Evaluation In the first instance this stage is likely to comprise a series of meetings between the venture capitalist and managers/directors of the applicant firm. Thereafter, and crucially, due diligence is undertaken. As a minimum, this is likely to include: a thorough analysis of the financial viability of the proposition and the accuracy, or appropriateness, of financial projections; credit searches on the company and its owners; and an appraisal of the firm's operating history.

Structuring Having decided to invest in principle, this stage involves negotiations over the nature of the investment. At its simplest, the issue may be thought of as, 'how much equity, for how much money?' However, the provision of third party equity is usually only one element in the final deal. Additional sources of finance may also include secured and unsecured debt from banks, loan notes and various convertible instruments. Clearly, this is liable to be the most sensitive stage in the investment process, as entrepreneurs become anxious over perceived inequities.

Monitoring 'One of the characteristics of venture finance is an *active* interest in the performance of investee companies ... a combination of capital and consulting'[40] (pp. 40–2, emphasis added). In general, as an agency problem, the emphasis is upon effective communication and the flow of information. In this circumstance, the venture capitalist normally takes a non-executive seat on the board. However, more occasionally, the VC may assume a more 'hands-on' approach, where this course of action is deemed necessary.

The above process lays out, in simple terms, the role of venture capitalists in identifying, appraising, investing and subsequently monitoring and advising business projects. It also makes clear the various points at which investment decisions are made. For instance, Murray[4] notes that approximately 80 per cent of applications are rejected at the initial screening stage, often for tangible reasons associated with the size of investment or industry of activity; although in the Boocock and Wood study, 31 per cent of rejections were as a result of an 'incomplete plan'.[40] Further rejections are likely to occur as a result of due diligence – finding 'skeletons in the closet' – or the inability to settle on an agreed deal structure. However, for obvious reasons, rejections become less common as the investment process progresses. Notwithstanding this, the general objective of the process is to pare down the many applications to a few attractive investment opportunities.

While the foregoing gives an idea of *when* the investment decision occurs, given low investment rates, it is important to also understand *why* the decision to invest is made, or not. To this end, myriad criteria are invariably identified by academic studies, many of which correspond with those employed by banks to assess lending proposals (see Chapter 5). On the whole, the approach tends to emphasize the balance between negative risk factors and positive return factors.[44] Specifically, these may include the attractiveness of the proposed market, the intended company strategy (e.g. level of product differentiation, existence of proprietary product, etc.), the size and stage of investment, the investors' technological or product market familiarity, the entrepreneur's own commitment and the geographic location of the venture. However, as Murray[4] notes, there has been a surprising degree of convergence among the many academic studies in this area. To illustrate he quotes MacMillan *et al.*,[46] such that:

"There is no question that irrespective of the horse (product), horse race (market), or odds (financial criteria), it is the jockey (entrepreneur) who fundamentally determines whether the venture capitalist will place the bet at all."

Clearly, certain baseline criteria must be established in respect of the 'horse', 'horse race' and 'odds'. However, the key point is that 'shortcomings of senior management' is the most commonly cited reason for failure in investment applications.

INFORMAL VENTURE CAPITAL AND BUSINESS ANGELS

Earlier in the chapter we hinted at the potential role business angels may play as 'gap funders'. That is, there is a generally held belief that:

"Business Angels fill the financing gap between founder, family and friends (the 3 'F's) . . . and the stage at which institutional venture capital funds might become interested. Because of their high transaction costs, venture capital funds typically have a high minimum investment size, a minimum efficient overall fund size and a correspondingly restricted number of portfolio companies which can be evaluated, invested in and monitored . . . In the UK there are very few funds that are willing to invest less than £500,000, and the average investment by a venture capital fund in an early stage investment is over £1 million."[47] (p. 137)

Business angels are private, high net-worth individuals who make direct investments in unquoted companies in which they have no family connection. It has been assumed that the bulk of angels are 'cashed-out' entrepreneurs who seek to act as value-added investors, contributing commercial acumen, contacts and entrepreneurial skills. In this sense, informal venture capital may be thought of as 'smart money'.[48] However, a study of 144 business angels in Scotland found that the majority were not previous entrepreneurs but had careers in large firms and financial institutions.[49] Far more than institutional venture capitalists, business angels adopt a hands-on role providing an array of strategic, monitoring and supporting inputs. Research indicates that entrepreneurs who have raised finance from angels report that their most valuable contribution is as a sounding board for management. Moreover, angels invest predominantly at seed and start-up stages and provide relatively small amounts of capital. For instance, while the average investment by a venture capital fund in an early stage investment is over £1 million, business angels typically invest less than £100,000 – although larger amounts are possible in situations where deals are syndicated. However, given their hands-on involvement, business angels are fairly infrequent investors, managing only a few investments at a time.

Furthermore, it is important to understand that business angels are not philanthropists or altruists. They are motivated, first and foremost, by capital gain – typically in the region of 20 per cent per annum – over the life of the investment, though they may derive some 'psychological income' from being involved with a new business and helping to develop the next generation of entrepreneurs. Given that the primary reason for investing is pecuniary, it is hardly surprising to find that business angels are at least as selective as formal venture capitalists. For instance, one study of Canadian private investors noted that 72.6 per cent of deals were rejected on the basis of 'first impressions', while a further 15.9 per cent were rejected after a detailed reading of the business plan.[50] In other words, a cumulative 88.5 per cent were rejected without ever meeting the principals of the business. Moreover, given similarities in objectives and context, one should anticipate that the investment process would be broadly similar to that utilized in the case of formal venture capital, though perhaps with less attendant bureaucracy in the form of professional advisers and, crucially, over a shorter time frame. This notwithstanding, Mason and Harrison[48] have suggested that business angels, in deciding whether to invest, are primarily concerned to answer four key questions:

1. Is there a market for the product or service, is it growing and how competitive is it?

2. Will the product or service be competitive? Does it merely represent a 'me-too' product or service?

3. Is the entrepreneurial team credible? What is the experience and expertise of the management team?

4. What is the upside potential of the venture? Relatedly, why is the money being sought and to what use will it be put?

Again, the essence of these questions is not remarkable and simply paraphrases the criteria employed by other investors or providers of external finance. The key issue, however, is the private investor's ability to adequately assess these concerns. That is, since business angels frequently invest in areas where they have prior experience or a declared interest, one may anticipate that they will often be uniquely placed, in the sense of having a comparative advantage, to accurately gauge the potential of a given opportunity.

However, irrespective of process, the consensus holds that private, or informal, investors are the primary source of external equity for new firms (i.e. for those seeking seed or start-up capital). Yet this axiom relies heavily on anecdotal evidence and on speculation, or estimation. As noted earlier, the bulk of informal venture capital is invisible and there is simply no way to accurately measure the scale of business angel activity. That is:

"Most business angels strive to preserve their anonymity, although some have a high profile. There are no directories which list business angels and there are no public records of their investments. It is therefore impossible to say how many business angels there are or how much they invest in aggregate."[48] (p. 110)

However, notwithstanding these difficulties, attempts have been made to estimate the size of the informal venture capital market. One recent effort extrapolated from the visible proportion of the UK market ('the tip of the iceberg').[47] This visible proportion is represented by Business Angel Networks (BANs). BANs are essentially intermediary organizations, of which there are currently 48, which seek to reduce inefficiencies in the market by acting as an information conduit, or dating agency, bringing investors and entrepreneurs together. Accordingly, and taking BANs as a starting point, these authors estimate that, in 1999, private investors made (at least) 1,800 *early stage* investments involving a total investment of £220 million. When one contrasts this with the 241 investments, involving a total investment of £228 million, made by venture capital funds in the same period, then the considerable contribution, especially in the provision of smaller amounts of capital, made by business angels becomes clear. Moreover, while the authors admit that the evidence on which this estimate is based is somewhat 'flimsy', they maintain that, at worst, it is likely to significantly understate the level of business angel activity.

The general implication is that, in situations where entrepreneurs are seeking less than £250,000, they may, more appropriately, direct their efforts towards the informal venture capital market rather than institutional venture capital funds.

THINK POINTS 6.3

Raising entrepreneurial finance

1. 'There are only ever going to be a small number of firms suitable as venture finance investments.' Give reasons for this statement from demand and supply perspectives.

2. What are the main stages in the venture capital cycle? And why is it a cycle?

3. What are the major differences between business angel investors and venture capital companies?

4. What are the advantages of business angels (over VC companies) for an entrepreneur seeking to raise entrepreneurial finance?

5. How would you advise such an entrepreneur, seeking to raise venture finance, on the best ways to find a business angel investor?

CONCLUSIONS

This chapter sought to outline the role of venture capital, as genuine risk capital, in supporting the start-up and development of high-risk, but high-growth potential, new and small firms. Given the higher levels of information asymmetries, which are invariably associated with higher-risk projects, and the necessarily longer-term investment horizon, it is suggested that the sale of equity, through venture capital intermediaries, may be a more appropriate source of funding than bank debt. This is likely to be particularly true for firms in high and new technology-based industries.

However, the chapter also noted the formal venture capitalist's preference for later stage and larger-scale investments, most especially MBOs/MBIs. In light of the disproportionately high transaction costs associated with investments in smaller and younger firms, this is not, in itself, remarkable. Yet, it has led to the identification, by many, of a 'new equity gap', impacting upon firms seeking relatively small amounts of 'classic' venture capital. In other words, formal venture capitalists are unlikely to be attracted by investments of less than £250,000, in firms with little or no track record, or in emerging, but untested, technologies. Clearly there is a role for public/private partnerships in ameliorating these concerns, and some positive signals are being sent, most notably by the development of regional venture capital funds in England. However, the 'gap' may more usefully, or more significantly, be met by independent or syndicated private investors or business angels. Notwithstanding the foregoing, it is important that we recognize that this is not merely a supply-side issue. Many venture capital funds and business angels bemoan the quality of proposals that come their way. Moreover, many entrepreneurs eschew equity funding, viewing it as dissolution of their control. If autonomy was central to the start-up decision, this is understandable. However, it is important to educate entrepreneurs that it may be better to own part of an orchard rather than the whole of an apple.

Finally, with respect to the investment decision-making process, we detailed some of the myriad, and logical, factors that influence the investor's judgement. However, we noted the common finding that both venture capital funds and business angels invest, first and foremost, in people.

SUGGESTED ASSIGNMENTS

1. Identify and interview an entrepreneur about their attitude towards sharing equity.
2. List the pros and cons associated with investing in the different investment stages.
3. As an entrepreneur, list the pros and cons associated with both formal and informal venture capital.
4. Visit the following websites and compile a report on the level of venture capital activity in the UK, US and Europe:
   www.bvca.co.uk
   www.evca.com
   www.nvca.com

REFERENCES

1. Cressy, R. (1996) 'Are business start-ups debt-rationed?' *Economic Journal*, vol. 106, pp. 1253–70.
2. Storey, D. (1994) *Understanding the Small Business Sector*, Routledge, London.
3. Cosh, A. and Hughes, A. (eds) (2000) *British Enterprise in Transition*, Centre for Business Research, University of Cambridge.
4. Murray, G. (1996) 'Venture Capital,' in Burns, P. and Dewhurst, J. (eds) *Small Business and Entrepreneurship*, Macmillan, London.
5. MacMillan (1931) *Report of the Committee on Finance and Industry*, Cmnd. 3897, HMSO, London.
6. Bolton (1971) *Report of the Committee of Inquiry on Small Firms*, Cmnd. 4811, HMSO, London.
7. Wilson (1979) *The Financing of Small Firms*, Interim Report of the Committee to Review the Functioning of the Financial Institutions, Cmnd. 7503, HMSO, London.

8. Williams (1989) *Financing of High Technology Business: A Report to the Paymaster General*, HM Treasury, London, November.

9. Mason, C. and Harrison, R. (1999) 'Venture Capital: rationale, aims and scope', editorial, *Venture Capital*, vol. 1, no. 1, pp. 1–46.

10. McNally, K. (1995) 'Corporate venture capital: the financing of technology businesses', *International Journal of Entrepreneurial Behaviour and Research*, vol. 1, no. 3, pp. 9–43.

11. Doran, A. and Bannock, G. (2000) 'Publicly sponsored regional venture capital: What can the UK learn from the US experience?' *Venture Capital*, vol. 2, pp. 255–86.

12. Harrison, R. and Mason, C. (2000) editorial, 'The role of the public sector in the development of a regional venture capital industry,' *Venture Capital*, vol. 2, pp. 243–54.

13. Bygrave, W. and Timmons, J. (1992) *Venture Capital at the Crossroads*, Harvard Business School Press, Boston, MA.

14. Wright, M. and Robbie, K. (1998) 'Venture capital and private equity: a review and synthesis', *Journal of Business Finance Accounting*, vol. 25, pp. 521–70.

15. Timmons, J. (1999) *New Venture Creation: Entrepreneurship for the 21st Century*, McGraw-Hill, Boston, MA.

16. Murray, G. (1992) 'A challenging market place for venture capital', *Long Range Planning*, vol. 25, pp. 79–86.

17. Baygan, G. and Freudenberg, M. (2000) 'The internationalisation of venture capital activity in OECD countries: implications for measurement and policy', STI WP 2000/7, OECD, Paris.

18. Amit, R., Brander, J. and Zott, C. (1998) 'Why do venture capital firms exist? Theory and Canadian evidence', *Journal of Business Venturing*, vol. 13, pp. 441–66.

19. Coopers and Lybrand/Venture One (1996) *Seventh Annual Economic Impact of Venture Capital Study*, NVCA, Arlington, VA.

20. Coopers and Lybrand LLP (1997) *The Economic Impact of Venture Capital in Europe*, EVCA, Belgium.

21. Tylecote, A. (1994) 'Financial Systems and Innovation', in Dodgson, M. and Rothwell, R. (1994) *The Handbook of Industrial Innovation*, pp. 259–67, Edward Elgar, Cheltenham.

22. BVCA (1998) *A Guide to Venture Capital*, BVCA, London.

23. Brouwer, M. and Hendrix, B. (1998) 'Two worlds of venture capital: what happened to US and Dutch early stage investment', *Small Business Economics*, vol. 10, pp. 333–48.

24. CBI (1996) *Tech Stars: Breaking the growth barriers for technology-based SMEs*, CBI, London.

25. Bank of England (1996) *The Financing of Technology-Based Small Firms*, London, October.

26. HM Treasury (1998) *Financing of High Technology Businesses: A report to the Paymaster General*, London, November.

27. BVCA (2000) *Report on Investment Activity 1999*, BVCA, London.

28. Mason, C. and Harrison, R. (1995) 'Closing the regional equity gap: the role of informal venture capital', *Small Business Economics*, vol. 7, pp. 153–72.

29. Admati, A. and Pfleiderer, P. (1994) 'Robust financial contracting and the role of venture capitalists', *The Journal of Finance*, vol. 49, pp. 371–402.

30. Reid, G. (1999) 'The application of principal–agent methods to investor–investee relations in the UK venture capital industry', *Venture Capital*, vol. 1, pp. 285–302.

31. Akerlof, G. (1970) 'The market for lemons: Quality uncertainty and the market mechanism', *Quarterly Journal of Economics*, vol. 84, pp. 488–500.

32. Seaton, J. and Walker, I. (1997) 'The pattern of R&D finance for small UK companies', in Oakey, R. and Mukhtar, S-M. (eds) *New technology-based firms in the 1990s, Volume III*, pp. 71–91, Paul Chapman, London.

33. Jensen, M. and Meckling, W. (1976) 'Theory of the firm: managerial behaviour, agency costs and ownership structure', *Journal of Financial Economics*, vol. 3, pp. 305–60.

34. Goodacre, A. and Tonks, I. (1995) 'Finance and Technological Change', in Stoneman, P. *Handbook of the Economics of Innovation and Technological Change*, pp. 298–341, Blackwell, Oxford.

35. Moore, I. and Garnsey, E. (1993) 'Funding for innovation in small firms: the role of government', *Research Policy*, vol. 22, pp. 507–19.

36. Lerner, J. (1994) 'The syndication of venture capital investments', *The Financier*, vol. 23, pp. 16–27.

37. Ross, S. (1977) 'The determination of financial structure: the incentive-signalling approach', *Bell Journal of Economics*, vol. 8, pp. 23–40.

38. Myers, S. and Majluf, N. (1984) 'Corporate financing and investment decisions when firms have information that investors do not', *Journal of Financial Economics*, vol. 13, pp. 187–221.

39. Giudici, G. and Paleari, S. (2000) 'The provision of finance to innovation: a survey

conducted among Italian technology-based small firms', *Small Business Economics*, vol. 14, pp. 37–53.

40. Boocock, G. and Wood, M. (1997) 'The evaluation criteria used by venture capitalists: Evidence from a UK venture fund', *International Small Business Journal*, vol. 16, pp. 36–57.

41. Silver, A. (1985) *Venture Capital: The complete guide for investors*, John Wiley and Sons, New York.

42. Hall, G. (1989) 'Lack of finance as a constraint on the expansion of innovatory small firms', in Barber, J., Metcalfe, J. and Porteous, M. (eds) *Barriers to Growth in Small Firms*, Routledge, London.

43. Fried, V. and Hisrich, R. (1994) 'Toward a model of venture capital investment decision making', *Financial Management*, vol. 23, pp. 28–37.

44. Tybejee, T. and Bruno, A. (1984) 'A model of venture capital investment activity', *Management Science*, vol. 30, pp. 1051–66.

45. Sweeting, R. (1991) 'UK venture capital funds and the funding of new technology-based businesses: Process and relationships', *Journal of Management Studies*, vol. 28, pp. 601–22.

46. MacMillan, I., Siegal, R. and Subba Narishima, P. (1985) 'Criteria used by venture capitalists to evaluate new venture proposals', *Journal of Business Venturing*, vol. 1, pp. 126–41.

47. Mason, C. and Harrison, R. (2000) 'The size of the informal venture capital market in the United Kingdom', *Small Business Economics*, vol. 15, pp. 137–48.

48. Mason, C. and Harrison, R. (1997) 'Business angels are the answer to the entrepreneur's prayer', in Birley, S. and Muzyka, D. (eds) *Master Entrepreneurship*, FT/Prentice Hall, London, pp. 110–14.

49. Paul, S., Johnston, J., Whittam, G. and Wilson, L. (2002) 'Are business angels entrepreneurs?' paper presented to the Small Business and Enterprise Development Conference, Nottingham, April.

50. Feeney, L., Haines, G. and Riding, A. (1999) 'Private investors' investment criteria: insights from qualitative data', *Venture Capital*, vol. 2, pp. 121–45.

RECOMMENDED READING

Amit, R., Brander, J. and Zott, C. (1998) 'Why do venture capital firms exist? Theory and Canadian evidence', *Journal of Business Venturing*, vol. 13, pp. 441–66.

BVCA (1998) *A Guide to Venture Capital*, BVCA, London.

Mason, C. and Harrison, R. (1999) 'Venture Capital: rationale, aims and scope', editorial, *Venture Capital*, vol. 1, no. 1, pp. 1–46.

Murray, G. (1996) 'Venture Capital', in Burns, P. and Dewhurst, J. (eds) *Small Business and Entrepreneurship*, Macmillan, London.

Tybejee, T. and Bruno, A. (1984) 'A model of venture capital investment activity', *Management Science*, vol. 30, pp. 1051–66.

Wright, M. and Robbie, K. (1998) 'Venture capital and private equity: a review and synthesis', *Journal of Business Finance Accounting*, vol. 25, pp. 521–70.

7

INNOVATION AND ENTREPRENEURSHIP

LEARNING OUTCOMES

At the end of this chapter you should be able to:

1. Define innovation in the context of the entrepreneurship process.
2. Describe advantages and disadvantages of small firms in the innovation process.
3. Discuss the importance of external linkages for small firms with the innovation process.
4. Describe the issues that innovative entrepreneurs face with securing funding.
5. Discuss how policy-makers might intervene to assist small firms with the innovation process.
6. Apply entrepreneurial concepts to the innovation process.

He that will not apply new remedies must expect new evils; for time is the greatest innovator.

Francis Bacon

There is nothing more difficult to take in hand, more perilous to conduct, or more uncertain in its success, than to take the lead in the introduction of a new order of things.

Niccolo Machiavelli

INTRODUCTION

Academics and policy-makers rarely understate the importance of industrial innovation. In a world where such consensuses are rare, the common view[1] holds that '[i]n all highly-industrialised nations the long-term growth of business and (thus) of regions [and, one may safely assume, nations] stems from their ability to continually develop and produce innovative products' (p. 391). Indeed, Chris Freeman, the doyen of innovation theorists, goes further,[2] suggesting that 'not to innovate is to die' (p. 266). While one may quibble about the appropriateness of such imperatives, it is nonetheless clear that innovations, of varying scale and scope, positively impact upon the aggregate performance of firms and, by implication, economies.[3,4,5] Moreover, in contrast to earlier convictions, it has gradually become clear that there is no firm size unequivocally optimal for innovation. That is, both large and small firms have significant, and often complementary, roles to perform in the process of technological development and innovation broadly defined.[6] With this in mind, the current chapter seeks to delineate the distinct contribution made by smaller firms to industrial innovation and outlines some key enabling and constraining factors.

What do we Mean by Innovation?

The most obvious link between innovation and entrepreneurship, or innovation and small firms, may arguably be traced to the early work of Joseph Schumpeter.[7] With respect to the nature of innovation, Schumpeter identified five principal sources of 'creative destruction':

- **the introduction of a new good (or a significant improvement in the quality of an existing good);**
- **the introduction of a new method of production (i.e. an innovation in processes);**
- **the opening of a new market (in particular an export market in a new territory);**
- **the 'conquest of a new source of supply of raw materials or half-manufactured goods';**
- **the creation of a new type of industrial organization (i.e. an administrative innovation).**

Clearly, then, this conception is far broader than simply technical advance, narrowly defined, though Schumpeter was unambiguous in excluding merely marginal or aesthetic changes. Moreover, this more eclectic view is certainly attractive. As a recent OECD[8] workshop on SMEs concluded:

> ***"Most high growth firms are not innovative in a technical sense, but may include marketing innovations or cross-national alliances. Most high-tech firms are not high growth. [and] Most new jobs are created by low innovation, low growth traditional firms." (pp. 57–8)***

In other words, the best performing firms are those occupying mature industries and engaged in marketing or administrative innovations and *not* the high technology or new technology-based firms which dominate policy deliberations. However, notwithstanding this observation, convention, and common usage of the term innovation, carry connotations of technical change narrowly defined. That is, innovation concerned with substantive changes in the technology underlying processes or products. Furthermore, while there may be some ambivalence with regards to the performance of individual firms, innovations of this type undoubtedly impact upon aggregate economic performance and economic growth generally. Accordingly, technical innovations are the focus of this chapter.

So, adopting this narrow definition, what do we mean by innovation? To begin with, innovation is emphatically not invention. Invention is only part of the process. The concept of innovation is more holistic and involves the commercial application of inventions (often for the first time). Thus, innovation incorporates both creation or discovery aspects and diffusion or utilization aspects. The obvious inference to draw from this is that innovation, as a commercial phenomenon, is somehow a linear process, beginning with basic science and ending in sales – or vice versa. Indeed, just such a conception dominated academic and industrial thinking from the 1950s up until the early 1970s; conceived of as either 'science-push' innovation (in which the emergence of new opportunities based upon new technologies drives the process) or 'demand-pull' innovation (reflecting more stationary technology, an increase in the importance of marketing to firm growth and a 'needs'-driven innovation agenda) (See Figures 7.1 and 7.2). Rothwell[9] terms these linear approaches the 'First generation Innovation Process' and the 'Second generation Innovation Process' respectively and notes that systematic empirical evidence, available for the first time in the mid 1970s, had suggested that 'the technology-push or need-pull models of innovation were extreme and atypical examples of a more general process of *interaction* between, on the one hand, technological capabilities and, on the other, market needs" (p. 9, emphasis added). It is this idea of interaction that underpins current thinking.

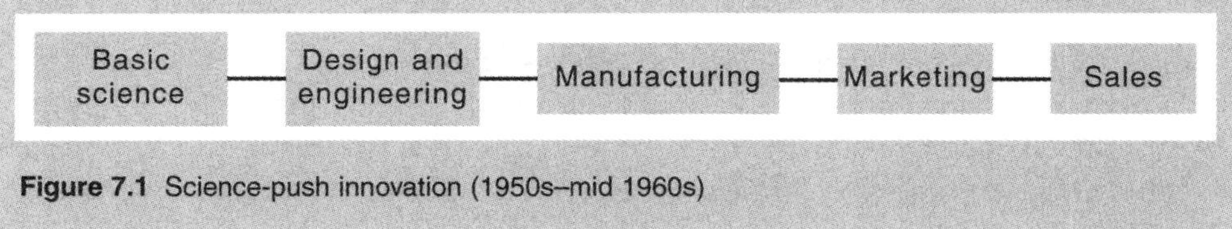

Figure 7.1 Science-push innovation (1950s–mid 1960s)

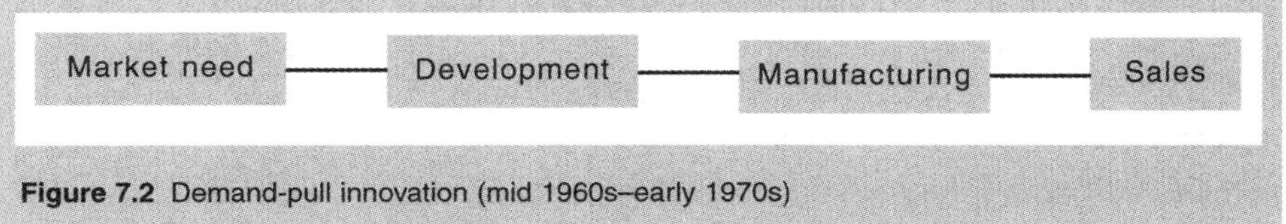

Figure 7.2 Demand-pull innovation (mid 1960s–early 1970s)

This view of innovation, as a process of complex links and feedback mechanisms, is most notably represented by Kline and Rosenberg's 'chain-linked' model[10] and by Rothwell and Zegveld's 'coupling' model (Figure 7.3).[11] In these models innovation is conceived of as a network of inter-organizational and extra-organizational communication paths, linking the various in-house functions and allowing the firm to articulate with both the market place and the wider scientific and technological community. At each stage of the development process, innovation endeavours may be informed by internal and external user constituencies and by the external technological state of the art. Clearly this is a more satisfactory representation of the intricacy one would anticipate, given the degree of market and technological

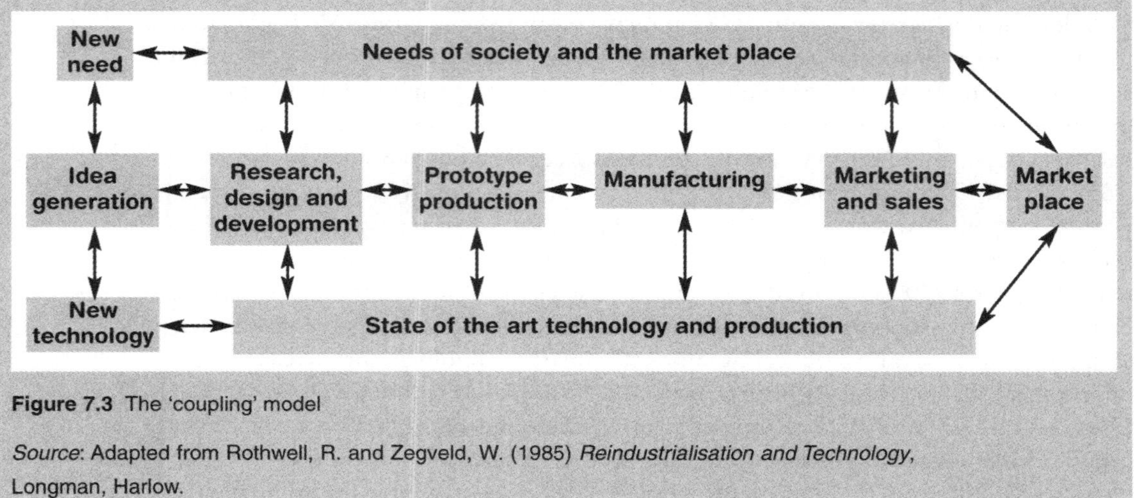

Figure 7.3 The 'coupling' model

Source: Adapted from Rothwell, R. and Zegveld, W. (1985) *Reindustrialisation and Technology*, Longman, Harlow.

uncertainties involved. Moreover, persistent internal and external feedback mechanisms and reference points are likely to reduce waste and increase the speed of acceptance of the final product or process, thus contributing, ultimately, to innovation success.

Although initially compelling, 'coupling' models of innovation suffer from a number of weaknesses, most notably the implicit assumption that innovation remains a linear, though occasionally iterative, process enacted by organizations, or more usually firms, as discrete entities. Thus, while the functional units within the organization intermittently interact with each other or with an external agency, the principal innovation tasks are undertaken with relative autonomy. By contrast, contemporary and prevailing opinion has begun to view innovation as a systemic phenomenon. Kenneth Boulding[12] defines a system, at its most fundamental, as 'anything that is not chaos'. In this sense, conceptions of innovation have long been systemic. Clearly, the linear 'technology-push' or 'demand-pull' views of innovation, discussed above, are not chaos. Yet, contemporary understanding of systems, at least in the context of innovation theory, carries connotations beyond these simple models. Systems approaches to innovation are driven by the pervasive idea that[13] 'innovation by firms cannot be understood purely in terms of independent decision-making at the level of the firm' (p. 73). Rather, innovation is viewed as an iterative, cumulative and co-operative phenomenon[14] in which 'interactive learning and collective entrepreneurship are fundamental' (p. 9). Systems of innovation (SI) extend 'Third generation' coupling models to incorporate not only a series of phased, bilateral or dyadic interactions involving users, producers, existing scientific knowledge and the science base,[14] but also, more inclusively, all 'elements and relationships which interact in the production, diffusion of new, and economically useful, knowledge' (p. 2). That is, since innovation involves the cumulative or path-dependent creation of new knowledge, or novel recombination of existing knowledge, innovation is essentially concerned with learning. Learning in its turn is largely a social process – most especially in the context of the transfer or accumulation of tacit knowledge[15,16] – and is likely to involve considerably more than two actors. In this vein, any innovation system is likely to be socially embedded in such a way that the innovativeness of individual firms will be influenced by socially specific factors such as the infrastructure of financial institutions, labour markets, policy and provision of workforce training, mechanisms governing the support of business start-ups and development, attitudes and policy concerned with science and technology and so on.[17] That is, SI[18] 'are conditioned by a wide array of factors ranging from the cultural habits and tastes of a community and the institutional topography of an industry or region, to the physical and intellectual resources of states as well as their policy or managerial carrying capacities' (p. 102).

A systems approach allows for the interaction of environmental factors (e.g. cultural, social and economic) with institutions such as academic universities and state research institutions, as illustrated by Figure 7.4.[19]

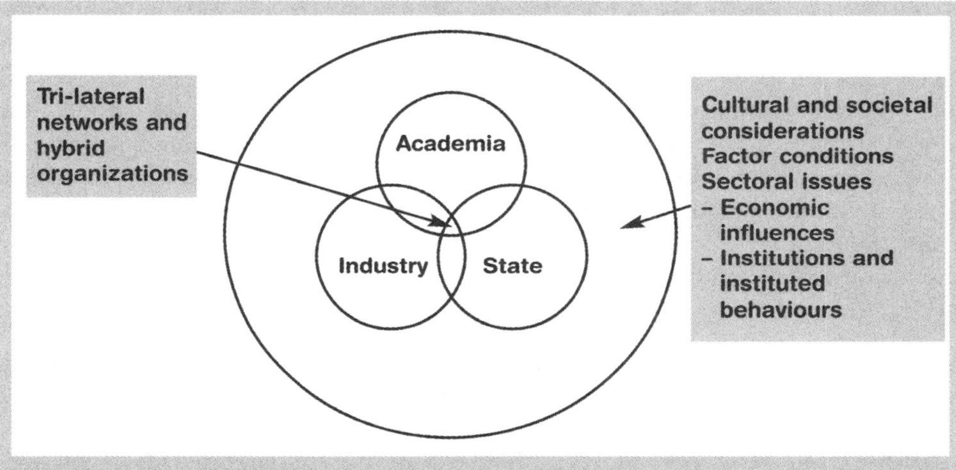

Figure 7.4 A systems approach

Source: Adapted from Etzkowitz, H. and Leydesdorff, L. (2000) 'The dynamics of innovation: from National Systems and "Mode 2" to a Triple Helix of university-industry-government relations', *Research Policy*, vol. 29, no. 2, pp. 109–24.

ENTREPRENEURSHIP AND INNOVATION

No firm is an island

The basic premise of systems approaches to innovation, and similarly motivated network aproaches, is that no firm may function efficiently as an island entire of itself.[20]

Frequently, advocates of network aproaches to innovation-induced economic development highlight an increasing division of labour among organizations as a first principle, compelling collaboration or interaction.[1] That is, increasing uncertainty, associated with changing technology and global competition, has encouraged many firms (and, indeed, many nations) to concentrate on fewer and fewer core competencies, relying upon trade, or co-operation, for others.[21] See also the discussion on globalization in Chapter 11.

This effective disintegration of the vertical value chain has been taken as evidence of a move from hierarchical governance structures (based on threat and coercion) to network governance structures (based on reciprocity and trust).[22] That is, in contrast to the pre-eminence of Fordist and Taylorist practices during the immediate post-war period, the efficient organization of production is increasingly associated with vertical disintegration and flexibility.[23,24] Fundamentally, however, the conclusion one is asked to reach is that[25] 'a high level of co-operation and communication typically affects innovation activities positively' (p. 467). While internal resources (such as expenditure on research and development and the technical skills of staff) and strategies will impact upon the firm's ability to innovate, it is increasingly the case that (particularly small) firms will also require external resources and know-how to successfully innovate. A belief in the necessary combination of external and internal resources and interactions drives much of public policy (e.g. regional innovation strategies, cluster policies and science parks) and helps delineate the discussion that follows.

ENTREPRENEURSHIP AND INNOVATION

Benefits of networking

As discussed above, the development of environments that encourage networking, such as business incubators, have been the focus of recent development. Networking of entrepreneurs encourages innovation due to:

- the ability to call on different skills to solve technical problems;
- firms interact to develop new ideas;
- access to resouces and funding may be more likely;
- prototypes may be enhanced by testing and development through interaction;
- encouragement of the development of an innovative and entrepreneurial culture.

INNOVATION AND FIRM SIZE

Before turning to specific issues affecting small firms seeking to innovate, it is clearly appropriate to briefly comment on the question of how firm size affects innovation. Indeed, notwithstanding the enduring ambivalence, this question has given rise to the second largest corpus of empirical literature in the field of industrial organization.[26] As noted earlier, much of the work favouring small firm contributions owes a great deal to the early writings of Joseph Schumpeter. In his initial deliberations, what one may term 'Schumpeter Mark 1', Schumpeter[7] proposed that it was the exceptional creative drive of independent entrepreneurs which led to the introduction of radical new products and the creation of new industry structures which, in turn, undermined the status quo and impelled changes in existing market structures (see also Chapter 1). This is the Schumpeter who takes pride of place in many undergraduate entrepreneurship courses. However, in *Capitalism, Socialism and Democracy*,[27] as cited in the work of Acs and Andretsch,[28] Schumpeter adopts what appears to be a diametrically opposite position, arguing that:

> ***"The monopolist firm will generate a larger supply of innovations because there are advantages which, though not strictly unattainable on the competitive level of enterprise, are as a matter of fact secured only on the monopoly level."***

Essentially, this later Schumpeter ('Schumpeter Mark 2') suggests that, since the process, or task, of innovation has become increasingly routinized (over the first half of the twentieth century), admitting increasing returns to scale, large firms are likely to possess advantages over smaller rivals. For instance, large firms may be able to spread the risk of innovation over a number of projects, adopting a portfolio approach, whereas smaller firms are often constrained to put 'all their eggs in one basket'. Moreover, if firms are liable to innovate only where positive post-innovation returns, accounting for development costs, are anticipated, one may plausibly assume that a high degree of market power (i.e. the ability to set prices above marginal cost), frequently associated with larger size, would be the first best condition for innovation. Indeed, a belief in the importance of monopoly power, in stimulating innovation, underpins the international system of patents. At the risk of oversimplifying, successful patents, conferring exclusive rights to make and sell a given product, create fixed-term monopolies, preventing imitation and allowing firms to recoup research and development expenses.

Support for this later hypothesis is provided by, among others, J.K. Galbraith.[29,30] As cited in Acs and Andretsch,[28] with respect to technological innovation Galbraith[29] argued that:

> ***"Because development is costly, it follows that it can be carried on only by a firm that has the resources which are associated with considerable size."***

That is, large firms have the advantage of being able to spread the considerable fixed costs over a large sales volume.

THINK POINTS 7.1

Entrepreneurship and innovation

1. Why does Schumpeter have two diametrically opposed views on the role of the entrepreneur in innovation (Schumpeter Mark 1 and Mark 2)?

2. What are Schumpeter's forces of creative destruction?

3. To what extent is the Internet revolution an example of creative destruction?

   Hint: see also Chapters 1 and 8.

4. How can innovation occur through demand-pull and cost-push forces?

5. How would you advise a local development agency wishing to encourgae innovative entrepreneurship, particularly in relation to the creation of conducive environments?

Small Firms v. Large Firms

The view that 'big is best', or that large firms are at the heart of the process of innovation and wealth and welfare creation, has, until relatively recently, prevailed. However, over the last twenty years, a 'new learning' has emerged.[28] Empirical studies in both the USA and the UK[31,32,33,34] noted that, subject to certain sectoral variations, 'small firms can keep up with large firms in the field of innovation'[35] (p. 335) and, indeed, may more efficiently use R&D inputs to generate innovation outputs. In other words, rather than searching for some firm size uniquely and unequivocally optimal for innovation, it is vital that we recognize that small and large firms may fulfil different and often complementary roles – what Rothwell terms 'dynamic complementarity'.[6]

Moreover, the relative importance of small and large firms may vary over the business cycle or industry life cycle. That is, small firms may enjoy comparative advantages as innovators in embryonic industries. However, once a dominant design has been established, the focus switches from product development activities to minor product improvements and cost-saving process technology. In the later stages of the cycle, innovation activities become relatively routinized and scale economies become more important. This dynamic view of a changing innovation-firm size relationship is supported by casual observation of industrial population data. For instance, Figure 7.5 below provides approximate data on the number of automotive manufacturers in the US over the course of the twentieth century. Figure 7.5 clearly indicates considerable industry 'shake-out' as technology becomes more stable.

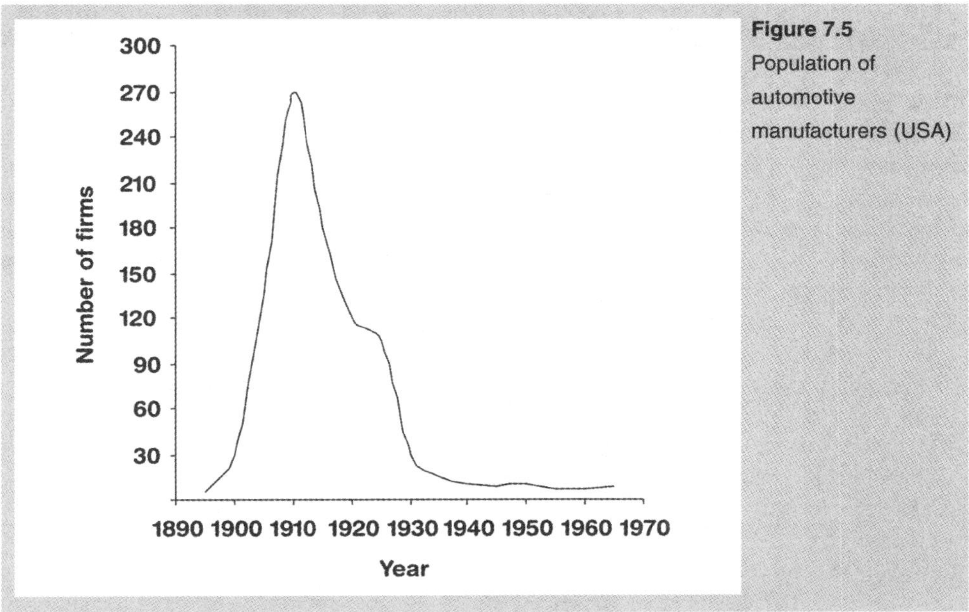

Figure 7.5
Population of automotive manufacturers (USA)

Similar trends may be noted for industries as diverse as televisions, tyres and penicillin.[36] Indeed, we may be observing the seeds of 'shake-out' in recent 'high-profile' dotcom failures.

Further evidence in support of this 'dynamic complementarity' is provided by the observation that large firms dominate innovation activities in mature industries (such as consumer durables), while small firms are disproportionately responsible for innovations in new and emergent sectors, such as bio-technology and E-commerce. However, notwithstanding the increasing rate of technological change and associated shortening of product life cycles, the sustainability of small firm comparative advantages, in anything other than narrow market niches, must be in doubt. This aside, the general inference that is drawn is that:[31]

“Industries which are capital-intensive, concentrated and advertising intensive tend to promote innovation in large firms. The small-firm innovation advantage, however, tends to occur in industries in the early stages of the life-cycle, where total innovation and the use of skilled labour play a large role.” (p. 573)

To rephrase, while fundamental or radical invention and process innovation ordinarily takes place within either large firms or large public laboratories, small firms are disproportionately responsible for near-to-market developments and initial market diffusion. That small firms enjoy innovation advantages in certain industries, and at certain levels of technological maturity, is now fairly well established and generally accepted. Accordingly, the discussion turns now to the basis of such advantages and associated disadvantages, as illustrated in Table 7.1.

Advantages	Disadvantages
Management: Lack of bureaucracy; greater risk acceptance; entrepreneurial management; rapid decision-making	Lack of formal management skills
Marketing: Nearness to markets ensures fast reaction to changing market requirements; may dominate niche markets	Little or no market power; poor distribution an servicing facilities; geographic market expansi may prove prohibitively costly
Technical manpower: Considerable scope for cross-functionality; technologists often 'plugged-in' to other departments	Often lack suitably qualified specialists (which may also constrain external networking); often unable to support formal R&D efforts
Communications: Efficient and informal internal communication facilitates rapid internal problem solving	Lack of time and resources to forge external technological linkages
Finance: SMEs often considered more 'R&D efficient' (i.e. innovation can be relatively less costly); 'bootstrapping' possible	Difficulties accessing external finance; cost of capital relatively high; reliance on short-term debt; inability to spread risk
Growth: Potential for growth through 'niche' or differentiation strategies	Difficulties accessing finance for growth; entrepreneurs often unable to manage growth
Government schemes: Government schemes established to facilitate small firm innovation (e.g. SPUR, SMART)	High transaction costs involved in accessing schemes; few resources available to manage collaborative schemes; lack of awareness
Regulation: Some regulations are applied less rigorously to small firms	In general, however, the relative unit cost of regulatory compliance is higher for small firms patent system prohibitively complex and costly
Collaboration: Flexibility and rapid decision-making may make firms attractive partners	Firms suffer from power asymmetries in collaboration with larger partners; little or no supply chain influence
Organization: Suffer less from routinization and inertia	Suffer more from uncertainties and associated costs
Human resources: Flat management structures and local project ownership are likely	High staff turnover; little formal training

Source: Adapted from Rothwell, R. (1984) 'The role of small firms in the emergence of new technologies', *Omega*, vol. 12, no. 1, pp.19–29.

Table 7.1 Advantages and disadvantages of small firms in innovation

As the earlier discussion hinted, in fulfilling the role of product developer and diffuser, small firms enjoyed unique advantages associated with lack of bureaucracy, flat management structures, efficient, often informal, internal communications systems, and flexibility and adaptability through nearness to markets. By contrast, small firms faced constraints associated with lack of technically qualified labour, poor use of external information and expertise, difficulty in attracting/securing finance and related inability to spread risk, unsuitability of original management beyond initial prescription, and high cost of regulatory compliance. However, notwithstanding these particulars, the most striking feature of Table 7.1 is that the advantages enjoyed by small firms are fundamentally *behavioural*, while constraints relate to *resource*. In the process of industrial innovation, small firms are behaviourally advantaged and resource constrained.

The challenge, then, for firm strategy and public policy is to alleviate resource constraints while maintaining behavioural advantages. This resolution of this dilemma is not a simple as one might initially anticipate. For instance, as stage models of firm growth indicate (see Chapter 10), increasing firm size is invariably accompanied by problems of control. That is, as the firm gets larger, it becomes more difficult for the entrepreneur to effectively monitor and supervise all facets of the firm's activities. Moreover, the measures employed to affect control, reduce waste or prevent unilateralism by subordinates commonly reduce flexibility. Layers (or hierarchies) of management are introduced, ways of doing things become proceduralized and routinized, and paper systems evolve. In essence, the organization becomes less an entrepreneurial firm and more a bureaucratic firm. There is an implicit trade-off between the alleviation of resource constraints and the preservation of behavioural advantages. This is simply a rephrasing of the 'innovator's dilemma'.[37] However, as the earlier discussion hinted, one solution may be for small firms to engage in innovation networks, thereby accessing the necessary resources for innovation through external linkages (with supplier, customers, etc.) while maintaining the flexibility and adaptability associated with smaller size.

THINK POINTS 7.2

Entrepreneurship and innovation: small firms v. large firms

1. What are the advantages of small firms over large firms in the entrepreneurship and innovation process?
2. Why has technological change encouraged innovative activity associated with entrepreneurial small firms?

   Hint: see also Chapter 2.
3. Why are large firms suited to innovative activity in certain sectors? What are these sectors?
4. Is innovative activity linked to a firm's life cycle?

   Hint: see also Chapter 10.

INNOVATION AND EXTERNAL LINKAGES

Links with Suppliers and Subcontractors

Bought-out items account for over 50 per cent of total costs for the average UK manufacturing firm.[38] Accordingly, there can be little doubt that the supplier relationship plays a considerable role in determining competitiveness and, ultimately, innovative capability. As Sako[39] notes, '[t]he extent to which suppliers are asked to contribute to the design and development of products ... is a crucial dimension affecting the scope for innovation' (p. 269). While there are dangers involved in encouraging upstream innovation – related, in part, to the devolution of value creation sources – benefits are presumed to arise through greater cross-fertilization, reduced costs and improved efficiency. In essence, the firm is able to gain many of the advantages of vertical integration (and larger size) while reducing the transaction costs involved.[40] Additionally, one may anticipate that the use of subcontracted services will allow the small firm to alleviate internal resource limitations. Where the relationship with the external service provider is sufficiently longitudinal, and the requisite knowledge is embedded in technology or people, there exists scope for the transfer of tacit knowledge that may otherwise be unattainable.[41] Reviewing data from a variety of studies, Rothwell and Dodgson[42,43] suggest that 'subcontracting ... can enable firms to innovate products requiring new production techniques, without having to invest initially heavily in expensive, sophisticated production equipment'[42] (p. 105). Yet, as a caveat, it is important to note that subcontracting processes which add considerable value to the firm's profitability, or those which are key to the development of the company's core competence, may reduce the innovative capability of the buyer firm. Notwithstanding this, one may anticipate that small firm capacity for innovation will be enhanced by the extended knowledge base offered through extensive supplier/subcontractor links. Indeed, from their review Rothwell and Dodgson find that, in the case of 'significant innovation', 10 per cent of innovations involved collaboration with customers only, compared with 55 per cent which involved collaboration with both customers *and* suppliers. These figures can be contrasted with those for 'incremental' innovation, where 40 per cent of innovations involved collaboration solely with customers and only 20 per cent involved collaboration with customers *and* suppliers.[43]

Links with Customers

The relationship of the customer, or user, to the efficacy of industrial innovation has received much attention in the academic literature. However, while accepting that understanding user need is crucial to the success of innovations,[44] it is with the more formal collaboration and feedback loops we are currently interested. To this end, the innovation process has been characterized as 'user-dominated'[45] in which 'continuous user-manufacturer interaction ... identifies re-innovation opportunities, new uses and new users'[46] (p. 127, tense changed). Indeed it has been further argued that there is scope for considerable gain through involving the user in the product design and development processes.[47] These gains are believed to be principally fourfold:

1. Firms may be able to supplement their internal design and development activities by accessing the technical and managerial skills resident within their customers.

2. User involvement is likely to be the ideal way to establish the optimum price/performance combination and, consequently, the optimum specification.

3. Involving the user in the product design and development stages is likely to reduce the post-delivery learning required on their part (and, accordingly, this may result in strong demonstration effects, attracting other customers and accelerating the innovation acceptance process).

4. Where user involvement engenders a strong relationship, this may result in user feedback and associated product improvements that serve to lengthen the product life cycle.

In general, one would anticipate that the most innovative firms would be more likely to have non-exchange-related links with customers and that these links, in turn, are likely to be stronger and more formal.

Links with Competitors and other Firms

Inter-firm linkages, outside the value chain, are those that have been the subject of greatest attention within the small firms literature. Lawson, for instance, notes '[t]he importance of "horizontal" linkages ... rather than simply supply chain "vertical" linkages'[48] (p. 44). However, the interest has gone further than simple agglomeration economies resulting from Marshall's externalities, and seeks to investigate the way in which local clusters of (mainly) small enterprises alternately co-operate and compete.[49] This not to suggest that firms are unable to gain benefit simply through geographic proximity. Indeed, improvements in local infrastructure and related trades and the flow and spill-over of knowledge are all likely to improve the firm's position, while requiring minimal direct action.[50] However, in the present context, we are concerned primarily with the gains that arise through direct collaboration between small firms and the impact it has upon their innovative capability. In this vein, the literature suggests that the principal benefits to be gained through collaboration involve: complementing and supplementing internal product development efforts,[43] cost and risk sharing,[51] accessing new markets[52] and the transfer of both (embedded) technology and (tacit) knowledge[53] (see also Chapter 8). Dodgson goes as far as to suggest that inter-firm collaboration can lead to 'positive sum gains' – i.e. firms can obtain mutual benefits that could not be achieved independently.[51]

Links with Universities and Colleges

Accepted wisdom holds that the success of Route 128 Boston and Silicon Valley is due, in no small part, to their proximity to MIT and Stanford University respectively.[54] Attempts to replicate this phenomenon in the UK have taken the form of an increasing number of science parks adjacent to universities. Two principal reasons are posited to support the notion that university links are likely to improve small firm innovative capability: first, it is argued that 'university research is a source of significant innovation-generating knowledge which diffuses initially through personal contacts to adjacent firms'[55] (p. 2). Supporting this, evidence from the USA has suggested that university research drives industry R&D rather than vice versa.[56] Second, it is suggested that small firms are able to alleviate internal resource deficiencies by accessing university resource networks.[57] Thus, as with other forms of external collaborative arrangements, small firms are able to gain access to sophisticated technology and technical expertise, whose direct employment is prohibitively costly.

Despite these presumptions there is little evidence available to substantiate the role of near-to-university science parks in encouraging small firm innovation or, more generally, improved performance. Work on UK science parks[57,58] found no statistical difference between firms located on or off science parks with regard to degree of innovation. Indeed, Westhead reports that 'it is the similarities between independent Science Park firms and comparable off-Park firms which are striking, rather than the contrasts'[58] (p. 57). Taking the argument further, Oakey suggests that any benefits from location on a science park are, at best, neutral, while the costs of such 'prestige' premises tend to be above the market average.[59] Irrespective of the value of the (rather artificial) clustering that science parks represent, the bulk of the literature maintains that links between small firms and higher education institutes (HEIs) are likely to have a favourable effect on innovation.[60] Undeterred by finding no relationship between science park location and innovation, Westhead goes on to suggest that 'the focus of policy, in any region, has to be to . . . actively promote links between HEIs and technology-based firms'[58] (p. 58). The rationale for this conclusion lies in the paucity of firm–university links, which were found to exist both on and off science parks.[57] Empirical support is offered by Wilkinson *et al.* who found that 90 per cent of the most innovative firms, in their study, had formal links with a university.[61]

Links with Government and Support Agencies

If the principal benefits to collaboration relate to supplementing internal managerial and technical resources, it is sometimes unclear what function (other than as a dating service) enterprise support agencies, and indeed government, can play. In the case of Business Links, for example, Oughton suggests that the 'encouragement of networking relationships between firms to establish collective economies of scale'[62] (p. 1479) is one of a number of worthy features of such organizations. Such economies arise through the pooling of fixed costs within a network of collaborators.[63] Indeed, it is known that the Business Links network has increased the number of technology-specialist personal business advisers (PBAs).[64] The argument that Business Links, or in Scotland Local Enterprise Companies (LECs), should be able to provide specialist advice and information, or an introductory service, holds equally well for chambers of commerce or trade associations. Unfortunately, Business Link and LEC relationships with small firms are, in practice, bilateral and are unlikely to be well placed to promote inter-firm co-operation.[63] (Further discussion of the role of support agencies such as Business Links and LECs is given in more detail in Chapter 9.)

In the case of UK government departments, we may anticipate that the small firm relationship is of a more direct and longitudinal nature. This is due, in part, to the expectation that government will employ the requisite expertise or have easy access to such through its considerable resource networks. Alternatively, and perhaps more realistically, government may play a network management role. As the competitiveness White Paper suggests, 'there may be a role for government in brokering greater collaboration between firms or between firms and universities'[65] (p. 24).

The Empirical Picture

Notwithstanding the foregoing, empirical studies of small firms tend to indicate a lower degree of innovation-related networking than one might anticipate.[66,67] In other words, it appears 'that internal strategies relying on the firms' own capacities are significantly more important than strategies involving external partners'[68] (p. 33). Moreover, where innovation-related links are observed, these occur predominantly along the value chain, with relatively few firms engaged in networks involving university, competitor or public sector organizations. Again, one may not consider this surprising, providing, as it does, empirical confirmation of Nooteboom's conceptual framework. Nooteboom[69] suggests that, when internal knowledge, competence or resource limitations are appreciated, the rational entrepreneur will conclude that there is a need to delegate or share responsibility for those decisions, or processes, upon which the limitations impact. Successful delegation or, in this case, co-operation 'requires trust in a dual sense: the other party (to whom judgement is delegated) has no interest in giving wrong advice (disinterestedness), and is capable of giving good advice (competence)'[69] (p. 342). The requirement for both disinterestedness and competence is likely to lead small firms to interact, first, with those agencies with which they have daily contact, such as customers and suppliers and, thereafter, with frequent local contacts (e.g. banks and accountants – considered subcontractors/suppliers in Figure 7.6. Interaction with competitors, universities and public sector agencies is likely to be lower. While competitors are likely to be highly competent (incorporating an appreciation of the relevant priorities), there exist question marks over their disinterestedness. With regards to public sector support agencies and universities, the reverse may be true – i.e. high levels of disinterestedness but low levels of competence. In the absence of prior evidence of trustworthiness, the individual firm is unlikely to commit to joint ventures in which it has limited control over final appropriability (other than through costly legal means – either *ex ante* contracts or *ex post* legislation). Trust is an iterative process, based on the social programming of values and routinization of co-operative conduct. And routinization, in its turn, 'is based on proven past performance and reliability of a co-operative relationship.'[70] A recent study of small manufacturing firms, for instance, suggested that small firms consistently (irrespective of whether they are classed as innovators or non-innovators) rank 'established long-term relationships' and 'frequency of contact' as the key factors stimulating collaboration.[66] The likely absence of such trust-creating mechanisms militates against collaboration with competitors, while their likely presence favours value chain linkages.

Clearly, if the network model of innovation is to be seen as the panacea for small firm resource constraints, much remains to be done.

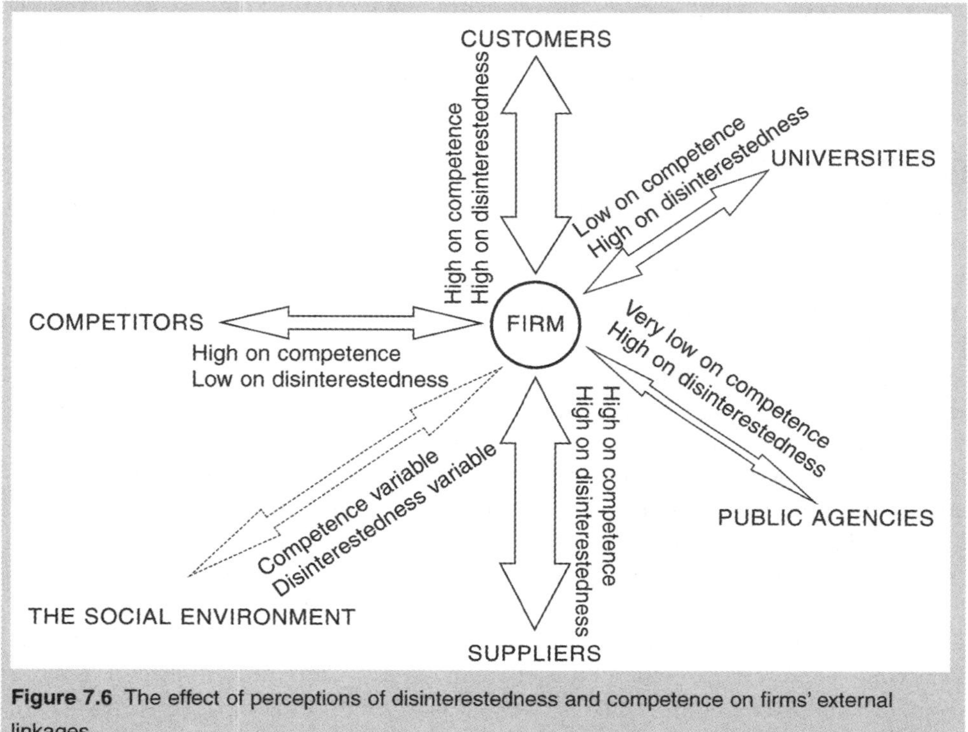

Figure 7.6 The effect of perceptions of disinterestedness and competence on firms' external linkages

THINK POINTS 7.3

Entrepreneurship and innovation

1. What are the external interactions that can exist for innovative entrepreneurs that will influence the process of innovation?
2. How does your answer relate to the question of networking by firms and innovative activity (Think Points 7.2)?
3. What are principal ways that customers can be used to advantage by innovative entrepreneurs?

4. Is there any empirical evidence that entrepreneurs located on science parks are more innovative than others?

5. What might account for your answer to Q4?

6. What role could support agencies take with innovative entrepreneurs?

Hint: see also Chapter 9.

FINANCING INNOVATION

The final issue we turn to is that of finance for innovation (the reader should also see the discussion on the finance of technology-based small firms in Chapter 5). While there is some ambivalence over the extent to which access to external finance acts as a barrier to the development of small firms generally, the financing of small firm innovation is commonly considered a special case.[71]

It is generally held that 'a strict reliance on a market system will result in underinvestment in innovation, relative to the socially desirable level'[72] (p. 438). Innovation is essentially a speculative process. In the main, resources must be committed prior to receipt of revenues from the sale of products or services that these resources generate (see Figure 7.7).[73] Yet, costs and revenues are inevitably difficult to anticipate with any precision.[74] R&D projects (whether formal and discrete or otherwise), for instance, 'typically require large fixed costs which are independent of the size of the market for the innovation'[75] (p. 17). Moreover, these costs are effectively sunk. That is, they are committed prior to production and are *independent* of the gross return from innovation. Moreover, further uncertainty relates to the level of expected future cash flows and the firm's ability to adequately appropriate the returns (in the face of, for example, imitating competitors).[76] Assuming that firms exploit innovations through their own output, this is particularly disadvantageous for small firms – in which the ability of gross rates of return (i.e. their expected sales) to meet initial costs is often marginal at best.[26] The consequence of the foregoing is a high degree of project risk, in the face of an uncertain return.

As Arrow suggested, a rational organization's likelihood of investing in high-risk projects will invariably be a function of its ability to transfer or spread risk.[77] Firms commonly transfer risk through insurance.[78] Unfortunately, in the classic Knightian sense, the success or failure of an innovative venture cannot be assigned some probability value and cannot be insured against.[79] Yet, as noted earlier, for the large firm, risk may be effectively spread through a portfolio of investments. That is, 'large firms may diversify their innovative projects and obtain more stable cash flows'[80] (p. 40). By contrast, small firms more often develop single research projects that require considerable funding, relative to turnover base. Moreover, if finance is required (i.e.

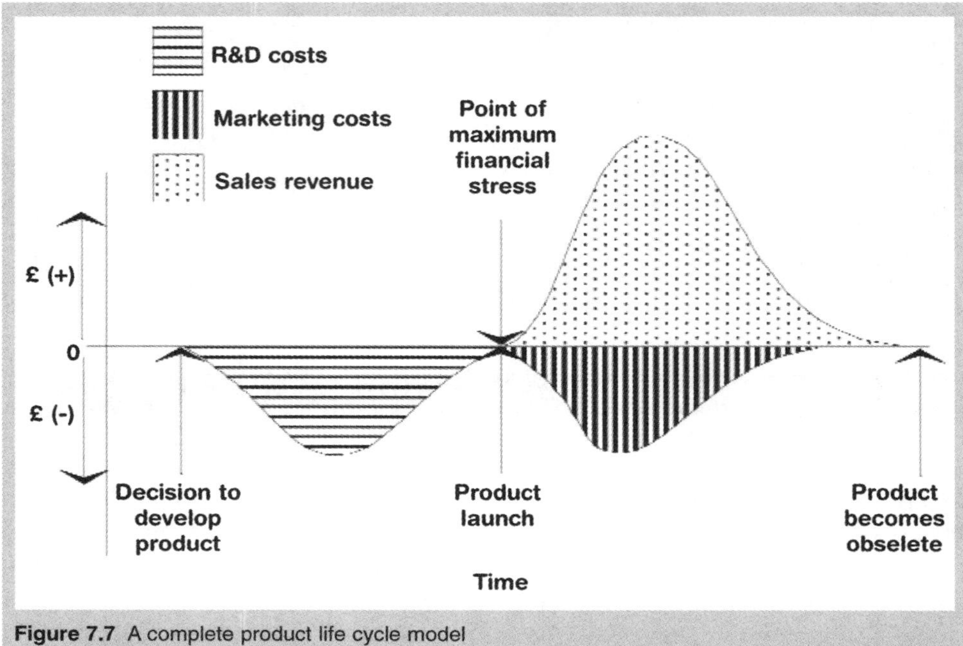

Figure 7.7 A complete product life cycle model

Source: Adapted from Oakey, R. (1997) *A review of policy and practice relating to high technology small frims in the United Kingdom*, WP 359, MBS, University of Manchester.

factor inputs must be paid for) in advance of receipt of revenues from the sale of project outcomes, 'then the growth of the project will always require funding from outside the project'[73] (p. 65). In large firms this may involve the reinvestment of retained profits or the annexing of alternative income streams. In small firms, though internal resources are frequently the most significant source of funding, significant projects are likely to require at least some external finance.

It is widely believed that small firms, generally, are disadvantaged in capital markets in relation to larger firms. The reasons conjectured to explain this apparent inequity are numerous. However, principal among these is a presumed high level of risk due to: the higher relative probability of failure,[81] fixed costs in assessing applications for finance,[75] greater scope for information asymmetry and moral hazard[82] and proportionately higher due diligence and monitoring costs.[83] For a detailed discussion of these concepts the reader should consult Chapters 5 and 6. This risk differential is further widened for funding applications based on an intended product innovation. This is related, in part, to uncertain and intangible pay-backs and an inability, on the part of funding providers, to adequately assess technological viability and related market potential.[84] Additionally, the high-risk profile of innovative small firms is likely to be heightened by the notion that much of the input to the innovation process has no residual or scrap value should the project not reap the anticipated rewards. This supposition is supported by recent research, which reports a large proportion of small firms citing access to finance as a considerable barrier to innovation.[85,86]

At the risk of oversimplifying, identified concerns are broadly fivefold:

1. The scope for innovative ventures to be denied access to finance in the absence of specialist loan officers with adequate knowledge of the technology or product market.

2. The potential unsuitability of current, capital-based institutional venture appraisal procedures in light of the unique risk/return profile innovative small firms present (i.e. an emphasis on gearing and collateral).

3. The over-reliance on short-term debt finance (in particular overdrafts) to fund innovation.

4. The inadequate supply and awareness of genuine risk capital.

5. The under-exploitation of grant finance, with the potential to validate technology and act as security, against which further finance may be leveraged

Of these, the likelihood that innovators will be denied access to finance, as result of deficiencies in assessment procedures, and the reliance on short-term debt give greatest cause for concern. With regards to the former, it should be noted that, while empirical studies do point to lower success rates in accessing external finance for innovative small firms, the absolute success rates, at least in the case of bank debt, are relatively high. For instance, data from a recent survey of small manufacturing firms in the West Midlands (Figure 7.8) noted that approximately 80 per cent of innovators applying for either overdraft funding or short-term debt (i.e. the most common sources sought) to finance innovation were successful. While lower than the equivalent figure for non-innovators (93 per cent), it still does not suggest a high degree of rationing, at least not acutely so. It may be that current bank assessment procedures are less appropriate for firms seeking to innovate. Equally, however (recalling that debt proposals are not homogeneously good), it may be that innovative firms, presenting projects with higher risks and less certain returns, are simply less attractive to banks or, taken as a whole, they include more 'bad' proposals. In either case, it is in no one's interest to counsel banks to accept bad debt.

The reliance on short-term debt to fund innovation is more pressing. Recent 'expert' reports[52,84,87] have been in accord in concluding that policy measures determined to improve the financing of small firm innovation should aim at[52] 'reducing the risk for private investors ... and increasing the supply of risk capital' (p. 7), and that[87] 'the distinctive requirement ... is for genuine risk capital' (p. 6).

In light of what is known of seed capital requirements and lagged, uncertain pay-backs, this reliance on short-term debt is clearly sub-optimal. In the case of high-technology small firms, for example, it has been suggested that the cyclical nature of R&D expenditure and sales is likely to be accompanied by a lack of uniformity in profits, raising questions about the innovative firm's ability to repay debt.[88] What

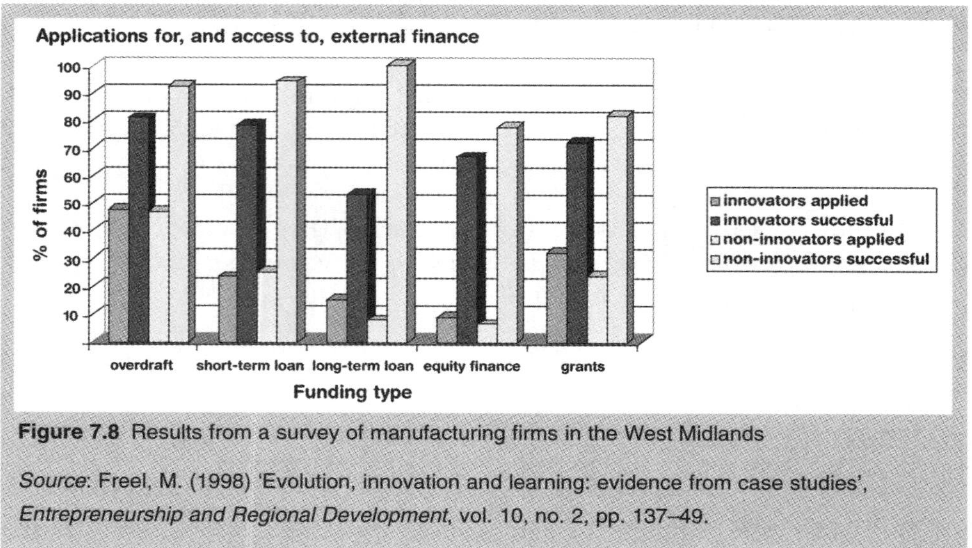

Figure 7.8 Results from a survey of manufacturing firms in the West Midlands

Source: Freel, M. (1998) 'Evolution, innovation and learning: evidence from case studies', *Entrepreneurship and Regional Development*, vol. 10, no. 2, pp. 137–49.

innovating firms require is true 'risk' capital, returns to which are contingent upon the success of the venture and pay-back may, more realistically, be judged in terms of a five- to ten-year period.[59] However, it is generally believed that the availability of risk capital is limited within the UK. The classic ACOST Report,[89] for instance, noted that, within the UK, 'there is a major shortfall in the amount and diversity of sources of funds available to finance business experimentation and growth' (p. 68). In other words, the under-utilisation of equity finance and the over-reliance on debt is commonly considered a supply-side issue. There are simply not enough funds available and the blame is laid squarely at the feet of venture capitalists (who concentrate their resources on relatively low risk management but-outs and management buy-ins) or business angels (whose investment behaviour is erratic and fickle and who interfere excessively post-investment). Certainly, there is some evidence to support this point of view (see Chapter 6). However, a focus on supply-side issues tells only half the story. As Figure 7.8 makes clear, there is an obvious pecking order with respect to the source external finance firms seek. For both innovators and non-innovators, overdraft funding is more commonly sought than short-term loans, short-term loans than long-terms loans and equity funding (i.e. risk capital) is sought very infrequently. For example, only 9 per cent of innovators and 6.5 per cent of non-innovators attempted to access either formal venture capital or business angel finance over the three years covered by this study. The same 'pecking order' has been found in similarly motivated studies.[90,80]

Unquestionably, the low success rates (typically in the region of 1–2 per cent), high transaction costs and time involved will serve to steer firms towards alternative external (or, indeed, internal) sources of finance. However, there is growing evidence which suggests that a large proportion of small firms eschew equity finance, which is consistent with much of the anecdotal evidence small firms researchers bring to bear.[91] In other words, small firms may trade-off the sub-optimality of debt, of internal bootstrapping or of not undertaking a given project against continued independence or autonomy. Additionally,[92] 'various studies confirm that the majority of business angels cannot find sufficient investment opportunities' (p. 16). It is not clear to what extent the documented poor use of equity finance for innovation is a supply-side or a demand-side issue. Accordingly, we must be cautious about criticizing institutions and individuals without simultaneously educating firms.

THINK POINTS 7.4

Entrepreneurship and innovation

1. Why do innovative entrepreneurs face special funding problems?
2. Why should this be of concern to policy-makers?
3. Why should innovative entrepreneurs also face special insurance problems?
4. What is meant by a 'pecking order' for funding by technology-based entrepreneurs.

Hint: See also Chapter 5.

CONCLUSIONS

Innovation, or the presence of novelty, is often taken as a prerequisite for entrepreneurship. Moreover, the rhetoric of policy-makers and small firm academics frequently implies that small firms enjoy a comparative advantage with respect to certain types of industrial innovation. In this chapter we have argued that the innovative contributions of small firms varies across industry sectors and through the industry life cycle, at least with respect to technical innovations. In new industries, where technology is still evolving, small firms have a more significant role to play than in mature industries, where the innovation focus has switched to cost-reducing process innovation and minor product enhancements. However, in mature industries small firms may benefit from innovations in structure, supply or markets.

As innovators, in dynamic embryonic industries, small firms enjoy a number of advantages. These advantages are fundamentally behavioural and relate to the internal organization of activities and the manner in which small firms may articulate with markets. Flexibility and speed are at the root of the small firm's innovation advantage. Yet, notwithstanding these advantages, studies regularly report in excess of 40 per cent of firms introducing no new products.[93] Why might this be the case? Since studies consistently point to a higher innovative intent than actual innovative output, it is likely that at least some firms are constrained in their innovative activities. It is clear that, while small firms are behaviourally advantaged, they are also resource constrained. This chapter outlined the role that networking may play in alleviating internal resource constraints. However, we also noted the relative dearth of innovation-related external linkages and highlighted the 'need to do more' in this respect. Policy has identified, for itself, a role as network facilitator and this is encouraging.

Finally, we discussed the sub-optimality of much of the financing of innovation in small firms. The greater likelihood that small innovators will be denied access to external finance certainly gives cause for concern. However, of greater concern is the reliance on short-term debt, rather than equity, to fund innovation. Nevertheless, supply-side issues alone are not to blame for the current predicament and any policy measures must be aimed at both improving the funding environment and educating firms.

This chapter concludes with the case study of Aquamotive Ltd. The case provides a vehicle for the discussion and practical illustration of many of the issues in this chapter, including the nature of the innovation process and entrepreneurship, learning of small firms, the finance of innovative small firms and barriers in the innovation process.

CASE STUDY: AQUAMOTIVE LTD

Introduction: Mauchline Business Services

Mauchline Business Services (MBS) was a precursor business start-up by two partners: Marion Welsh and Alex Howie. This service-based business was started by Marion and Alex in light of their successful experience in the effective daily operation and control of their previous employment. MBS offered a consultancy service to other SMEs. It was the partners' intention to offer a holistic, global solution to the administrative needs of small firms and to provide a 'one-stop shop'.

During the initial start-up phase, the partners were able to take customers (from their previous employer) with them, but Marion and Alex faced difficulties in sourcing initial custom to create a broader, more secure customer base. MBS faced a further obstacle in the longer term – the nature of the service that they were offering and the market they were targeting was such that their customer base was necessarily 'churning'. The essence of the service offered by MBS was the provision of administrative and commercial support to new start and micro-firms until such times as these firms had enjoyed sufficient growth to enable them to bring these functions in-house. Although custom from individual client organizations was often on a repeat basis, this custom had a finite lifetime, averaging in the region of two years. As a result, MBS was required to find new clients to replace those they had helped to grow. In effect they were assisting organizations to reach a situation whereby they no longer needed the services of MBS.

After two years trading, MBS had achieved a turnover marginally in excess of £50,000 and was employing one additional member of staff in a clerical/administrative role. Although this situation was considerably short of the original targets the partners had set themselves, the company pre-tax profit (excluding partner remuneration) was £40,925. At this stage the temptation would have been to seek the consolidation and limited growth which marks the 'lifestyle firm', content with generating an acceptable level of personal income and enjoying continued autonomy. However, the partners remained intent on growing the business. A possible opportunity was soon to present itself.

Alex had received several phone calls from his brother, who was a maintenance foreman at a fish farm, asking advice on a feeding system that didn't work very well. There had been several lengthy sessions on the phone and eventually his brother invited Alex and Marion to the site of the fish farm. The feeding system was manufactured in Norway, with the result that obtaining service and an engineer from Norway was both time consuming and very expensive. Alex and Marion visited the site and, on opening the control panel box, they found a programme logic controller (PLC). This was exactly the type of technology they had been working with in their former employment. They found that the system in place at the fish farm was adapted from other land-based systems. They were able to repair the system but, as they were leaving, they both thought: *There has got to be a better way of engineering a fish-feeding system*. In addition, they were of the opinion that the existing technology was being utilized in an incomplete and piecemeal manner which, they felt, created as many difficulties as it was able to solve.

Aquamotive Control Systems Limited

From the outset it had been the intention of Marion Welsh and Alex Howie to become involved in electronic control systems design. However, they realized that, if this course was to be followed exclusively, the finances and time involved in creating a product/service range and establishing a reputation and customer base would render the venture unfeasible. Although the partners had no direct prior experience with regard to control systems within the fish farming industry, it is true that many of the concepts involved were generic across industries. It was as a result of this truism that the partners felt problems were arising.

Product Development

These problems revolved around issues relating to:

- the harshness of the environment and the inherent difficulties arising from exposure of electrical devices and other equipment;
- the high maintenance requirements/costs of existing equipment in the event of blockages and disruption;
- wastage, destruction and uneven dispersal of foodstuff;
- algal growth and pollution.

After some initial market survey work, designed to establish whether the problems they had identified where indeed prevalent throughout the fish farming industry, the partners were determined to develop a prototype system which would provide a global solution for the sector. Prototype development was begun. The original intention in developing a system and its companion software had been to utilize existing technology in a more efficient and comprehensive manner; however, during the design process they were to discover that the necessary technology was unable to meet adequately the requirements which they had set the system.

Fish farming involves a significant amount of water. The risks and potential costs involved when electricity comes into close proximity with water led the partners to the conviction that traditional control systems, involving on-site electrical currents, could not be the cheapest and most effective method of meeting control requirements. The task with which they were faced was to design a system which would withdraw the necessary electrical components from the site and the water tanks. To facilitate the development project that was to be at the centre of their activities, the company were able to secure a public sector innovation grant which represented 50 per cent of estimated costs involved (including wages, travelling expenses, etc. – amounting to £25,000).

The key innovative elements of this finished system were the Aquamatic Control Valves. These valves effectively take hydraulics into the realms of digital computing. Current systems use 1 valve : 1 hydraulic line. By digitizing the system, the addition of one hydraulic line doubles the number of valves which can be controlled, such that 16 valves can be controlled by 4 hydraulic lines. Control was therefore by means of a digital address. This address, however, was created by means of (water) pressure and not from electrical signals. In addition to the obvious electrical safety considerations, this system offered another principal benefit, in the event of leakage, in its use of (salt)water as the hydraulic fluid as opposed to the more conventional oil. Hence, the hydraulic fluid used is free, in plentiful supply, non-toxic and safe.

Market Positioning

The technology had originally been developed to create a more efficient automated fish-feeding system. However, it became obvious to the partners during, and immediately after, the design stage of their project that the breadth of applicability of their 'invention' was far greater than they had originally appreciated.

For example, it could be adapted for application in the:

- horticulture industry (primarily large-scale greenhouse facilities);
- oil and gas industry (including extraction, transport and storage activities);
- chemical industry (principally transport and storage activities).

Despite this diverse technological applicability it was decided that the company should concentrate its initial activities on tailoring, and subsequently marketing, the technology for one distinct industry. The rationale for this decision lay, in part, in the desire to maintain effective control of the company's growth and, in part, in the limiting nature of finance – fearing that potential financiers would perceive the company to be spreading themselves too thinly. Superficially it could be assumed that concentration on one or more of these alternative market opportunities would offer greater scope for remuneration than that offered by the low-profile, 'unfashionable' fish farming industry. However, in deciding on their initial market positioning and developing a market strategy, the partners highlighted several drawbacks associated with entry into these alternative markets:

- Development for the oil and gas or chemical industries would prove to be too costly at this stage of the company's development (e.g. due to material and time costs, valves for petrochemical industries would cost in the region of £300 as opposed to £30 for the fish farming industry).
- There are no technological barriers to development specifically for the horticulture market. Specification limits and tolerances are of a similarly low nature to those required for the fish farming market and the valves themselves would require little further research and development time. However, the profit margins and attitudes to investment within these markets are such that investment in automation would only be undertaken at prices incompatible with development costs to date.

By contrast, the fish farming industry offered some distinct benefits, such as:

- Comparatively low levels of competition. There existed no direct competition for the valve component of the system and automation in general is relatively low, though a growth area within the industry.
- Low materials costs, and subsequent relative selling price (due to looseness of technical specification requirements).
- Direct and obvious applicability of technology.
- Immediate potential customer base.
- Proximity of potential test facility offering mutual benefit (i.e. opportunity for 'real-life' testing allowing problem identification and resolution – in addition, potential subsequent saleability at reduced cost).

Marketing Strategy

Given that feed costs for the average medium-sized fish farm were circa £30,000/month and that the technology for such an enterprise, costing £10,000–£30,000 (depending on complexity of system), promised savings in the region of 30 per cent, farmers investing in the system could expect it to pay for itself within a year of purchase.

Appreciating the fact that technological value and associated benefits were not in themselves guarantors of success, the partners sought to develop a profile of potential customers who would be targeted in the first instance – dividing the overall market into groupings by type and size. To this end it was decided that the immediate focus of attention would be directed at salmon farms, with a least 8 cages and having 2–3 sites, where profit margins and potential returns to investment were greatest. Having established a customer base within this market and developed a degree of visibility within the industry, it would then be possible to consider diversification into freshwater and other specialist fish farming fields.

Previous promotion and marketing activities for the administrative and system-related services of MBS comprised advertising in the local press, local exhibitions and direct personal selling. The company recognized that, due to the nature of the product and services that were offered by Aquamotive Control Systems Limited and the relative dimensions of the proposed market place, a different approach should be taken.

The activities identified for involvement in the process of gearing up for the launch of the Aquamatic Control Valves and the Aquamotive Control Systems for the fish farming industry included:

- Development of a new company image; to protect their identity, Aquamotive Control Systems Limited was registered as a company name, professional brochures and marketing material were commissioned under this name, and the company began trading under the trade-name/trademark Aquamotive Control Systems (though still through the 'books' of the original company, MBS).

- Construction of a beta-test facility; construction of this facility was nearing completion and provided the company with exact information regarding the capabilities of the system, allowing it to detail more accurately the expected benefits and savings associated with farm investment in this area. Once the facility had been established, the intention was to produce a video to act as a complementary promotional tool.

- Establishment of a network of contacts within the industry; in addition to farm contacts established during the prototype development stage, and with the assistance of the agency funding, the company was able to make visits to Sweden, in the first instance, and then other European/Scandinavian countries. These trips were made with a view to making direct contacts with firms operating in a similar sphere to determine the possibility of some form of co-operative venture whereby Aquamotive would be willing to act as an agent for other organizations' products if a reciprocal agreement could be reached. On a more direct sales front the company attended the industry's annual trade fair to gauge market reactions to their technology.

Perhaps of greatest importance in establishing a reputation from which to build a client base is the role played by 'word of mouth' and referral business within the industry. Market research undertaken by the company had shown that 'the majority of technological advancements within the industry are as a result of recommendations made between the fish farms themselves'. In light of this, the beta-test facility on the new site of an established and prominent fish farm was important to achieve demonstration and hence recommendation. 'Word of mouth' had already led to two requests from fish farms for the design and implementation of comprehensive feed-control systems (values circa £30,000 each).

In a supplementary move to further increase the company's profile within the industry Aquamotive have been involved in the design and implementation of a crustacean feeding control system which, although not incorporating the innovative valves, has allowed them a smooth introduction to the market. An order was placed for this system by the North Atlantic Fisheries College in Shetland (circa £25,000), after having seen a ¼ scale prototype demonstration. The college intends to expand to five such systems, while several other establishments are keeping a close eye on the system's progress (including an institution in Wales which has invited the company to tender for a system valued in the region of £120,000 – arising through industry 'word of mouth').

Licensing

The company was approached by five separate organizations from Chile and Norway with a view to these organizations manufacturing under license the technology currently being developed at Aquamotive Control Systems Limited. Though these proposals were declined, this was not as a result of an aversion in principle to the concepts involved, but rather to a general 'unreadiness', on the company's part, to become involved in such a venture. The company felt that it will prove to be the ideal way in which to surmount the barriers to entry associated with international markets where competition and technological sophistication is far greater than those that will be encountered in the domestic market. The primary reasons for rejecting interest at the time were threefold:

- Financial – the partners felt that they would like to 'learn to walk before we run' and were in danger of driving the company too fast.

- Uncertainty and lack of knowledge with respect to individual organizations and foreign markets; though lack of knowledge of foreign markets was seen as a barrier to direct entry, relative naivety and asymmetric information were also seen as barriers to licensing. Consequently the company was determined to become more familiar with the environment in which it will be dealing and the actors within that arena before making a decision on this issue.

- Inability to adequately police the use of technology once it was made available to external interests.

Patenting

Although patents have been applied for, and the company is confident of having its application accepted, completion of the patent application process is expected to take in the region of 3–4 years. As a result, the company was reluctant to license their technology for manufacture without advice from the appropriate quarters and a fuller understanding of the risks involved. The patenting process itself will prove to be a considerable financial burden on a company of this size. The original patent application cost circa £2,500, while costs for further patents covering individual countries will be in the region of £2,000. Thus, with 20 countries immediately within the intended scope of coverage, final costs will be in excess of £40,000.

Short-Term Developments

In the short term the company's aims revolved around initial market penetration and active direct product sales (discussed above), the establishment of a manufacturing facility and the corresponding internal organizational development.

The need to establish a manufacturing facility in the immediate future was of paramount importance. One requirement, associated with the development work being carried out to date, which in turn has created an ongoing dilemma for the partners, revolves around the issue of premises. The company occupies reasonable premises on a small industrial complex, which ideally suited the function of MBS in the provision of administrative and rudimentary systems support. For the research and development and subsequent manufacturing activities in which Aquamotive were involved, these facilities were inadequate. The specific systems being developed for the fish farming market naturally, if testing is to be rigorous, require large quantities of water. This should be part of a recycling process, incorporating water storage facilities, to ensure maximum efficiency and minimum waste.

As a temporary measure the company took a short-term lease on an additional unit within its current industrial estate. This step, though providing sufficient accommodation, has insufficient facilities for further development work and was only suitable for small-scale production runs. Thus, the company is exploring the possibility of purchasing or custom building premises with adequate scope for future growth in line with manufacturing output.

At the time, only one individual (in a clerical and administrative capacity) was employed by the company. With the move to manufacturing, staffing levels will have to increase to fully service both the new custom generated by Aquamotive Control Systems Limited and existing/future business undertaken by MBS (dependent on any decision regarding the operating future of MBS). With this in mind, Marion Welsh devised a proposed medium-term staffing structure which, it was hoped, would be achieved in a progressive manner (Figure 7.9).

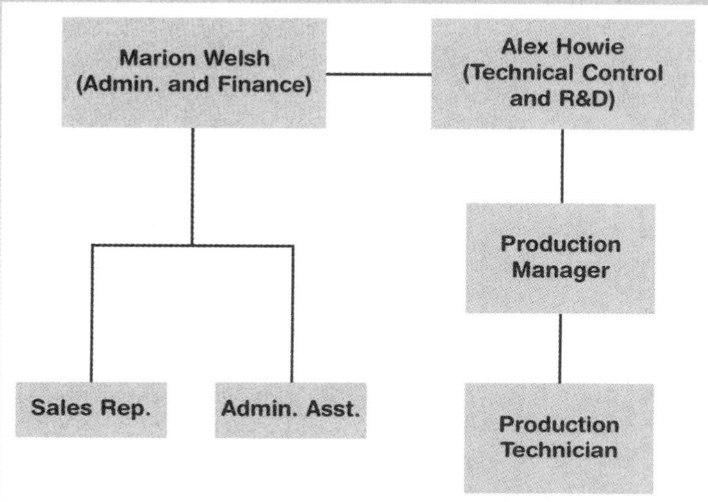

Figure 7.9 Organizational structure of aquamotive

The short-term/immediate plans with regard to this recruitment and organizational development process will involve the employment of a graduate electronic engineer to fill the position of production technician ('Though he will wear forty hats like the rest of us.') with a view to promotion to the role of production manager when sales and output warrant the recruitment of further technical members of staff. A member of staff dedicated to sales will be employed once initial industry contacts have been established, production is underway and it is felt that the partners are unable to devote sufficient time to this function. Any moves in this direction were dependent on finance being made available.

Funding

Although the partners had identified aims, objectives and strategies for growth and development these, in turn, were reliant upon the injection of considerable capital to allow their initial implementation and achievement, regardless of the probability of ultimate success. The estimated financial package required to launch the first stage plans for Aquamotive (namely the initial small-scale manufacturing and sales) was between £50,000 and £60,000, depending on whether premises were bought, custom built or leased. In raising all, or part, of the necessary finance the company had several avenues which could be explored:

1. Further government/quasi-government grants and/or loans. This naturally represented the preferred option for the company whereby they are able to

secure grants or low-interest loans via central government (as was the case for the previous Innovation Grant), agencies or the local authority. With this in mind the company had targeted a regional assistance manufacturing grant available through the government (though the application process for this had not formally begun).

2. Bank/financial institution funding. Since it was unlikely that government funding would fully satisfy the financial needs of initial development, overdraft extensions or bank loans would be sought to make up the shortfall. At the time, the company had received an overdraft extension from £14,000 to £35,000 to allow the leasing of temporary premises (discussed above). This figure was expected to fall to £23,000 once the second instalment of the Innovation Grant had been received and was further expected to fall to zero on sale of the first feeding system. The company enjoyed an excellent relationship with their bank and required no guarantee for this facility.

3. Venture capital/external stakeholding. The entrepreneurs were not averse, in principle, to the notion of an external shareholding in their company, and the external influences that may come with this, believing in Marion's words, 'It is better to own part of something than all of nothing.' The company had no formal approaches from venture capitalists; however, the feeling within the networks they had established was that this would not prove to be a problem (particularly once small-scale manufacturing had begun and the first sales had been achieved).

4. Business angel venture financing. An individual angel may be more interested in providing the required funding level of £50,000 to £60,000.

5. Manufacturing under licence. Despite the fact that approaches to this effect had been dismissed for reasons discussed previously, this course of action would offer an initial lump sum and a guaranteed income thereafter. If the concerns highlighted above could be adequately addressed, this would offer a partial solution to the financial needs of the company corresponding with organizational development.

The Future

Marion and Alex began to look forward to the future with some confidence and excitement. They felt that they had a sound trading record that counted highly with the bank, a solution to the fish farming industry's problem, a patentable product with a global market, good knowledge from market research on the fish farming industry and good contacts and high levels of interest from overseas at their exhibitions. However, to realize the potential of Aquamotive Control Systems, they needed to raise additional finance.

Financial Forecasts for Aquamotive Control Systems Ltd

Profit & loss account forecast	Year 1 £		Year 2 £		Year 3 £	
SALES FORECAST						
Administration	24,000		12,000		12,000	
Technical services	7,500		10,000		15,000	
Aquamatic systems	40,000		120,000		180,000	
Other fish farm equipment	10,000		24,000		24,000	
	81,500	81,500	166,000	166,000	231,000	231,000
COST OF SALES						
Administration	420		420		420	
Technical services	1,000		2,000		3,000	
Aquamatic systems	20,000		60,000		90,000	
Other fish farm equipment	5,000		12,000		12,000	
	26,420		74,420		105,420	
GROSS PROFIT		55,080		91,580		125,580
Grants		25,000		0		0
OVERHEADS						
Wages & salaries	0		9,300		28,400	
PAYE & NI	0		4,700		14,700	
Prototype materials	5,000		0		0	
Heat & light	1,200		1,200		1,800	
Rent & rates	2,650		2,650		2,650	
Motor & travel	5,000		5,500		6,050	
Post, stationery & adv.	4,400		2,500		4,400	
Telephones	2,000		2,200		2,420	
Office costs	500		550		605	
Insurance	2,200		2,420		2,662	
Repair & renewals	500		550		605	
Sundry expenses	500		550		605	
Accountancy fees	1,000		1,000		1,000	
Patent fees	2,000		20,000		2,000	
Bank charges	280		550		605	
Bank interest	0		0		0	
HP interest	1,122		1,224		1,224	
Loan interest	0		0		0	
Depreciation	7,050		7,050		7,050	
Bad debt provision	4,075		8,300		11,550	
	39,477	39,477	70,244	70,244	88,326	88,326
NET PROFIT		40,603		21,336		37,254

Balance sheet forecast	Year 1 £		Year 2 £		Year 3 £	
FIXED ASSETS						
Motor vehicle opening	0		6,375		4,250	
Motor vehicle additions	8,500		0		0	
Motor vehicle disposals	0		0		0	
Motor vehicle depreciation	2,125		2,125		2,125	
		6,375		4,250		2,125
Plant & equipment opening	0		9,750		6,500	
Plant & equipment additions	13,000		0		0	
Plant & equipment disposals	0		0		0	
Plant & equipment depreciation	3,250		3,250		3,250	
		9,750		6,500		3,250
Computer equip opening	1,603		2,553		1,403	
Computer equip additions	2,100		0		0	
Computer equip disposals	0		0		0	
Computer equip depreciation	1,150		1,150		1,150	
		2,553		1,403		253
Fixtures opening	88		1,563		1,038	
Fixtures additions	2,000		0		0	
Fixtures disposals	0		0		0	
Fixtures depreciation	525		525		525	
		1,563		1,038		513
TOTAL FIXED ASSETS		20,241		13,191		6,141
CURRENT ASSESTS						
Debtors	17,184		16,255		22,618	
Cash in bank	15,305		19,470		40,829	
Cash in hand	68		68		68	
	32,557		35,793		63,515	
CURRENT LIABILITIES						
Creditors	7,777		7,287		10,322	
HP creditor	9,510		4,755		0	
PAYE	0		392		1,225	
VAT	2,498		3,397		5,648	
Bad debt provision	4,075		12,375		23,925	
	23,860		28,206		41,120	
NET CURRENT ASSETS		8,697		7,587		22,395
SURPLUS FINANCED BY		28,938		20,778		28,536
Loans	0		0		0	
Capital account	17,831		28,938		20,778	
Less drawings	(29,496)		(29,496)		(29,496)	
Period profit/loss	40,603		21,336		37,254	
		28,938		20,778		28,536

Cash flow projection Year 1	Month 1 £	Month 2 £	Month 3 £	Month 4 £	Month 5 £	Month 6 £	Month 7 £	Month 8 £	Month 9 £	Month 10 £	Month 11 £	Month 12 £	Year1 End
INFLOW													
Administration	0	2,350	2,350	2,350	2,350	2,350	2,350	2,350	2,350	2,350	2,350	2,350	25,850
Technical services	0	734	734	734	734	734	734	734	734	734	734	734	8,074
Aquamatic systems	0	0	0	0	0	0	0	0	0	11,750	11,750	11,750	35,250
Other fish farm equipment	0	0	0	1,175	1,175	1,175	1,175	1,175	1,175	1,175	1,175	1,175	10,575
Debtors	19,727	0	0	0	0	0	0	0	0	0	0	0	19,727
Grants	0	0	12,500	0	0	0	0	12,500	0	0	0	0	25,000
												0	
TOTAL CASH INFLOW	19,727	3,084	15,584	4,259	4,259	4,259	4,259	16,759	4,259	16,009	16,009	16,009	124,476
OUTFLOW													
Administration	0	41	41	41	41	41	41	41	41	41	41	41	451
Technical services	0	98	98	98	98	98	98	98	98	98	98	98	1,078
Aquamatic systems	0	0	0	0	0	0	0	0	0	5, 875	5,875	5,875	17,625
Other fish farm equipment	0	0	0	587	588	587	588	587	588	587	588	587	5,287
Creditors	3,878	0	0	0	0	0	0	0	0	0	0	0	3,878
OVERHEADS													
Wages & salaries	0	0	0	0	0	0	0	0	0	0	0	0	0
PAYE & NI	0	0	0	0	0	0	0	0	0	0	0	0	0
Prototype materials	2,350	0	0	2,350	0	1,175	0	0	0	0	0	0	5,875
Heat & light	353	0	0	352	0	0	353	0	0	352	0	0	1,410
Rent & rates	221	221	220	221	221	220	221	221	221	221	221	221	2,650
Motor & travel	489	490	489	490	489	490	490	489	490	490	489	490	5,875
Postage, stationery & adv.	1,175	150	150	150	150	150	150	2,350	150	150	100	100	4,925
Telephones	0	587	0	0	587	0	0	587	0	0	587	0	2,348
Office equipment costs	543	0	0	0	0	0	0	0	0	0	0	0	543
Insurance	184	183	183	184	183	184	183	183	183	184	183	183	2,200
Repair & renewals	543	0	0	0	0	0	0	0	0	0	0	0	543
Sundry expenses	543	0	0	0	0	0	0	0	0	0	0	0	543
Accountancy fees	0	0	293	0	0	0	0	294	0	0	0	588	1,175
Patent fees	0	0	0	0	0	0	0	2,350	0	0	0	0	2,350
Bank charges	15	15	15	15	15	15	15	15	40	40	40	40	280
Bank interest	0	0	0	0	0	0	0	0	0	0	0	00	
HP interest	0	102	102	102	102	102	102	102	102	102	102	102	1,122
Loan interest	0	0	0	0	0	0	0	0	0	0	0	0	0
VAT	1,384	0	0	(2,316)	0	0	1,159	0	0	1,815	0	0	2,042
HP repayments – cars	850	219	218	219	218	219	218	219	218	219	218	219	3,254
HP repayments – equip	1,510	177	7,550	178	177	178	177	178	177	178	178	178	10,836
Capital equipment	2,642	2,350	0	0	0	0	0	0	0	0	0	0	4,992
Income tax payments	0	0	0	0	0	0	0	3,000	0	0	0	3,000	6,000
Drawings	1,958	1,958	1,958	1,958	1,958	1,958	1,958	1,958	1,958	1,958	1,958	1,958	23,496
TOTAL OUTFLOW	18,638	6,591	11,317	4,629	4,827	5,417	5,753	12,672	4,266	12,310	10,678	13,680	110,778
NET CASHFLOW	1,089	(3,507)	4,267	(370)	(568)	(1,158)	(1,494)	4,087	(7)	3,699	5,331	2,329	13,698
Opening bank balance	1,607	2,696	(811)	3,456	3,086	2,518	1,360	(134)	3,953	3,946	7,645	12,976	1,607
CLOSING BANK BALANCE	2,696	(811)	3,456	3,086	2,518	1,360	(134)	3,953	3,946	7,645	12,976	15,305	15,305

Cash flow projection Year 2	Qrt 1 £	Qrt 2 £	Qrt 3 £	Qrt 4 £
INFLOW				
Administration	2,350	3,525	3,525	3,525
Technical services	2,206	2,940	2,940	2,940
Aquamatic systems	23,500	35,250	35,250	35,250
Other fish farm equipment	4,700	7,050	7,050	7,050
Debtors	17,184	0	0	0
Loans	0	0	0	0
TOTAL CASH INFLOW	49,940	48,765	48,765	48,765
OUTFLOW				
Administration	82	123	123	123
Technical services	490	588	588	588
Aquamatic systems	11,750	17,625	17,625	17,625
Other fish farm equipment	2,350	3,525	3,525	3,525
Creditors	7,777	0	0	0
OVERHEADS				
Wages & salaries	2,325	2,325	2,325	2,325
PAYE & NI	783	1,175	1,175	1,175
Prototype materials	0	0	0	0
Heat & light	352	353	352	353
Rent & rates	663	662	663	662
Motor & travel	1,615	1,615	1,615	1,615
Postage, stationary & adv.	1,175	255	1,175	250
Telephones	646	646	646	646
Office equipment costs	161	162	161	162
Insurance	605	605	605	605
Repair & renewals	161	162	161	162
Sundry expenses	161	162	161	162
Accountancy fees	0	0	0	1,175
Patent fees	0	23,500	0	0
Bank charges	137	138	137	138
Bank interest	0	0	0	0
HP interest	306	306	306	306
VAT	2,498	3,396	123	3,396
HP repayments – cars	656	656	656	655
HP repayments – equip	533	533	533	533
Drawings	5,874	8,874	5,874	8,874
TOTAL OUTFLOW	41,100	67,386	38,529	45,055
NET CASHFLOW	8,840	(18,621)	10,236	3,710
Opening bank balance	15,305	24,145	5,524	15,760
CLOSING BANK BALANCE	24,145	5,524	15,760	19,470

Cash Flow Projection Year 3	Qrt 1 £	Qrt 2 £	Qrt 3 £	Qrt 4 £
INFLOW				
Administration	2,350	3,525	3,525	3,525
Technical services	3,426	4,406	4,406	4,406
Aquamatic systems	41,125	52,875	52,875	52,875
Other fish farm equipment	4,700	7,050	7,050	7,050
Debtors	16,255	0	0	0
Loans	0	0	0	0
TOTAL CASH INFLOW	67,856	67,856	67,856	67,856
OUTFLOW				
Administration	82	123	123	123
Technical services	686	882	882	882
Aquamatic systems	20,562	26,437	26,437	26,437
Other fish farm equipment	2,350	3,525	3,525	3,525
Creditors	7,287	0	0	0
OVERHEADS				
Wages & salaries	7,100	7,100	7,100	7,100
PAYE & NI	2,842	3,675	3,675	3,675
Prototype materials	0	0	0	0
Heat & light	528	528	528	528
Rent & rates	663	662	663	662
Motor & travel	1,777	1,777	1,777	1,777
Postage, stationery & adv.	1,475	450	2,650	350
Telephones	711	711	711	711
Office equipment costs	177	177	177	177
Insurance	665	666	665	666
Repair & renewals	177	177	177	177
Sundry expenses	177	177	177	177
Accountancy fees	0	0	0	1,175
Patent fees	2,350	0	0	0
Bank charges	151	151	151	152
Bank interest	0	0	0	0
HP interest	306	306	306	306
VAT	3,397	5,253	5,822	5,428
HP Repayments – cars	656	656	656	655
HP Repayments – equip	533	533	533	533
Drawings	5,874	8,874	5,874	8,874
TOTAL OUTFLOW	60,526	62,840	62,609	64,090
NET CASHFLOW	7,330	5,016	5,247	3,766
Opening bank balance	19,470	26,800	31,816	37,063
CLOSING BANK BALANCE	26,800	31,816	37,063	40,829

SUGGESTED ASSIGNMENTS

Questions on Aquamotive case study

As a basis for discussion

1. With hindsight, was the strategy to use MBS to gain time and finance as well as business experience correct?

2. What are the difficulties faced by entrepreneurs in the innovation process as demonstrated by Aquamotive?

3. How can these be overcome?

4. What are the risks for a potential investor in Aquamotive?

As a role play

Students are allocated roles through a briefing sheet which asks them to adopt one of the following roles:

- 2 students play the role of Alex and Marion.
- 1 student plays the role of a 'business angel' who has £100,000 to invest and is searching for an engineering opportunity.

Students that take on the role of Marion and Alex must sell their idea to the business angel who then has to justify his/her decision of whether or not to invest in Aquamotive.

Additional assignments

1. Identify a significant innovation introduced by a small firm or solo entrepreneur. What factors may have contributed to the success of this innovation? What barriers might the firm or entrepreneur have faced? This is likely to be a web-based exercise.

2. Identify a local small firm who have recently (in the last three years) introduced a new product and/or process. Interview the lead entrepreneur with respect to the motivation driving their innovation, the difficulties encountered and the success achieved.

3. Discussion around the theme of E-commerce generally and dotcom enterprises specifically. What opportunities are available to small firms? What factors are likely to determine the success of dotcoms?

REFERENCES

1. Sternberg, R. (2000) 'Innovation networks and regional development evidence from the European Regional Innovation Survey (ERIS): Theoretical concepts, methodological approach, empirical basis and introduction to the theme issue', *European Planning Studies*, vol. 8, pp. 389–407.

2. Freeman, C. And Soete, L. (1997) *The Economics of Industrial Innovation*, 3rd edn, Pinter, London.

3. Geroski, P. and Machin, S. (1992) 'Do innovating firms outperform non-innovators?' *Business Strategy Review*, Summer, pp. 79–90.

4. Geroski, P. and Machin, S. (1993) 'Innovation, profitability and growth over the business cycle', *Empirica*, vol. 20, pp. 35–50.

5. Freel, M. (2001) 'Do small innovating firms outperform non-innovators?' *Small Business Economics*, vol. 14, pp. 195–210.

6. Rothwell, R. (1983) 'Innovation and firm size: a case for dynamic complementarity; or is small really beautiful?' *Journal of General Management*, vol. 8, no. 3, pp. 5–25.

7. Schumpeter, J. (1934) *The Theory of Economic Development*, Harvard University Press, Cambridge, MA.

8. OECD (1996) *SMEs: Employment, Innovation and Growth – The Washington Workshop*.

9. Rothwell, R. (1994) 'Towards the fifth-generation innovation process', *International Marketing Review*, vol. 11, pp. 7–31.

10. Kline, S. and Rosenberg, N. (1986) 'An Overview of Innovation', in Landua, R. and Rosenberg, N. (eds) *The Positive Sum Strategy: Harnessing Technology for Economic Growth*, National Academic Press, Washington, DC.

11. Rothwell, R. and Zegveld, W. (1985) *Reindustrialization and Technology*, Longman, Harlow.

12. Boulding, K. (1985) *The World as a Total System*, Sage, Beverley Hills.

13. Smith, K. (2000) 'Innovation as a systemic phenomenon: Rethinking the role of policy', *Enterprise and Innovation Management Studies*, vol. 1, pp. 73–102.

14. Lundvall, B. (1995) *National Systems of Innovation: Towards a Theory of Innovation and Interactive Learning*, Pinter, London (first published 1992).

15. Polyani, M. (1966) *The Tacit Dimension*, Routledge, London.

16. Howells, J. (1996) *Tacit Knowledge and Technology Transfer*, WP16, Centre for Business Research, University of Cambridge.

17. Dosi, G. (1999) 'Some notes on national systems of innovation and production, and their implications for economic analysis', in Archibugi, D., Howells, J. and Michie, J. (eds) *Innovation Policy in a Global Economy*, CUP, Cambridge, pp. 35–48.

18. de la Mothe, J. and Paquet, G. (1998) 'National Innovation Systems, "Real Economies" and instituted process', *Small Business Economics*, vol. 11, pp. 101–11.

19. Etzkowitz, H. and Leydesdorff, L. (2000) 'The dynamics of innovation: from National Systems and "Mode 2" to a Triple Helix of university-industry-government relations', *Research Policy*, vol. 29, no. 2, pp. 109–24.

20. Håkansson, H. (1987) 'Product Development in Networks', in Håkansson, H. (ed.) *Industrial Technological Development: A Network Approach*, Croom Helm, London.

21. Archibugi, D., Howells, J. and Michie, J. (1999) 'Innovation systems and policy in a global economy', in Archibugi, D., Howells, J. and Michie, J. (eds) *Innovation Policy in a Global Economy*, CUP, Cambridge, pp. 1–18.

22. Nelson, R. (2000) 'National Innovation Systems', in Acs, Z. (ed.) *Regional Innovation, Knowledge and Global Change*, Pinter, London, pp. 11–26.

23. Hansen, N. (1990) 'Innovative regional milieux, small firms and regional development: Evidence from Mediterranean France', *Annals of Regional Science*, vol. 24, pp. 107–23.

24. Lawson, C. (1999) 'Towards a competence theory of the region', *Cambridge Journal of Economics*, 23, pp. 151–66.

25. Arndt, O. and Sternberg, R. (2000) 'Do manufacturing firms profit from intraregional innovation linkages? An empirical based answer', *European Planning Studies*, 8, pp. 465–85.

26. Cohen, W. (1995) 'Empirical studies of innovative activity', in Stoneman, P. *Handbook of the Economics of Innovation and Technological Change*, pp. 182–264, Blackwell, Oxford.

27. Schumpeter, J. (1950) *Capitalism, Socialism and Democracy*, 3rd edn, Harper Row, New York.

28. Acs, Z. and Audretsch, D. (1993) 'Innovation and firm size: the new learning', *International Journal of Technology Management*, pp. 23–35.

29. Galbraith J.K. (1957) *American Capitalism*, Hamilton, London.

30. Galbraith, J.K. (1956) *American Capitalism: The Concept of Countervailing Power*, revised edition, Houton Mifflin, Boston, MA.

31. Acs, Z. and Audretsch, D. (1987) 'Innovation, Market Structure and Firm Size', *The Review of Economics and Statistics*, vol. 69, no. 4, pp. 567–74.

32. Acs, Z. and Audretsch, D. (1988) 'Innovation in Large and Small Firms: An Empirical Analysis', *The American Economic Review*, vol. 78, no. 4, pp. 678–690.

33. Rothwell, R. (1989) 'Small Firms, Innovation and Industrial Change', *Small Business Economics*, vol. 1, no. 1, pp. 51–64.

34. Pavitt, K., Robson, M. and Townsend, J. (1987) 'The size distribution of innovating firms in the UK: 1945–1983', *Journal of Industrial Economics*, vol. 35, pp. 297–316.

35. Van Dijk, B., Den Hertog, R., Menkveld, B. and Thurik, R. (1997) 'Some new evidence on the determinants of large and small firm innovation', *Small Business Economics*, vol. 9, pp. 335–43.

36. Simons, K.L. (1995) *Technological Change and Firm Survival in New Manufacturing Industries*, unpublished PhD thesis, Carnegie Mellon University.

37. Miller, D. and Friesen, P. (1982) 'Innovation in Conservative and Entrepreneurial Firms: Two Models of Strategic Momentum', *Strategic Management Journal*, vol. 3, pp. 1–25.

38. Turnbull, P., Oliver, N. and Wilkinson, B. (1992) 'Buyer-supplier relations in the UK automotive industry: strategic implications of the Japanese manufacturing model', *Strategic Management Journal*, vol. 13, pp. 159–68.

39. Sako, M. (1994) 'Supplier relations and innovation', in Dodgson, M. and Rothwell, R. (eds) *The Handbook of Industrial Innovation*, Edward Elgar, Cheltenham.

40. MacPherson, A. (1997) 'The contribution of external service inputs to the product development efforts of small manufacturing firms', *R&D Management*, vol. 27, no. 2, pp. 127–45.

41. Freel, M. (1998) 'Evolution, innovation and learning: evidence from case studies', *Entrepreneurship and Regional Development*, vol. 10, no. 2, pp. 137–49.

42. Rothwell, R. (1991) 'External networking and innovation in small and medium-sized manufacturing firms', *Technovation*, vol. 11, no. 2, pp. 93–112.

43. Rothwell, R. and Dodgson, M. (1991) 'External linkages and innovation in small and medium-sized enterprises', *R&D Management*, vol. 21, no. 2, pp. 125–37.

44. Rothwell, R. (1977) 'The characteristics of successful innovators and technically progressive firms', *R&D Management*, vol. 7, pp. 191–206.

45. von Hippel, E. (1978) 'Successful industrial products from customer ideas', *Journal of Marketing*, vol. 42, pp. 39–49.

46. Shaw, B. (1991) 'Developing technological innovations within networks', *Entrepreneurship and Regional Development*, vol. 3, no. 2, pp. 111–28.

47. Gardiner, P. and Rothwell, R. (1985) 'Tough customers: good designs', *Design Studies*, vol. 6, no. 1.

48. Lawson, C. (1997) 'Local inter-firm networking by high-technology firms in the Cambridge region', in Keeble, D. and Lawson, C. (eds) *Network Links and Large Firm Impacts on the Evolution of Regional Clusters of High-Technology SMEs in Europe*, Dept. of Applied Economics, University of Cambridge.

49. Staber, U. (1998) 'Inter-firm co-operation and competition in industrial districts', Organizational Studies, vol. 19, no. 4, pp. 701–25.

50. Fujita, M. and Thisse, J. (1996) 'Economics of agglomeration', *Journal of the Japanese and International Economies*, 10, pp. 339–78.

51. Dodgson, M. (1994) 'Technological collaboration and innovation', in Dodgson, M. and Rothwell, R. (eds) *The Handbook of Industrial Innovation*, Edward Elgar, Cheltenham.

52. CBI (1997) *Tech Stars: Breaking the growth barriers for technology-based SMEs*, CBI, London.

53. Karlsson, C. and Olsson, O. (1998) 'Product innovation in small and large enterprises', *Small Business Economics*, vol. 10, pp. 31–46.

54. Acs, Z. (1993) *US High Technology Clusters*, discussion paper no. 9315, CRIEFF, University of St Andrews.

55. Acs, Z., FitzRoy, F. and Smith, I. (1994) *High Technology Employment and University R&D Spillovers: Evidence from US Cities*, occasional paper no. 50, CIBER, University of Maryland.

56. Jaffe, A. (1989) 'Real effects of academic research', *American Economic Review*, vol. 79, pp. 957–70.

57. Westhead, P. and Storey, D. (1995) 'Links between higher education institutions and high technology firms', *Omega*, vol. 23, no. 4, pp. 345–60.

58. Westhead, P. (1997) 'R&D "inputs" and "outputs" of technology-based firms located on and off Science Parks', *R&D Management*, vol. 27, no. 1, pp. 45–62.

59. Oakey, R. (1997) *A review of policy and practice relating to high technology small firms in the United Kingdom*, WP 359, MBS, University of Manchester.

60. Johnson, D. and Tilley, F. (1999) 'HEI and SME linkages: recommendations for the future', *International Small Business Journal*, vol. 17, pp. 66–81.

61. Wilkinson, F., Lawson, C., Keeble, D., Lawton-Smith, H. and Moore, B. (1996) 'Innovative behaviour of technology-based SMEs', paper presented at the joint CBR/Warwick SME Centre conference on *Innovation in Small Firms*, University of Cambridge.

62. Oughton, C. (1997) 'Competitiveness Policy in the 1990s', *Economic Journal*, vol. 107, no. 444, pp. 1486–1503.

63. Oughton, C. and Whittam, G. (1997) 'Competition and co-operation in the small firm sector', *Scottish Journal of Political Economy*, vol. 44, no. 1, pp. 1–30.

64. DTI (1998) *Our Competitive Future: building the knowledge economy*, White Paper, Cm 4176, London, HMSO.

65. DTI (1998) *Our Competitive Future: building the knowledge economy*, White Paper, Cm 4176, London, HMSO.

66. Freel, M. (2000) 'External linkages and product innovation in small manufacturing firms', *Entrepreneurship and Regional Development*, vol. 12, pp. 245–66.

67. Oerlemans, L., Meeus, M., and Boekema, F. (1998) 'Do networks matter for innovation? The usefulness of the economic network approach in analysing innovation', *Tijdschrift voor Economische en Sociale Geografie*, 89, 298–309.

68. Kaufmann, A. and Todtling, F. (2000) 'Systems of Innovation in Traditional Industrial Regions: The case of Styria in a comparative perspective', *Regional Studies*, 34, pp. 29–40.

69. Nooteboom, B. (1994) 'Innovation and Diffusion in Small Firms: Theory and Evidence', *Small Business Economics*, vol. 6, pp. 327–47.

70. Nooteboom, B. (1999) 'Innovation, Learning and Industrial Organisation', *Cambridge Journal of Economics*, 23, 127–50.

71. Storey, D. (1994) *Understanding the Small Business Sector*, Routledge, London.

72. Martin, S. and Scott, J. (2000) 'The nature of innovation market failure and the design of public support for private innovation', *Research Policy*, vol. 29, nos. 4–5, pp. 437–48.

73. Brophy, D. and Shulman, J. (1993) 'Financial Factors which Stimulate Innovation', *Entrepreneurship Theory and Practice*, vol. 17, pp. 61–75.

74. Moore, I. and Garnsey, E. (1993) 'Funding for innovation in small firms: the role of government', *Research Policy*, vol. 22, pp. 507–19.

75. Symeonidis, G. (1996) *Innovation, Firm Size and Market Structure: Schumpeterian Hypotheses and Some New Themes*, Economics Dept. WP 161, OECD, Paris.

76. Seaton, J. and Walker, I. (1997) 'The pattern of R&D finance for small UK companies', in

Oakey, R. and Mukhtar, S-M. (eds) *New technology-based firms in the 1990s, Volume III*, pp. 71–91, Paul Chapman, London.

77. Arrow, K. (1971) 'Economic Welfare and the Allocation of Resources for Invention', in Arrow, K. *Essays in the Theory of Risk-Bearing*, Markham, Chicago.

78. Deakins, D., Paddison, A. and Bentley, P. (1997) 'Risk management, insurance and the high technology firm', *Small Business and Enterprise Development*, vol. 4, no. 1, pp. 21–30.

79. Knight, F. (1921) *Risk, Uncertainty and Profit*, Houghton Mifflin, New York.

80. Giudici, G. and Paleari, S. (2000) 'The provision of finance to innovation: a survey conducted among Italian technology-based small firms', *Small Business Economics*, vol. 14, pp. 37–53.

81. Jensen, J.B. and McGuckin, R.H. (1997) 'Firm Performance and Evolution: Empirical Regularities in the US Microdata', *Industrial and Corporate Change*, vol. 6, no. 1, pp. 25–47.

82. Ennew, C. and Binks, M. (1995) 'The provision of finance to small firms: does the banking relationship constrain performance?' *Journal of Small Business Economics*, vol. 4. no. 1, pp. 69–85.

83. Boocock, G. and Woods, M. (1997) 'The evaluation criteria used by venture capitalists: evidence from a UK venture fund', *International Small Business Journal*, vol. 16, no. 1, pp. 36–57.

84. HM Treasury (1998) *Financing of High Technology Businesses: A report to the Paymaster General*, London, November.

85. Hoffman, K., Milady, P., Bessant, J. and Perren, L. (1998) 'Small firms, R&D, technology and innovation in the UK: a literature review', *Technovation*, vol. 18, no. 1, pp. 39–55.

86. CBR (1998) *Enterprise Britain*, Department of Applied Economics, University of Cambridge.

87. Bank of England (1996) *The Financing of Technology-Based Small Firms*, London, October.

88. Oakey, R. (1984) *High Technology Small Firms: Innovation and regional development in Britain and the United States*, Frances Pinter, London.

89. ACOST (1990) *The Enterprise Challenge: Overcoming Barriers to Growth in Small Firms*, HMSO, London.

90. Oakey, R., Rothwell, R. and Cooper, S. (1988) *Management of Innovation in High Technology Small Firms*, Pinter, London.

91. Walsh, V., Niosi, J. and Mustar, P. (1995) 'Small firm formation in biotechnology: a comparison of France, Britain and Canada', *Technovation*, vol. 15, no. 5.

92. Mason, C., McNally, K. and Harrison, R. (1996) 'Sources of equity capital for small growing firms: ACOST's "Enterprise Challenge" revisited', in Oakey, R. (ed.) *New technology-based firms in the 1990s, Volume II*, pp. 8–24, Paul Chapman, London.

93. CBR (2000) *British Enterprise in Transition*, Department of Applied Economics, University of Cambridge.

RECOMMENDED READING

Rothwell, R. (1994) 'Towards the fifth-generation innovation process', *International Marketing Review*, vol. 11, pp. 7–31.

Rothwell, R. (1983) 'Innovation and firm size: a case for dynamic complementarity; or is small really beautiful?' *Journal of General Management*, vol. 8, no. 3, pp. 5–25.

Rothwell, R. (1984) 'The role of small firms in the emergence of new technologies', *Omega*, vol. 12, no. 1, pp. 19–29.

Hoffman, K., Milady, P., Bessant, J. and Perren, L. (1998) 'Small firms, R&D, technology and innovation in the UK: a literature review', *Technovation*, vol. 18, no. 1, pp. 39–55.

Moore, I. and Garnsey, E. (1993) 'Funding for innovation in small firms: the role of government', *Research Policy*, vol. 22, pp. 507–19.

Nooteboom, B. (1994) 'Innovation and Diffusion in Small Firms: Theory and Evidence', *Small Business Economics*, vol. 6, pp. 327–47.

8

E-BUSINESS, THE SMALL FIRM AND THE KNOWLEDGE-BASED ECONOMY

By Professor William Keogh and Dr Laura Galloway*

Acknowledgements

Part of the research included in this chapter was supported by ESF, Objective 4 – Programme number 984200UK4, project reference 991017SO4. The Research Assistant on that project was Victoria Stewart, Robert Gordon University with support from Angela Mulvie, researcher on the Investors in People phase of the study.

* Thanks to Andrew Jardine at the University of Strathclyde for technical advice.

LEARNING OUTCOMES

At the end of this chapter you will be able to:

1. Describe the importance of the knowledge economy for small firms.
2. Describe different types of knowledge.
3. Describe the role of the Internet and E-commerce in the knowledge economy.
4. Discuss the importance of knowledge management for the modern economy.
5. Describe the advantages of small firms in a knowledge-based economy.
6. Discuss future trends affecting the knowledge-based economy.
7. Evaluate the importance of the main factors underlying the growth in the knowledge economy.

INTRODUCTION

This chapter deals with the issue of the impact of E-business and the associated development of the knowledge-based economy on entrepreneurs and small firms. We will explain what is meant by 'the knowledge economy', what policy-makers are concerned with and we will examine factors affecting future trends. The knowledge economy can have a variety of different interpretations and elements – a selection is shown below (see box).

ELEMENTS OF THE KNOWLEDGE ECONOMY

- the use of information systems and information technology;
- the development of people in society;
- commercialization (spin-out) of research from companies and the public sector research institutions;
- the development of new world markets;
- new ways of working in entrepreneurship, E-business and other methods of communication.

The focus of much of the chapter, however, is on the elements of E-business and its implications for entrepreneurs and small firms, but we also discuss the importance of knowledge management for the modern economy. The concept of knowledge is explored in relation to innovative entrepreneurs and small firms and examples are given of the types of knowledge available within knowledge-based small firms. As repositories of knowledge and the use of that knowledge in differentiation of their niche markets, these knowledge-based small firms may struggle to market their innovative product and services. Some characteristics of knowledge-based small firms are given below (see box).

CHARACTERISTICS OF KNOWLEDGE-BASED SMALL FIRMS

- operate in global markets;
- dependent on highly qualified staff with key skills;
- human resources are their key assets;
- reward systems for staff based on share options and wealth creation, rather than mere income;
- continuous refinement and development of their products and service.

Later in this chapter, some research results will be presented on the importance of such characteristics and practices in knowledge-based small firms, but first we turn to the impact of E-business and the way it affects all firms in a modern knowledge-based economy.

E-BUSINESS AND SMALL FIRMS

E-business affects all small firms and entrepreneurs, whether in traditional or emergent sectors, whether characterized by knowledge management or not. We have referred to the Internet bubble in previous chapters (for example, Chapter 1) and it will reoccur in Chapter 12. At the time (1998–2000), there was speculation that traditional sector firms could be swept away, that E-business represented a threat to traditional small manufacturing firms; yet with hindsight E-business provided traditional small firms with advantages through the opening of new markets and new forms of trading. In fact, as chronicled elsewhere (see Chapters 1 and 12), it was the dotcom firms that struggled to stay in existence. Early use of E-business focused on the provision of information and online brochures, but as trading electronically grew firms realized that they could exploit the Internet for direct sales and distributing information.[1]

Governments have noted E-business and E-commerce activities.[2] A major aspect of operating in E-business, as well as the information systems, information technology and information computer technologies aspects, is the necessity of finding the right people. For example, the E-people Survey surveyed 1200 high-flyers working across 63 nations involved in E-business.[3] The focus was on young talented graduates who were trying to make a career for themselves in the world of dotcoms and E-business. The Report sees the dotcom crash as a blip in the use of E-business. It highlights the importance of the talents of the people involved for successful exploitation of E-business, whether it involves a firm in traditional or emergent sectors. Drucker has also pointed to the importance of people needed to manage, as new technologies affect all innovative firms.[4]

E-business is just one part of the knowledge-based economy, where information and knowledge are valuable commodities. For example, Roos *et al.* highlight knowledge and information as prime commodities and they explain why there is an increase in the amount of knowledge and information, particularly in the business world.[5] They give four main areas of development:

1. Technological progress and the speed of information.

2. Communication technologies and closer connections between geographically separate countries.

3. The level of sophistication in the consumer population, e.g. expressing their needs and wants clearer than ever before.

4. A structural shift in the economy from industry to service.

At the macro (and micro) economic levels, such developments are of major concern for the Government, with issues such as labour supply, education and training in new technology applications. Prime Minister Tony Blair has remarked:

"This new, knowledge driven economy is a major change. I believe it is the equivalent of the machine driven economy of the Industrial Revolution." [6]

The importance of E-business and the implications for the knowledge-based economy are reflected in new priorities in policy, given the development of the knowledge-based economy. Elements of Government policy in relation to this are shown below (see box).[6]

THE KNOWLEDGE-BASED ECONOMY

The policy response

1. To ensure stability is central to the new economy to enable businesses to plan.

2. To ensure that IT would play a vital role in many aspects of developing the new economy, even assisting many small companies to operate in a global market.

3. To unleash the potential of the people by reforming welfare and establishing the work ethic for the whole society, with social inclusion and education for as many people as possible.

4. To ensure that businesses, whether high-tech or not, could exploit the new opportunities.

5. To ensure innovation through acting in different ways and applying different techniques to achieve and goals, e.g. in ways of logistical thinking and servicing contracts, with learning as key to the individual's success and the organization's success.

Internationally, the developments in E-business and the development of knowledge-based industry have also had implications for international co-operation and development. This has been recognized, for example, by a UK minister.[7] In relation to the advent of new technologies she commented:

"The new technologies are making it possible to embed computing power – intelligence – and transmission capability – connectivity – in every object, connecting people to people and things to things, in ubiquitous networks."

A number of challenges have been identified that face nations globally:[7]

1. Competition and co-operation between nations as they partner to create stable frameworks for trade and environmental issues to create the environment that will lead to success.

2. The construction of legal and market frameworks to make co-operation work.

3. To help people make sense of economic and social transformations that are taking place or, in other words, change and its impact.

Definitions of the Knowledge Economy

1. *At a policy level.* This has translated into an emphasis on knowledge, skills, creativity and knowledge transfer from the science and engineering base into the market place. There has been more concern with commercialization, technology transfer and science enterprise.[8]

2. *Paradoxes of knowledge.* For example, in Australia,[9,10] one response is illustrated by the following: 'using knowledge does not consume it, transferring knowledge does not lose it,' and ironically, as will be explained later in this chapter, 'much of it walks out the door at the end of the day.' Thus, although there is a knowledge economy, knowledge very often resides in individuals and it is what is made of that knowledge that creates the economy.

3. *Technology-based change.* For example, in New Zealand, technology creates change through know-how and even basic production processes, providing added value. At an early date they widened access for schoolchildren and introduced interactive technological environments so that 83 per cent of primary and 94 per cent of secondary schools had Internet access as early as 1988; a reflection of the recognition that they were working in a global economy.[11]

4. *Recognition and management of knowledge.* For example, at the organizational level, key issues in developing companies are fostering innovation,[12,13] developing expert workforces[14] and developing people.

THINK POINTS 8.1

1. What elements do you consider are characteristic of the knowledge-based economy?

2. What factors have influenced the growth of the knowledge-based economy?

3. How do approaches to the knowledge economy differ in different countries?

This section has focused on the characteristics of the knowledge-based economy; we have stressed that it is a global phenomenon, not restricted to developed nations. We have noted that E-business is an integral part of the development of the knowledge-based economy. We turn now to focus more explicitly on this element, the growth of E-business and the significance of the Internet for business.

Small Firms and the Internet

The Internet varies in its impact on the way that small firms operate; as a result there are three types of small firm:

- **those which exist in traditional physical form and do not engage in E-business;**
- **those which exist entirely on the Internet (for example lastminute.com);**
- **those which exist in both states.**

This latter type of firm is usually referred to as a 'hybrid' business. Examples of hybrid firms include the traditional large companies, for example Tesco, which uses the Internet for marketing as well as trading through online shopping and ordering facilities, and Toys Я Us, which has an online brochure and purchasing facility through Amazon.

There are varying degrees to which a small firm may have Internet presence. Thelwall identifies five types of business website:[15]

TYPES OF BUSINESS WEBSITE

1. Sites having company information and contact details and are advertised on a search engine.
2. Sites having company information and contact details *and* information about a specific product or service.
3. Sites having an online catalogue – details about the company's range of products are included.
4. Sites having an online mail-order catalogue – includes the opportunity to order online or by fax, phone, etc.
5. Sites having a cyberstore – the ability to accept payment online through an automated process.

The importance for small firms of having an Internet presence has been illustrated by Chaston, who observes that 62 per cent of US online trade is through traditional firms with an Internet presence, rather than 'pure' dotcoms.[16] In addition, E-business trading is predicted to grow. Many statistics exist which show real and projected figures for increases in online spending; for example see E-Insight (www.e-insight.com), Commerzbank (www.commerzbank.com) and BT (www.bt.com). What these sources of data have in common is that the amount of online trade, both business-to-business and business-to-consumer, is constantly increasing. The benefits to businesses with Internet presence over those without are therefore obvious; more important, it is the entrepreneurial firms that have exploited E-business opportunities to ensure continued growth that have really benefited. For example, entrepreneurial firms such as Ryanair and easyJet have exploited the Internet to maintain their strategy of low-cost fares to gain market share. Their approach to the Internet is a part of their integrated business strategies that have paid off, with their business still growing despite the effects on air travel of the terrorist events of 11 September 2001. This demonstrates that, today, the Internet and E-business needs to be an integral part of a small firm's marketing strategy and fit with its overall business strategy. Although E-business has opened up new opportunities, it is mainly established existing firms that have exploited those opportunities.

Websites

Despite the spectacular success of some online firms, such as Amazon and easyJet, the most common means of online trade is not retail; rather, it is business-to-business (up to 80 per cent of online trade). It implies that the business-to-business infrastructure is benefiting from the ease, speed and lower cost of ordering and purchasing materials and services, which the Internet can allow, compared with the traditional supply chain infrastructure.

In order to have Internet presence, a website is an obvious necessity. A domain name is also necessary, and there are several facilities for domain name registration available, including 123Domain Names (www.123domainnames.co.uk), Nominet (www.nic.uk) and Verio (www.verio.com). A firm can either launch a site on its own server or buy space from an Internet Service Provider (ISP). ISPs provide connection to the Internet and charges range from being a one-off fee to a monthly/yearly/biyearly/etc. fee. As discussed above, a firm's website needs to be an integral part of its strategy. It may be significantly important that business strategy is built around its website, or the website may be an element of marketing strategy. Whatever the role of the website, this clearly needs to be identified by the entrepreneur. This will be important whatever stage the firm is at – even at start-up a website could perform an important function and provide an alternative means of revenue (see also Chapter 12).

Regardless of the type or capability of the website, an entrepreneur must ensure that the site is aesthetically appealing, easy to understand and easy to use. For example, customers will be quickly turned off by a site which is difficult to navigate or which has inconsistencies. Also important to remember is how your customers access the Internet. If your customers are home Internet users or small businesses, where access to the Internet is via the relatively slow telephone line/modem connection, they will not be prepared to wait long for graphics, sound, movement, etc. to load, no matter how spectacular they are. One estimate is that Internet users will wait an average of 10 seconds before giving up on a site and moving on. Hence, attention must be given to how a firm is found on the Internet.

Getting found on the Internet

Whatever type of Internet presence a small firm has, it would be worthless if nobody knew it was there. Attracting visitors and potential customers to a site is a very important part of business Internet use, and has to be maintained. Table 8.1 identifies different ways that consumers and businesses locate sites.[17]

	Consumers	Business users
Word of mouth	100%	71%
Links from websites	83%	88%
TV, Radio, posters	67%	76%
Magazine articles	61%	94%
Newspaper articles	50%	53%
Conferences	17%	47%

Source: Cognitiative (1999), press release, April, www.cognitiative.com.

Table 8.1 Locating information on websites

Search engines and directories

Search engines and directories are different things. Search engines (e.g. Lycos, www.lycos.co.uk, and Northern Light, www.nothernlight.com) tend to use software called spiders or crawlers to search the Internet for key words, for example a brand, product or service. When changes are made to a website, crawlers/spiders will find the changes, and a small firm's listing can be affected. Although a search engine can locate a site without that site being registered with the search engine, registration is important as it maintains a firm's presence even when changes to the site are made. It used to be the case that the greater amount of key words embedded into the text of a website, the more likely a search engine was to locate that site. This meant that websites which had nothing to do with the key word, but which belonged to firms or individuals that wanted traffic to their site in the hope of 'capturing' it, could embed many lexical items in their site – often invisibly – and could be included in the search results. This exploitation has been counteracted to a large extent by greater sophistication of search engine software. Some search engines (e.g. AltaVista, www.altavista.co.uk, and Google, www.google.co.uk) include a supplementary directory service.

Directories (e.g. Yahoo! www.yahoo.co.uk) use human assessment of a website. An entrepreneur has to apply for inclusion in a directory and a *person* assesses the application and the website before accepting it.

Meta-search facilities, such as AskJeeves (www.ask.co.uk), are also available. These use a variety of engines and directories for a search. A good guide to search facility inclusion is Search Engine Watch (www.searchenginewatch.com).

Whatever the type of search facility, a small firm will want its website to be found and to be one of the first results of a search. In order to do this a small firm must maintain its registration with search engines and directories. There are online companies which, for a price, will do this, so that the small firm entrepreneur does not have to spend time regularly maintaining their inclusion.

Links

Other methods of online advertising include banners (small advertisements which appear on another website, usually at a price), affiliate programs and associates, where a small firm can pay for a link from a related site to their own, or has a mutually beneficial link agreement on an associated website (i.e. links to each other appear in each site). Again, there are online companies which will source and contact potential associates and affiliates for an entrepreneur (e.g. Click Trade, www.click-trade.com, and Link Share, www.linkshareuk.com).

Low-tech methods

There are a number of effective methods and techniques that allow an entrepreneur, even in a small firm, to maintain their presence and market their name on the Internet. For example, effective means of advertising a small firm's web presence include:[18]

- **adding the web address to all Emails using a signature file (included in Email programs);**
- **mentioning the web address on the answerphone message;**
- **including the web address in all traditional advertising;**
- **adding the web address to stationery, business cards, etc.;**
- **maintaining the site and product/service details regularly.**

The Internet Market

The most obvious advantage of the Internet for small firms is the access to the global market. It is estimated that there are 332 million Internet users worldwide, and the proportion of them who purchase online is increasing as use and faith in the Internet as a medium for financial transaction increases. For example, Ernst & Young found that the proportion of Internet users who purchase online rose from 43 per cent in 1999 to 61 per cent in 2000.[19]

The number of small firms with Internet access is also significant in terms of market potential. In terms of access to customers, location and size are less limiting than they once were. For example, with an effective website and sound online transaction facilities a young, small firm can appear to be more established than it is, and as such can be in a position to compete with older, larger and more experienced firms. Thus an effective Internet strategy is something to consider when developing a start-up business plan.

Although access to large global markets is appealing, it has to be very carefully managed. Customer loyalty is of utmost importance on the Internet as competitors are only a click away, and customers will defect to competitors if the quality of experience is poor. Because of this, trade facilitated by the Internet – be that in the form of a website advertisement or by the availability of a fully equipped E-commerce site – must be both attractive to customers and reliable. Advertised costs, product descriptions, special online offers, delivery times, prices (including taxes and, if appropriate, postage costs) must be clearly stated, unambiguous and fulfilled as promised. For example, a small firm can find itself in huge trouble if it has underestimated the marketing potential of the Internet, or has overestimated its ability to provide goods or services to other businesses or consumers. In either case a small firm may be unable to fulfil customer orders on time.

Personalized customer service, on the other hand, is one of the most appealing advantages of the Internet for businesses in that it has the potential to increase customer loyalty. Small firms can develop and keep a profile of customers relatively easily, either by monitoring their purchases or by asking customers directly to divulge information about themselves.[a] For example, if an online travel agent knows that a customer usually purchases weekend city breaks it can target its advertising to that customer appropriately. It can further refine this tailored service if it has information about customers' personal details, e.g. posting or Emailing offers of reduced price children's facilities to customers with no children would not only be an unnecessary expense, but would also be a waste of both the firm's and the customer's time.

Security

With customer service an optimal part of a small firm's online trade, security is critical issue with E-business and Internet trading. The reasons are given below (see box).

[a] If the latter method is used, it is prudent to give customers the choice as to whether or not they divulge personal details, and to make explicit the company's policy on the use of customer data. It is counter-productive for a company's customer service methods to alienate customers or to contravene Data Protection regulations.

THE NEED FOR SECURITY ON WEBSITES

1. To limit the amount of damage to your site by Internet vandals.
2. To ensure that employees do not waste company time and money on Internet activities other than those associated with their jobs.
3. To ensure that sensitive customer and company data – especially financial data – are not available.
4. To prevent Emails of a defamatory or derogatory nature becoming public (it can take only a matter of minutes for Email to reach the public domain due to its speed and copy functions).

There are means of protecting a website. For instance, various IT methods can be used, such as firewalls to stop hackers and software which disallows the use of websites containing 'barred' lexical items to stop employees abusing company time on the Internet. It is also a good idea for a small firm to have disclaimers attached to all employees' Emails clearly stating that the firm is not responsible for the text of the Email. A small firm may not have the resources to deal with these measures but they can be out-sourced to companies such as Click Sure (www.clicksure.com) and Zeuros Network Solutions (www.zeuros.co.uk) which specialize in these areas.

In addition to electronic security, there are several low-tech means of adding security (see box).

LOW-TECH WAYS OF ADDING SECURITY

- Restricting Internet access to employees who work directly with the Internet trade side of the company or require access for some other work-related reason.
- Having computers clearly visible within an office to restrict those with Internet access to relevant use.
- Storing all financial data – including company data as well as customers' credit card details – offline, preferably on a separate offline computer.
- Requiring employees to sign a non-disclosure agreement as part of their contract to ensure that they do not abuse access to customer data such as Email addresses, home addresses, telephone numbers, etc., as well as company information.

Business on the Internet

For a small firm, as for all companies, Internet trading needs to be part of an overall business/growth strategy to be of optimum benefit. It is not enough to create a website and post it on the Internet. Even if the website is merely an online advertisement with no E-commerce capability, it is important to update product/ service details regularly. A site with more sophisticated facilities such as online ordering and payment requires close monitoring and maintenance. For some small firms this is best served by having expertise and responsibility for Internet trading in-house, and for others it will be more cost-effective to receive support from external sources. There are many independent web-hosting, maintenance, IT and online solutions companies including inyourcity (http://design.inyourcity.com) (see case study), MHz (www.mhzscotland.com) and It's Not Rocket Science (www.inrs.-co.uk).

SUMMARY OF THE IMPORTANCE OF BUSINESS ON THE INTERNET

Throughout the late 1990s the dotcom industry boomed. Entirely Internet-based businesses were created and grown, usually at massive expense and often 'burning out' before profit was ever made. What is emerging from this as the sustainable face of Internet business is not, in fact, 'Internet business' at all, but rather it is traditional business that uses the Internet to best advantage. With Internet use and, more importantly, purchasing on the Internet continuing to increase, saturation is inevitable. The Internet and ICT are already establishing themselves as mainstays of modern culture. The impact for many businesses is, as Hugh Aitken of Sun Microsystems predicts, 'if you're not an Internet company by 2005, you won't be a company at all'.[20]

THINK POINTS 8.2

1. How can small entrepreneurial firms use the Internet to compete with large firms?
2. What are the different ways that firms may use the Internet?
3. How would you advise an entrepreneur looking to start a new firm on developing an Internet strategy?

Discussion questions on the following case study are given at the end of the chapter. In the section that follows the case study, we turn to the broader topic of knowledge management which, like E-business, is an issue that concerns all small firms in the modern economy.

ENTREPRENEURSHIP IN ACTION: STARTING AN E-BUSINESS: inyourcity.com

Background

At the age of 27, Forbes Manson already had experience of IT and the Internet, having worked for a small company in the games and entertainment sector and having completed a degree in Business Information Technology at his local university. Forbes believed that the Internet held many opportunities and, as a student, he elected to study entrepreneurship alongside his core subjects, and look for gaps in the online market. He identified that at that time there were no detailed guides to facilities, attractions and information about his native city, Glasgow.

Development of the Idea

Forbes's entrepreneurship elective at university provided him the opportunity to research and develop a business idea and complete a feasibility study. It also required him to prepare a working business plan. Forbes used his idea of an online information service and guide to Glasgow as his focus for these assignments, and through this was able to develop and refine the idea.

Competition

Forbes identified that information sites about Glasgow tended to be specific to one particular aspect of the city (e.g. history or pubs) but there was no site which constituted a comprehensive information service about the city, including history, culture, places to go, etc. Forbes also noted that information sites about Glasgow did not offer visitors much in the way of linked information. So, while competition did exist, Forbes concluded that he could provide a service with a broader range, and at a lower cost, than his competitors. This more holistic service links up information in such a way that if customers access his site for information about, for example, movies being shown in the city, they will not only receive a list of appropriate cinemas with links to route maps, film titles, times and dates, etc., but also will receive information on other related facilities within a one-mile radius, e.g. pubs, restaurants and nightclubs, again including links to maps and other appropriate information, e.g. restaurant menus and prices. Additionally, unlike his competitors, an availability and booking service is offered at no extra charge to business.

Realization

Forbes's vision of a comprehensive online guide to Glasgow first started to become a reality when he registered the domain names www.virtualscotland.net and www.inyourcity.com. Virtual Scotland is registered as a limited company and offers web-hosting, design, maintenance, advice and advertising via local directories. The first of these local directories is inyourcity for Glasgow. Glasgowinyourcity.com generates revenue from advertising the services included, providing links to their sites, and where there is no site, creating one. Services and information available through inyourcity include local information, news, weather, events (e.g. concerts, exhibitions), cinema, shopping, area guides, virtual tours (e.g. of museums) and a business search facility.

As a means of attracting and maintaining interest in the site, Forbes also was keen to establish a community 'feel' to the service. Chat rooms and noticeboards are key features of inyourcity and are mainly responsible for the fact that inyourcity.com attracted between 7,000 and 8,000 visitors a month *before* any businesses had bought into the service and before any target advertising had taken place.

Organization

Forbes and his mother own Virtual Scotland, each with a 50 per cent interest. As the operational partner, Forbes is the managing director of the company, while his mother is the company's secretary. There are two other employees who work on an ad hoc basis to assist Forbes with website content, design and creation. The intention is to have these employees full-time salaried as soon as is feasible.

Web-hosting is rented from a third party, which deals with all back-up and security issues.

Virtual Scotland is based within Glasgow city centre, at the heart of the city's business and entertainment communities.

Start-up Costs

Virtual Scotland operates from office space owned by Forbes's family. There is, therefore, no office rental to pay. Equipment and fees for start-up were estimated at £20,000. While banks and other external types of funding were considered, both directors' savings were sufficient to cover the cost of start-up, so debt finance was not necessary.

Sales

It has taken almost a year to complete the infrastructure necessary for inyourcity.com to start to generate revenue. With the site finished, Forbes and his team must sell the idea to businesses. Initially restaurants, sport venues, nightclubs and bars will be targeted. Though there will be discounted rates available for early takers, inclusion with inyourcity will cost £60 per month, with no extra charges (e.g. for menu changes throughout the month). While focusing on sales to businesses, the inyourcity team consistently advertise throughout Glasgow to those who comprise a market for these businesses. As Forbes puts it, 'Unlike our competitiors, we intend to avoid a massive advertising campaign at the start which will increase visitors in numbers not matched by the amount and variety of businesses we are facilitating online. Instead, what we intend doing is to slowly but consistently increase the profile of the company. By taking this bit-by-bit long-term approach we plan to avoid being missed by the target market, and to gradually establish our name within people's consciousness.'

KNOWLEDGE MANAGEMENT

Small firms, across all industries, are beginning to realize that it is their human assets, or intangible assets in the form of knowledge, that provide the key to their continued success. In many areas small firms are seeking to identify and manage their knowledge base more efficiently and effectively. This is achieved by implementing a range of initiatives addressing issues such as behavioural or technological processes. Critical aspects of this can be seen from the benefits derived in sharing knowledge both inside and outside the company. As discussed at the beginning of this chapter, it is evident that knowledge management has different interpretations. Much debate has gone on as to what is termed knowledge.[13] However, it is evident that competitive advantage can from identification and realization of the knowledge resource within small firms; as discussed below, this knowledge lies not in physical assets of the firm, but in its workforce.

THE KNOWLEDGE-BASED ECONOMY

The importance of knowledge in individuals

Much of the knowledge in small firms resides in, and is unique within, individuals. This is known as tacit knowledge and a key problem for many organizations is how to capture and utilize such a knowledge base. The nature of the job market within certain industries (e.g. software) impacts on the knowledge base within other firms. Other industries suffer from people leaving the industry with them (e.g. the oil and gas industry). This knowledge is often not captured or transferred within the organizations and consequently may lead to increased costs due to training new people in the areas, or through buying in the knowledge that they have lost, or through the extension of projects due to inexperienced staff operating on them.

Types of Knowledge

Definitions of knowledge have been suggested by writers,[21,22,23] but what is evident is that there are different types of knowledge:

1. *Technical knowledge*, where knowledge of a specific discipline or process can be learned by individuals.

2. *Case-based knowledge*, where knowledge has been gained from specific projects and then used heuristically for other projects.

3. *Others aspects of knowledge* may include the *environmental aspects* such as the business environment of a firm, including the customer base and competitor details.

4. *Explicit and tacit knowledge*. Knowledge which can be learned and is used within the organization can be known as *explicit* knowledge and *tacit*

knowledge exists within the individual. This may begin as an aptitude or something that they can do intuitively and can be honed to meet other requirements. The distinction is very important because this will affect how knowledge may be transferred within the small firm or across different firms. Thus, if key individuals leave then it may be very difficult to replace their own individual skills or tacit knowledge.

Different knowledge types within small firms can come together so that operating on a particular case or project may mean that technical knowledge or environmental knowledge and other aspects come together in order to satisfy the requirements for retention. In the small firm it may mean that the individual or small group of people operating on a project may have to know a great deal about different areas.

The Need to Update Knowledge

The constant need to update knowledge within small firms, particularly in relation to the customer base and the additional value, is generally seen as an essential part in maintaining a market niche position. Knowledge requirements to achieve success in a niche market tend to bring together aspects such as market information, individual knowledge of the sales team and the technical teams and also the drive and determination of the management teams (or entrepreneurs). Updating this knowledge and learning is vitally important for such small firms. They may well spend a great deal of time trying to keep in touch with their market place, thus their main efforts may be spent on tracking individuals.[24] Updating knowledge and learning is vital for small firms, particularly if they are technology-based.

Argyris[25] explains that, to be successful in the market place, key individuals require further learning, as discussed below (see box).

THE KNOWLEDGE-BASED ECONOMY

Individual learning in small firms

In order to get others to learn within a small firm requires an internal infrastructure and support mechanism to help them learn and aid the technology transfer processes. This requires a broader perspective, so that by focusing on organizational learning and seeking to continuously improve the processes, the people and the organization, changes can be targeted more effectively. If the knowledge is shared then the intellectual property of the organization is not just invested in the projects or services offered in the market place. Indeed, a great strength is the knowledge which is developed within the individuals and small firms will grow in their intellectual capital. It is important that there is a greater recognition of the intellectual capital. It is important that there is a greater recognition of the intellectual work of individuals and lessons are still there to be learned, as will be seen in the practical explanations of technology-based small firms which follow. Examples of this deal with the placement of individuals with tacit knowledge and key skills and their ability to communicate, as demonstrated by the role of the entrepreneurs within these firms.[26]

Management of knowledge within small firms is therefore a vital requirement and knowledge sharing is a major focus for some of the emerging knowledge management literature.[27] For small firms to be innovative, they must encourage key staff to think and develop new ideas and concepts which will find their way to the market place. A greater awareness and understanding of systems and processes in businesses are vital for small firms and much has been done by authors such as Senge[28] in investigating the inter-relationships between process dynamics and systems theories.

One key challenge, after the identification of the knowledge base and the determination of where the tacit and explicit knowledge resides, is how to go about capturing that knowledge. The subsequent exploitation of that knowledge leads to another series of opportunities in the global market place. Porter has identified the importance of applying the aspects of added value.[29] By investigating this further we can see that applying knowledge that way for a small firm really involves the application of resources at strategic points in the process. Thus, the management specialist may intervene in parts of the process where added value is most important. This may occur in the process of managing innovative projects, where output from the knowledge base aids small firms in differentiating their products or services and enables them to occupy their niche markets.[30] This also acts as an aid for strategic awareness and planning for entrepreneurs, who can begin to target their scarce resources into key areas.

Knowledge of this kind also plays a major part in the identification of network opportunities and the importance of realizing that shared knowledge can lead to complementary strengths where specialist groups are working together and may even lead to reduction in costs over time (e.g. in supply chain agreements).

Knowledge and Learning

The need to update knowledge within technology-based small firms has been made apparent through various studies and examples will be discussed later in this chapter. As stated above, this is important in the adding of value in processes within the small firm and also for the customer base. In some industries there has been a move over the past few years towards joint ventures, partnerships and strategic alliances.[31] This is essentially part of the supply chain strategies operated by large firms, but may exclude small firms on the basis that they cannot share the same degree of risk in financial terms as large firms.[24] However, it is the tacit knowledge of the specialist small firms that differentiates them within the market place and allows them to be key suppliers within very complex systems. In order for the small firm to achieve this, knowledge requirements bring together market information, individual knowledge and the drive of the entrepreneur.

Senge identified key dimensions in the learning process that are important for small firms in the modern knowledge-based economy.[28] These are given below (see box).

THE KNOWLEDGE-BASED ECONOMY

Critical dimensions in learning

- systems thinkings;
- personal mastery;
- mental models;
- building shared vision;
- team learning.

In some situations it is not always clear which of these dimensions are incorporated into small firms. Certainly entrepreneurs may intuitively move towards team learning and attempting to build a shared vision with key staff members.

The process governing the management of knowledge in small firms can be affected by a range of factors that have to be considered for the implementation of any knowledge management initiative, consciously or unconsciously. For example, there is a need for the small firm to manage its knowledge and manage the knowledge-based processes more effectively. This was emphazised by Garvin, who argues that organizations need to transform into 'learning organizations'.[32] He defines a learning organization as:

> ***"an organization skilled at creating, acquiring, and transferring knowledge, and at modifying its behaviour to reflect new knowledge and insights."***

Many small firms do this, either through their strategic plans or perhaps through the vision of the entrepreneur. What is important is the way that small firms learn, as this has a bearing on their effectiveness. Senge pointed out that survival learning, or what is more usually termed adaptive learning, is important.[28] Indeed it is necessary, but, for a small firm, adaptive learning must be joined by generative learning, in other words, learning that enhances the capacity to create.

Within any small firm, the complexity of what key staff are trying to do must be supported by some form of infrastructure or plan. Recognition of what the firm is trying to do is very important. As stated through the OECD, the distribution of knowledge through formal and informal networks is essential to economic performance.[33] Therefore, as small firms develop they will add to the economic development of their own country.

The Knowledge Management Survey has attempted to develop an understanding of the effectiveness of organizations (across a range of industries and sectors) managing knowledge.[34] Despite a large number (92 per cent of respondents) stating that they worked in knowledge-intense organizations, of this only 6 per cent indicated that their organizations were very effective in leveraging knowledge to improve their business performances and results. Another study on knowledge management conducted by KPMG, also discovered that, although 70 per cent of the organizations involved identified knowledge as a key internal issue, 45 per cent stated that they were not learning organizations.[35] Therefore, small firms may be aware of the importance of what they are trying to do and the use of knowledge as an asset, but they may be unaware of how to take advantage of this. It may be that large firms can learn from some of the small firms which have to survive through doing many different things.

Garvin states that learning organizations are skilled at five main activities:[36]

THE KNOWLEDGE-BASED ECONOMY

Features of learning in organisations

- systematic problem solving;
- experimentation with new approach;
- learning from their own experience and past history;
- learning from the experience and best practice of others;
- transferring knowledge quickly and efficiently throughout the organization.

In order to take advantage of the situation and to overcome the range of factors which may inhibit the development in organizations, they would have to become fairly skilled in each of the areas above. Indeed, when viewed from this perspective, many small firms do these things naturally.

As well as the key issues of how to identify which knowledge is valuable to a small firm, as well as how to manage the knowledge workers, another aspect is the use and advent of *enabling technologies*. These technologies can make things happen much quicker in small firms, but there are problems in knowing what type of knowledge to try to capture. Other aspects, such as economic pressures, resulted in a loss of corporate memory in large firms through, for example, downsizing. However, changes in international trade and globalization have resulted in new logistical techniques and the availability of new sources of supply.[37] Davis and Bodkin defined knowledge as the application and productive use of information.[38] They also identified characteristics of knowledge-based firms which include the following: knowledge-based products, services that have relatively short life cycles and the fact that the more a firm uses knowledge-based offerings, the smarter the small firm can get.

As can be seen from the introduction to this chapter, there is a challenge for policy-makers at both local and national levels to try to broaden the focus and understanding of knowledge requirements and to assist emerging entrepreneurial small firms.

Knowledge Transfer

The issue of transferring learning and knowledge exists between companies as well as within them and a good example of this is the use of the supply chain, where knowledge can be transferred.[39,40]

Knowledge transfer skills are important to companies operating within supply chains, where they can be used to identify potential suppliers, to identify customers, to promote their technology and skills, and to promote the unique offering that the small firm can provide. The use of the supply chain operates as an effective conduit so that knowledge can be transferred, but to some extent this is dependent on which form that knowledge takes. Explicit knowledge, of course, may be transferred relatively simply, but the tacit knowledge which resides in the individuals is more difficult to transfer. For example, difficulties occur when a large firm buys a controlling interest in a small firm or takes it over. It is important for the organization to ensure that the knowledge still resides in the firm and that the key individuals concerned do not leave. As mentioned earlier, added value is an area where small firms can leverage their worth within the supply chain in which they operate. An example would be where the small firm is the only supplier of a unique product, but it is underselling its services. So added value does not just have to be in the province of those companies which offer manufacturing. It can also relate to engineering and software services.

Added value comes from the change in the form of information, the availability of the product or service, and the market in which the small firm operates.[41] The importance of identifying added-value activities has been explored by a number of authors, including Manganelli and Klein,[42] who explain that the easiest way to identify the steps which add value involves the consideration of the impact that the step has in relation to certain performance measures that are determined for and within that process. The steps, which may be non-value added, can be categorized as 'control' or 'other', where 'other' includes communication and administration. In the case of small firms, they may wish to map out their process carefully, identifying the steps and relationships between what they do and where it adds value to their customers. This detailed examination of the process can result in the elimination of non-value added steps in the value process. In Porter's model of the value chain, value activities are divided into primary and support activities, with primary activities consisting of activities involved in the development of the product or service.[29] Support activities include issues such as human resource management, technology development and procurement. In the case of small firms, depending on the size and type of organization, there is a possibility that the entrepreneur will be directly responsible for controlling activities in relation to the innovative capacity of the firm.

Small Firms and the Knowledge-based Economy

In this section we examine a two-year research study conducted by the author with innovative small firms that were working to develop new products and services and were concerned with the recruitment, training and the retention of their staff (the most important asset to an organization).

The information requirements of innovative small firms tend to be focused on the goals identified by management; for example, on company growth and capturing market share. The 'can do' attitude of the management, which tends to lead to working informally, can easily be interpreted as unsophisticated. However, this is not always the case and may be a flexible way of achieving goals. Where there may be a lack of management skills, contact with customers and a willingness to co-operate in order to solve problems for the customer requires flexibility and the application of the intellectual capital of the firm. According to Stewart:

"Intellectual capital is the sum of everything everybody in a company knows that gives it a competitive edge."[43]

It was evident from all the firms in the sample that data were gathered constantly with a view to spotting market opportunities. Key aspects of the use of information and intellectual capacity can be illustrated by exploring issues such as innovation and human resource development.

In order to maximize and maintain their output all the small firms involved in the study needed to be helped to develop and work on a continuing improvement basis, particularly as firms were growing.[43] Major events for growing include raising finance for growth or becoming a target for acquisition.[44] During the course of the two-year research study, five small firms were bought by larger organizations and changed. Many changes occur in the firm as it grows;[45] for instance, the entrepreneur may deal with problems through very simple lines of communication to begin with, but these tend to become more complex as staff members grow to a different degree of complexity.[46]

Small firms face difficulties in trying to identify their own real needs and necessary support mechanisms in order to grow and deal with the practical needs of the organization.[47] Figure 8.1 illustrates a suggested model for managing change in the knowledge-based economy and deals with the processes involved in knowledge management and identifying key components.

The data relating to small firms in the study are shown in Table 8.2.

From Table 8.2 it can be seen that one became a large firm due to takeovers of other small firms, developments within the organization and expansion abroad through internationalization. This company was in turn taken over by a large national organization. The five different categories (sectors) of companies relate to organizations that were trying to grow and develop. The bio-science related

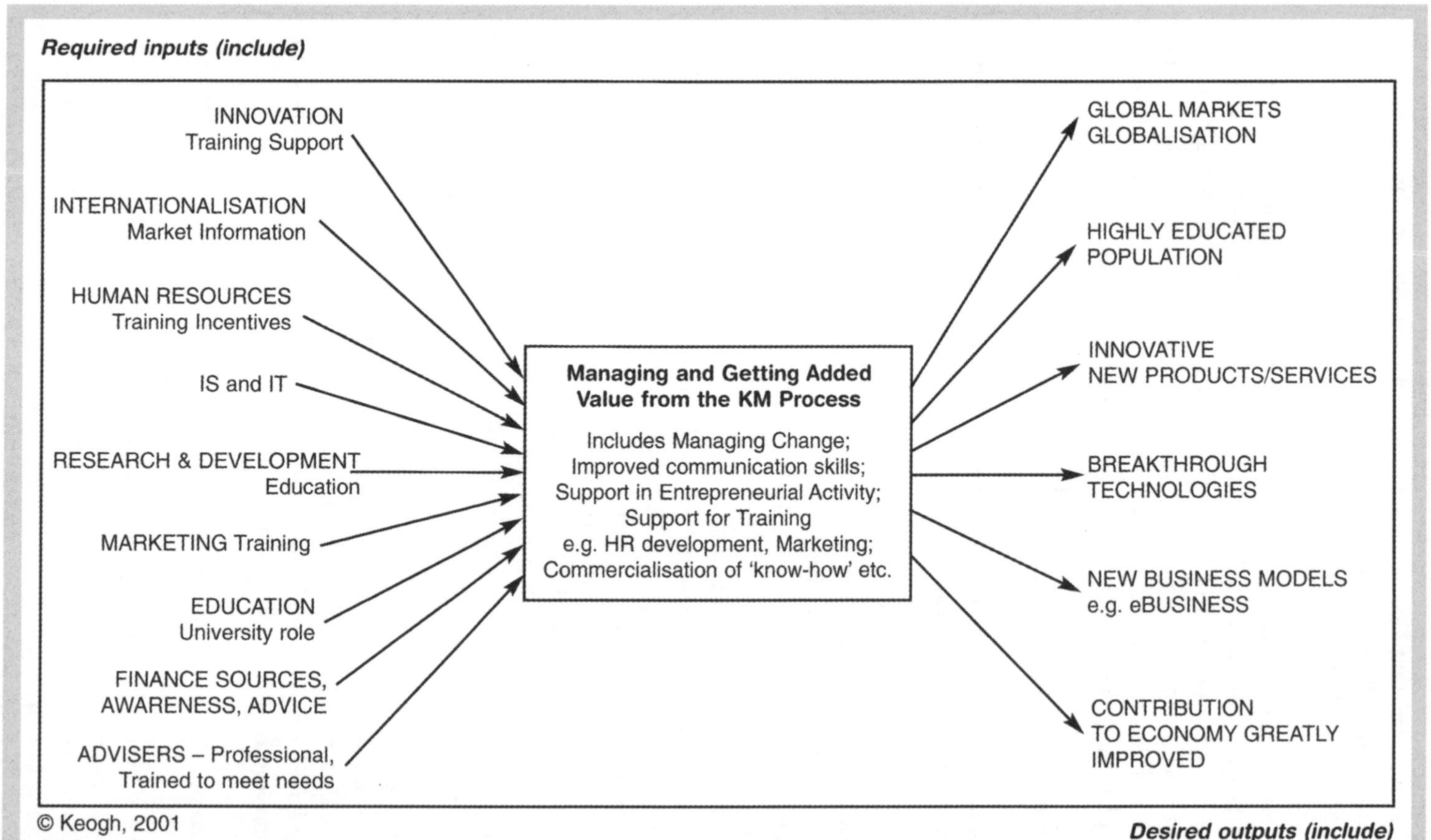

Figure 8.1 Model of managing change in the knowledge economy

Size of firms	Year 2	Year 1	Total firms
Micro (<9 employees)	13	1	14
Small (10 < 50 employees)	15	9	24
Medium (50 < 250 employees)	12	9	21
Large (>250 employees)		1	1
Totals	40	20	60

Sector	Year 2	Year 1	Total firms
Software	8	4	12
Engineering	7	7	14
Analytical services	8	4	12
Instrumentation	9	4	13
Bio-science related	8	1	9
Totals	40	20	60

Table 8.2 Study firm profiles

companies were not all bio-science researchers as it was difficult to identify small firms in the geographic area in which the study took place. Therefore, some of these firms were users of some form of bio-science.

It was of critical importance to the small firms that their staff were experienced and trained to address the many external pressures that they faced. It was also important that the staff members were organized and motivated in such a way as to facilitate and assist the development of systems within the firm and co-operative working within the network in which they operated. Therefore individuals within the firm – and their knowledge – could also use this with some of the incentives to aid their own potential. It can be seen in Figure 8.1 that one of the desired outputs from the knowledge economy is a highly educated workforce.

At a policy level, the UK Government has developed policies over the years to support competitiveness, which places a strong emphasis on 'raising the average level of attainment'[48] and also the development of a skilled and adaptable workforce.[49] These policies have been reflected in the objectives and priorities at regional level and they marry quite well with the knowledge-based economy measures. However, this is not all plain sailing and evidence has emerged to show the problems with many small firms in relation to the training that they have and acquire. The British Chambers of Commerce in their Small Firms Survey of Furthering Skills makes it clear that the firms' skills shortages have an adverse effect on competitiveness.[50] Although it can be seen from the introduction to this chapter that steps are being taken in the UK, problems will still remain and it will take some time to put the strategies into operation.

The 60 innovative small firms taking part in the study reported that they operated in niche markets in highly competitive environments. They could ill-afford to waste resources and they tended to work in a flexible manner with little waste and within tight schedules. Small firms such as these survive through a number of transitions in the development of their organizations and most of those organizations could demonstrate that they have been innovative as well as able to adapt to changing market needs and customer requirements. The firms indicated problems in attempting to support training and development, for example insufficient capacity to undertake skills analysis and planning and also a lack of contact with appropriate facilitators such as training organizations. In one excellent example of a software firm, each member of staff had a work and continuing professional development (CPD) programme mapped out for them and they had their own record of training. This could be transferred when they went to other organizations within the software industry.

All 60 firms took part in phase one of the project, which involved investigation of issues such as strategy, innovation and internationalization. The second phase focused on people needs and, over the two years, 43 companies took part. Figure 8.2 illustrates the education level attained at degree and above.

Engineering firms' employees had relatively low qualifications; however, a fairly large number of employees had HNC/HND level qualifications. As might be expected, other sectors, especially bio-science firms had high employee qualifications. Thus it can be seen that, within the small firms that are innovative, educational levels were high. One or two firms in specialist areas had very large PhD numbers in their organization in percentage terms. Previous analysis of the research data has indicated the heavy reliance of the sample upon technical staff.[51] It may be that there is a lack of technical support within certain small firms and many of those employees in support functions, such as sales, were ex-technical staff.

In many instances senior management also came from technical backgrounds. This should not really be a problem but was highlighted by a number of the interviews because of their lack of business and commercial skills and experience among other senior managers. From Figure 8.1 we can see that the required inputs of some of the key aspects of training, such as marketing and finance and HR, could be made available in a different form to senior management in innovative small firms.

Harrison has defined human resource development as:

> ***“ the all important process to which individual and organisational growth can through time achieve its fullest potential. ”***[52]

This means that small firms must ensure that they have the right people, with the correct skills and use them in the right place. In practice, the human resource strategy integrated with business strategy can be a complex process. Developing employees rather than just having them on staff training programmes is a much bigger issue and the knowledge of these employees, as indicated earlier, could be used to enhance the reputation of the firm.

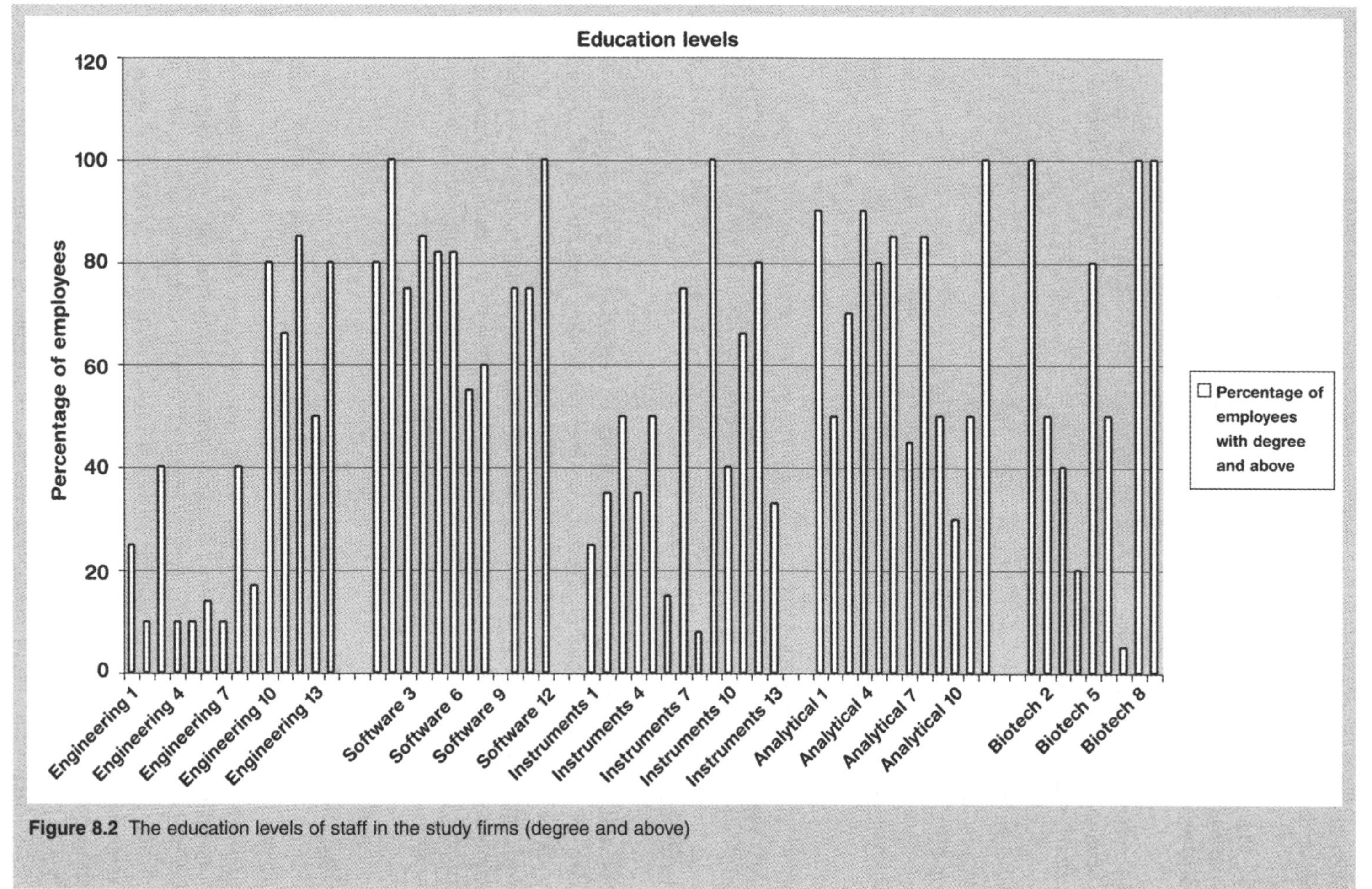

Figure 8.2 The education levels of staff in the study firms (degree and above)

Working with technology for individuals in the dynamic environment can also prove to be difficult. Scott *et al.* argue that:

> ***"the successful exploitation of technology in a dynamic environment depends crucially upon a skill base capable of identifying opportunities for and managing technological development."*** [53]

In other words, in order to achieve strategic goals, planning must take place throughout the organization and the skill requirements must be identified in an appropriate manner.

Recruiting the right staff begins with the identification of job and person requirements and this can be seen again from Figure 8.1, where the process of making use of knowledge management would include skills such as the management of change for managers in small firms. Improving communication skills for the managers and working with their teams is vital, as is supporting them in entrepreneurial activity where they may be lacking in new skills as they may well come from technological or scientific backgrounds. Other aspects, such as HR development and marketing, may well come under 'support for training'. In part, this may well be relieved from the advice being given as business advisers professionalize. A key aspect is the commercialization of know-how, using and understanding innovation and reaching global markets, all of which are vital for the small firm and its staff.

As well as developing the staff, the issue of the retention of technological staff can also prove to be difficult. We can consider the widely reported Y2K problem in software, where many small firms were having great difficulties in obtaining people with software skills. In order to keep people, the sample firms devised several methods. In one case, a company band was supported by the senior management, in another, a football team was supported. Others offered share inducements in the organizations and some tried to develop CPD incentives.

The Innovation Process and Use of Knowledge

The 60 firms in the survey were all regarded as innovative in some way or another. This was determined from their own peer group, where they were identified as being innovative, and from the standards and awards they had won. However, the innovation cycle itself had been in many cases, the linchpin on which the firm had been founded; for example, where the idea of the entrepreneur had been taken through the process of invention to reach the market place. Many examples were given by the 60 firms and the processes that deal with this particular aspect varied from company to company. Figure 8.3 illustrates just some of the issues involved.

Ideas often came from customers and the requirements of the customers. Also, working with the staff and developing the staff meant that in-house ideas could be taken further. From the sales forces, competitors' ideas were fed back and, of course,

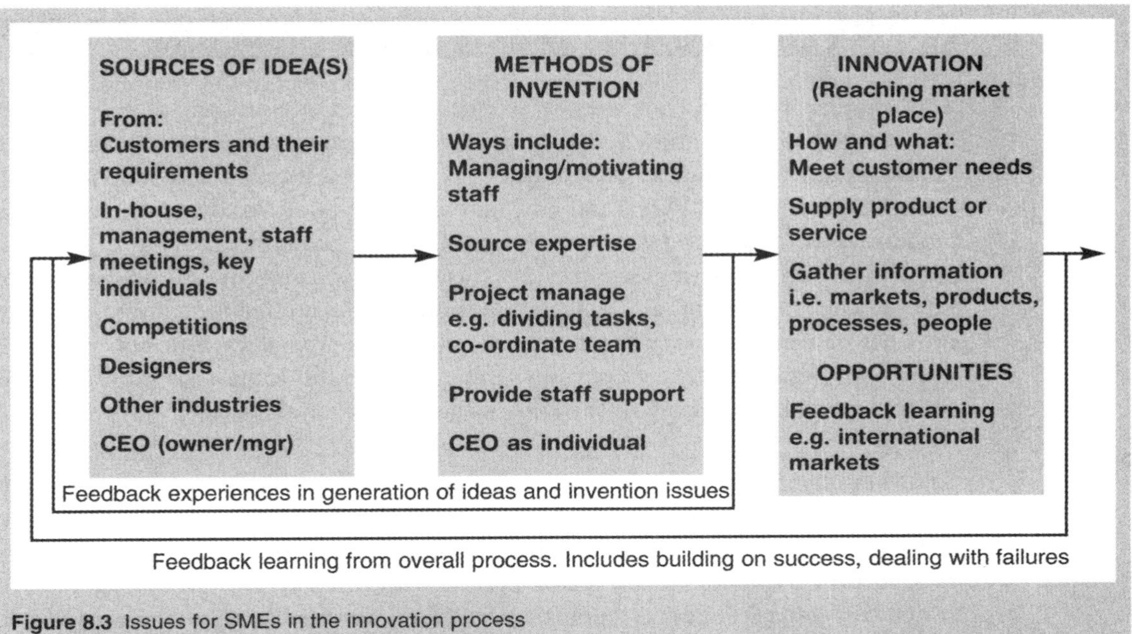

Figure 8.3 Issues for SMEs in the innovation process

bringing in items from other industries was always a possibility. Under the methods of invention, every company worked differently. In one case, the entrepreneur managed the project team to an extent that he had sourced or identified external specialists who came into the organization to help him prepare sub-assemblies of the new innovations. In another, the idea came from the entrepreneur and he worked with groups in-house until they had taken the idea through the invention stage and were ready to bring it into production as an innovation. At the innovation stage, meeting the customers' needs was the prime requirement but the products and services supplied also allowed the firm to feedback other requirements into the sources of ideas by identifying new opportunities. In many cases, companies were moving from one industry to another from the supply base; for example, a firm may move from sub-sea within the oil and gas industry to sub-sea within some other industry and in other parts of the world – which requires innovation.

THINK POINTS 8.3

1. If you were advising an innovative entrepreneur, what are the features of knowledge management that he or she needs to be aware of?
2. What examples can you give of rewards and incentives to retain staff in knowledge-intensive companies?
3. Why do such companies have to be innovative? And why are they in global markets?

CONCLUSIONS

This chapter began by looking at the features and importance of the modern knowledge-based economy. One important feature, of course, has been the development of E-business. We have examined how this has impacted on entrepreneurs and small firms and how entrepreneurs can take advantage. In today's modern knowledge-based economy, E-business must be an integral part of business and marketing strategy. This applies whether the small firm is classified as an Internet company or not, as a dotcom or a traditional manufacturing firm, as service provider or manufacturing firm, as a technology-based small firm or not. All small firms need to identify the most appropriate use and advantages of E-business for themselves while operating in the knowledge-based economy.

Some key issues have been identified, for example the use of information systems and information technology, and the concept of taking new innovations and commercializing these. There are other issues, such as the development of people as a primary resource, the fact that a persons's knowledge can be leveraged and, of course, the impact of new technologies. Following this, the concept of knowledge in context was explored. It is through a firm's learning that individuals with their tacit knowledge, and the knowledge within the firm, can be developed further. It was indicated that a major area of concern is that knowledge may leave the small firm in one way or another. Sometimes this is not recognized by entrepreneurs, but by using methods to identify key individuals the entrepreneur can then try to codify or record aspects of their knowledge and then develop other people to the same standards. Because of the nature of tacit knowledge, this may not be possible in many cases (it is tacit knowledge that makes a great sportsman or writer different from anybody else).

Next, examples were given of a study of 60 innovative small firms where the education levels were illustrated and the numbers of employees were shown to give something of their profile. These small firms where all involved in potential internationalization and globalization of their products or services. To have the right people in the right place at the right time was essential for them.

The knowledge-based economy itself has many components and in the model presented here of feedback from the components it should, in turn, result in information being available to the policy-making process. Governments around the world are looking at output-driven measures, but the input is essential in order to achieve the desired output measures. It is only by putting in support mechanisms and making information available that small firms will be able to use their own knowledge in order to transform the inputs available into meeting the outputs identified by the governments. These outputs, as stated earlier, focus on internationalization, globalization and breaking into new international markets with new innovative products or services. In order to do this, a highly educated workforce is required and, through the innovation process itself, the workforce would be enhanced to an even higher level by the knowledge that they acquired through these aspects. It is through people who have high education levels and those entrepreneurs who are innovative that breakthrough technologies will come. By exploiting these through new business models, such as the use of E-business or the use of international networks, small firms will be able to develop and grow.

SUGGESTED ASSIGNMENTS

Using material from the inyourcity.com case study:

1. As the initial targets for sale are nightclubs, sports venues, restaurants and bars, what is the target market that inyourcity should be aiming their advertising at in order to generate sales to these types of businesses?

2. As a start-up company with limited cash, how would you advertise to this market?

3. Once revenue is established, would you change your advertising strategy and, if so, how?

4. A major problem inyourcity has faced is that their bank refuses to allow them to set up a direct debit arrangement with companies, claiming that it is more cost-effective for them if payments are made by standing order. From the point of view of both the business customers and inyourcity, a direct debit arrangement is best because it means that transaction occurs with least hassle for the business customer. The bank are refusing to allow a direct debit arrangement because they consider it too costly to set up when currently there are few sales.

   How would you deal with this catch-22 situation of being unable to generate sales fully because you don't have a direct debit facility to transact them?

5. What should inyourcity's short-, medium- and long-term strategy be?

REFERENCES

1. Chaston, I., Badger, B., Mangles, T. and Sadler-Smith, E. (2002) 'Knowledge-based Services and the Internet: an investigation of small UK accountancy practices', *Journal of Small Business and Enterprise Development*, vol. 9, no. 1, pp. 49–60.

2. HM Government (1988) *White Paper: Employment for the 1990s*, HMSO, London.

3. Graham, C. and Jackson, J (2001) *e-people: engaging talent in the entrepreneurial age*, Career Innovation, Oxford.

4. Drucker, P.F. (1995) *Managing in a Time of Great Change*, BCA, London.

5. Roos, J., Roos G., Dragonetti, N.C. and Edvinsson, L. (1997) *Intellectual Capital: Navigating the New Business Landscape*, Macmillan Press, Basingstoke.

6. DTI (1999) *Information Society Initiative: Moving into the Information Age 1999 – International Benchmarking Study*, HMSO, London.

7. Hewitt, The Rt. Hon. Patricia (2000) 'Creating Competitive Advantage in the Knowledge Economy', Said Business School, University of Oxford, November.

8. The Scottish Office (1999) *Scotland: Towards the Knowledge Economy* (the Report of the Knowledge Economy Taskforce), The Scottish Office, Edinburgh.

9. Swan, J. (1999) 'Case Studies in Knowledge Management', in *Issues in People Management*, IPD, London.

10. Vaile, M. (2000) 'Australia and the Knowledge Economy', Speech by Australian Minister for Trade, The Economist Intelligence Unit, Canberra, 31 October.

11. Information Technology Advisory Group (ITAG) (2001) 'The Knowledge Economy', Ministry of Economic Development, Manatu Ohanga: http://www.knowledge.gen.nz.

12. De Geus, A. (1988) 'Planning as learning', *Harvard Business Review*, March–April, pp. 70–4.

13. Von Krogh, G. and Roos, J. (1996) *Managing Knowledge: Perspectives on cooperation and competition*, Sage Publications, London.

14. Fleck, J. and Tierney, M. (1991) 'The management of expertise: knowledge, power and the economics of expert labour', Edinburgh PICT Working Paper No. 29, Research Centre for Social Science, University of Edinburgh.

15. Thelwall, M. (2000) 'Effective websites for small and medium sized enterprises', *Journal of Small Business and Enterprise Development*, vol. 10, no. 2, pp. 149–59.

16. Chaston, I. (2000) 'Small Firms and the Impact of the Internet', paper presented to ISBA seminar, Business Link, Lincolnshire, July.

17. Cognitiative (1999) press release, April: www.cognitiative.com.

18. Coussins, C. (1999) *11 Point Plan for Business on the Internet*, Hullachan, Glasgow.

19. Ernst & Young (2000) www.ey.com/global/gcr.nsf/UK/.

20. Aitken, H. (2001) 'Don't believe the hype', *New Business*, Issue 6, April/May.

21. Kanter, R.M. (1999) 'Knowledge management, practically speaking', *Information Systems Management*, Fall, pp. 7–15.

22. Amidon, D.M. (1997) *Innovation Strategy for the Knowledge Economy: The Ken Awakening*, Butterworth-Heinemann, Newton, MA.

23. Boisot, M.H. (1998) *Knowledge Assets: Securing Competitive Advantage in the Information Economy*, Oxford University Press, Oxford.

24. Nonaka, I. and Takeuchi, H. (1995) *The Knowledge-Creating Company*, Oxford University Press, Oxford.

25. Argyris, C. (1996) *On Organisational Learning*, Blackwell, Oxford.

26. Albert, S. and Bradley, K. (1997) *Managing Knowledge: Experts, Agencies and Organisations*, Cambridge University Press, Cambridge.

27. Hendriks, P. (1999) 'Why share knowledge? The influence of ICT on the motivation for knowledge sharing', *Knowledge and Process Management*, vol. 6, no. 2, pp. 91–100.

28. Senge, P.M. (1990) *The Fifth Discipline*, Century Business, London.

29. Porter, M.E. (1990) *The Competitive Advantage of Nations*, MacMillan Press, London.

30. Braganza, A., Edwards, C. and Lambert, R. (1999) 'A taxonomy of knowledge projects to underpin organisational innovation and competitiveness', *Knowledge and Process Management*, vol. 6, no. 2, pp. 83–90.

31. Bower, D.J. and Keogh, W. (1997) 'Conflict and co-operation in technology-based alliances', *International Journal of Innovation Management*, vol. 1, no. 4, pp. 387–409.

32. Garvin, D.A. (1993) 'Building a learning organization', *Harvard Business Review*, July–August, pp. 78–91.

33. OECD (1996) *The Knowledge-Based Economy*, OECD, Paris.

34. Chase, R. (1997) European KM Survey: http://www.knowledgebusiness.com/european.html.

35. KPMG (1998) *Knowledge Management Research Report*, KPMG Management Consulting, London: http://kpmg.interact.nl/publication/survey.shtml.

36. Garvin, D.A. (1998) 'Building the learning organization', *Harvard Business Review* on *Knowledge Management*, Harvard Business School Press, Boston.

37. Rajan, A., Lank, E. and Chapple, K. (1999) *Good Practices in Knowledge Management and Exchange*, Focus, London.

38. Davis, S. and Bodkin, J. (1994) 'The Coming of Knowledge-Based Business', *Harvard Business Review*, September–October, pp. 165–70.

39. Grant, R.M. and Baden-Fuller, C. (2000) 'Knowledge and Economic Organization: An Application to the Analysis of Interfirm Collaboration', in von Krogh, G., Nonaka, I. and Nishiguchi, T. (eds) *Knowledge Creation: A Source of Value*, MacMillan Press, Basingstoke.

40. Nishiguchi, T. and Beaudet, A. (2000) 'Fractal Design: Self-organising Links in Supply Chain Management', in von Krogh, G., Nonaka, I. and Nishiguchi, T. (eds) *Knowledge Creation: A Source of Value*, MacMillan Press, Basingstoke.

41. Cox, B. (1979) *Value Added*, Heinemann, London.

42. Manganelli, R.L. and Klein, M.M. (1994) *The Reengineering Handbook*, Amacom, New York.

43. Stewart, T. (1997) *Intellectual Capital: The New Wealth of Organisations*, Nicholas Brealey Publishing, London.

44. Oakey, R.P. (1995) *High-technology New Firms: Variable Barriers to Growth*, Paul Chapman, London.

45. Keogh, W., Evans, G. and Blaydon C. (1999) 'The deployment of strategies for growth within NTBFs in the Aberdeen area of Scotland', in Oakey, R., During, W. and Mukhtar, S-M. (eds) *New Technology-Based Firms in the 1990s, Vol. VI*, Paul Chapman, London.

46. Mintzberg, H. (1989) *Mintzberg on Management*, Free Press, New York.

47. Autio, E. and Klofsten, M. (1998) 'A Comparative Study of Two European Business Incubators', *Journal of Small Business Management*, vol. 36, no. 1, pp. 30–43.

48. HM Government (1994) *Competitiveness – Helping Business to Win*, HMSO, London.

49. HM Government (1997) *The Development of Skills and Adaptable Workforces United Kingdom Action Plan: The New Agenda*, HMSO, London.

50. British Chambers of Commerce (in association with Alex Lawrie) (1998) *Small Firms Survey: Skills*, British Chambers of Commerce, London.

51. Keogh, W. and Stewart, V. (2001) 'Identifying the skill requirements of the workforce in SMEs: Findings from a European Social Fund Project', *Journal of Small Business and Enterprise Development*, vol. 8, no. 2, pp. 140–9.

52. Harrison, R. (1998) *Employee Development*, 2nd edn, IPD, London.

53. Scott, P., Jones, B., Bramley, A. and Bolton, B. (1996) 'Enhancing Technology and Skills in Small and Medium-Sized Manufacturing Firms: Problems And Prospects', *International Small Business Journal*, vol. 14, no. 3, pp. 85–99.

RECOMMENDED READING

Argyris, C. (1996) *On Organisational Learning*, Blackwell, Oxford.

Foresight Information, Communications and Media Panel (2000) *Let's Get Digital*, DTI, London.

Foresight (2001) *Electronic Commerce Task Force Report*, DTI, London.

Foresight Financial Services Panel SME Sub-Group (2001) *Financing the Enterprise Society*, DTI, London.

Institute of Personnel and Development (1999) *Case Studies in Knowledge Management*, IPD, London.

Internet Sources

For statistics

www.e-insight.com
www.bt.com

For search engines

www.altavista.co.uk
www.google.co.uk
www.ask.co.uk

For directories

www.yahoo.co.uk

Useful links

www.clubtrade.com
www.linkshare.com

9

ENTERPRISE SUPPORT AND GOVERNMENT POLICY

LEARNING OUTCOMES

At the end of this chapter students should be able to:

1. Describe the range and diversity of government enterprise initiatives designed to encourage and foster the development of the enterprise culture.
2. Describe examples of business development support provision.
3. Discuss the roles of different support agencies and the level of UK enterprise support provision.
4. Describe the advantages of networking between agencies and other institutions involved in the support of new ventures.
5. Compare UK levels of networking to the German and French experience and the role of German and French Chambers of Commerce.
6. Describe criteria that can be used to evaluate state schemes.
7. Discuss problems with the term 'enterprise culture'.
8. Discuss both positive and negative aspects of the attempt to create an enterprise culture.

INTRODUCTION

Government intervention and public sector funded support for enterprise has matched the growth of enterprise activity in the UK, as described in Chapter 2. For example, during the 1980s, the philosophy of the Thatcher administration fitted the more important role given to enterprise and entrepreneurship. At the time, the small firm and 'enterprise' were seen as the key to reducing unemployment and evidence was also beginning to emerge that small firms could be important for future job creation.[1] Successive administrations since then have continued to foster enterprise support, although the mechanisms and agencies used to deliver enterprise support have changed with each newly elected government, with the most recent change coming with the introduction of the Small Business Service, modelled, at least partly, on the USA's Small Business Administration.[2] In this chapter we examine the principles of government and publicly-funded intervention, discuss the many changes that have occurred in the UK and make some comparisons with other systems of enterprise support in Europe.

A simplified version of the framework of support agencies that will be referred to in this chapter is shown, for England and Wales, in Figure 9.1, and for Scotland, which has different support agencies, the equivalent structure is shown by Figure 9.2. These illustrations do not attempt to show all the agencies involved in providing advice and

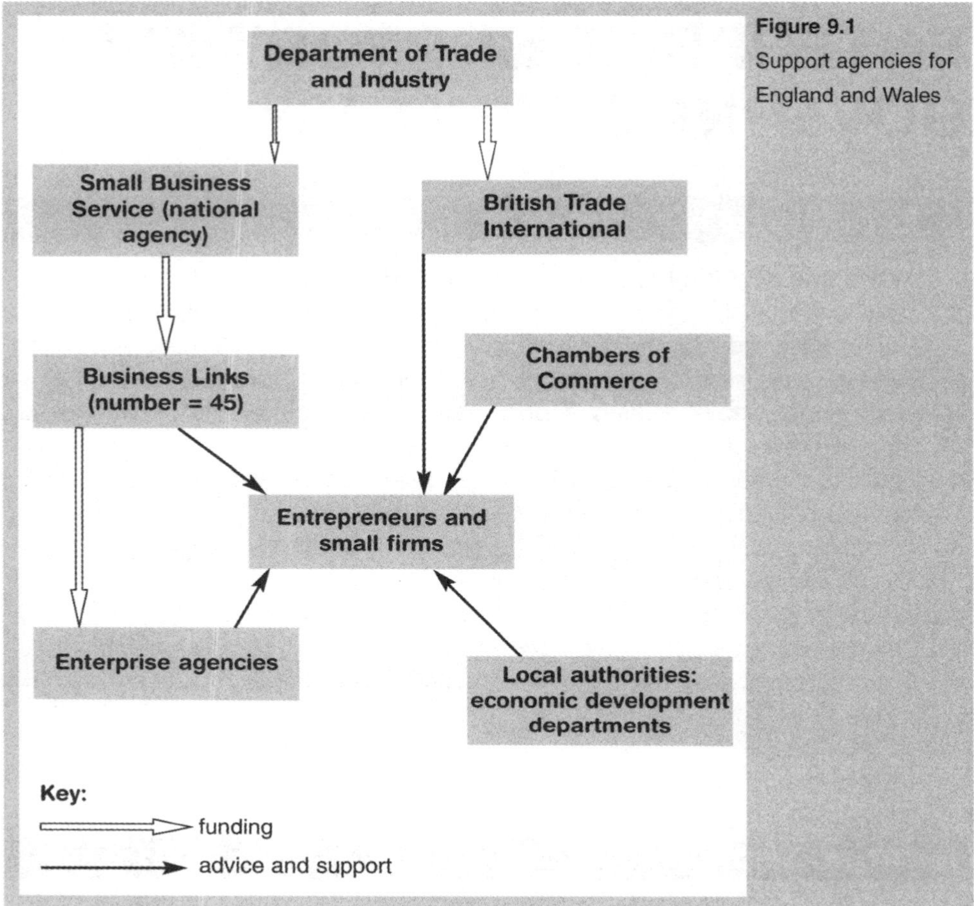

Figure 9.1 Support agencies for England and Wales

support to entrepreneurs and small firms, but show the relative funding links between different agencies.

What is Enterprise Support?

Throughout this chapter we will refer to business and enterprise support, but what does this mean and what forms can it take? Enterprise support may range form intensive one-to-one counselling and adviser support to individual entrepreneurs, to the mere provision of additional information. The entrepreneur–adviser relationship may also vary in intensity over time, from days to years, with longer periods for these relationships usually referred to as mentoring relationships. Figure 9.3 illustrates the different nature of enterprise support, the role of the support agency, which may employ the adviser or pay a consultant to provide the advice, and the entrepreneur–adviser relationship.

Before we discuss the nature of enterprise support provision, it is worth noting that it is debatable whether to provide enterprise support through publicly-funded agencies

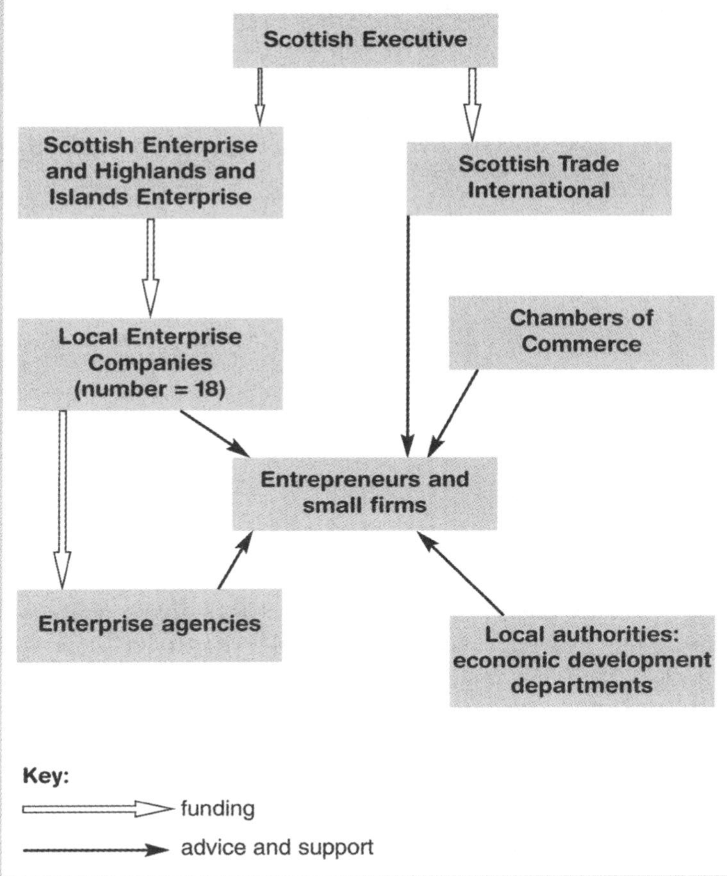

Scottish Executive
Scottish Enterprise and Highlands and Islands Enterprise
Scottish Trade International
Chambers of Commerce
Local Enterprise Companies (number = 18)
Entrepreneurs and small firms
Enterprise agencies
Local authorities: economic development departments
Key:
funding
advice and support

Figure 9.2
Support agencies for Scotland

Entrepreneur
Information and funding
Fee-based advice
Counselling advice
Business adviser
Consultant
Employed
Funded
Enterprise support agency

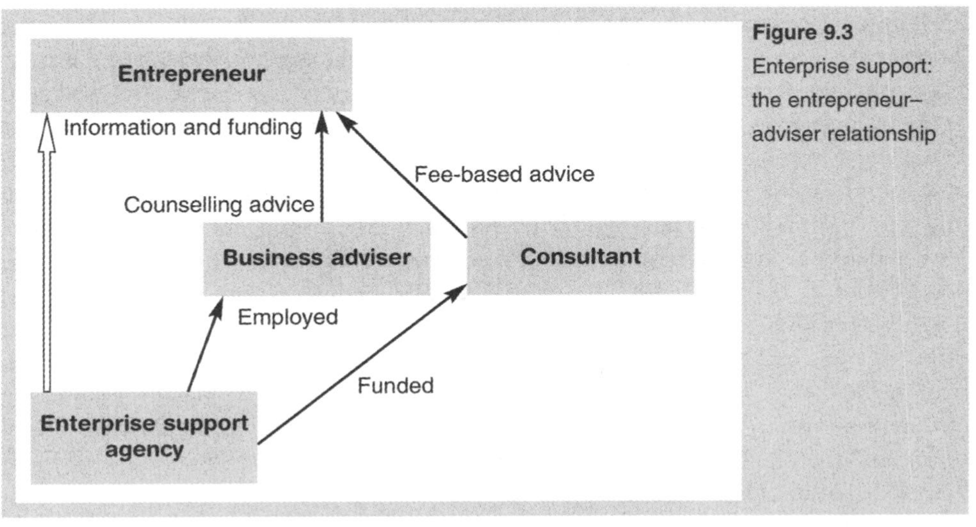

Figure 9.3
Enterprise support: the entrepreneur–adviser relationship

at all. For example, Curran has argued that although there has been extensive provision, the take-up of such support has been very low and has not been cost-effective.[3] Gibb has also argued that support policies have been based on shaky assumptions of small firm entrepreneurial performance.[4] We will discuss the value of enterprise support provision in more detail later in this chapter, but first we describe the nature and type of support provision.

To provide a framework to discuss the principles of support provision it is useful to use a categorization as follows:

1. Business start-up and aftercare support

2. General business development support

3. Export and trade development

1. Business Start-up and Aftercare Support

Start-up support is designed to provide some initial pre-start advice and basic business training to ensure that new start businesses are better prepared to cope with the difficult early months of trading. New start-up businesses are vulnerable to failure (UK figures from the SME statistics unit suggest up to 30 per cent failure rates in the first year), but start-up support can have dramatic effects on improving survival rates, especially when start-up advice and training is combined with aftercare support. Aftercare support, where provided, is designed to provide a one-to-one advisory support structure over the early trading months of a business. Aftercare may vary from a few months to several years. In the UK, at best, we can say that start-up support and aftercare has varied, dependent on the objectives of state policy. For example, in the 1980s the Enterprise Allowance Scheme (EAS) provided an incentive for business start-up, but this was replaced in the 1990s with a shift in focus to support for established firms only through the Business Link network (outside Scotland). Finally, more recently the introduction of the Small Business Service, from April 2001, has shifted focus to supporting targeted, growth-based start-up businesses.[2] The extent of aftercare support, when and where provided, has also varied from one geographical locality to another. The extent has varied from a few months to up to three years. Even within one area, large variations can exist in the type of support and training, where individual enterprise agencies deliver support rather than one agency or organization across an administrative area, such as those identified for Training and Enterprise Councils (TECs) (from 1990 to 2000 in England and Wales) and Local Enterprise Companies (LECs) in Scotland. Each TEC/LEC area has had different patterns of support, delivered by different agencies, even within their own area. These differences in delivery are not explained by targeting different groups. To add to confusion and potential duplication, the Prince's Youth Business Trust (PYBT) has provided selective start-up and aftercare support for those under 26 years across all the TEC/LEC areas with a standard 18-month period of aftercare support.

Segmentation

New start-up ventures, like all small firms, are characterized by *diversity*. Even where start-up support has been part of policy (such as Scotland), such diversity has resulted in the segmentation of support. Every start-up entrepreneur, potentially, requires a different level of support; lifestyle businesses have different requirements from start-up companies with high growth potential. Hence, there is a need to reconcile consistency with flexibility through the integration of support services. Providing adviser-based start-up support to all businesses is expensive for any length of time beyond an initial start-up advice service; however, economic and environmental trends support a policy that encourages new start entrepreneurship. Segmentation provides scope to reconcile the twin aims of consistency and flexibility. For example, in Scotland, most of the LECs provided some segmentation of support for new start businesses with both a volume provision and more selective support for higher growth potential start-up businesses during the 1990s. This selectivity has also been driven by different European funding regimes.

START-UP AND AFTERCARE SUPPORT: SELECTIVITY

It is too expensive to provide business advice to all new business owners on a one-to-one basis. Business advisers have to meet their clients frequently and may have intensive periods of counselling sessions.

Example

In the Strathclyde European Partnership (SEP) Objective 2 area, in recent years, it has only been possible to get ERDF money for start-up support for growth businesses (defined by SEP as a start-up business having growth potential of £100,000 turnover or the ability to employ more than one person after one year). This has tended to drive the nature of aftercare support for start-ups in Strathclyde, leading to the segmentation of aftercare support between volume businesses and growth businesses. To illustrate this, in Dunbartonshire, where three Enterprise Trusts delivered the programme, start-up and aftercare business support has been rationalized from a previous 18-month period for all start-ups to just an initial advisory/basic training support for volume business and a more intensive aftercare support for the growth potential businesses of 18 months.[5]

Continuity

It is arguable that some businesses will need the continuity of pre-start, start-up, aftercare and business development adviser support. In the same way that start-up support has varied across areas and, historically, practice has varied, not only has the extent and length of aftercare varied, but also the continuity of support has varied. In principle, early stage clients may be passed on to general business development adviser support, but in practice there has been a sharp division of support, with different agencies focusing on different types of support and in some cases overlapping areas of responsibility.[6] However, many early stage business clients, perhaps at a critical stage in their development, will not have access to further support. Segmentation, driven by public and European funding (ERDF), has meant that only the higher growth potential clients have received intensive and proactive aftercare support in a limited number of areas in England and Wales.

Integrated Model: The Business Link Model

Business Links (introduced in the early 1990s) were meant to be an integrated model of business support, a one-stop shop. This has some attractions since resources, information and delivery can all be provided in the one location. Advisers can easily speak to each other and with trainers, managers and specialist advisers. The Business Links were also meant to combine different initiatives under one roof, such as the DTI Information Society Initiative to provide, for example, an IT centre for training, advice and consultation. However, as reviewed by a number of writers, the provision of such an integrated one-stop shop has been highly variable.[7,8]

Special Needs Groups

The provision of volume adviser support, where limited start-up advice is given, can ignore the needs of special groups where there is case for more targeted and more specialized support. For example, in Birmingham specialized agencies, such as Black Business in Birmingham (3bs), aim to cater for the needs of ethnic minorities in business. In Glasgow the Wellpark Enterprise Centre has been promoted as an example of specialized support for women from socially excluded groups by a Bank of England report.[9] Other cities have similar targeted support agencies. The advantage of providing specialized, targeted support at special needs groups is that it can integrate business development with economic inclusion and establish business forums that maintain links with such business groups. For example, in Scotland the Scottish Ethnic Minority Business Forum operates in both the west and east of Scotland to provide a networking forum representing the needs of EMBs and is a valuable mechanism for communicating initiatives targeted at the EMB sector (see also a discussion of networking in Chapter 4).

It is arguable that technology-based start-ups should receive specialized start-up support and longer aftercare provision, given their special requirements for funding and, in some cases, R&D. The current focus on exploiting commercialization is important for the UK's economy and some Business Links and LECs have integrated support linked to HEIs. For example, in the east of scotland, Dundee Technopole combined with BioDundee has established a partnership linking to world-class expertise in the University of Dundee in bio-sciences resulting in an incubator and Medipark and a successful bio-science cluster.

The complexity of the support picture across the UK is illustrated by the confusing range of specialist support agencies that may provide advice to technology-based start-up firms, women-in-business, ethnic minority firms and other categories of firm which may qualify for a range of support, funding and specialized advice.

ENTREPRENEURSHIP IN ACTION

Should enterprise support for women be delivered by specialist centres?

Targeting enterprise support through specialized support for women may have beneficial effects. In Glasgow, the Wellpark Centre was highlighted by the Bank of England.[9] Wellpark operated as a specialized managed workspace for women's enterprise. A recent policy report on women's enterprise for the Industrial Society was remarkable for the finding that there had been little change in the issues facing women in enterprise over the past 15 years and called for a national centre for women's enterprise as a necessary development to shift assumptions and profile women's enterprise.[10]

The advantage of a national centre is that it can raise the profile of women in enterprise, promote role models, lobby for developments in training that cater for more diversity, provide information and deliver support. It would have a role that went beyond the delivery of enterprise support for women. Such centres exist in the USA through Women's Business Centers, but they are not engaged directly in women's enterprise support delivery.

An alternative approach is to ensure that women's support is adequately catered for through the provision of cultural and social diversity awareness training with business advisers. Women in business may not need women business advisers but, in order for them to be able to place confidence in their advisers, they do need advisers who are sensitive to their needs and aware of issues that they face. Although improvements have been made in the accreditation and training of advisers through programmes introduced by the SBS in England and Wales and Scottish Enterprise in Scotland, a study by the author and colleagues indicated that greater attention was required to issues of diversity awareness and training with business advisers and support networks.[11]

Similar arguments could be applied to the need to develop distinctive enterprise support policies aimed at ethnic minority and young entrepreneurs.

2. General Business Development Support

Small firms do not have the resources to employ specialists and general business development support may be designed to meet specific short-term needs of companies, for example in IT or finance. Support may be designed to meet longer-term needs through more general development advice. This is more likely to involve business advisers (from Business Links) operating in a facilitation role, which recognizes that a company's needs will change over time. Thus, to explain provision in this section, we classify support into the following categories or levels of general business development support programmes:

(a) Short-term and episodic part-funded external consultancy (including marketing, finance, IT and HRM), such as 'expert help'.

(b) Medium-term programmes targeted at specific aspects of business development, such as innovation.

(c) Longer-term relationships such as mentoring and key adviser support.

(a) Short-term Support

The principle of short-term 'expert' help assumes that a company's need for support will be essentially sporadic and short-lived. It assumes that the business client can self-diagnose their problems and need for help; yet such support is often driven by assumed needs of small firms rather than diagnosed individual needs. Such support will meet a one-off need for help in a specific area such as finance, marketing or IT management systems. In England with the Business Links and in Scotland with the LECs, a wide variety of schemes have had the same essential characteristics – all have variants of programmes that provide scope for complexity in the provision of services and in the business community.

(b) Medium-term Programmes

Medium-term support programmes attempt to build a longer working relationship based on client need. Examples include the Regional Innovation Strategies (RIS) developed with European funding in the West Midlands, Yorkshire and Humberside and Strathclyde. Such a RIS is developed into local area programmes by the TECs/ LECs working with client companies over an extended period to instill management change within the company. Another example includes UK national initiatives, such as Quality Management (ISO 9000) and Investors in People, which review firm performance and take the business through a planned strategy of improvements which may be introduced in a phased manner over an extended period of time; that may take several years to implement.

(c) Longer-term Relationships

The pattern of support provided generally by Business Links matches the shorter-term approaches with personal business advisers (PBAs) operating from Business Links to deliver short-term, semi-diagnostic support. This has been episodic in nature and, as discussed above, varies from one locality to another. Overlaying this pattern of support have been mentoring-related initiatives introduced in England and Wales by the DTI and in Scotland by the Scottish Executive. For example, in Scotland, a Scotland-wide national mentoring scheme, Business Mentoring Scotland, was introduced in 2000 with the aim of using successful entrepreneurs in a long-term relationship with a small company to help them achieve better growth and performance.

Quality of Advice

The quality of business advice available has been highlighted as an area of concern by small firm pressure groups and business communities.[12] As a result, with the introduction of the Small Business Service a major concern has been to establish an accreditation system for PBAs.[13] In contrast to England and Wales, it is only recently that moves to establish an accreditation system for business advisers in Scotland have been introduced by Scottish Enterprise.

SUMMARY

General business development support

- Overall a notable lack of consistency and potential duplication dominates the provision of general business development support for established businesses. We have discussed the diversity that characterizes the SME sector; this diversity gives rise to a proliferation of different needs which may involve short-, medium- or longer-term needs for help.
- Business development support programmes will meet some specific needs but they also contribute to confusion due to the variety of schemes and the range of agencies and authorities involved. They vary from one Business Link area to another, which cannot be ascribed merely to differences in European Objective status.
- A complaint of the business community, that the existence and levels of support varies across different Business Link/LEC areas (i.e. the lack of a consistent 'level playing field'), is particularly relevant in this category of business development support.

3. Export and Trade Development

Small firm entrepreneurs face difficulties in exporting due to the greater financial requirements, longer credit terms required and knowledge about overseas trade regulations. Historically, successive UK governments have attempted to provide support that met the perceived needs of small firms through finance (export credits), access to information and an 'export help' service provided through the DTI. However, there was still local variety in the form of advice provided and it is only recently that a national strategy has been developed that co-ordinates such support at a local level.

British Trade International has developed a national export development strategy that seeks to provide local assistance through locally based Local Export Partnerships. These represent a local partnership that combines the work of local agencies which may include Chambers of Commerce, local authorities and Business Links/LECs. The role of each body varies, but generally Business Links work with small firms to develop capacity and awareness, chambers provide information, documentation and training, and local councils, where they are involved, may provide support for international trade missions.

As a result of a special study undertaken by the author and colleagues for the Scottish Parliament,[12] two case examples of local provision of exporting help are given below (see boxes).

ENTREPRENEURSHIP IN ACTION: SUPPORT FOR EXPORTERS

Case Example 1: Central Scotland: Forth Valley

The Trade Development Centre (TDC) is funded by Forth Valley Enterprise, three local authorities (Falkirk, Stirling and Clackmannanshire) and the Chamber of Commerce for Central Scotland. The Centre has the advantage of providing a single access point for all export services to companies in the local area of Central Scotland.

The Centre's services include export advisory services, export documentation, information and intelligence-gathering services, developing export plans with individual companies, export-related training and the normal links and support into trade missions and overseas exhibitions. The TDC is able to run a series of export-related events and training seminars at the TDC.

The TDC has been able to use its integrated facility to develop a website, www.scotexport.org.uk, to provide online help and advice. Local exporting companies are offered a free web page listing in the Forth Valley Trade Directory, enabling access via the website to a potential worldwide market.

ENTREPRENEURSHIP IN ACTION: SUPPORT FOR EXPORTERS

Case Example 2: Highlands and Islands Trade and Export Partnership

The Highlands and Islands Trade and Export Partnership (HITEP) is funded by Highlands and Islands Enterprise (HIE) and Scottish Trade International. It operates as a partnership between the Highlands and Islands LEC Network, the five local councils in the Highlands and Islands and Inverness and District Chamber of Commerce.

Integration is achieved through an Export Development Manager based at HIE in Inverness, who acts as a facilitator and co-ordinator of HITEP. HITEP provides an extensive exporting advisory and information service for companies in the Highlands and Islands. More intensive training and mentoring help is provided through export mentors and companies can also qualify for a range of assistance to help them break into new markets in Europe and overseas.

HITEP also operate an export club, the Highland Export Club, which provides a networking forum for local companies to exhange information, problems and experience and raise awareness of events, training and overseas trade missions and exhibitions.

Although there has been considerable improvement in the delivery of assistance to small exporting companies, the extent of successful integration in local area trade and export partnerships (TEPs) can vary. Practice varies because differences exist in the relative strengths of different Chambers of Commerce. Nevertheless, TEPs have been successful in co-ordinating different sources of export support and simplifying the point of access for exporting companies. The complexity of advice and support in this area is illustrated by the complexity of information. For example, information available from a Euroinfo Centre on one enquiry ran to 99 pages. In such circumstances there is danger that a company will be overwhelmed by the sheer scale of different and complex information. It could be considered essential to provide clarity and guidance for the initial enquiry. Integration at one centre has the advantage that correct signposting is more likely to be achieved.

THINK POINTS 9.1

1. What examples can you give of the different relationships that might exist between entrepreneurs and business advisers/consultants?
2. What role can enterprise support agencies take in your examples given in your answer to Q1?
3. Argue the case for start-up enterprise support.
4. Give examples of good practice in enterprise support; what principles are illustrated by such examples?

SUPPORTING ENTERPRISE

Successive governments' desire to support enterprise and develop an 'enterprise culture' in the UK can be traced back to Lord Young's statement in the mid 1980s:[14] 'The restoration of enterprise in Britain has played a major role in the revival of growth, employment and prosperity' (p. 34). Since the 1980s, governments have claimed that they have created the right environment for successful enterprise and entrepreneurship. This can be seen even in recent documents. For example, a key aim of the recently established Small Business Service[13,15] is to make Britain 'the best place in the world in which to start and grow a new business'[13] (p. 6).

Over this time a network of different enterprise support agencies has been established along with, in particular, the development of the enterprise agencies (or, in Scotland, enterprise trusts), Training and Enterprise Councils (TECs) and in Scotland the Local Enterprise Companies (LECs). By the 1990s the confusing haphazard pattern of enterprise agencies led to the establishment of the Business Link network, created in an attempt to co-ordinate support provision in England and Wales. (Scotland has Business Shops, but here their role is more concerned with signposting rather than a co-ordinating role. In 2001–2 delivery of enterprise support is now the responsibility of a national Small Business Gateway in Scotland.) In the 1990s the provision of enterprise support as part of government policy has lost much of its political dimension. For example, the election of a Labour Government in 1997 has, if anything, reinforced enterprise support policy. For example, Barbara Roche, the Small Firms' Minister at the time (1997), indicated that Business Links were to be the prime vehicle of support for small firms.[16] Since then the introduction of the Small Business Service (SBS) in 2000–01 has seen the role of TECs redefined and relaunched as Learning and Skills Councils and the merger of a number of Business Links as they have tendered for the local franchises for the SBS. The potential for overlap and duplication remains, however, with the introduction of Regional Development Agencies, which have the power to develop their own enterprise support strategy.[17] See for example the Yorkshire Forward's (Yorkshire and Humberside's RDA) Business Birth Rate Strategy.[18]

Although Business Links are often seen as the primary vehicle for enterprise support, there are in practice many organizations involved in the infrastructure of enterprise support in any one area. These organizations include local authorities, Chambers of Commerce, banks, training agencies and others.

TYPE AND METHOD OF SUPPORT

As can be seen from the discussion so far in this chapter, there are considerable differences in the way that support can be provided. For example, there may be provision of short-term (part-funded) consultancy to meet a specific short-term need for expert advice; alternatively other programmes may provide longer-term support to meet an ongoing need for general business advice. These different forms of advice/counselling may be supplemented by other support such as grant aid, access to finance and training. We discuss below some of the issues in the different types of support provided.

Part-funded Consultancy

The use of business consultants has grown dramatically in both the private sector and the public sector in the last decade. As a result, consultancy has become a virtual industry in its own right, with nearly 12,000 consultancy firms by the 1990s.[19] One of the reasons for this growth has been the availability and use of (part) publicly funded consultants, in the belief that SMEs do not have the resources or the time to undertake specialized market research or other functions that larger firms can carry out, but would benefit from having greater access to such expertise.

Much of the research on the impact of consultancy utilizes satisfaction measures.[20,21] For example, the study by Segal *et al.* into the government's Consultancy Initiatives used two main measures, turnover and value added, to reflect different types of the potential impact of consultancy on businesses.[22] The satisfaction measures were high (77 per cent of the firms rated the scheme as satisfactory or better in terms of their part of the consultancy cost), whereas the hard measures demonstrated a substantial shortfall between what consultants promised and subsequently delivered (on average, gross impact, as measured at the follow-up interview, was 40 per cent of the forecast of impact made at the initial interview). However, there was a striking variation on the impact of the initiative. For the smallest firms, those with less than 10 employees, actual gross impact was only 9 per cent of the forecast; for firms with 100–249 employees the corresponding figure was 10 per cent; however, for other size groups, actual/forecast gross impact on turnover ranged from 40 per cent to 167 per cent.

Most models of the consulting process follow Schein's classic consulting typology in which he advocates a collaborative, non-expert role for the consultant with the focus on the process and helping the client to define diagnostic interventions.[23] Schein's vision of the consultant is in a non-expert, collaborative capacity. This difference between the process and task consultants is particularly important for the appropriate role of the consultant with small firms. For smaller firms, it is suggested that Schein's process consultation role is more appropriate than the expert role. Under the expert role, which frequently occurs when small firm owner-managers are referred for specialist help, successful outcomes are crucially dependent on self-diagnosis by the small firm entrepreneur. Under the process consultation role, the consultant is involved through helping clients help themselves, and assumes that the client is unable to diagnose the problem. As a result, the key to successful consultation is diagnosis. Since it can be questioned whether small firm entrepreneurs can successfully self-diagnose, it is arguable that the process consultation model or role is more appropriate for small firms. As a further result, there is then a role, in theory, for support agencies in the diagnosis process.

Research carried out by the author and colleagues into one part-funded consultancy scheme found that there was an inappropriate match between the use of expert consultancy and the needs of small firms on the scheme.[24]

Longer-term Relationships with Small Firms

There are a variety of ways in which longer-term relationships may be developed. For example, Business Links have introduced the principle of an in-depth diagnostic service available to growth-seeking companies. It can be disputed whether PBAs see themselves as consultants, but as one survey of PBAs points out, 'a number of pressures are shifting the focus of the role of PBAs to that of consultant.'[25] The creation of Business Links – and hence PBAs – which have a pivotal role at the crux of the Business Link service, has been the subject of some criticism;[26] the expense associated with providing an extensive up-front consultancy service, available on demand, places large-scale support provision in some jeopardy.[27] The creation of Business Links and the pivotal role of the PBA has been made at considerable public expense, but with little knowledge of the potential value of the 'mentoring' role of the PBA/consultant with small firms and little previous research into this relationship and the impact that it can have on small firm development. Hence the critical review by Curran that calls into question, after 20 years, the value of having enterprise support at all.[3]

Research by the author and colleagues with a local scheme in Scotland, which provided mentors for selected start-up small firms, found that there was considerable value added as a result of the mentoring support.[28] The study confirmed that the programme of mentoring support was highly valued by the clients. Following the second stage analysis it was possible to identify the main areas of value added by the mentoring support as:

- **clients had a clearer focus on achieving objectives;**
- **clients were more likely to use business planning;**
- **clients were focused on profitability rather than just turnover or cash;**
- **helping new entrepreneurs to learn, manage their businesses and cope with change.**

Value added of such impacts cannot be measured precisely, but mentoring support did have results in terms of better performance of new start businesses, better competitiveness and hence better survival rates. The impacts on performance and achieving objectives were validated through the performance of the clients in the sample who, on average, met or exceeded their projected performance targets from the first stage.

Providing publicly funded long-term support, however, may be prohibitively expensive for some agencies. Agencies can overcome this through having a free diagnostic service, followed by a fee-based advice/counselling service. As stated above, this can increase pressure on PBAs to become consultants. An alternative that may be appropriate for some small firms, particularly strong growth performers, is to provide an initial mentoring service which may convert into the mentor taking a non-executive director (NED) role in the later development of the company. Research by the author and colleagues into the role of NEDs in small companies found largely positive findings.[29] For carefully selected firms, NEDs provided a close model of the mentor relationship for small, growing firms. Such selected firms could be encouraged to appoint a NED on a purely commercial basis. Agencies could promote and support the development of a list of appropriate people to be NEDs in such growing small firms.

The Role of Support Agencies

Enterprise Agencies (EAs) and Business Links (BLs) have mirrored the development of state concern with support for small firms. At one time there were over 300 such agencies in the UK. Part of their role has been to nurture the growth of start-up business, to unlock the potential for entrepreneurial activity and to raise enterprise awareness. The ad hoc development of the support agency movement means that provision of support, spatially and vertically, is the result of chance, accidents of geography and the economic mix of the environment that happened to exist at the time that different agencies were formed. Despite the considerable framework of support that now exists (established in the 1990s), the delivery of small business advice varies considerably from agency to agency. There are huge asymmetries in the size, staffing and operation of individual agencies. Some agencies provide merely basic counselling advice for start-ups; others have a full range of training and consultancy services for the SME community. An earlier study by the author revealed that a range of support services was common, such as business clubs, financial support, clerical services, databases and additional business services.[30] There was an uneven geographical pattern of support, with over-provision of support in some areas and under-provision in others.

TECs and LECs also vary in size (and budget) even though they were supposed to be based on local labour markets with populations of 250,000. There have been a number of studies that have examined the concept and remit of TECs. Bennett *et al.* have argued that the TECs were given insufficient empowerment:[31]

> ***“ The key impediments to business development in the UK is that not enough power has yet been given out to redress a century long imbalance that has frustrated Britain's economic growth. ” (p. vii)***

TECs have had a relatively short life of less than 10 years. Their remit has been refocused on learning and skills development and they have been renamed Learning and Skills Councils. Their enterprise support role has now been taken over by the Small Business Service, which will continue to operate through the Business Links (in England and Wales). In their short life, TECs have still attracted criticism. For example, Topham *et al.* compared the budgets of TECs to social and business needs of their areas.[32] Ranking by budget did not match local needs, the implicit conclusion being that many TECs were not able to meet local needs. Curran has argued that there was a low level of awareness of local TECs by the small business community and concluded that TECs were unable to reach small firms and provide appropriate enterprise support.[33] However, more recent evidence did indicate that TECs had raised their profile with the local enterprise community.[34]

Whether support agency intervention makes an effective difference to small business development is a moot point. If agencies are to be effective then their role lies in unlocking latent entrepreneurial talent. This is obviously difficult to achieve, but is associated with their effectiveness in raising their profile in the small business community and the extent to which members of the community can be targeted. Since agencies have been criticized for their low profile, it is possible to argue they have had little impact on small business development. For example, Casson has argued that empirical evidence suggests that interventions to promote small firm start-ups are unlikely to stimulate entrepreneurship.[35] Business In The Community (BITC) reports suggest support is effective in creating sustainable businesses but the actual difference that the agency makes is difficult to assess.[36] Moore[37] has suggested that the impact of EAs can vary from 'marginal to significant' (pp. 24–25). More recent studies, however, have suggested that there is tentative evidence of positive impacts from the Business Links.[38,39] A review of the evidence by Storey suggested that the level of enterprise support is not a significant factor in the development of SMEs.[40] However, an evaluation of TEC services for the DTI by PA Cambridge Consultants[41] concluded that:

> ***“[Overall] some jobs are created – but are largely offset – by displacement ... the more significant benefits arise through increased efficiency and profitability in small firms.” (p. 1)***

SUMMARY

The role of support agencies

- The quality of support in the UK has, so far, been very variable.
- The effectiveness of support is determined by the degree of selectivity, of co-ordination and collaboration of different agencies and the profile of the agency.
- Previous research has suggested that the collaboration and co-ordination between different support agencies is very limited when compared to other levels of networking that take place, for example in Germany.[42]
- Links between agencies and other institutions in the infrastructure of support are relatively undeveloped.[43]
- Co-ordination of support between EAs and other institutions has been slow to develop. While there is continual changes in the structure of support and funding mechanisms this lack of co-ordination is likely to remain.

The Role of Support Agencies: Example of a Business Link

Business Links were charged with the role of bringing together the often confusing pattern of support that faces the entrepreneur or small firm owner. In a paper addressing specifically the role of Business Links, Bennett claimed that such institutions have the potential to meet the needs of SMEs for assistance, but policy suffered from bureaucratic and financial constraints.[44] We draw upon the example of Business Link Birmingham (BLB) to illustrate the role of Business Links. BLB saw itself as a single gateway for existing firms seeking assistance with their business problems. In general, Business Links provide support in the following areas: marketing, business survival, staff and management training, quality management, corporate and business planning, European issues and information.[45] In BLB's case, eight areas had been identified: exporting, sales and marketing, quality, team development, management and finance, legal and regulation, property and technology.

BLB offered help at three levels. The first level was information and advice in response to enquiries through an easy-to-remember phone number. The second level involved the business adviser service. If the client wished, they could be allocated a personal business adviser (PBA) whose role was to carry out a diagnostic check or 'health check' on the business. For example, an officer commented:

" It is at that point that we bring the PBA in, which is a free service, which is working with the client anything up to three days to assess the real needs of the business. "

The third level involves the referral of the client to an agency, which will attempt to carry out the PBA's recommendations. It was regarded that this was more than a simple referral, with a continual review by the PBA, who is charged with the responsibility of ensuring that the project is completed successfully.

Business Links, via the role of the Small Business Service, have been charged with helping to support new start innovative growth firms;[46] previously their remit had focused on established firms employing more than 10 staff. Supporting new starts selectively, however, introduces a targeting approach. In the case of BLB, the idea that Business Links could target 'winners' was not backed by any criteria for targeting such firms beyond a belief that they would be self-selecting. In BLB's case it was believed that such firms would select themselves by coming forward for assistance.

The creation of Business Links has offered an opportunity both to rationalize support in the UK (by reducing duplication) and to develop some specialization by different EAs. However, we found that, in the case of Birmingham, there was little attempt to do either. Some provision for targeted support to ethnic minority clients was provided, as might be expected, but there was no attempt to encourage specialization beyond that which already existed. For example, the director of BLB was of the opinion that:

"I do not see it [rationalization] personally as a saving; I see it as an opportunity to spot the gaps – and retrain the resource to the gaps which we may well define as a service that is needed."

THINK POINTS 9.2

The role of support agencies

1. What enterprise support agencies exist in the UK?

2. Which of the following characteristics apply to enterprise support provision in the UK?
   - Consistency
   - Quality
   - Integrated
   - Networked
   - Segmented support
   - Value for money

   What factors account for your answer?

3. What is the role of the personal business adviser (PBA)?

4. How does the role of the PBA differ from that of a paid consultant?

COMPARATIVE PRACTICE IN ENTERPRISE SUPPORT

Figure 9.4 illustrates the more simplified model of support in Germany. The primary source of advice for most small firms is the Industrie-und Handelskammern (IHK), the local Chambers of Commerce. Membership of the IHK is compulsory for most small firms and, hence, these institutions are much stronger than UK Chambers of Commerce and play a much more pivotal role in promotion and dissemination of information. There is also a greater diversity of financial institutions.

The regional states, the Länder, have considerable independence and power to implement their own investment and funding programmes. In the UK there are no such powerful organizations as the IHK and the Länder. In the West Midlands, during the 1990s alone there were 10 TECs and we have argued that such agencies are too small to make an effective difference to the level of enterprise support and training.[42] However, the Regional Development Agencies established in England and Wales do have considerable powers (for example to introduce their own regional venture capital funds) and may be able to make more significant interventions.

In Baden-Württemberg the IHK was able to provide specialist support and training for high-technology small firms by having a director who specialized in technology.

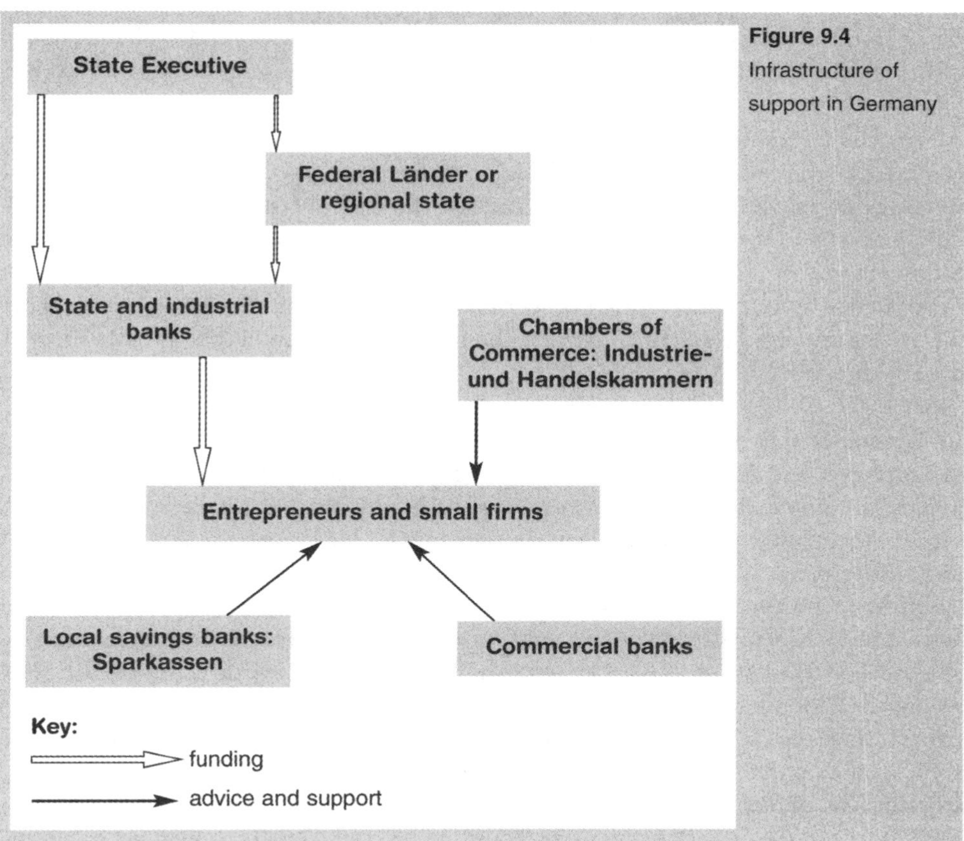

Figure 9.4 Infrastructure of support in Germany

His role was seen as that of promoting the interests of technology-based firms, co-ordinating resources and support. Specialized start-up support was available at the Chamber even though their members were small and medium-sized manufacturing firms. The difference in support was the way in which the Chamber could bring its influence to bear on other institutions, such as the banks, to provide support. The co-ordinating role was more effective than equivalent organizations in the UK. This included providing information and seminars for the local banks as well as venture capital providers. For example, a comment by a representative of one of the local banks was that: 'The IHK, once a year, hold special seminars on advice to small firms, which bank staff attend.'

In Baden-Württemberg there was also a range of special assistance to help different industrial sectors, such as high-technology small firms. This was in the form of grants, subsidies, guarantees and soft loans. But beyond industrial sectors there was little in the way of targeting assistance to other categories. Similar to both the UK and France, the Chamber provided seminars on specialized help for areas such as exporting, marketing and development. The IHK saw the promotional role as being more important than direct support, especially with start-up concerns. In this way it could co-ordinate support such as finance or other requirements of its members.

One survey of British and German Chambers of Commerce found that the resources of British Chambers were, on average, only 7 per cent of those in Germany and they had only 17 per cent of the staff.[47] For example, the Germans do not have to bid for contracts like an enterprise agency and their income from year to year can be calculated with relative certainty. This contrasts with the relative uncertainty of funding for local EAs in the UK. When we carried out the interviews with EA directors, some of them were not only unsure what their income would be for the following year, but in some cases they were also unsure whether they would still be in existence in a year's time. The periodic revamping of the enterprise support infrastructure only serves to emphasize the uncertainty of funding that faces support agency directors.

In Germany, the certainty of income allows the IHK to plan support, training programmes and counselling. By the nature of provision, the German system also avoids any duplication. Other institutions work with the IHK rather than trying to set up their own support system. For example, local authorities and regional authorities provide schemes that complement the provision of the IHK rather than set up agencies that may be in competition or offer duplication of support from the IHK. The IHK is relatively independent, powerful and is able, as a result, to employ specialist staff. For example, we were able to interview a director of the IHK responsible for advice and support for technology-based firms. Where other agencies existed they met a specific and identified need and complemented the work of the IHK. For example, in Pforzheim, a specialized agency for the jewellery industry existed, the Creditoren-Verein (CV). This agency's role was to provide debt collecting for the jewellery industry where debt collection was seen as a specific problem. Again, the agency had the characteristics of independence, membership by subscription and power that was supported by law.

By contrast, in the UK there is little co-operation and networking between agencies and, hence, business advisers tend to be generalists rather than specialist consultants.[30] In the UK, the diversity of the pattern of small business support provided by EAs gave them the flexibility to meet local needs. However, this very diversity can operate as an inhibitor to developing an effective and collaborative network. Asymmetries between agencies in size, resources, sponsorship, personnel and attitudes operated to prevent integration. For example, the study in Scotland found 18 different agencies in Glasgow alone, where jealous guarding of roles and boundaries militated against much integration.[48]

There were similarities between the German Chambers of Commerce and French Chambers of Commerce. Our study compared the role of agencies in Clermont-Ferrand.[42] A simplified version of the infrastructure of support based on Clermont-Ferrand is illustrated in Figure 9.5.

The local Chambre de Commerce et d'Industrie was independent, powerful and membership was again compulsory. The agencies concerned with support and regeneration in Clermont-Ferrand proved to be atypical for France, because there

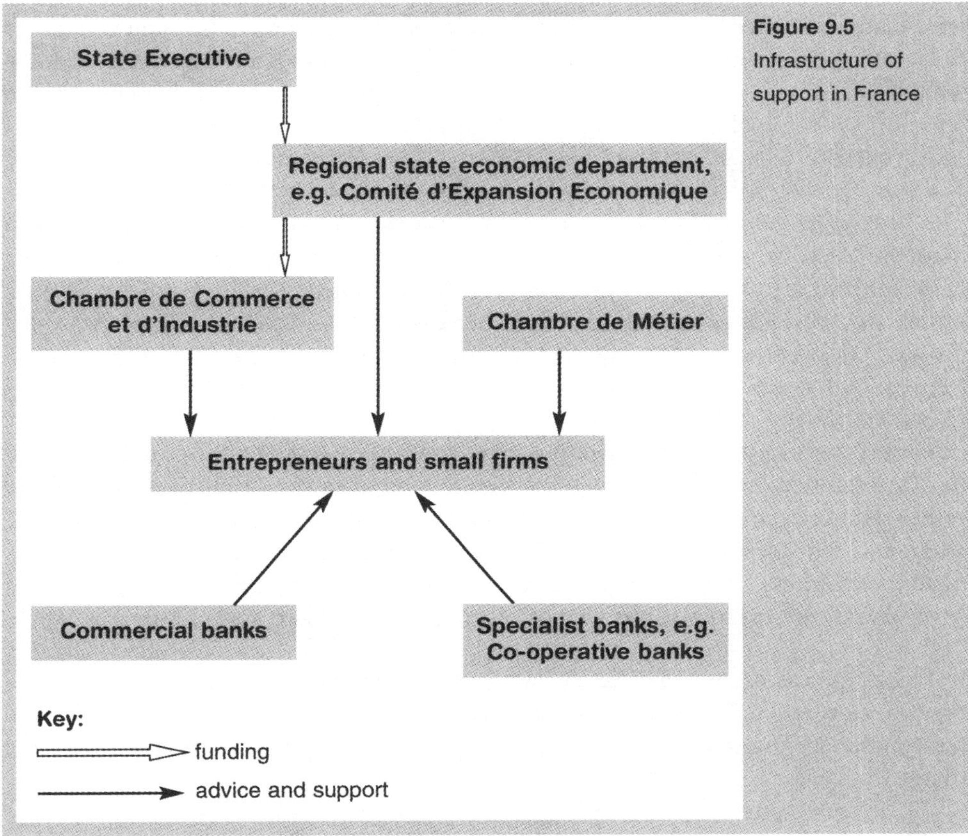

Figure 9.5 Infrastructure of support in France

was special provision due to the need to reconstruct and diversify the local economy from its dependence on Michelin as a major employer. However, there was evidence of co-operation between these agencies concerned with enterprise support. For example, a director from the Chambre commented:

“We work together [with the Development Commission] but . . . there is some competition.”

This point was developed by an officer from the Comité d'Expansion Economique (of the Puy de Dôme Département). He considered that the relationship with the Chambre was:

“A sort of partnership, yes. The success depends on the relationship between the entrepreneur and the Chambre. If things are going well between the entrepreneur and the Chambre then they will stay with the Chambre. If not, they will come here and vice versa.”

In addition there are a number of smaller Chambres for shopkeepers and smaller firms: the Chambres de Métier. There was one Chambre de Métier in the Département (the Puy de Dôme). The services of this smaller Chamber, however, were distinctly different from the main Chambers of Commerce. The main Chambers of Commerce have member firms whose employment varies from 10 to 100 workers, whereas the Chambre de Métier is more likely to serve the 'petite de commerce', the self-employed and skilled tradespeople. Thus, there was some competition, but co-operation also seemed to be effective between different support institutions.

The level of collaboration that existed in Germany between support agencies and financial institutions means that better quality start-ups were ensured. We commented that it may be more difficult to establish a new business because informational requirements were higher, but the quality of those start-ups was also higher.[42] One of the problems in the UK is that the extent of new small firm creation has been subject to much volatility, as discussed in Chapter 2.[49,50]

In Germany there was some selectivity of support. The IHK, by its nature, will tend to direct support more to existing firms and respond to the needs of existing firms rather than start-ups. Seminars were provided, not for start-ups or to raise enterprise awareness, but for retraining, technology or exporting. The programme was a series of support seminars and training that was geared at existing firms and at Germany's Mittelstand, the medium-sized firm of 50 to 200 employees.

In France, a similar emphasis on developing firms rather than directing aid at start-ups was normal. Start-up clients were more likely to go to the Département agency, the Comité d'Expansion Economique. For example the officer concerned considered that, of his clients:

“One-third are people who want to start a new business; one-third are clients who want to develop an existing business; and one-third are people who are facing difficulties.”

The director of the Chambre considered that his typical client was a 'medium-sized firm' and considered that he wished to develop a long-term relationship with these medium-sized firms, although they did provide advice and support for the creation of new firms.

There were parallels with the development of Business Links in the UK and some of the work and emphasis of French and German Chambers of Commerce. In the UK there are the beginnings of the development of longer-term relationships with existing firms, providing support more in response to a firm's needs, when it is required, rather than some policies which have been seen as top-down and 'off the shelf' by some commentators.[31]

ADDITIONAL ENTERPRISE INITIATIVES

There have been, over time, a large number of state initiatives designed to encourage small firm start-up and growth. At the same time, set in the background to these initiatives has been a general withdrawal of the state from the production and provision of goods and services. The extensive programme of privatization and other major economic changes, such as changes in income taxes, and corporation taxes, cannot be discussed here, but they form the background of general state measures designed to increase and promote the opportunities for private sector enterprise and development. Specific state measures designed to encourage small firm formation and growth are much more limited. They concentrate on relieving perceived constraints on small firm formation and growth. As such, they tend to concentrate on funding and other resource constraints. The main schemes are identified below; we merely list and describe them briefly before turning to an examination of whether there has been any significant change, as result, in our culture.

(a) The Creation of Enterprise Zones

Enterprise zones were created in a limited number of areas and were designed to provide special conditions that would foster the growth of new businesses. They represented a special 'tax free' zone where the firm did not have to pay local authority rates. Each zone was created for 10 years. The most famous enterprise zone has been the Isle of Dogs, since it attracted the Canary Wharf investment and development. The Isle of Dogs illustrated the major problem with enterprise zones: they have attracted large-scale firms and funding, which, it is arguable, would have been invested in anyway, but in other localities, where firms would have more long-term viability. In addition, enterprise zones do not have the infrastructure to support long-term growth and viability. The Isle of Dogs, for example, has continued to suffer from poor transport links compared to the City of London and it has never attracted the amount of office space that it needed to establish itself as a major centre of regeneration. Amin and Tomaney, in a study of the north-east, were critical of the creation of enterprise zones, where investment has gone into property development rather than into manufacturing.[51]

(b) The Enterprise Allowance Scheme (EAS)

Designed to encourage unemployed people to start their own businesses, now the EAS has been withdrawn, although some Business Links have had variations of this scheme funded with European assistance. The original requirement, that an individual had to be unemployed for a period of up to six months, has been dropped. Like the pattern of UK support discussed above, there was diversity in this support. There could, for example, be different levels of enterprise training and requirements under the scheme depending on the TEC/LEC that was responsible. In general, however, the EAS has been criticized for creating businesses that may not be viable, for subsidising inefficient businesses, for creating unemployment (since other businesses may be forced to stop trading through 'unfair competition)', and for not tackling the problem of the long-term unemployed, for which group it was designed to help.[52] Official evaluation reports can often paint a rosy picture. For example, one MSC report claimed survival rates of 74 per cent after 18 months for businesses on the scheme.[53] However, such crude survival rates tell us little about the effective quality of such start-ups. The repeated criticism of the EAS is that jobs and businesses were being created at the expense of others, that is, that displacement rates were high.

(c) The Small Firms' Loan Guarantee Scheme (SFLGS)

Finance was seen as a potential constraint on individual enterprise. This scheme was designed to relieve problems that might exist in raising finance for viable ventures that lacked security. As discussed in Chapter 5, the problem with this scheme has been that banks have to put forward a venture to qualify, and the banks have not been enthusiastic supporters. Compared to similar schemes in Germany, UK take-up rates have at different times been at only 10 per cent of German levels.[54] Since the scheme was enhanced (in 1993), take-up rates have improved[55] but levels are still below other countries' equivalent schemes and default rates have remained high.[56]

As discussed above, the extent and level of networking is one of the reasons for the higher take-up of an equivalent scheme in Germany. The role of institutions such as the IHK meant that the promotion and subsequent take-up of such a scheme was on a higher level. The lower take-up in the UK reflects, in part, the lack of collaboration and effective networking between the banks and external support agencies.

(d) The Enterprise Initiative

A Department of Trade and Industry (DTI) scheme which offered help to small businesses to get professional advice and consultancy. It was part of the government's switch from specific help with funding to more emphasis on advice and consultancy. It was designed particularly to help existing small businesses to expand by providing financial assistance for small firms to employ consultants. The Enterprise Initiative scheme seems to have had some impact although it can be argued, as with other schemes, that take-up rates were low.[57] The main problem with the scheme seems to have been lack of adequate follow-through on implementation by firms and the perception that the scheme was more suited to medium-sized firms rather than small firms. An evaluation of the scheme claimed considerable value added but, as with many such schemes, assessing additionality is difficult because of the subjective nature of advice as part of the consultancy provided under the scheme.[22] For example, it is very difficult to place a value on 'expert' advice, and it may take considerable time for the benefits of such advice to materialize. The evaluation did attempt to track changes in firms before and after the consultancy but, as with most such evaluation, such assessments are inevitably retrospective and rely (as a result) on subjective assessments.[58]

(e) The Enterprise Investment Scheme (EIS)

The EIS is designed to encourage potential investors to invest in small amounts of equity. In particular it encourages individual investors, business angels, to invest in small entrepreneurial firms with tax breaks on capital gains. One survey of business angels found that the EIS was a popular investment vehicle.[59] The EIS replaced the old Business Expansion Scheme (BES), which was withdrawn because it became a vehicle for property investment.

(f) Other Schemes

A number of other semi-official schemes were established, all designed to encourage small firm start-ups. For example, in some areas funding was available under British

Coal redundancy schemes. British Steel also had similar schemes; and there was the role of Task Force Funding in inner-city areas.

When added together, the combination of these different enterprise initiatives and the background of the broadbrush government economic changes in taxation and privatization provides the basis for claims that successive governments have created an 'enterprise culture'. However, this is a much more difficult concept to evaluate. To some extent, there has been a debate about whether there has been sufficient changes in society to talk about the creation of an enterprise culture. We briefly consider some of the contributions to the debate.

Developing an Enterprise Culture

We concentrate on whether successive governments (since 1979) have successfully changed the attitudes to enterprise in the UK. Obviously implicit in this claim is that there has been some change in the attitudes and beliefs of society since 1979. To claim that there has been this change it is necessary to show that society, in 1979, was different in perceptions and attitudes. It has been claimed that, before 1979, society did not provide an environment that fostered entrepreneurship and enterprise development; that enterprise skills were insufficiently rewarded; that there was insufficient motivation and reward to start your own business; and that existing businesses were stifled for lack of opportunity and the right climate for development and growth. It is claimed that the development of enterprise skills, whether in large or small organizations, was not fostered by the culture and environment that existed before the 1990s.

The debate has drawn comments from a wide academic background and contributions have ranged from theologians and sociologists [60,61] to economists and politicians.[62,63] Advocates of the existence of the enterprise culture have been enthusiastic in their claims. For example, Bannock has gone so far as to call this a 'sea change' in social attitudes.[64]

Claims for the creation and existence of an enterprise culture suffer from a number of problems. First, it is difficult to define precisely what is meant by the term 'enterprise culture'. It is a term which is full of ambiguities and has led to different attempts at definition.[65] MacDonald and Coffield[66] have compared the term 'enterprise' to 'Heffalump'– the mythical creature of supposed vast importance but which no one has ever seen. Second, as pointed out in this chapter, evaluation reports on the effectiveness of state initiatives give misleading impressions of their effectiveness and impact. Mills,[67] commenting on the EAS, said:

> ***"The rhetoric of the EAS claims to create an Enterprise Culture and encourage the growth of entrepreneurs in Britain. In practice it seems to have been a means of reducing the unemployment statistics."* *(p. 93)***

Third, it is very difficult to assess the much more tenuous question of whether there has been any noticeable change in the culture of society. For example, Amin and

Tomaney,[51] in their study of the north-east, assess the impact of enterprise initiatives and comment that it has been the 'expressed aim of the Conservative administration to foster an entrepreneurial culture and to use this as a main plank for local economic generation' (p. 479). This study is critical of the government initiatives (such as enterprise zones) and the gradual rundown of state regional grant aid. Even the creation of the Nissan plant in the region comes in for criticism as being a relatively costly investment. Other initiatives are criticized for encouraging investment in property rather than manufacturing, such as the Tyne and Wear Urban Development Corporation.

Fourth, there have been long-term changes that have been taking place in the structure of the UK economy. For example, the decline of traditional industries and structural change involving a shift out of manufacturing has been in evidence for some time.

An attempt to change cultural attitudes to entrepreneurship has been undertaken in Scotland, through a national strategy targeted at changing attitudes in institutions and in the population. A national enquiry in Scotland (as discussed in Chapter 1) revealed that entrepreneurs (and entrepreneurship) were perceived as low status (and as a career) and that this was a factor affecting the low rate of participation.[68] After seven years of a major campaign in Scotland, to influence attitudes to entrepreneurs and to starting a business, the strategy does seem to have had an effect. For example, a repeat of the Mori opinion poll showed a significant increase in the numbers 'committed to starting a business'.[69] This seems to show that a major campaign targeted at improving the profile of entrepreneurs, and the education system, can have effects on society's attitudes to enterprise. It is also notable that some RDAs have copied the Scottish Enterprise approach by introducing their own regional enterprise strategies. Furthermore, a study by the IPPR has suggested that a range of government measures still need to be taken if the UK is to develop an entrepreneurial society.[70] The authors of this report comment:

> ***“Our proposals range from broad measures to foster a culture of enterprise to some of the detail of business support schemes ... which are certainly in need of reappraisal and overhaul.” (p. v)***

The recent GEM studies in the UK have attempted to measure entrepreneurial attitudes as well as entrepreneurial activity.[71] Their findings suggest stability in attitudes rather than changes, although there is evidence of changing attitudes in younger people in more positive approaches to an 'enterprise culture'.

It is likely that forces for change in society's attitudes are much more complex and, if changes have taken place, they have been set in train by forces in society that were changing long before. It may be that the enterprise initiatives introduced by the government have given these changes a boost and brought them forward. However, many of the claims for the impact of these initiatives must be treated with caution.

THINK POINTS 9.3

Enterprise support

1. Compare and contrast European systems of enterprise support with that of Britain. What are the main differences?

2. Why is it possible to talk about a raft of measures to stimulate enterprise in the UK over several decades? What examples can you give?

3. What factors need to be taken into account when discussing whether there has been a shift in attitudes to enterprise in the UK?

4. What factors might account for the more positive attitudes to enterprise by younger people in the UK?

CONCLUSIONS

The development of a network of support agencies has seen large private and public sector investments in supporting enterprise development of new and small businesses. Whether this investment will ever be adequately evaluated is doubtful. Despite the additional creation of the Small Business Service, the level of support is still confusing and suffers from a number of inadequacies. We are still some way from the German model of effective intervention, collaboration and networking that supports the creation of viable and high-quality small businesses.

The introduction of the Small Business Service in 2000–01, and the revamping of Business Links, have been a welcome rationalization and refocusing of enterprise support (for example on start-ups). This has also been paralleled in Scotland by a revamping of support, now delivered through a national (to Scotland) Small Business Gateway. However, the development of the support agency movement has left the UK with an unplanned and confusing mixture of public and independent support that owes more to historical accidents of provision and individual promotion rather than any policy of consistent and planned support targeted to areas and firms that need the support. Duplication of support provision remains a problem in the UK. The creation of the Small Business Service has been beneficial in acting as a catalyst to force support agencies to work together; however, limited co-operation still remains a problem.

State enterprise initiatives have met with limited success. But, often, the true cost of these initiatives is not appreciated (or admitted) for example there are many people who would not be in business if more jobs were available. Wider criteria need to be applied to evaluation of state schemes, that is, the quality of jobs created, longitudinal criteria (how long do the jobs last for?), assessment of the externalities of the schemes, and suggestions for improvement of the schemes.

There is welcome change, however, to considering whether the right type of people are being encouraged into business. In the past, the associated suffering of families of the people who are encouraged to start their own businesses, that later fail, has been ignored. Often these business failures are accompanied by the loss of personal equity, property and homes. Families which may have enjoyed a good standard of living have, in some cases, been left destitute and with large personal debts. The social costs of this greater concern with the enterprise culture have sometimes been ignored. The 'downside' aspects of running a small business are often not appreciated by the people who are encouraged to start their own businesses due to an emphasis on success and achievement. The associated social costs can include, for example, strains on married life and family relationships, long hours of work and the lack of fringe benefits such as non-contributory pension schemes. While it remains true that the UK needs to promote an enterprise culture, this needs to be done in a balanced way that ensures appropriate people are encouraged to enter entrepreneurship.

SUGGESTED ASSIGNMENTS

1. You are a consultant to a local firm wishing to obtain advice on exporting to Eastern Europe. Write a report detailing national and local assistance, indicating differences in the nature of local and national support provided in your region or local area.

2. Interview your local support agencies and identify their primary role and objectives. How do these match national policies?

3. Obtain the policy of your Regional Development Agency on 'enterprise support'. What are the objectives in terms of developing a local supportive enterprise culture? Discuss whether these objectives are feasible.

REFERENCES

1. Birch, D.L. (1979) 'The job generation process', *MIT study on neighbourhood and regional change*, MIT, Boston.

2. DTI (1999) *The Small Business Service: A Public Consultation*, DTI, London.

3. Curran, J. (2000) 'What is Small Business Policy in the UK for? Evaluating and Assessing Small Business Support Policies', *International Small Business Journal*, vol. 18, no. 3, pp. 36–50.

4. Gibb, A.A. (2000) 'SME Policy, Academic Research and the Growth of Ignorance: Mythical Concepts, Myths, Assumptions, Rituals and Confusions', *International Small Business Journal*, vol. 18, No. 3, pp. 13–35.

5. PERC (1998) *Enterprise Works: Evaluation Report*, Dunbartonshire Enterprise (not publicly available).

6. Ram, M. (1996) 'Supporting Ethnic Minority Enterprise: Views from the Providers', paper presented to the 19th ISBA National Small Firms Policy and Research Conference, Birmingham, November.

7. Bennett, R., Robson, P. and Bratton, W. (2000) 'Government Advice Networks for SMEs: An Assessment of the Influence of Local Context on Business Link Use, Impact and Satisfaction', Working Paper No. 182, Centre for Business Research, University of Cambridge, Cambridge.

8. Mole, K. (1999) 'Heuristics of Personal Business Advisers', unpublished PhD thesis, University of Wolverhampton.

9. Bank of England (2000) *Finance for Small Businesses in Deprived Communities*, Bank of England, London.

10. Shaw, E., Carter, S. and Brierton, J. (2001) *Unequal Entrepreneurs: Why female enterprise is an uphill business*, The Industrial Society, Policy Paper, London.

11. Deakins, D., Whittam., G. and Wilson, L. (2002) *National Centre for Women's Enterprise: Feasibility Study*, for Department of Enterprise and Lifelong Learning, Scottish Executive, Glasgow.

12. Danson, M., Deakins, D., Whittam, G. and Fairly, J. (2001) *Final Report on Economic Development Services in Scotland*, for the Enterprise and Lifelong Learning Committee, Scottish Parliament, Edinburgh, Scotland.

13. Small Business Service (2001) *Think Small First Supporting Smaller Businesses in the UK – a challenge for Government*, HMSO, London.

14. Lord Young (1992) 'Enterprise Regained', in Heelas, P. and Morris, P. (eds) *The Values of The Enterprise Culture: the moral debate*, Routledge, London.

15. Small Business Service (2000) *Research Strategy*, SBS, Sheffield.

16. The Guardian, 25 November, 1997.

17. HM Government (1998), White Paper, *Regional Development Agencies*, HMSO, London.

18. Yorkshire Forward (2001) *Can Do – Will Do: A Business Birth Rate Strategy for Yorkshire and Humberside*, Yorkshire Forward, Leeds.

19. Schlegelmilch, B.B., Diamantopoulos, A. and Moore, S.A. (1992) 'The Market for Management Consulting in Britain: An Analysis of Demand and Supply', *Management Decision*, vol. 30, no. 2, pp. 46–54.

20. HRD Partnership Report (1992) 'UK Management Consultants and the Small/Medium Firm: HRD Study of the BGT Option 3 Programme', Esprit Consulting, London.

21. Payne, A. (1986) 'Effective Use of Professional Management Services', *Management Decision*, vol. 24, no. 6, pp. 16–24.

22. Segal, Quince and Wicksteed (1994) *Evaluation of the Consultancy Initiatives* (4th Stage), HMSO, London.

23. Schein, E.H. (1987) *Process Consultation, Vol. II*, Addison-Wesley, Massachusetts, USA.

24. Deakins, D., Levinson, D., O'Neill, E. and Paul, S. (1996) *The Use and Impact of Business Consultancy in Scotland*, Paisley Enterprise Research Centre, University of Paisley, Scotland.

25. Sear, L. and Agar, J. (1996) *A Survey of Business Link PBAs*, Small Business Centre, Durham University Business School, Durham.

26. Jones, M. (1996) 'Business Link: A critical commentary', *Local Economy*, vol. 11, no. 1, pp. 71–8.

27. Bryson, J., Daniels, P. and Ingram, D. (1999) 'Evaluating the Impact of Business Links and Profitability of SMEs in the UK', *Policy Studies*, vol. 20, no. 2, pp. 95–105.

28. Deakins, D., Graham, L., Sullivan, R. and Whittam, G. (1998) 'New Venture Support: an analysis of mentoring support', 1st Stage Report to Renfrewshire Enterprise, Paisley Enterprise Research Centre, University of Paisley, Scotland.

29. Deakins, D., Mileham, P. and O'Neill, E. (1998) 'The Role and Influence of Non-Executive Directors in Growing Small Companies', Research Report for the ACCA, Paisley Enterprise Research Centre, University of Paisley, Scotland.

30. Deakins, D. (1993) 'What Role for Support Agencies? A case study of UK Enterprise Agencies', *Local Economy*, vol. 8, no.1, pp. 57–68.

31. Bennett, R.J., Wicks, P.J. and McCoshan, A. (1994) *Local Empowerment and Business Services: Britain's Experiment with TECs*, UCL Press, London.

32. Topham, N., Padmore, K. and Twoney, J. (1994) *English TECs: Ranking, Requirement and Resources*, Salford University, Salford.

33. Curran, J. (1993) 'TECs and Small Firms: Can TECs Reach the Small Firms Other Strategies have Failed to Reach?' paper presented to the House of Commons Social and Science Policy Group, Kingston University, Kingston.

34. Curran, J., Blackburn, R., Kitching, J. and North, J. (1996) 'Small Firms and Workforce Training', paper presented to the 19th National Small Firms Policy and Research Conference, Birmingham.

35. Casson, M. (ed.) (1990) *Entrepreneurship*, Edward Elgar, London.

36. Business In The Community (1988) *The future for enterprise agencies*, BITC, London.

37. Moore, C. (1988) 'Enterprise Agencies: privatisation or partnership?' *Local Economy*, vol. 3, no. 1, pp. 21–30.

38. Ernst & Young (1996) *Evaluation of Business Links*, DTI, London.

39. PACEC (1998) *Business Links: Value for Money, Evaluation Final Report*, DTI, London.

40. Storey, D.J. (1994) *Understanding the Small Business Sector*, Routledge, London.

41. PA Cambridge Consultants (1995) *Evaluation of DTI-funded TEC Services in Support of SMEs*, HMSO, London.

42. Deakins, D. and Philpott, T. (1993) *Comparative European Practices in the Finance of Small Firms: UK, Germany and Holland*, University of Central England, Birmingham.

43. Coopers and Lybrand Deloitte and Business In The Community (1991) *Local support for enterprise*, BITC, London.

44. Bennett, R.J. (1996) 'SMEs and Public Policy: present dilemmas, future priorities and the case of Business Links', paper presented to the 19th ISBA National Small Firms Conference, Birmingham.

45. Cutler, D. (1994) 'Gearing Up for Business Link', *Local Economy*, vol. 8, no. 4, pp. 365–8.

46. Roper, S., Hart, M., Bramley, G., Dale, I. and Anderson, C. (2001) 'Paradise Regained: The Business Link Tracker Study', paper presented to the 24th ISBA National Small Firms Policy and Research Conference.

47. Bennett, M.J., Krebs, G. and Zimmerman, H. (1993) *Chambers of Commerce in Britain and Germany and The Single Market*, Anglo-German Foundation, Poole.

48. Danson, M., Deakins, D. and Whittam, G. (2000) *Interim Report on Economic Development Services in Scotland*, to the Enterprise and Lifelong Learning Committee, Scottish Parliament, Edinburgh.

49. Daly, M. and McCann, A. (1992) 'How Many Small Firms?' *Employment Gazette*, April, pp. 47–51.

50. Daly, M., Campbell, M., Robson, G. and Gallagher, C. (1992) 'Job Creation 1987–89: The Contributions of Small and Large Firms', *Employment Gazette*, April, pp. 589–94.

51. Amin, A. and Tomaney, J. (1991) 'Creating an Enterprise Culture in the North East? The impact of Urban and Regional Policies of the 1980s', *Regional Studies*, vol. 25, no. 5, pp. 479–87.

52. Gray, C. (1990) 'Some Economic and Psychological Considerations on the effects of the Enterprise Allowance Scheme', *Small Business*, vol.1, pp. 111–124.

53. Simkin, C. and Allen, D. (1988) *Enterprise Allowance Scheme Evaluation: Second Eighteen-Month National Survey, Final Report*, MSC, London.

54. Batchelor, C. (1993) *Financial Times*, 23 March.

55. Bank of England (2001) *Finance for Small Firms, An Eighth Report*, Bank of England, London.

56. Cowling, M. and Clay, N. (1994) 'An Assessment of the Loan Guarantee Scheme', *Journal of Small Business and Enterprise Development*, vol. 1, no. 3, pp. 7–13.

57. National Economic Research Association (1990) *An Evaluation of the Loan Guarantee Scheme*, Department of Employment, London.

58. Segal, Quince and Wicksteed (1989) *Evaluation of the Consultancy Initiatives*, HMSO, London.

59. Paul, S., Johnston, J. and Whittam, G. (2001) *Business Angels Made in Heaven: An Assessment of the Investment Activity of Business Angels in Scotland*, LINC Scotland, Glasgow.

60. Morris, P. (1991) 'Freeing the Spirit of Enterprise', in Keat, R. and Abercrombie, N. (eds) *Enterprise Culture*, Routledge, London, pp. 21–37.

61. Abercrombie, N. (1991) 'The privilege of the producer', in Keat, R. and Abercrombie, N. (eds) *Enterprise Culture*, Routledge, London, pp. 171–85.

62. Ricketts, M. (1987) *The Economics of Business Enterprise*, Wheatsheaf Books, London.

63. Lawson, N. (1984) *The British Experiment*, Fifth Mais Lecture, HM Treasury.

64. Bannock, G. (1991) *Venture Capital and the Equity Gap*, National Westminster Bank, London.

65. Ritchie, J. (1991) 'Chasing Shadows: Enterprise Culture as an Educational Phenomenon', *Journal of Education Policy*, vol. 6, no. 3, pp. 315–25.

66. MacDonald, R. and Coffield, F. (1991) *Risky Business: Youth and the Enterprise Culture*, Falmer Press, London.

67. Mills, V. (1991) 'Review of Some Economic and Psychological Considerations on the Effects of the EAS', *International Small Business Journal*, vol. 9, no. 4, pp. 91–4.

68. Scottish Enterprise (1993) *Scotland's Business Birth Rate: A National Enquiry*, Scottish Enterprise, Glasgow.

69. Scottish Enterprise (1998) 'The Business Birth Rate 5th Anniversary: press release', Scottish Enterprise, Glasgow.

70. Gavron, R., Cowling, M., Holtham, G. and Westall, A. (1996) *The Entrepreneurial Society*, IPPR, London.

71. GEM (2002) *The UK 2001 Report*, GEM, Babson College, USA.

RECOMMENDED READING

Curran, J. (2000) 'What is Small Business Policy in the UK For? Evaluating and Assessing Small Business Support Policies', *International Small Business Journal*, vol. 18, no. 3, pp. 36–50.

Gibb, A.A. (2000) 'SME Policy, Academic Research and the Growth of Ignorance: Mythical Concepts, Myths, Assumptions, Rituals and Confusions', *International Small Business Journal*, vol. 18, no. 3, pp. 13–35.

GEM (2002) *The UK 2001 Report*, GEM, Babson College, USA.

Gray, C. (1999) *Enterprise Culture*, Routledge, London.

10

ENTREPRENEURIAL AND GROWTH FIRMS

LEARNING OUTCOMES

At the end of this chapter you should be able to:

1. Discuss the strengths and weaknesses of the main entrepreneurial growth theories.
2. Identify and describe some of the important factors which may affect growth in small firms.
3. Explain the importance of an understanding of the process of growth to the development of small firms' policy.
4. Describe and discuss the complexity of growth.
5. Evaluate the current developments in growth theory with reference to empirical evidence and existing knowledge.

INTRODUCTION

There is a basic distinction between the person or entrepreneur that wishes to go into self-employment to pursue their own interests (and perhaps enters self-employment because there is no or little alternative) and the person or entrepreneur that enters small business ownership because they have desires to develop their businesses, to achieve growth, expand employment and grow into a medium-sized or a large firm. The former type of small business owner has very different managerial objectives from the latter. Objectives of the first will be concerned with survival and maintenance of lifestyle, whereas those of the second type will be concerned with growth and expansion, with the entrepreneur eventually owning several companies.

Many people who were made redundant due to 'downsizing' of traditional manufacturing firms in the 1980s entered self-employment as small business owners. They were normally sole traders, employed few or no people and their major objectives were likely to be concerned with survival and ensuring that the business provided them and their family with sufficient income. These small businesses, which are the overwhelming majority of small firms in the UK, are sometimes called 'lifestyle' businesses. In other words, the owner-manager is only concerned with maintaining a lifestyle that he or she may have been accustomed to in a previous form of employment. A minority of small firms may be called 'entrepreneurial firms'; their owners will be concerned mainly with the strategic objective of achieving growth and will often go on to own more than one firm.

There has been much speculation about whether such 'entrepreneurial firms' can be identified *ex ante*, that is, before they achieve growth, rather than *ex post*, after they have demonstrated growth. This presents a problem for researchers, policy-makers and investors, such as venture capitalists who will want to identify high-growth and high-performing firms. It is a classical adverse selection problem created by uncertainty and limited (if not asymmetric) information. Despite the inherent difficulties of identifying such growth firms, this has not stopped policy-makers from establishing agencies, such as the Business Links, to support growth firms. This problem has also not stopped researchers from attempting to identify the characteristics and features of such growth firms and their entrepreneurs.

There is no agreement on exactly what measure to use to distinguish a high-performing firm. Should performance be measured on the basis of employment created or by some other criterion, such as profits, turnover or financial assets? Attention has, nonetheless, focused on identifying growth firms rather than identifying constraints that may block the growth potential of many entrepreneurs and small firms. The inherent problem for policy-makers, however, is that environments that favour the expansion of some firms may not remain stable. There are only certain windows of marketing opportunity that can lead to success of entrepreneurs and growth firms. The right timing has proved to be crucial in many circumstances, even if other equally crucial factors might be in place. We saw with the Aquamotive case in Chapter 7 that the right product may not lead to growth and success if the timing is wrong and the environment has not been supportive. Even very successful entrepreneurs such as Bill Gates may not be able to recreate their success. There may be a unique combination of circumstances and perhaps the right combination of people that produce the high-growth firm. The rest of this chapter reviews theory, evidence and approaches to growth firms.

Almost forty years ago Edith Penrose[1] classically noted that:

> ***“The differences in the administrative structures of the very small and the very large firms are so great that in many ways it is hard to see that the two species are of the same genus . . . we cannot define a caterpillar and use the same definition for a butterfly.” (p. 19)***

Yet, logically, there must exist a process through which small becomes large – one need only look at such visible exemplars as Microsoft, Apple or Dell. This process of growth and growth firms themselves have been, and remain, among the main foci of research into entrepreneurship and small firms. The focus is further heightened by the contention that only a few small firms enjoy the bulk of growth in any given period. That is to say:

> ***“job creation amongst small firms is heavily concentrated within very few such firms.”[2] (p. 35)***

This view, drawing impetus and support from the work of Colin Gallagher and others, has, in effect, become accepted wisdom in the small firms literature.[3,4,5] As a rule of thumb, 'out of every 100 small firms 4 will be responsible for 50% of the employment created in a given time period'. Further, this body of research has had considerable influence upon small firms policy. Accordingly, blanket and early stage support schemes, such as EAS and BSUS, have all but been abandoned in England, left to the discretion of Business Links, while in Scotland many of the LECs, though persisting with versions of these schemes, have begun to shift a proportion of their resources towards targeted support. In essence, the aim now is to 'pick winners' or, in Scottish Enterprise parlance,[6] 'create winners'.[a]

Given limited resources and the desire to maximize returns or minimize losses, the attraction of a satisfactory predictive model, or growth theory, to policy-makers, financial institutions, support services and potential investors is clear. As a result, a commendable amount of research has attempted to articulate the process of growth or identify those characteristics that distinguish growth firms from their stable or declining counterparts. The purpose of this chapter is to review the major contributions to date and to make some comment on the future direction of work in this area.

THE (NEOCLASSICAL) ECONOMICS APPROACH

From the perspective of standard (or neoclassical) economics *all* firms within an industry are compelled, by the existence of a U-shaped average cost curve (Figure 10.1) and by universal profit maximizing behaviour, to expand their size until they reach (but do not exceed) the scale corresponding (given available technology) to the minimum feasible cost. In other words, all firms must grow until such time that the minimum efficient scale (MES) is reached. That is, the process of growth is at an end insofar as this process of optimization is ended.

The MES is the point at which all scale economies are exhausted. Thereafter, the balance of diseconomies of scale serves to increase the average cost of each unit of production – leading to the U-shaped short-run average cost (SRAC) curve depicted in Figure 10.1. Moreover, as Figure 10.1 suggests, for very low levels of output, costs are lowest with plant size $SRAC_1$. Costs for plant size $SRAC_2$ are relatively high for these lower levels of output because of the higher fixed costs associated with this plant size. However, as output expands, plant size $SRAC_1$ would be required to operate beyond designed capacity, incurring high variable costs and accruing scale diseconomies. At these higher levels of output, $SRAC_2$ becomes the 'optimum' plant size. This argument can be progressed for the total number of feasible plant sizes,

[a] It is of interest to note that Scottish Enterprise[6] persist with the conviction that 'improving the number of new ventures is a prerequisite to increasing the number of fast-growing businesses' (p. 16) – a notion running counter to the Storey and Johnson[2] contention that 'policies which artificially raise the number of business formations lead to higher death rates of businesses and to a radical reduction in the number of successful firms and hence of employment' (p. 39).

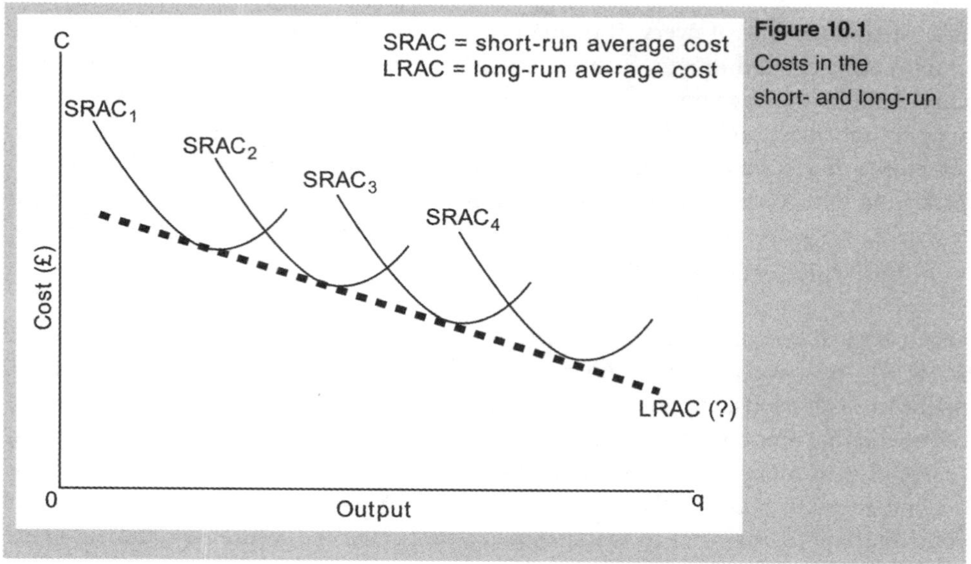

Figure 10.1 Costs in the short- and long-run

with the long-run average cost (LRAC) curve represented by the minimum point on each successive SRAC curve.

Following this logic, it becomes clear that, in the short-run, growth is constrained by the fixity of capital – by each firm's ability to expand plant and machinery or, most simplistically, to expand factory capacity or build new factories. In the long-run, growth will be limited only by market demand, or the willingness of consumers to purchase expanding output. As Marshall[7] noted, in this view, the long-run size of the firm will only be increased, 'other things being equal, by the general expansion of the industry' (p. 460). However, Penrose[1] points out that, 'To say that the expansion of a firm which can produce unspecified new products is limited by "demand", is to say that there are no products that the firm could produce profitably' (p. 13). In a world of conglomerates this is clearly an erroneous position. While there may be some 'optimum' output for each of the firm's product lines, there is unlikely to be an 'optimum' output for the firm as a whole. As such, under neoclassical theory, there can be no limits to the size of firms as long as there exist product markets that may be profitably exploited.

Problems arise when one confronts this elegant theory with empirical evidence. In this event, as Ijiri and Simon[8] note, 'the theory either predicts the facts incorrectly or makes no predictions at all' (p. 10). Clearly, firms in the 'real world', within any given industry, are not of a uniform size (subject to some 'frictional' disequilibria), as the theory would suggest. In fact, firm size distributions within modern industrial economies tend to be highly skewed – with a small number of large firms dominating. Moreover, the theory fails to explain the changes in business concentration witnessed over the last 60 years (namely, the rise in concentration post-Second World War up to the end of the 1960s, and the reversal of this pattern from the mid 1970s).

There are a number of fairly obvious reasons why the theory fails to converge with 'real world' observations. Perhaps the most important involves recognizing that competition is never perfect and is rarely pure. In other words:

"Many small firms, even if they are not efficient, may reach the minimum efficient size for their industry by selling to relatively uncompetitive and partially protected local and regional markets."[9] (p. 1366)

The essential corollary to this is to note that business firms are not faced with the same cost curves. Without doubt, firms are marked by differences in their ability to access, *inter alia*, managerial resources, skills, technology and finance – and by the relative efficacy of these resources. In other words, firm competencies vary and, relatedly, relative costs vary. Moreover, firm strategies vary. A great many firms do not grow, at least in part because they do not wish to grow. To talk in terms of an 'average' or 'representative' firm, as this theory implies, is clearly inappropriate and unhelpful when trying to comprehend the underlying factors which influence the occasional growth of individual firms. An appreciation that firms differ is an essential starting point for understanding why they differ – i.e. why some firms grow and others do not.

CHANCE MODELS

As noted above, causal observation of real-world data on firm size suggests a highly skewed size distribution, with a few large firms and a larger tail of smaller firms. Such skewed distributions, of which the lognormal is perhaps the most familiar, may be generated by a stochastic process in which the variate (i.e. the size of firms) is subjected to cumulative random shocks over time. That is, with a sufficient number of observations, a mechanical chance model can be used to infer the size distribution of a population of firms that resembles actual empirical distributions. In other words, viewed in aggregate, firm size follows a 'random walk'. This 'fact' is the almost universal conclusion of econometric studies of both large and small firm growth.

The first, and most famous, exposition of this theory is Robert Gibrat's 'Law of Proportionate Effect'.[10] Leaving aside the associated mathematics, Gibrat suggested that:

1. The causes of size change are numerous.

2. No single cause exerts a major influence on the phenomenon.

3. Any influence is independent of firm size.

The final premise (that growth is independent of size), which gives the law its name, may be rephrased as 'the probability of a given proportionate change in size during a specified period is the same for all firms in a given industry – regardless of their size at the beginning of the period'[11] (p. 1031). It is this element of Gibrat's Law that has been subjected to the most rigorous testing, with generally negative conclusions. All in all, empirical results show a general tendency for growth rates to be negatively correlated with size, while their variance appears to decrease as size increases. In other words, taken in aggregate, small firms exhibit higher, but more erratic, growth rates. However, notwithstanding the falsifiablity of Gibrat's proportionality hypothesis, it is the first two premises that, conceptually, present the most compelling logic. To illustrate, consider a study by Westhead and Birley;[12] having identified 88 variables hypothesized to influence firm growth, and having subsequently conducted a large-scale postal survey, they found 2 (in the case of manufacturing) or 3 (in the case of services) factors exerted a statistically significant influence on growth rates. However, the authors acknowledged that these factors ' "explain[ed]" a relatively small proportion of the variance [in sample firm growth]' (p. 28). Many factors may be thought to influence firm growth, but their influence is seldom significant or consistent.

Obviously, to suggest that all successful businesses or entrepreneurs were merely lucky is to considerably overstate the case. However, Reid and Jacobsen,[13] while acknowledging that eliminating all factors but chance from the equation is to put the case too strongly, suggest that 'it is a necessary caution to those who would ignore the role of chance in determining the fortunes of a small entrepreneurial firm' (p. 81). These authors go on to offer anecdotal evidence, from their experiences with entrepreneurs and business owners, in support of the attribution of significance to the role of chance – of 'lucky breaks' and grateful perplexion, as well as the predictable 'hard luck stories'. Such evidence, though lacking in academic or scientific rigour, is likely to be echoed in the experiences of most small firm researchers. It is surely undeniable that, in the presence of uncertainty and bounded rationality, fortune will play a significant, if variable, role in determining which firms will succeed. As Nelson and Winter[14] note, 'luck is the principal factor that finally distinguishes winners from near-winners – although vast differentials of skills and competence may separate contenders from non-contenders.'

Yet, in spite of a general belief in the influence of serendipity, it is clear that abstract stochastic models, of the type developed by econometricians, have little predictive or explanatory power at the level of the individual firm. Crucially, a better understanding of the growth processes of individual firms is central to the agenda of small firm academics and the business and public policy communities.

THINK POINTS 10.1

Entrepreneurial and growth firms

1. How small is the proportion of new firms that may achieve significant growth?
2. Why are policies to select 'growth firms' attractive to policy-makers?

3. Is there any evidence to support Gibrat's Law that growth will be independent of firm size? Explain your answer.

4. Why do you think 'chance' plays a large part in successful (or unsuccessful) firm growth? Do any of the case studies discussed in this text support the role of chance in growth?

STAGE MODELS OF GROWTH

With respect to the development of firm-level models of growth, much of the early theoretical and empirical work, during the 1970s and 1980s, attempted to conceptualize the metamorphosis of Penrose's caterpillar in terms of stage, or life cycle, models of firm growth. These models, normally incorporating five stages, envisage an inevitable and gradual movement along a known growth trajectory – the classic 'S-curve' (Figure 10.2). At each stage the organization undergoes changes in management practices and style, organizational structure and degree of internal formality of systems and strategy, in such a way that the stage-five firm is truly distinct from the stage-one firm from which it derived.

In this section we briefly discuss two of the most commonly cited stage models of growth: Greiner[15] and Churchill and Lewis.[16] Taking them chronologically, the Greiner model posits a linear, continuous relationship between time and growth, postulating periods of incremental, trouble-free growth (evolution) punctuated by explicitly defined crises (revolution). Each period of evolution has a clear set of

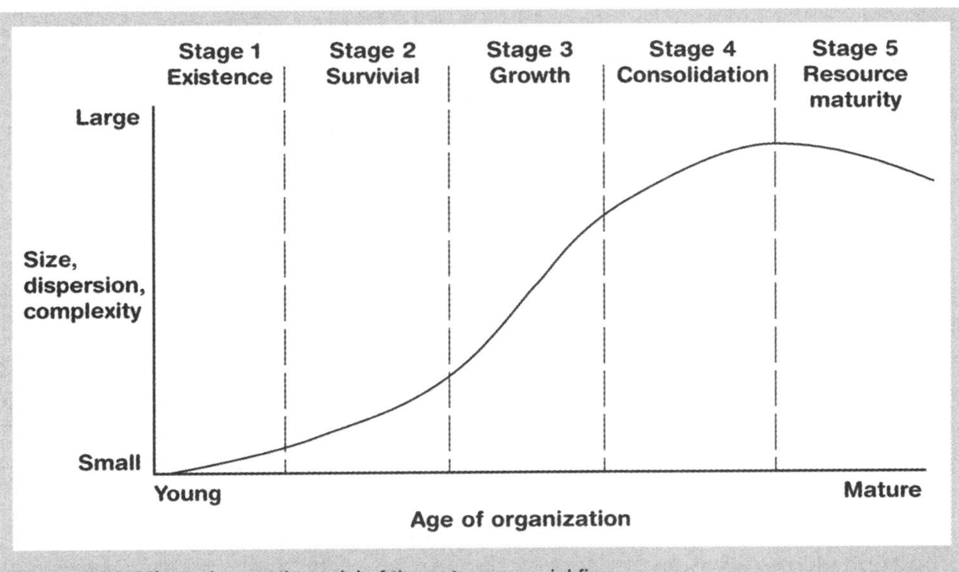

Figure 10.2 Life cycle growth model of the entrepreneurial firm

Attribute	Phase 1 Creativity	Phase 2 Direction	Phase 3 Delegation	Phase 4 Co-ordination	Phase 5 Collaboration
Management focus	Make and sell	Efficiency of operations	Expansion of market	Consolidation of organization	Problem solving and innovation
Organization structure	Informal	Centralized and functional	Decentralized and geographical	Line-staff and product groups	Matrix of teams
Top management style	Individualistic and entrepreneurial	Directive	Delegative	Watchdog	Participative
Control system	Market results	Standards and cost centres	Reports and profit centres	Plans and investment centres	Mutual goal setting
Management reward emphasis	Ownership	Salary and merit increases	Individual bonus	Profit sharing and stock options	Team bonus
Crises	Crisis of leadership	Crisis of autonomy	Crisis of control	Crisis of red tape	Crisis of ?

Table 10.1 Greiner's model of firm growth

attributes that characterize it and each stage, which ultimately degenerates into crisis, is a solution to the crisis of the previous stage (Table 10.1).

The crises outlined by Greiner form the bottom row of Table 10.1. In more detail these are:

Crisis of leadership: the shift from a phase 1 firm to a phase 2 firm is triggered by a crisis of leadership. More sophisticated knowledge and competencies are required to operate larger production runs and manage an expanding workforce. Capital must be secured to underpin further growth and financial controls must be put in place. The company must hire additional executive resource and restructure to meet these challenges.

Crisis of autonomy: the control mechanisms implemented as a result of the first crisis become less appropriate as the physical size of the company increases. Line employees and line managers become frustrated with the bureaucracy attendant upon a centralized hierarchy. Line staff are more familiar with markets and machinery than executives and become 'torn between following procedures and taking initiative' (p. 42). It has become necessary for the company to delegate to allow sufficient discretion in operating decision-making.

Crisis of control: top executives begin to perceive a loss of control as a consequence of excessive discretion resting with middle and lower managers. There exists little co-ordination across divisions, plants or functions – 'Freedom breeds a parochial attitude' (p. 43). Top management must seek to regain control, not through recentralization, but through the use of (undefined) 'special co-ordination techniques'.

Crisis of red tape: the 'watchdog' approach adopted by senior management in phase 4 and the proliferation of systems and programmes leads to a crisis of confidence and red tape. Line managers object to excessive direction and senior managers view line managers as uncooperative and disruptive. Both groups are unhappy with the cumbersome paper system that evolved to meet the challenges of the previous period. The company has become too large and complex to be managed through an extensive framework of formal procedures and controls. Movement to phase 5 requires a shift to 'interpersonal collaboration'.

Crisis of ?: the crisis into which phase 5 degenerates remains undefined in Greiner's model. He can find no 'consistent' empirical evidence which points to the nature of this crisis and the subsequent phase 6. However, he hypothesizes that this crisis will revolve around the 'psychological saturation' of employees which will occur as a logical result of the information age. Consequently organizations will evolve with dual structures of 'habit' and 'reflection', allowing employees to move periodically between the two for periods of rest – or some alternative format whereby 'spent' staff can refuel their energies.

The revolutionary components of Greiner's paradigm are perhaps atypical of the broader set of stage models (although Scott and Bruce imply a similar set of crisis triggers).[17] By contrast, Churchill and Lewis, although commenting upon Greiner, present a more general depiction of growth models where transition from stage to stage has no explicit trigger (Table 10.2). Further, Churchill and Lewis include a sixth stage by dividing the standard 'Success', or 'Growth', stage into growth firms and what may be described as 'comfort' or 'lifestyle' firms. Comfort firms (stage 3-D) are those which, having achieved economic viability and chosen not to proactively seek further growth, can be assured of average, or above average, profits in the long-run, providing managerial incompetence is avoided and the environment does not change to destroy their market niche.

In addition to those represented in Table 10.2, Churchill and Lewis include a further two factors in their paradigm which do not allow for easy tabulation – 'Organization' and 'Business and Owner'. Addressing 'Organization', in the first instance, the authors posit an internal organizational structure of progressively increasing horizontal and vertical complexity, thus allowing for greater managerial sophistication and delegation. In the first instance, 'the organization is a simple one – the owner does everything and directly supervises subordinates'[16] (p. 33). Ultimately, however, as resources allow and complex operations require, 'the management is decentralized, adequately staffed, and experienced'; extended hierarchies have evolved with detailed reporting relationships.

With regards to the 'Business and Owner' factor, this tracks the importance of the original owner-manager from an initially increasing central role to an eventual

	Stage 1 Existence	Stage 2 Survival	Stage 3-D Success-Disengage	Stage 3-G Success-Growth	Stage 4 Take-off	Stage 5 Maturity
Management style	Direct supervision	Supervised supervision	Functional	Functional	Divisional	Line and staff
Extent of formal systems	Minimal to non-existent	Minimal	Basic	Developing	Maturing	Extensive
Major strategy	Existence	Survival	Maintaining profitable status quo	Get resources for growth	Growth	Return on investment

Table 10.2: The Churchill and Lewis model of firm growth

peripheral capacity when the organization has reached 'Resource maturity' (Figure 10.3). In the early stages the owner is the business. He/she performs all the major tasks and is the principal supplier of energy, direction and capital. In contrast, by the resource maturity stage, the 'owner and the business are quite separate both financially and operationally' (p. 40).

Figure 10.3 Business and owner*

* Smaller circle represents owner; larger circle represents business.

Source: Adapted from Ijiri, Y. and Simon, H. (1997) *Skew Distributions and the Sizes of Business Firms*, North-Holland, Amsterdam.

Following both Tables 10.1 and 10.2 along individual rows from left to right we see a logical progression in the sophistication of the individual factors. The implication appears to be that firms move from an informal and ad hoc birth, through a quasi-Taylorist state, culminating in the highest level of managerial and organizational refinement yet imagined. While there are obvious differences in the nuances of these models, they are sufficiently alike to permit consolidation. Thus, generalizing, explicitly these models are intended to facilitate owner-managers and senior executives in recognizing the stage at which their organization stands and consequently identifying the skills required for further progression or, in the case of Greiner, the likely impending crises. Yet, while these models have the advantage of highlighting the notion that managerial skill requirements are not of a 'once and for all time' nature, there are fundamental flaws associated with the rigidity of these models. From the literature,[18,19] the standard critique is fourfold:

- First, most firms experience little or no growth and therefore are unlikely to ever reach stages 3, 4 or 5. While Greiner allows for the conscious decision to remain in a particular stage and Churchill and Lewis provide numerous 'break-off' paths for disengagement or failure, it nonetheless remains implicit that the 'norm' for firms is to follow and complete the process.

- Second, the models do not allow for a backward movement along the continuum or for the 'skipping' of stages. It is surely conceivable that many firms will reach 'Take-off' only to find themselves plunged back into a struggle for survival due to unexpected changes in markets, technology or consumer preferences. In addition, the requirement for the firm to complete each individual stage, before moving forward, seems excessively limiting. In the case of the Churchill and Lewis model, we can envisage some firms moving from 'Existence' to 'Growth' with such speed that 'Survival' is either negligible or non-existent. We can also conceive of a start-up which is sufficiently large as to fulfil the criteria for Churchill and Lewis's Stage 3-G.

- Third, and perhaps most significant, the models do not permit firms to exhibit characteristics from one or more stage, to become hybrids. As brief illustrations, from Greiner we can conjecture a situation whereby top management style is participative (Phase 5) while the organization structure is informal (Phase 1); from Churchill and Lewis, a situation such that formal systems are either maturing (Stage 4) or extensive (Stage 5) and yet the major strategy is survival (a new franchisee may be one such example).

- Fourth, the idea that firms are occasionally able to learn and adjust with greater effect in response to crises than in periods of relative stability seems entirely plausible. Yet, that crises occur in the non-random manner suggested, given the inherent uncertainty within which firms operate, is far less credible. It is conceivable that some firms will lurch from crisis to crisis and that these crises will not be of leadership, autonomy, control and red tape, but of market stagnation, market saturation, technology, finance or skills (i.e. a mixture of internal and external crises, rather than the purely internal crises Greiner conjectures). It is also conceivable that other firms will enjoy smooth growth over a relatively uninterrupted horizon.

Stage models do place a welcome emphasis on the role of history in defining the future shape and success of an organization. Greiner explicitly notes the importance of 'historical actions ... [as] ... determinants of what happens to the company at a much later date' (pp. 45–6). Where difficulties arise is in the interpretation of this historicity, path dependency and crisis-stimulated growth. The frameworks suggested are overly rigid. The inevitability of each stage and each crisis is implausible. To assume that firms move from one stage to another along a narrow path, shaped only by periods of regularly recurring crises, ignores the variability and complexity of firm growth, the copious causes and the inconsistency of their influence.

PREDICTIVE MODELLING OF GROWTH

In his final criticism of stage models, Storey[18] notes that the 'models describe, rather than predict' (p. 122). Accordingly, it is to the body of literature concerned with predictive modelling of firm growth that we turn to in this section.

Financial Models

The early work undertaken by Storey *et al.*[20] concentrated on the role of standard financial variables in predicting successful small firms. This method, adapted from use with large corporations, adopted an inverted approach to predicting small firm success – predicting failure and identifying success by implication. After initial testing of 'univariate ratio analysis' (consideration of individual financial ratios in progression rather than as a composite) proved inappropriate, Storey and colleagues shifted their focus towards methods of multivariate inquiry (principally 'multiple discriminant analysis'). In short, while univariate analysis suggested, predictably, that low profitability and high gearing ratios were positive correlates of small firm failure, the researchers' 'optimum' multivariate model utilized cashflow and asset structure variables as their primary predictors. On the basis of this final model, Storey *et al.* claimed a 75 per cent success rate in distinguishing between failed firms and survivors.

Several criticisms can be levelled at this technique:[b]

CRITICISM OF PREDICTIVE FINANCIAL MODELS

1. The technique offers no historical insight. That is, there is little consistent evidence to suggest that the variables alter significantly as the companies approach failure; nor is there any indication of the underlying causes of failure.

2. As a predictive model for rapid growth firms, the technique would appear inadequate. Since its purpose is to identify firms that will fail, the model is unable to distinguish between the small proportion of growth firms and the bulk of survivors.

3. The model takes little account of the human capital factors that assuredly play a considerable role in determining survival and growth.[21,22]

Characteristics Approach

Subsequent efforts to distinguish growth firms from their stable or declining contemporaries have tended to place a greater emphasis on non-financial characteristics of the owner-manager and the firm. In a comprehensive review and

[b] For a more detailed critique, see Reid and Jacobsen[13] (pp. 78–83).

synthesis of the research literature,[c] Storey postulates that small firm growth is driven by three integral component sets: characteristics of the entrepreneur (identifiable pre-start); characteristics of the firm (identifiable at start); and characteristics of the corporate strategy (identifiable post-start).[18] From the empirical studies reviewed, Storey isolates those factors where 'consistent' evidence of influence was available (Table 10.3).

Entrepreneur	Firm	Strategy
Motivation	Age	External equity
Education	Legal form	Market positioning
Managerial experience	Location	New product introduction
Teams	Size	Management recruitment
Age	Market/sector	
	Ownership	

Table 10.3 Storey's characteristics approach

The Entrepreneur

Motivation

The conjectured influence of motivation has a tidy, intuitive and appealing logic. It is suggested that individuals who are 'pulled' into business ownership, and whose motivations are consequently positive, are more likely to develop growth firms than those who are 'pushed' and whose motivations are correspondingly negative. However, in common with other areas of entrepreneurship, motivation is likely to be a more complex process, often the result of an interplay of factors.[23] Simplifying motivation into an artificial dichotomy ('pull' versus 'push') is likely to be misleading.

Education

There are two contrasting hypotheses presented for this factor. First, it may be argued that education provides a foundation from which the entrepreneur can undertake the personal and professional development necessary for successful entrepreneurship and that education will endow the entrepreneur with greater confidence in dealing with bankers, customers and suppliers. This, again, seems entirely plausible. Second, and conversely, however, it may also be argued that 'business ownership is not an intellectual activity' (p. 129) and that the educated entrepreneur will quickly become wearied with the many tedious tasks which form the remit of most owner-managers. From the 18 studies that form Storey's review, evidence is found to support the former hypothesis in preference to the latter. More specifically, further research has indicated that, while a first degree in a science or engineering subject may be most appropriate for high-technology entrepreneurs, it is likely that a trade qualification is more suited to success in many mainstream firms.[24]

[c] Summarized effectively in Barkham *et al.*[25] (Ch. 2).

It would appear that education, not to a level but of a type, influences the entrepreneur's ability in the given environment and, consequently, the firm's chances of growth. However, since little effort is made to explain the effect education has on firm processes we cannot explain why various types or levels of education *occasionally* influence growth. For instance, Barkham *et al.*,[25] in their four-region study of the determinants of growth, note that 'Education matters ... but in an indirect way, and the disadvantage of poorer education can be overcome by those who adopt similar strategies to graduates' (p. 140); the authors suggest that education per se does not influence growth, but rather education influences strategic choice which, in turn, influences growth. The underlying process issues remain hidden.

Managerial experience

Management is literally concerned with the management of people. In this vein, it is often suggested that, in all but the very smallest firms, the principal activity of the entrepreneur is the co-ordination of the work of other individuals. Hence prior managerial experience and, consequently, experience in the co-ordination role will allow the entrepreneur to attend more effectively to his remit and subsequently meet business objectives. There is also a parallel argument regarding the higher 'reservation wages' those with managerial experience are likely to have. Individuals with high reservation wages are unlikely to enter into self-employment without a corresponding high degree of confidence in a successful outcome. In either instance, prior managerial experience is thought to positively impact upon firm growth.

Teams

Storey[18] notes that, 'Since the management of a business requires a range of skills ... businesses owned by more than a single individual are more likely to grow than businesses owned by a single person' (p. 130). This view is often taken to be axiomatic by both academics and policy-makers. However, from his research with high-technology firms (often viewed as the industrial sector representing greatest growth potential), Oakey[26] noted that 'rapid firm growth is strongly related to "single founder" businesses' (p. 16). On a different note, but perhaps as significantly, Vyakarnam *et al.* argue that the core competence of successful entrepreneurs is the ability to build and manage effective teams – not the team itself.[27] In this way, we may more appropriately conceive of the 'entrepreneurial team' as a dynamic and evolutionary phenomenon rather the static entity implied by characteristics or predictive models of firm growth. It is further argued by Vyakarnam *et al.* that the team building process itself is 'non-linear, chaotic and unique', raising questions about the scope for policy to artificially contrive teams.

Age

In line with the evidence viewed by Storey, Cressy argues that the critical characteristics of growth firms are associated with human capital variables – most significantly founder(s) age and team size.[24] Much as with Gibb and Richie's 'social dynamic' model, age may be used as a proxy for accumulated capital (both human and material), though Gibb and Richie imply a degree of trade-off between accumulated capital, on the one hand, and energy and tolerance of risk, on the other. Notwithstanding this, it is interesting to note that research frequently points to a strongly increasing self-employment rate up to the 35–44 age group, declining thereafter, before rising dramatically again to peak in the post-65 age range.

The Firm

Legal status

In his review, Storey[18] finds overwhelming support for the contention that 'United Kingdom studies consistently point to more rapid growth being experienced by limited companies' (p. 140). Credibility with customers, suppliers and financial institutions is argued to be the principal benefit of incorporation. Although limited liability is often circumvented through the provision of personal guarantees to funding providers, it is difficult in the face of the evidence to dispute this hypothesis. However, from the perspective of predictive modelling it should be noted that legal form is by no means stationary. As Storey points out, 'we cannot reject the hypothesis that current legal status is a consequence rather than a cause of growth' (p. 141).

Age and size

The issues of firm size and age are often dealt with concurrently since it can be safely assumed that they are often related variables. While the relationship between size and age is by no means linear, we can plausibly suggest that in aggregate "[t]he more a firm grows (the bigger it is) the more likely it is to survive another period (the older it is).'[28] With regards to growth, accepted wisdom states that small firms grow faster than large firms and that younger firms grow faster than older firms. From the point of view of policy, logic would superficially seem to endorse the support of small, new firms as a means to achieving employment policy objectives. On a cautionary note it should be understood that most studies deal with changing *rates* of growth and not with absolute growth. An additional caveat would be to note that, since in practice all failures are omitted from empirical samples, there is a tendency to overestimate small firm growth rates in relation to their larger counterparts.[29] Further, as recent research has noted, employement growth within the small firm sector is primarily a result of existing business expansion rather than new firm creation.[30,31] Indirectly allied to this is the notion that 'The probability of a firm failing falls as it increases in size and as it increases in age'[21] (p. 17).

Location

Since the bulk of small firms operate in localized markets, location (as a proxy for the buoyancy of these local markets) will presumably influence firm performance. In this vein, Storey suggests that, on balance, the empirical evidence indicates a higher propensity to grow more rapidly for firms located in accessible rural areas than for firms located both in urban areas and in remote rural areas – although no attempt is made to rationalize this finding. By contrast, more recent work by Westhead[32] found that 'the majority of firms suggested more than half their customers were located outside the county region of the businesses main operating premises' (pp. 375–6) and that 'urban firms had recorded the largest absolute and standardised employment increases since business start-up' (p. 375). Fundamentally, the literature is decidedly equivocal on this point. Even the studies reviewed by Storey fail to reach consensus. Regardless, this factor does little to enhance our understanding of cause and effect. Location itself does not directly influence growth; rather, a number of inconsistently related variables – such as physical and support infrastructure, resource munificence and availability of skilled labour – are the 'true' factors for which location acts as a fallible proxy variable.

Market/industry sector

With regards to markets or industry sector, high-technology small firms have often been viewed as a potential panacea for the structural unemployment which was attendant upon the decline of traditional industries over the last 30 years. This view is reflected in the plethora of policy initiatives directed at this sector of the economy. However, as Oakey stresses, what little evidence there is available to support this contention has been extrapolated from mainly American data.[26] In contrast, and at the risk of repetition, recall the recent OECD[(33)] conclusion that 'Most high growth firms are not innovative in a technical sense, but may include marketing innovations or cross-national alliances. Most high-tech firms are not high growth, [and] Most new jobs are created by low innovation, low growth traditional firms' (pp. 57–8). Concerned by policy-makers' excessively optimistic view of high- and new-technology small firms, Tether[34] notes that 'expectations of small firms as "atomistic" innovators and employment creators have become over-inflated' (p. 109).

Ownership

A number of recent academic studies have indicated that a considerable amount of small firm growth is inorganic, i.e. growth through acquisition and through the development, by individual entrepreneurs, of other distinct business. The latter notion, often called 'portfolio entrepreneurship', has enjoyed a considerable surge in popularity.[35,36,37] Scott and Rosa contend that the predilection of small firm researchers for firm-level analysis fails to recognize the contribution of the individual entrepreneur to wealth and capital accumulation.[38] While this might be true, the survey-based methodologies employed have a tendency to overstate the case. For example, such remote, and often general, studies are unable to distinguish between those who have started another trading business and those who have merely registered another company for legal reasons. In addition, regardless of the merits of identifying portfolio entrepreneurs and shifting the focus of research from firm-level to individual-level analysis, the substance of the research findings to date have not advanced our ability to 'explain' the process through which wealth and capital are accumulated.

The Strategy

External equity

It is generally accepted that the sources of finance accessed and the corresponding financial structures of small firms will influence their propensity to grow. The relative reliance of firms on short-term, often overdraft, debt finance is clearly far from ideal.[39] To this end, Storey suggests that those firms which have either shared external equity or have been willing to allow an external holding in their company are more likely to grow than those which have, or are, not. This capital for equity exchange allows firms to circumvent the constraint imposed by short-term debt funding. Yet, we note two points which indicate the need for caution: first, as Storey himself points out, it may be the case that the only firms which attract external equity are those which have grown or exhibit obvious potential for growth. Consequently, there is no indication of the direction of causation. Second, irrespective of the inclination, or indeed disinclination, of small firms towards equity sharing, there undoubtedly exists some form of 'equity gap' (see Chapters 5 and 6).[40] In other words, many small firms, regardless of desire and strategic stance, are unable to obtain equity funding. It may be that this factor is, in part, not a true measure of strategy but is, instead, a measure of the beneficence of the external environment – an exogenous variable rather than an endogenous variable.

Market positioning

The temptation has always existed to characterize small firm competition as either perfect or pure in the economic sense.[41] In this way firms become price takers and are bereft of any market power, consequently unable to adopt price competition strategies, erect entry barriers and are overly vulnerable to the vagaries of the ensuing market uncertainty. Since perfect competition requires, *inter alia*, perfect knowledge about present and future states, perfect factor mobility and perfectly rational maximizing actors, this has always been a surprising and implausible assertion. Pure competition, which relaxes the first and second of these assumption,[d] is slightly more credible and is attractive, given that, superficially, we can identify in many industries or markets a large number of small firms competing. The argument, then, for market positioning is that growth firms overcome this lack of market power and pricing discretion by inhabiting niches or Penrosean interstices. Competition becomes monopolistic and the firm is able to set prices above marginal cost – making above normal profits which help to finance growth and increase relative market share (thus reducing uncertainty). Yet, casual observation might lead one to suggest that price competition is, on the whole, becoming less common. It is likely that most firms undertake some form of differentiation strategy, be it direct product characteristics, customer demographics or product quality. Although a niche strategy is undoubtedly advantageous, on aggregate, it is likely to be neither a sufficient nor, indeed, a necessary condition for growth. Indeed, there is some concern over the appropriateness of niches for sustainable growth. Barber *et al.*[42] for instance, suggest that '[t]he challenge facing the growing firm can be stated in terms of a move from relatively narrow market niches in which it exploits a narrow range of distinctive assets into a situation in which it serves a larger number of market segments with a much broader skills and knowledge base' (pp. 15–16).

Another, and related, component of market position involves competitor characteristics. It may be plausibly argued that fast growth firms, occupying market niches, see

[d] Nor in practice is the assumption of perfectly rational maximizing actors held to be true.

their primary competitors as other small firms occupying the same or adjacent niches.[41] Conversely, poorer performing firms would be in direct competition with large firms where no niche exists. Accordingly, the large firms are able to take advantage of a relatively large market share to the detriment of the small firm. While there is an internal logic to this argument, the empirical evidence is, once again, inconclusive. For instance, Westhead and Birley[12] note that '[Growth] firms are associated with a strategic stance of competing with large employment sized firms rather than a decision to operate in markets saturated by fellow new and small firms' (p. 28).

New product introduction

New product introduction is, as a means of differentiating one firm's products from another's, related to the above discussion of product differentiation and market niches. However, it is not clear whether the measure addresses products new to the market and industry or simply those new to the firm (i.e. and extension of an individual firms product range). Truly new products (i.e. those new to the market and/or industry) are often taken as a measure of innovative activity and it is suggested that innovative firms perform better than non-innovative firms.[43,44] However, as we have seen in the discussion of the market/industry sector above, Oakey finds little evidence to support the contention that innovative firms enjoy super-growth.[26] This is supported, in part, by Wynarczyk and Thwaites,[45] who find that 'strong growth in employment is not a strong feature of the average innovative firm' (p. 186). Moreover, recent literature suggests that firms whose efforts at innovation fail are more likely to perform poorly than those that make no attempt to innovate.[46] To restate, it may be more appropriate to consider three innovation-derived sub-classifications – i.e. 'tried and succeeded', 'tried and failed' and 'not tried' – rather than two. Dichotomizing may serve to overstate the observed performance differential between innovative small firms and genuine non-innovators (i.e. those firms attempting no innovation), leading to the conclusion that firms not attempting to innovate are inevitably making an unwise choice. This is patently an erroneous position.

Turning to the second sub-factor, i.e. products new to the firm only, one may logically suggest that the broadening of product or service portfolios would insulate the firm against localized market shocks and consequently improve survival chances and increase likelihood of growth. Unfortunately, little or no work is available to support this final hypothesis.

Management recruitment

Recalling the stage models discussed in the earlier part of this chapter it can be seen that, as the firm grows, the managerial function becomes progressively more complex. This is likely to hold true, though perhaps not in the inevitable and incremental manner suggested by the stage models. As the firm grows, the manager can no longer maintain effective control over the minutiae of day-to-day operations and is required to delegate certain tasks to wage employees within the firm. The owner-manager's task becomes the identification or recruitment and motivation of suitable individuals who can 'manage' in his/her stead – sometimes characterized as a move from 'doing' to 'managing' to 'managing managers'. In a very general way, this is linked to the Penrosean competence/resource theory of firm growth (the link may also extend to the earlier discussion of teams). Penrose argued that the presence of a sufficiently experienced executive resource was required for confident planning and subsequent growth.[47] However, in the Penrosean model executive resource would ideally be internally experienced, whereas Storey suggests that growth firms are more likely to recruit managers externally. Regardless, as Storey notes, there has been insufficient research in this area. Intuitively, it is likely that management recruitment is both a consequence and a cause of growth and any subsequent growth will be significantly influenced, not by the presence of, but by the efficacy of new management.

In addition to his triumvirate, Storey notes the importance of the 'wish to grow' in achieving growth (pp. 119–21). This conjecture is supported by Smallbone *et al.*[48] who contend that 'One of the most important factors [in influencing growth] is the commitment of the leader of the company to achieving growth' (p. 59). While it can be plausibly argued that all small firms that grow do not do so willingly, occasionally being 'dragged' by a growing dominant customer, it would nonetheless seem prudent to include this factor in any predictive growth model.

The model described above clearly has a number of weaknesses – most of which are identified by Storey himself. Nonetheless, it represents the best available model, of its type. Moreover, the logic underlying the inclusion of individual variables is compelling and, in aggregate, they probably impact upon firms in much the way Storey envisages. Accordingly, it is emphatically not our intention to suggest that any of the factors discussed above do not influence firm growth – they undoubtedly do. Rather, there exists concern over the consistency of impact. And consistency is a prerequisite for prediction. Fundamentally, the influence of each variable is neither consistent nor, by consequence, predictable. Storey's model, and models of this ilk, do not describe, predict or, more importantly, explain very well. To this end, we would echo Smallbone *et al.*[48] in suggesting that '[w]hile it may be possible to identify key success factors that affect the growth of SMEs, it is unlikely that a comprehensive model with predictive capability will emerge'.

It should be noted that Storey, in his turn, is chary of 'picking-winners', most especially at start-up. Likening the process to a horse race, where the odds of backing a winner are unknown (though factors such as form or lineage may influence the outcome), Storey suggested that, when 'gambling' with public money, it would be better to back horses after a significant number of hurdles had been cleared; that is, after the high number of failures associated with the initial 2–3-year trading period have occurred.[49]

THINK POINTS 10.2

Entrepreneurial and growth firms

1. Compare Churchill and Lewis to Greiner's model of firm growth: Why are they characterized as life cycle models? How are they different?
2. What are the three broad categories of 'characteristics' in Storey's approach?
3. Can the characteristics approach explain firm growth?
4. Do any of the case studies given in this text fit a life cycle approach to entrepreneurial growth?

BARRIERS TO GROWTH

At the same time as the predictive modelling literature has grown, other commentators have argued that the focus of research and policy should be towards relieving barriers to growth for small firms rather than identifying generic characteristics or sets of characteristics.[23] Although such an approach does not concern itself directly with growth theories, it has merits which recommend its inclusion in a review chapter of this type. The suggestion that 'artificial' barriers to growth exist and that firms may grow more readily were these barriers to be removed may be viewed from a different perspective. Implicitly, this approach suggests that a particular external state or internal structure is more appropriate for growth than that which prevails in the absence of suggested interventions.

As part of an ACARD (Advisory Council for Applied Research and Development) and DTI sponsored study designed to examine the barriers to growth faced by 'high flyers', Barber *et al.*[42] summarizing the literature, suggest that these constraints consist of three types: management and motivation; resources; and market opportunities and structure.[e] Specifically, these would include, *inter alia*: lack of management training, relatively low qualifications, reluctance to delegate, and the need for new management skills and techniques as the organization grows; access to finance, access to skilled labour and access to technology; market growth rates, size and frequency of purchases, degree of segmentation and opportunities for collaboration or merger. Many of the factors in this list are complements of, or related to, variables discussed in the previous sections. For example, lack of management training may equate with prior management experience, low

[e] The work of the ACARD and DTI funded study was built upon by the later ACOST (Advisory Council on Science and Technology) study.[60] The findings of this second study served to support those of the first. In particular, it suggested that 'the ultimate barriers to growth relate to strategic management and lack of internal resources to make key business transitions' (p. v).

qualifications with education, degree of segmentation with market positioning and so on. However, the variable which sits least comfortably, although arguably loosely related to the earlier discussion of external equity, is that of access to finance. In addition, this is the most commonly cited and vigorously debated 'barrier' to growth.

Although the issue of finance was discussed in greater detail in Chapters 5 and 6, the following represents a brief recounting with a view to the current context. The argument generally focuses upon either the 'equity gap', discussed earlier, or access to bank finance – since most firms rely principally upon the latter method of funding. With regards to banks, it is often argued that some form of market failure or 'finance gap' in the provision of debt to small firms exists. In short, small firm demand for bank loans exceeds supply and the market fails to reach equilibrium at prevailing prices (interest rates set, by the Bank of England, below market equilibrium price). However, such an argument assumes homogeneous loan proposals, which is unlikely to be the case. Undoubtedly, some proposals will be of greater inherent worth than others. It is more likely that any difficulties relate to the relationship between small firms and their banks. Due to the nature of the banking relationship, in the presence of information asymmetries and moral hazard, adverse selection and credit rationing are liable to prevail. The risk averse character of banks may result in not selecting 'good' proposals in preference to selecting 'bad' proposals.[50] As a 'remedy' it is suggested that, while perfect information is an unattainable ideal, there exists scope to improve information flows between small firms and their bankers.[51] There are further issues regarding the inconsistency of criteria used in, and the often subjective nature of, bank appraisal procedures.[52] Regardless of the plausibility of the above argument, and the laudability of the suggested response, there exists little empirical evidence that access to finance represents a significant barrier to growth.[53]

On a more general note there exists a counter argument to the suggested lifting of presumed barriers to growth. It is implied that entrepreneurs, or small business owner-managers, trading in hostile environments are more likely to develop the characteristics of self-reliance and determination required to succeed.[54] Consequently, policy should avoid lowering barriers or providing incentives that dull the development of these attributes. This is a generally untested hypothesis built upon principally anecdotal and ad hoc observations and it is doubtful whether such an extreme position would be of value in the generality of policy. While we might feel a policy of erecting or maintaining barriers is a step too far, Cressy's suggestion that we should adopt a stricter German model which, by making start-up more difficult (or less easy), aims at raising the threshold quality of new ventures has some merit.[24]

THINK POINTS 10.3

Entrepreneurial and growth firms

1. Why might finance be regarded as a barrier to entrepreneurial firm growth?

2. In Chapter 9, it was suggested that support agencies such as the Business Links might attempt to target their support at entrepreneurial growth firms:

   Why does evidence presented in this chapter suggest that this policy might be unproductive?

3. From the previous discussion in this chapter, and the illustration shown in Figure 10.3, why might the legal ownership of an entrepreneurial firm be a large barrier to growth?

CONCLUSIONS

If this chapter were to provide a comprehensive review of all contributions to our understanding of small firm growth it would require a dedicated text in itself. Instead, we have contented ourselves with presenting key strands which have had considerable influence on public policy and mainstream academic debate. Of these, less attention has been given to the somewhat abstract neoclassical economics and stochastic approaches. At the level of the firm, their ability to throw light upon the process of growth is limited and their inclusion serves merely to highlight the weaknesses incumbent upon theorizing about averages or in aggregate.

The chapter also outlines two highly influential, though oft criticized, stage models of growth. While implausibly rigid, stage models are truly process-oriented and grant due attention to the role of history in determining the actions and structures of firms. However, we concur with Storey: the models describe rather than predict or, more significantly, explain (unless through equally implausible, non-random, defined crises).

On the other hand, the characteristics or predictive modelling approach to small firm growth has itself reached an impasse. The factors influencing growth are innumerable and are likely to defy classification in a simple, useable model. Attempting to isolate those where evidence of effect is 'consistent' appears fruitless. Perhaps more importantly, while many of the factors incorporated in such models *may* have considerable influence on the growth of small firms, any influence is likely to be contingent upon the given context.

More recently, emphasis has begun to shift from static analysis of (often categorical) proxy variables towards a more dynamic analysis of the processes of adaptation and learning.[55,56,57,58] Simplistically, it may be suggested that, since growth necessitates change, those firms that have enjoyed sustainable growth are those which were most receptive to change and/or have managed change most effectively. Within this context, learning is seen as a process of adaptation to changes in internal and external environments. This view owes much to Edith Penrose's early work on competence- or resource-based theories of the firm.[1] Penrose, for instance, noted that:

"the growing experience of management, its knowledge of the other resources of the firm and of the potential for using them in different ways, create incentives for further expansion as the firm searches for ways of using the services of its own resources more profitably." (p. xii)

Where limitations on growth exist, these relate to managerial competence and to the endowed resources (technology, skills, finance, etc.) of the firm. Moreover, in the sense that learning is cumulative, so the development of the firm is likely to be history- or path-dependent: 'Like the great men of whom Tolstoy wrote in *War and Peace*, "[e]very action of theirs, that seems to them an act of their own free will, is in bondage to the whole course of previous history".'[59] (p. 333)

The aim of such research is to discover and delineate the underlying processes of adaptive learning and growth, irrespective of context, or, indeed, to determine whether such processes exist. Unfortunately, no coherent, testable model has been developed to date. The development of a suitable process theory of (small) firm growth remains one of the major challenges in entrepreneurship and the wider social sciences, though interested students are directed to a recent paper by Elizabeth Garnsey, which serves as an excellent starting point.[58]

SUGGESTED ASSIGNMENTS

Resources

The following assignment is based on the Nichol McKay case study provided in the student online learning resources material. Further information on this case and teaching notes are also available in the *Lecturer's Manual*.

Required

Prepare a written report for a classroom discussion to answer the following:

1. Consider the Nichol McKay case in light of Storey's tripartite model. How closely does Nichol McKay fit the criteria suggested in the model?
2. Where possible, can the direction/nature of cause and effect be determined?
3. At start-up would we have predicted Nichol McKay's subsequent growth and success?

REFERENCES

1. Penrose, E. (1995/1959) *The Theory of the Growth of the Firm*, Blackwell, London.

2. Storey, D. and Johnson, S. (1987) *Are Small Firms the Answer to Unemployment?* Employment Institute, London.

3. Gallagher, C. and Stewart, H. (1985) 'Business Death and Firms Size in the UK', *International Small Business Journal*, vol. 4, no. 1, pp. 42–57.

4. Doyle, J. and Gallagher, C. (1987) 'Size Distribution, Growth Potential and Job Generation Contributions of UK Firms', *International Small Business Journal*, vol. 6, no. 1, pp. 31–56.

5. Gallagher, C. and Miller, P. (1991) 'New Fast Growing Companies Create Jobs', *Long Range Planning*, vol. 24, no. 1, pp. 96–101.

6. Scottish Enterprise (1993) *Improving the Business Birth Rate: A Strategy for Scotland*, Scottish Enterprise, Glasgow.

7. Marshall, A. (1920) *Principles of Economics*, 8th edn, Macmillan, London.

8. Ijiri, Y. and Simon, H. (1977) *Skew Distributions and the Sizes of Business Firms*, North-Holland, Amsterdam.

9. O'Farrell, P. and Hitchens, D. (1988) 'Alternative theories of small-firm growth: a critical review', *Environment and Planning A*, vol. 20, pp. 1365–83.

10. Gibrat, R. (1931) *Les Inégalités Economiques*, Sirey, Paris.

11. Mansfield, E. (1962) 'Entry, Gibrat's Law, innovation and the growth of firms', *American Economic Review*, 52, 1023–51.

12. Westhead, P. and Birley, S. (1995) 'Employment Growth in New Independent Owner-managed Firms in GB', *International Small Business Journal*, vol. 13, no. 3, pp. 11–34.

13. Reid, G. and Jacobsen, L. (1988) *The Small Entrepreneurial Firm*, Aberdeen University Press, Aberdeen.

14. Nelson, R. and Winters, S. (1978) 'Forces Generating and Limiting Concentration under Schumpeterian Competition', *Bell Journal of Economics*, vol. 9, pp. 524–48.

15. Greiner, L. (1972) 'Evolution and revolution as organisations grow', *Harvard Business Review*, vol. 50, July–August, pp. 37–46.

16. Churchill, N. and Lewis, V. (1983) 'The five stages of small business growth', *Harvard Business Review*, vol. 61, May–June, pp. 30–50.

17. Scott, M. And Bruce, R. (1987) 'Five Stages of Growth in Small Business', *Long Range Planning*, vol. 20, no. 3, pp. 45–52.

18. Storey, D. (1994) *Understanding the Small Business Sector*, Routledge, London.

19. Burns, P. and Harrison, J. (1996) 'Growth', in Burns, P. and Dewhurst, J. (eds) *Small Business and Entrepreneurship*, Macmillan, London.

20. Storey, D., Keasey, K., Watson, R. and Wynarczyk, P. (1987) *The Performance of Small Firms: Profits, Jobs and Failures*, Croom Helm, London.

21. Hall, G. (1995) *Surviving and Prospering in the Small Firm Sector*, Routledge, London.

22. Gallagher, C. and Robson, G. (1996) 'The Identification of High Growth SMEs', paper presented to the 19th National Small Firms Policy and Research Conference, Birmingham.

23. Freel, M. (1998) 'Policy, Prediction and Growth: picking start-up winners?' *Journal of Small Business and Enterprise Development*, vol. 5, no. 1, pp. 19–32.

24. Cressy, R. (1996) 'Are Business Start-ups Debt Rationed?' *The Economic Journal*, vol. 106, no. 438, pp. 1253–70.

25. Barkham, R., Gudgin, G., Hanvey, E. and Hart, M. (1996) *The Determinats of Small Firm Growth*, Jessica Kingsley, London.

26. Oakey, R. (1995) *High-Technology Small Firms: Variable Barriers to Growth*, Paul Chapman, London.

27. Vyakarnam, S., Jacobs, R. and Handelberg, J. (1996) 'Building and Managing Relationships: The core competence of rapid growth business', paper presented to the 19th National Small Firms Policy and Research Conference, Birmingham (unpublished amended version).

28. Jensen, J.B. and McGuckin, R.H. (1997) 'Firm Performance and Evolution: Empirical Regularities in the US Microdata', *Industrial and Corporate Change*, vol. 6, no. 1, pp. 25–47.

29. Jovanovic, B. (1982) 'Selection and the Evolution of Industry', *Econometrica*, vol. 50, no. 3, pp. 649–70.

30. ENSR (1994) *The European Observatory for SMEs: 2nd Annual Report*, ENSR/EIM.

31. Smallbone, D. and North, D. (1995) 'Targeting Established SMEs: Does Their Age Matter?' *International Small Business Journal*, vol. 13, no. 3, pp. 47–64.

32. Westhead, P. (1995) 'New Owner-managed Business in Rural and Urban Areas in Great Britain: A Matched Pairs Comparison' *Regional Studies*, vol. 29, no. 4, pp. 367–80.

33. OECD (1996) *SMEs: Employment, Innovation and Growth – The Washington Workshop*.

34. Tether, B. (2000) 'Small firms, innovation and employment creation in Britain and Europe: A question of expectations', *Technovation*, vol. 20, pp. 109–13.

35. Birley, S. and Westhead, P. (1994) 'A Comparison of New Businesses Established by "Novice" and "Habitual" Founders in GB', *International Small Business Journal*, vol. 12, no. 1, pp. 38–60.

36. Scott, M. and Rosa, P. (1996) 'Existing Business as Sources of New Firms: A missing topic in business formation research', paper presented to the Babson *Entrepreneurship Research Conference*, Seattle, USA.

37. Westhead, P. and Wright, M. (1997) 'Novice, Portfolio and Serial Founders: are they different?' paper presented to the Babson Entrepreneurship Research Conference, Boston, USA.

38. Scott, M. and Rosa, P. (1996) 'Has Firm Level Analysis Reached its Limits? Time for a Rethink', *International Small Business Journal*, vol. 14, no. 4, pp. 81–9.

39. Deakins, D. and Hussain, G. (1994) 'Financial Information, the Banker and Small Business: A Comment', *British Accounting Review*, vol. 26.

40. Murray, G. (1994) 'The Second "Equity Gap": Exit Problems for Seed and Early Stage Venture Capitalists and their Investee Companies', *International Small Business Journal*, vol. 12, no. 4, pp. 58–76.

41. Storey, D. and Sykes, N. (1996) 'Uncertainty, Innovation and Management', in Burns, P. and Dewhurst, J. (eds) *Small Business and Entrepreneurship*, Macmillan, London.

42. Barber, J., Metcalfe, S. and Porteous, M. (1989) 'Barriers to growth: the ACARD study', in Barber, J., Metcalfe, S. and Porteous, M. (eds) *Barriers to Growth in Small Firms*, Routledge, London.

43. Rothwell, R. and Zegveld, W. (1982) *Innovation and the Small and Medium Sized Firm*, Francis Pinter, London.

44. Gerowski, P. and Machin, S. (1992) 'Do Innovating Firms Outperform Non-Innovators?' *Business Strategy Review*, Summer, pp. 79–90.

45. Wynarczyk, P. and Thwaites, A. (1997) 'The Economic Performance, Survival and Non-Survival of Innovative Small Firms', in Oakey, R. And Muktar, S. (eds) *New Technology-Based Firms in the 1990s: Volume III*, Paul Chapman, London.

46. Audretsch, D. (1995) 'Innovation, growth and survival', *International Journal of Industrial Organisation*, 13, 441–57.

47. Penrose, E. (1971) 'Limits to the Size and Growth of Firms', in *The Growth of Firms, Middle East Oil and Other essays*, first published in *American Economic Review*, vol. 45, no. 2.

48. Smallbone, D., Leigh, R. and North, D. (1995) 'The characteristics and Strategies of High Growth SMEs', *International Journal of Entrepreneurial Behaviour and Research*, vol. 1, no. 3, pp. 44–62.

49. Storey, D. (1992) 'Should We Abandon the Support to Start Up Businesses?' paper presented to the 15th National Small Firms Policy and Research Conference, Southampton.

50. Deakins, D. and Hussain, G. (1991) *Risk Assessment by Bank Managers*, Birmingham Polytechnic Business School.

51. Binks, M. and Ennew, C. (1996) 'Financing Small Firms', in Burns, P. and Dewhurst, J. (eds) *Small Business and Entrepreneurship*, Macmillan, London.

52. Deakins, D., Hussian, G. and Ram, M. (1992) 'Overcoming the Adverse Selection Problem', paper presented to the 15th National Small Firms Policy and Research Conference, Southampton.

53. Cressy, R. (1996) 'Are Business Start-ups Debt Rationed?' *The Economic Journal*, vol. 106, no. 438, pp. 1253–70.

54. Dewhurst, J. (1996) 'The Entrepreneur', in Burns, P. and Dewhurst, J. (eds) *Small Business and Entrepreneurship*, Macmillan, London.

55. Freel, M. (1998) 'Evolution, innovation and learning: evidence from case studies', *Entrepreneurship and Regional Development*, vol. 10, no. 2, pp. 137–49.

56. Costello, N. (1996) 'Learning and Routines in High-Tech SMEs: Analysing Rich Case Study Material', *Journal of Economic Issues*, vol. 30, no. 2, pp. 591–7.

57. Wiklund, J. (1998) *Small Firm Growth and Performance: Entrepreneurship and Beyond*, dissertation series no. 3, Jönköping International Business School.

58. Garnsey, E. (1998) 'A Theory of the Early Growth of Firms', *Industrial and Corporate Change*, vol. 7, no. 3, pp. 523–56.

59. David, P. (1985) 'Clio and the Economics of QWERTY', *AEA Papers and Proceedings*, vol. 75, no. 2, pp. 332–37.

60. ACOST (1990) *The Enterprise Challenge: Overcoming Barriers to Growth in Small Firms*, HMSO, London.

RECOMMENDED READING

ACOST (1990) *The Enterprise Challenge: Overcoming Barriers to Growth in Small Firms*, HMSO, London.

Barkham, R., Gudgin, G., Hanvey, E. and Hart, M. (1996) *The Determinants of Small Firm Growth*, Jessica Kingsley, London.

Churchill, N. and Lewis, V. (1983) 'The five stages of small business growth', *Harvard Business Review*, vol. 61, May–June, pp. 30–50.

Freel, M. (1998) 'Policy, Prediction and Growth: picking start-up winners?' *Journal of Small Business and Enterprise Development*, vol. 5, no. 1, pp. 19–32.

Greiner, L. (1972) 'Evolution and revolution as organisations grow', *Harvard Business Review*, vol. 50, July–August, pp. 37–46.

Storey, D. (1994) *Understanding the Small Business Sector*, Routledge, London.

11

INTERNATIONAL ENTREPRENEURSHIP AND THE GLOBAL ECONOMY

LEARNING OUTCOMES

At the end of this chapter students should be able to:

1. Describe how different cultures can affect entrepreneurial activity.
2. Apply criteria to describe different levels of entrepreneurship in different nations, such as high levels and low levels of entrepreneurial activity.
3. Discuss the factors that affect the level of entrepreneurial activity in different nations.
4. Discuss how all entrepreneurs are affected by the global economy.
5. Discuss opportunities and threats posed by the global economy.
6. Describe examples of the nature of entrepreneurship in advanced, transition and emergent economies.

INTRODUCTION

The previous chapter examined some of the factors in the growth process. One factor likely to be involved in the growth process of an entrepreneurial firm is the ability to export or to internationalize through an overseas operation. For many fast growth firms, establishing overseas markets is an essential part of the growth process. Trading overseas requires some understanding of different cultures, different economies and different ways of 'doing business'. In this chapter we examine some of the characteristics of different cultures (which affect entrepreneurial behaviour), risk-taking and economic production methods in other nations – factors that need to be taken into account by entrepreneurs in the UK who are seeking to expand in overseas markets. We begin by noting the importance of the global economy, a trend, it is argued, that cannot be ignored by any small firm entrepreneur, whether trading internationally or not.

GLOBAL MARKETS

As we have stated a number of times before, the majority of small firm entrepreneurs do not wish to grow (and, by definition, do not wish to export or expand overseas). However, it is arguable that all entrepreneurs are affected by the globalization of the economy. A number of forces have led to increased globalization. All entrepreneurs have to trade in an economy that is affected by the trends or forces forming the global economy. Even if a firm's market is restricted to its local geographical area, it may face competitors that are based overseas and trading locally. Equally, the firm may be part of a supply chain whose end markets are global. For example, the West Midlands region of the UK is well known for the number of small firms that produce car components, supplying to local car manufacturers. All firms in the supply chain will be part of the global market and be unable to ignore trends in that market. A small firm producing car components in Coventry is probably affected more by events in Japan than by local events. While small firms can be embedded in local communities and dependent on the local infrastructure,[1] they are also dependent on global supply chains and markets.[2]

THE GLOBAL ECONOMY AND 11 SEPTEMBER 2001

Notwithstanding the tragic events of 11 September 2001, the immediacy of the effects of the terrorist acts unfortunately illustrated the dependency and interdependence of different sectors and economies that were felt by all sectors of the UK economy and by all entrepreneurial small firms.

The most publicized effects have concerned the major airlines and firms in the tourism sector, dependent on overseas visitors, yet it was unlikely that any firms were totally unaffected. Events organizers found that there were less people willing to travel to business conferences, insurance costs for business travel increased, time taken to travel to business meetings increased due to increased security checks, investment confidence was affected, prices in stock exchanges and financial markets were affected and there were changes in oil prices that further affected the costs of travel and moving goods.

Of course not all firms suffered adversely; we have already noted the contrasting fortunes of large airlines and tour operators with those of low-cost operators such as easyJet in Chapter 3, but the event, if in a very dramatic way, illustrated the interdependency and immediacy that characterizes trading relationships in the global economy.

Nowadays we are all affected by economic events in other economies whether they are taking place in Japan, Russia or closer to home. Ability to respond to these events, to manage with the increasing pace of change, will affect the sustainability and viability of all small firms; part of that increasing pace of change is the globalization of the economy. A number of factors have contributed to the development of the global economy, factors that are increasing in importance. Some of them are listed below (see box).

FACTORS CONTRIBUTING TO THE DEVELOPMENT OF THE GLOBAL ECONOMY

- the development of the knowledge economy, as discussed in detail in Chapter 8;
- greater mobility of the labour force and labour skills, as discussed in Chapter 8;
- improved forms of communication (and information);
- new technological developments that favour smaller firms (e.g. biotechnology/micro-technologies);
- reduction of barriers to trade through agreements formed under the General Agreement on Tariffs and Trade (GATT), now subsumed under the World Trade Association (WTA), and the increased importance of common trading areas such as the European Union;
- increased pace of change requiring flexible and speedy responses;
- privatization and reduced barriers in emerging nations, with the development of economies in transition, the emergence of 'tiger economies' and the emergence of China as a major overseas market;
- increased mobility of labour force and other resources;
- growth of global capital markets.

Implications for Entrepreneurs who Export

Growing companies have to assess how to tackle globalization and the penetration of overseas markets as a result. Operating abroad usually involves one of four approaches:

1. Production at home and *exporting* through partners or agents.
2. Production at home and *licensing* another firm to produce abroad.
3. Entering into a strategic joint venture agreement or partnership to exploit overseas markets (see below).
4. Owning and controlling an overseas operation, through either a *de novo* operation or buying an existing operation.

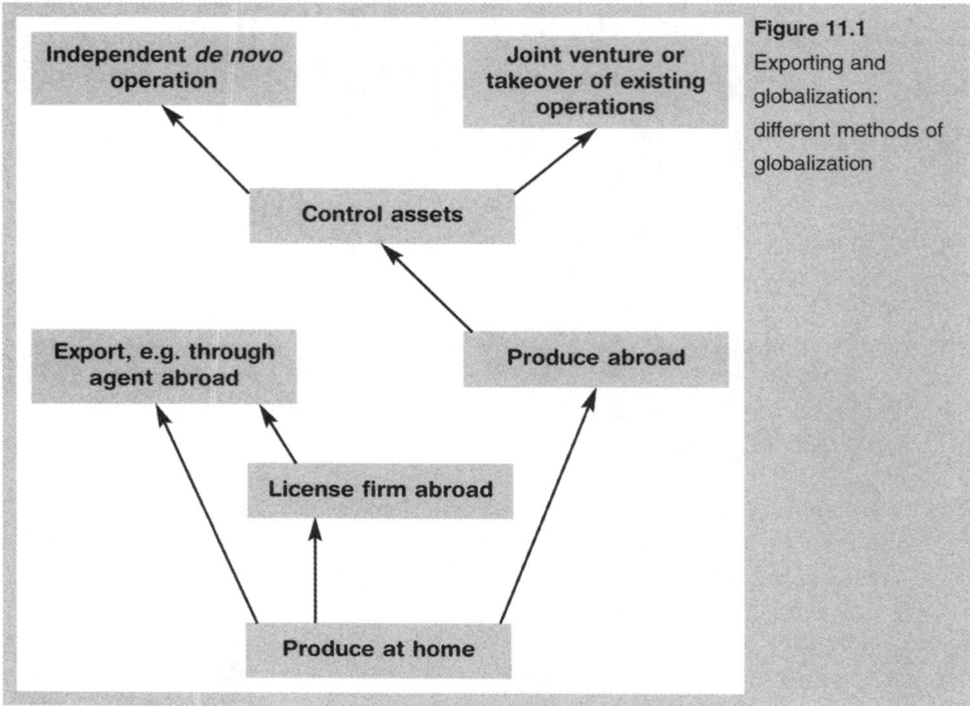

Figure 11.1 Exporting and globalization: different methods of globalization

These alternative methods are illustrated in Figure 11.1. The strategy adopted will depend on the nature of product or service, requirements of the customer and the growth aspirations of the international entrepreneurial firm.

These options represent different strategic choices for the entrepreneurial growth firm. The strategy chosen will depend on a number of factors, such as cost, availability of finance, regulations in different countries, risk involved, availability of strategic partners and exchange rate risks, but not least the entrepreneurial culture of different areas and nations. We have insufficient space for an adequate discussion of these factors; however, drawing on the example of the Aquamotive case study in Chapter 7, we saw there that the firm operated in global markets (supplying control-feeding systems to fish farms). The strategy adopted to exploit such global markets was to seek strategic partnerships. Aquamotive was at an early stage of the development of the product, was still operating on a small scale and with limited resources. Seeking strategic partners represented the best strategy for the firm, given its stage of development and given the resources it had available or could access. For a different firm, in a different technology, a different strategy might be preferable. For example, there are fast growth information technology firms which have quickly established overseas operations through expansion abroad by setting up overseas offices and production facilities and operating subsidiaries as a multinational enterprise. Factors such as the need to be near to their customers (users of new software) and the lower cost of operating abroad were important factors to such firms. This is further illustrated by the example of Nallatech (see Entrepreneurship in Action box, below).

ENTREPRENEURSHIP IN ACTION

Nallatech, by Tom Farrell

Technology-based companies, as illustrated in the previous case of Aquamotive, are often in global markets from their formation or first day of trading and even during their R&D and prototype development. This is further illustrated by the example of Nallatech.

Nallatech was founded in 1993 by Allan Cantle, who at the time was an electronics engineer with British Aerospace. He had been asked by a friend of the family to design a water pump controller, as there were no suitable products for the purpose on the market, and he agreed to do this in return for help in setting up the business. In the event, the design was not immediately commercialized and the company stayed dormant for a couple of years. In August 1995, Allan's wife Sarah, a computer scientist who had been running the IT department for Pegasus Critical Illness Insurance, was relocated when Pegasus was taken over by Abbey National. This was the spur to incorporate the business and Allan set up with a major design services contract from his previous employer BAe for a piece of design equipment used in training simulators. An entrepreneurship programme introduced him to Dr Malachy Devlin, whose PhD was in advanced computer algorithms and architectures. Dr Devlin's skills complemented those of the Cantles and he was invited to join the company.

The breakthrough for the company occurred in December 1998 when Xilinx awarded Nallatech a contract to develop a board for their own design equipment, which is now in regular production, and Nallatech was the first company in Europe to be appointed an expert consultant in the Xilinx XPERT programme. By 2002, 75 per cent of the company's sales were to blue-chip clients in 20 countries worldwide, including Sony, Philips, Texas Instruments, BAe, Xilinx and Motorola.

The demand for Nallatech's products had increased to such an extent that further organic growth could let competitors with deep pockets overtake the company's technological lead. In 2001, Nallatech appointed David Armour to facilitate a financing round. The result was a £2 million equity investment by a VC company. This will cover the company for the next 3–5 years of operation, in which time a marketing department will be created, an office set up in the USA, and the engineering department expanded.

Nallatech review questions

1. Why are technology-based entrepreneurs in global markets from an early stage?

2. Why is it often necessary for technology-based entrepreneurs to operate with an overseas office (rather than through an agent)?

The examples of Nallatech and Aquamotive serve to illustrate the importance of internationalization and global markets for technology-based firms. While noting the importance of such factors, for the rest of this chapter we focus on different cultures and how such cultures can affect entrepreneurial behaviour, a factor which will affect the strategy adopted by entrepreneurial firms to exploit the globalization of local economies.

DIFFERENT ENTREPRENEURIAL CULTURES

In Chapter 1 we discussed how the entrepreneur is increasingly seen as a key actor in the economy and an *agent* of economic change. To perform this function the entrepreneur becomes a *problem solver*, reconciling limited resources with the environment. The entrepreneur may be seen as having the same function in each economy yet the environment and resources will vary. In different economies, different cultures will affect the degree to which the entrepreneur is able to be the key actor and hence influence economic change. Some economies are perceived to contain environments that are more conducive to entrepreneurship than others. For example, the USA has an economy that is regarded as 'entrepreneurial', that is, favouring the entrepreneur as the key agent of economic change. In this section we examine some of the factors that determine whether the nature of the environment and culture in different economies is entrepreneurial.

ADVANCED ECONOMIES

Two contrasting attempts to assess the level of entrepreneurial culture and activity in different advanced nations are examined in this section. The first of these is the Global Entrepreneurship Monitor (GEM) approach,[3] which is contrasted with the second approach, that of Casson.[4]

The GEM approach proposes that a causal relationship exists between the level of entrepreneurial activity in an economy and the level of economic growth. Economies will differ in their level of entrepreneurial activity that will directly affect the growth of a nation's Gross Domestic Product (GDP). GEM further proposes that factors affecting the level of entrepreneurial activity can by represented by means of a model. The GEM model consists of demand-side and supply-side factors that can be measured, as represented in Figure 11.2. The demand-side is represented by entrepreneurial opportunities and the supply-side is represented by entrepreneurial capacity.

The 1999 GEM report[3] examined 10 countries and classified them into three categories of entrepreneurial activity as follows:

1. A group of countries with high rates of entrepreneurial activity, including the USA, Canada and Israel.

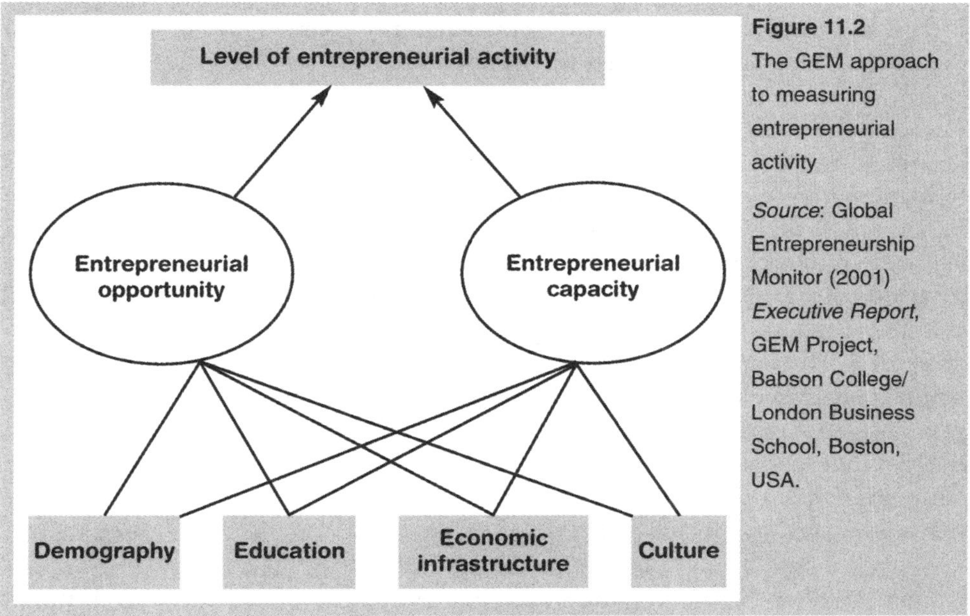

Figure 11.2 The GEM approach to measuring entrepreneurial activity

Source: Global Entrepreneurship Monitor (2001) *Executive Report*, GEM Project, Babson College/ London Business School, Boston, USA.

2. A group of countries with medium rates of entrepreneurial activity, including the UK and Italy.

3. A group of countries with low rates of entrepreneurial activity, including Denmark, Finland, France, Germany and Japan.

The 2001 GEM report expanded the number of countries to 29, including developing nations, which are surveyed annually to arrive at the measurement of entrepreneurial activity.[5] Comparisons across different cultures are obviously problematical. For example, GEM does not attempt to measure differences in culture. In addition, the use of a standard questionnaire survey across all 21 countries, when infrastructures are very different, is also, of course, problematical; nevertheless, the GEM reports have received much attention as a benchmarking approach to the level of entrepreneurial activity. The approach owes something to that of Casson[4] but is contrasted with it below.

Casson has attempted to analyse and classify the 'entrepreneurial' cultures of advanced, or developed, economies.[4] He makes a distinction between 'high level' entrepreneurial behaviour, which he claims is associated with the Schumpeterian concept of entrepreneurship, and 'low level' entrepreneurial behaviour, which he claims is associated with the Kirznerian concept of entrepreneurship (as discussed in Chapter 1, where an explanation is given of these contrasting entrepreneurship concepts). Casson compares seven advanced industrial economies (USA, Japan, UK, France, Canada, Sweden and Italy) and uses a scoring system for certain characteristics of cultural attitudes and environment, which are discussed below. Using this (weighted) scoring system he finds that Japan and the USA have the highest and most conducive entrepreneurial cultures, whereas (of the seven nations) the UK and Italy have the lowest ratings.

Casson claims that there are two groups of characteristics of national cultures that determine these ratings. First, technical aspects of a culture, which include attitudes to the importance of scientific measurement, to taking a systems view and hence to the degree of sophistication in decision making. Second, moral characteristics of a culture, which include the extent of voluntarism, types of commitment and attitudes to achievement. These groups of characteristics determine the extent to which a culture is conducive to 'high level' (Schumpeterian) entrepreneurship as opposed to 'low level' (Kirznerian) entrepreneurship. For example, Japan scores well on a national characteristic of a scientific approach to problems and a systems view to planning, which means a willingness to accept logistical planning and awareness of interdependency. Japan scores lower with voluntarism – the extent of willingness to allow freedom for transactions – an area where the USA scores highly. For example, this is explained by Casson[4] as:

"The philosophy of voluntarism ... supports a political framework within which people are free to transact with whomever they like. Voluntarism opposes the concentration of coercive powers on institutions such as the state." (p. 92)

Casson's hierarchy of national entrepreneurial cultures is an attempt to provide objective measurements of subjective and intangible values of different national cultures. As such, the measurements could be subject to widely different interpretations. For example, Germany is a rather surprising omission from Casson's countries chosen for comparison, and might score quite low on some of Casson's criteria, yet it would be accepted by many observers as a nation having a high level of entrepreneurial activity and behaviour. Casson's approach, nevertheless, is an interesting attempt to analyse different levels of entrepreneurial cultures in different economies. In identifying factors that affect attitudes to scientific endeavour, to moral codes, to commitments, the approach provides a useful framework for discussion of features of different national cultures and different levels of entrepreneurial activity.

It would be a mistake, however, to view certain economies as 'model' or prototypical entrepreneurial economies. Quite different cultures with different systems, attitudes and infrastructures can result in high-level, advanced entrepreneurship. For example, the Scottish Enterprise *Business Birth Rate Enquiry* investigated two advanced regional economies to examine factors that accounted for their relatively high levels of entrepreneurial behaviour.[6] The two contrasting regions, Massachusetts in the USA and Baden-Württemberg in Germany, had quite different attitudes, characteristics and environments. Massachusetts was characterized by little state intervention and a dependence on private sector venture capital to provide the risk capital to finance new ventures. Baden-Württemberg, however, was characterized by (regional) state-funded assistance and a reliance on bank loan finance to provide new venture capital. These two powerful regions demonstrate that different characteristics in society, and different infrastructures, can produce advanced high-level entrepreneurship.

THINK POINTS 11.1

International entrepreneurship and globalization

1. What are the main forces of increased globalization?
2. Why should no entrepreneur ignore these forces of globalization?
3. What methods and approaches might enable a firm to become international in operation? And why might international entrepreneurial strategies vary?
4. Distinguish between high-level and low-level entrepreneurial activity. Give examples of countries that demonstrate such different levels of entrepreneurial activity.
5. What are the main components of an economy that might affect the level of entrepreneurial activity according to the GEM approach?

The Importance of Developed Networks

The common feature of advanced entrepreneurial economies is the extent of networking. As discussed in Chapter 9, Baden-Württemberg contained advanced networks focused through local Chambers of Commerce. Massachusetts also had important networks, through venture capitalists and through integration with the Massachusetts Institute of Technology (MIT), which provided an important spin-out route for technology-based high-value start-ups. The importance of such support networks in Baden-Württemberg (B-W) has been highlighted by Kitching and Blackburn.[7] In a three-region study including B-W, Aarchus (Denmark) and London, they concluded that small engineering firms in London were disadvantaged by the lack of effective support networks. The level of networking and co-operative behaviour is not one of either the GEM or Casson's criteria; however, it is a recognized factor behind the success of areas such as the north-east of Italy, the *Third Italy*.

Scottish Enterprise, following its enquiry, identified networking arrangements among new firms as a way to achieve growth and hence job creation:[8]

“Networks are important: many of the solutions will be found in the actions of individual entrepreneurs, backed by their networks of family and friends. An important focus of action for the strategy is to improve the effectiveness of these networks and to make potential entrepreneurs more aware of what they can do themselves to achieve success. Part of this involves improving the

support given by the formal support networks in the private and public sectors.” (p. 4)

Similarly, in its more recent clustering strategy, Scottish Enterprise claims:[9]

“To compete, companies will need to build strong partnerships through which information and ideas can flow quickly and to best mutual advantage. Spanning customers, suppliers, competitors and other supporting institutions such as the universities, colleges, research bodies and the utilities, these specialist networks or 'clusters' create more of the sparks that fuel innovation and generate synergies that power them to greater competitiveness.” (p.1)

The benefits which can accrue to new firms operating in partnerships/networks/clusters are the potential advantages of economies of scope. Services and inputs, such as advertising, training, access to loan finance at advantageous rates, consultancy advice, financial services – items which a single firm cannot easily afford or secure when operating independently – can be secured when operating as part of a larger group. It has also been demonstrated that external linkages with other firms encourages innovation (See Chapter 7). For example, Edquist *et al.* have illustrated, in the case of Gothia in Sweden, the importance of networking for product innovation in small manufacturing firms.[10]

While the organizational structure of firms operating in some kind of cohesive way may be given the title 'networking', firms producing in any economy take on some of the attributes of a networking structure. For example, by engaging in production and trade a firm deals with suppliers and customers, which necessitates a degree of co-operation and trust. These factors are regarded as essential attributes to the successful functioning of a network. There is also an element of risk and uncertainty within any business relationship. Trust arises in response to the threat of risk and uncertainty. When trust exists it minimizes the potential risk and opportunism. Thompson underlines the importance of trust:[11]

“Co-operation is more secure and robust when agents have a trust because of the reputation of themselves and other agents in the network for honesty and consistency.” (p. 58)

Risk and opportunism can also be reduced via contracting but, as Macaulay notes, while detailed clauses are often written into contracts, they are seldom used:[12]

“contract and contract law are often thought unnecessary because there are many non-legal sanctions. Two norms are widely accepted.
(1) Commitments are to be honoured in almost all situations;
(2) One ought to produce a good product and stand behind it.” (p. 63)

In other words, an environment can develop where implicit contracting ensures a degree of trust and co-operation. Other, more established relationships can develop beyond that of a purely contractual kind. Sako[13] identifies two other kinds of trust: competence trust, being a belief that a trading partner will fulfil a particular task, and goodwill trust, which occurs in situations where initiatives are undertaken beyond the specific remit of a contract:[14]

“The role of goodwill trust extends beyond existing relations and includes the transfer of new ideas and new technology.” (p. 218)

While we have identified trust and co-operation as two attributes of an advanced economy, they can be strengthened to ensure the efficient operation of the network. This can be the key to the development of advanced entrepreneurial economies such as the Third Italy. For this to happen, contractual trust must be developed into goodwill trust. Economists using a game theoretical framework have demonstrated that where firms attach sufficient weight to future interactions, punishment strategies can be employed to secure co-operation. When joining a formal organization, such as a network, defectors and unco-operative players can be excluded. The problem with over-reliance on punishment strategies is that it could lead to distrust, which would threaten co-operation: 'If you trust me, why are you monitoring my behaviour?' Axelrod suggests that co-operation can evolve over a period of time, as firms gradually learn rules and norms of behaviour leading to co-operation.[15] In other words, through continual interaction and the belief of further interaction, the temptation to cheat diminishes. The participating firms build up reputations for co-operation and these reputations have to be protected.

We have indicated that where established networks exist, these can involve policing, by member firms, in an attempt to prevent opportunistic behaviour on behalf of the member firms. Where no existing meaningful networking arrangements exists, policy bodies could attempt to facilitate such developments. In local economies where this has proven to be more successful, such as the industirial districts of the Third Italy, this has occurred in conjuction with the key agents in the region, such as the small firm entrepreneurs themselves, the equivalent of the local Chambers of Commerce, the relevant financial institutions and the local authorities. In other words, the key players in the local economy have been involved in the design and implementation of the strategy, which is a major factor that these key players take on ownership of the organization.

Thus it has been argued that the level of co-operation, trust and networking is a key factor determining the level (high/medium/low) of entrepreneurship in different cultures. This networking may be characterized by different forms, but it seems to be a necessary condition for high levels of entrepreneurship. This may also explain why Mutual Guarantee Schemes (MGSs), which depend on trust, networking and co-operation, have been successfully established in some European economies but not in others (see discussion of MGSs in Chapter 5).

ECONOMIES IN TRANSITION

With the collapse of Communism in Eastern Europe and the old USSR, attention has focused on whether such nations can successfully transform into entrepreneurial economies (whether high level or low level). Such nations are regarded as emergent economies, as potential new areas for entrepreneurs seeking new markets. Therefore, if they can achieve the features of advanced economies, as discussed in the previous section, new opportunities for firms seeking growth become available. Such economies have been grouped together with the rather optimistic term of 'economies in transition'. As in Western Europe, this term hides a great diversity of development; different nations are at different stages in the transition process. This partly reflects the situation before the break-up of the old Soviet bloc, where some states had semi-market economies (such as Poland) and others were completely government controlled (such as the Baltic states). It also partly reflects the different features and characteristics of such nations.

These transition economies have certain features, as follows:

FEATURES OF ECONOMIES IN TRANSITION

- High levels of uncertainty and lack of information, implying opportunities for the Kirznerian entrepreneur.
- A lack of formal financial infrastructure and sources of finance.
- Limited markets and spending power within internal economies.
- No formal regulation, e.g. for regulating new firms/companies.
- Varying degrees of former 'market economies' giving different attitudes and approaches to entrepreneurial activity.
- Different levels of assistance, dependent on access to EU and Western development aid.

While there are obviously opportunities for entrepreneurship to flourish in such nations, innovative or high-level entrepreneurship is difficult due to the lack of infrastructure that can provide the level of finance or risk capital required; the lack of networks, co-operative behaviour and trust (identified above as important feature of advanced entrepreneurial regions) and the lack of infrastructure to support the small firm entrepreneur. In some nations, a tradition of co-operative ownership has led to problems with the establishment of individual entrepreneurship.[16]

Given the newness of 'economies in transition', there is still a limited literature on the characteristics of their culture and the way this affects entrepreneurial behaviour in such nations. However, a paper by Roberts and Tholen gives some insights into differences within these nations.[17] For example, their research showed considerable differences in Russia compared to other former Soviet bloc nations, with business development in Russia being more ad hoc and unplanned. Common characteristics across Eastern European nations included:

- **unstable political regimes and hence the need for businesses to grow quickly;**
- **a lack of tradition of business ownership and comparatively few family firms;**
- **the absence of support services.**

Differences were likely to be:

- **the source of new entrepreneurs (in Russia new entrepreneurs were former workers, whereas in other Eastern European nations they were more likely to come from management levels);**
- **higher growth ambitions in Eastern Europe compared to Russia;**
- **fewer women entrepreneurs in Russia (in other nations women entrepreneurs accounted for around 30 per cent of new business ownership);**
- **attitudes could vary to 'doing business' (entrepreneurs in Russia were likely to seek the 'big deal', whereas in other nations such as Poland, a more realistic incremental development was adopted by entrepreneurs).**

The transition economies of Eastern Europe and Russia can be seen as containing a wide spectrum of different stages of progression to higher levels of entrepreneurship. Undoubtedly, much of it is low level, characterized by Casson as Kirznerian, with some areas struggling to shake off attitudes that restrict creativity and innovative behaviour. In a comment that is probably representative of many such transition economies of Eastern Europe, one native writer on Slovenia comments perceptively that:[18]

"Traditionally, Slovenians have not been classified as exhibiting entrepreneurial traits. The collectivist culture, dependency upon the state, historical subordination by external powers and strong egalitarian values relative to the even distribution of social and material gains have combined with a conservative formal education system that rewarded obedience and diligence, and suppressed innovation and creativity." (p. 108)

Western European nations have been involved in assisting the development of infrastructures in transition economies in Eastern Europe; however, as one writer comments:[19]

> ***"It may well be that in the longer term, borrowing ideas which lead to a change in values and attitudes towards enterprise and small business, and which change norms of behaviour, is a critical task in ensuring that a culture sympathetic to small business is created." (p. 26)***

There can be considerable barriers to entrepreneurial and new firm development in the 'transition economies'. For example, adjustments have to be made by employees used to working for non-profit organizations to new cultures and working practices in small, privately owned firms. During periods of transition, recruitment of sufficiently motivated staff has been an issue.[20]

Smallbone and Welter, in a review paper, have summarized the key barriers to small and medium-sized firm development in countries in different stages of transition.[21] Those countries still at an early stage include the Ukraine and Belarus and are characterized by a number of barriers to the development of higher levels of entrepreneurial activity. The main barriers are identified below (see box).

ECONOMIES IN TRANSITION

Early stage barriers

- high levels of bureaucratic regulation;
- inadequate legal frameworks;
- inadequate financial institutions;
- high inflation;
- slow acceptance of private enterprise by government;
- the existence of relatively high levels of corruption.

By contrast, those countries at a later stage of transition, such as Poland, are characterized by the features given below (see box).

ECONOMIES IN TRANSITION

Later stage features

- essential legislative framework in place;
- financial infrastructure adjusting to needs of private sector;
- limited supply of investment finance;
- developing business support infrastructure but still not comprehensive;
- increasing competition from other indigenous entrepreneurs and small firms.

Lynn has also indicated that opportunities for entreprenurial small firm diversification vary across different economies in transition, providing greater entrepreneurial risk in those at earlier stages of transition.[22]

As illustrated above, transition economies are at very different individual stages of development, characterized by different levels of entrepreneurship. They face unique problems in transforming their society and cultures from former state dependency to ones where individual risk-taking is accepted and supported. The diversity of development, however, is such that to treat transition economies collectively is probably mistaken. Each nation, and indeed each region, will evolve their own entrepreneurial characteristics and activity. It would also be mistaken to prescribe solutions from the West. Lessons from emergent nations suggest that unique developments and infrastructures are required to overcome some of the barriers to entrepreneurial development. Some of these lessons are examined in the next section.

How important small firm entrepreneurs are in such transition economies has been the subject of some disagreement by writers. For example, one writer at least has claimed that small firms are still unimportant in such economies.[23] Others have claimed, in the case of Poland, that small firm entrepreneurs have become the engine of the Polish economy.[24] Such diametrically opposed opinions will take some time to reconcile, as the transition economies continue to evolve and further evidence of the different levels of entrepreneurial activity emerges.

THINK POINTS 11.2

International entrepreneurship and globalization

1. Give examples of nations that may be considered to be 'economies of transition' for the level of entrepreneurial activity.

2. Why are there likely to be large differences in the levels of entrepreneurial activity in such nations?

3. What features are likely to mark out the more advanced economies that are in this category?

4. Why should levels of networking, trust and co-operative behaviour affect the level of entrepreneurial activity in different economies, whether advanced, in transition or emergent?

EMERGING ECONOMIES

In contrast to transition economies, the emerging economies contain examples of nations in which the entrepreneur and the small firm have always played a role in their economic development. In India the small firm sector has been a prominent part of the economy for the past 50 years.[25] Other emerging nations, of course, provide examples where entrepreneurial behaviour has been far longer in developing. For example, Kenya is still considered to have low levels of entrepreneurial activity.[26] The most recent GEM report, at the time of writing, puts the emergent economies of Brazil, Mexico and Korea in its high band of entrepreneurial activity; India in its middle band; whereas some of the advanced industrial economies are in its low band, including the UK.[5]

There are obviously vast differences that exist in cultures and concomitant entrepreneurial levels of activity in different emergent nations. We do not attempt to discuss such diversity here. However, it is worth noting examples of successful entrepreneurial behaviour, how certain groups have overcome barriers to entrepreneurial development and the factors associated with such success. Such examples may have wider applications and lessons for advanced and transition economies.

In India, a high need for co-operation to overcome substantial limitations on resources has been observed and seems to be characteristic of entrepreneurial behaviour.[27] High levels of trust and co-operative behaviour have provided the basis for micro-credit unions,[28] examples of micro-business finance that have provided the basis for models of investment trusts in cities in advanced nations.[29] Demonstrating attributes of entrepreneurial behaviour that were discussed in our earlier section, India provides examples of flourishing networks and clusters.[30]

Other emergent nations often have complex factors that may have arisen from their history and inheritance as former colonial states, and which affect cultural attitudes to entrepreneurship. For example, South Africa, according to one writer:[31]

"with its many cultures and dynamic and transforming socio-political environment, represents a particularly problematic case study with respect of the application of arguments." (p. 27)

The legacy of apartheid in South Africa has caused some black entrepreneurs to respond entrepreneurially to adversity, whereas enterprise in other members of the black population has been stifled.[31]

The diversity of emergent economies is such that it is difficult to draw coherent patterns of factors that affect the level of entrepreneurship. For example, factors that may be important and conducive to entrepreneurial behaviour in one culture, such as co-operative behaviour and networks in India, may be restrictive in others. For instance, a study of small firm entrepreneurs in Turkey found that networks were dependent on traditional values, sectarian affiliations and the family environment.[32] The researcher claimed that such networks enforced their own inertia, preventing innovation in small firms in Turkey.

This complexity of factors reveals the infinite variety of entrepreneurial behaviour in emergent nations, variety to which we can only give the briefest of indications. In many cases we are only just beginning to learn about and appreciate this diversity. What is apparent is that we can't apply 'Western' solutions to such diversity.

THINK POINTS 11.3

International entrepreneurship and globalization

1. Give examples of nations that may be considered to be 'emergent economies' for the level of entrepreneurial activity.
2. Why are there likely to be large differences in the levels of entrepreneurial activity in such nations?
3. Using factors discussed in this chapter, why might they encourage high levels of entrepreneurial activity in such nations?

CONCLUSIONS

In this chapter we have argued that individual entrepreneurs cannot isolate themselves from the globalization of the economy. Every business trades in a global economy, which effectively means adopting strategies that enable the entrepreneur to optimize opportunities. These strategies will depend on resources available, key staff, type of product and the nature of technology. It may mean adopting joint venture strategies; it may mean adopting quality benchmarking techniques as part of a network of firms in a supply chain; it may mean forming networks to share resources, information and gain externalities. Entrepreneurs must think globally, even if they operate only in local markets.

Entrepreneurs who do 'internationalize' by operating in more than one country must be aware of different entrepreneurial cultures in different nations. We have examined how, in advanced economies, different regions can have very different cultures yet still be successful. We have suggested that advanced networks may hold one key to successful entrepreneurial development in advanced economies. In transition economies the legacy of Communism and state control has affected entrepreneurial development in different ways in different nations. Some have been more successful at overcoming this legacy; in others, lack of a recent history of business ownership has been more of a hindrance. Similarly, in emergent nations entrepreneurs have reacted in different ways to historical legacies, whether this is apartheid in South Africa or colonialism in the Indian subcontinent.

Casson has suggested that it is possible to identify characteristics in the cultures of different nations that will determine whether they have high or low levels of entrepreneurship. The GEM project has also attempted to identify factors affecting high- or low-level entrepreneurial activity. However, we have also seen that the infinite variety of international entrepreneurship defies classification and it can be claimed that inconsistent factors affect the level and success of entrepreneurial activity (such as networks). All entrepreneurs need to be aware of the global economy, but all entrepreneurs who wish to operate internationally must be aware of the infinite variety of cultures that still exist in the world economy.

SUGGESTED ASSIGNMENT

Students are required to work in a small group with an identified small firm entrepreneur in their locality. They are required to assess how the firm could be affected by the global economy. A group report should cover the following:

- introduction with case material on the firm;
- analysis of strengths and weaknesses;
- analysis of opportunities and threats with global economy;
- research with potential markets (DTI provides publications on overseas markets);
- conclusions.

REFERENCES

1. Atherton, A. and Sear, L. (2001) 'Are you one of us? An analysis of the interactions and linkages between small businesses and their local communities', paper presented to the 24th National ISBA Small Firms Policy and Research Conference, November, Leicester.

2. Curran, J. and Blackburn, R. (1993) *Local Economic Networks: The Death of the Local Economy*, Routledge, London.

3. Global Entrepreneurship Monitor (1999) *Executive Report*, GEM Project, Babson College/London Business School, Boston, USA.

4. Casson, M. (1990) *Enterprise and Competitiveness*, Clarendon Press, Oxford.

5. Global Entrepreneurship Monitor (2001) *Executive Report*, GEM Project, Babson College/London Business School, Boston, USA.

6. Scottish Enterprise (1993) *The Business Birth Rate Enquiry*, Scottish Enterprise, Glasgow.

7. Kitching, J. and Blackburn, R. (1999) 'Management Training and Networking in SMEs in Three European Regions: Implications for Business Support', *Government and Policy*, vol. 17, no. 5, pp. 621–36.

8. Scottish Enterprise (1993) *The Business Birth Rate Strategy*, Scottish Enterprise, Glasgow.

9. Scottish Enterprise (1998) *The Clusters Approach*, Scottish Enterprise, Glasgow.

10. Edquist, C., Eriksson, M-L, Sjögren, H. (2000) 'Collaboration in Product Innovation in the East Gothia Regional System of Innovation', *Enterprise and Innovation Management Studies*, vol. 1, no. 1, pp. 37–56.

11. Thompson, G. (1993) 'Network Coordination', in Maidment, R. and Thompson, G. (eds) *Managing the United Kingdom*, Sage, London.

12. Macaulay, S. (1963) 'Non-contractual relations in business: a preliminary study', *American Sociological Review*, vol. 45, pp. 55–69.

13. Sako, M. (1992) *Prices, Quality and Trust: Inter-Firm Relations in Britain and Japan*, CUP, Cambridge.

14. Burchell, B. and Wilkinson, F. (1997) 'Trust, business relationships and the contract environment', *Cambridge Journal of Economics*, vol. 21, no. 2, pp. 217–37.

15. Axelrod, R. (1981) 'The emergence of cooperation among egoists', *American Review of Political Science*, 75, 306–18.

16. Carlisle, B. and Gotlieb, A. (1995) 'Problems, Training and Consultancy Needs in SMEs in Russia – An Exploratory Study', paper presented to the 18th ISBA National Small Firms Policy and Research Conference, Paisley, November.

17. Roberts, K. and Tholen, J. (1997) 'Young Entrepreneurs in the New Market Economies', paper presented to a Conference on Enterprise in the Transition Economies, Wolverhampton, September.

18. Glas, M. (1998) 'Entrepreneurship in Slovenia', in Morrison, A. (ed.) *Entrepreneurship: An International Perspective*, Butterworth-Heinemann, Woburn, MA, pp. 108–124.

19. Batstone, S. (1998) 'SME Policy in Slovakia: The Role of Bi-Lateral and Multi-Lateral Aid', paper presented to a Conference on Enterprise in the Transition Economies, Wolverhampton, September.

20. A&O Research (1999) *Report on entrepreneurial activity in Görlitz: regional partnerships as a means of safeguarding employment*, A&O Research, Berlin.

21. Smallbone, D. and Welter, F. (2001) 'The Role of Government in SME Development in the Transition Economies of Central and Eastern Europe and the Newly Independent States', paper presented at the 4th International Conference on Enterprise in Transition, Hvar, Croatia.

22. Lynn, M. (1998) 'Patterns of Micro-Enterprise Diversification in Transitional Eurasian Economies', *International Small Business Journal*, vol. 16, no. 2, pp. 34–49.

23. Scase, R. (1998) 'The Role of Small Businesses in the Economic Transformation in Eastern Europe', *International Small Business Journal*, vol. 16, no. 1, pp. 13–21.

24. Erutku, C. and Vallée, L. (1997) 'Business Start-ups in Today's Poland: Who and How?' *Entrepreneurship and Regional Development*, vol. 9, no. 2, pp. 113–26.

25. Das, K. (1998) 'Collective Dynamism and Firm Strategy: a study of an Indian industrial cluster', *Entrepreneurship and Regional Development*, vol. 10, no. 1, pp. 33–50.

26. Dondo, A. and Ngumo, M. (1998) 'Entrepreneurship in Kenya', in Morrison, A. (ed.) *Entrepreneurship: An International Perspective*, Butterworth-Heinemann, Woburn, MA, pp. 27–41.

27. Schmitz, H. (1990) 'Small Firms and Flexible Specialisation in Developing Countries', *Labour and Society*, vol. 15, pp. 257–85.

28. Kashyap, S.P. (1988) 'Growth of small-scale enterprises in India: its nature and content', *World Development*, vol. 16, pp. 667–81.

29. Nicholson, B. (1998) 'Aston Reinvestment Trust', paper presented to the ESRC Seminar Series, The Finance of Small Firms, University of Middlesex, January.

30. Das, K. (1996) 'Flexibility together: surviving and growing in a garment cluster, Ahmedabad, India', *Journal of Entrepreneurship*, vol. 5, pp. 153–77.

31. Allie, F. and Human, L. (1998) 'Entrepreneurship in South Africa', in Morrison, A. (ed.) *Entrepreneurship: An International Perspective*, Butterworth-Heinemann, Woburn, MA, pp. 27–41.

32. Özcan, G.B. (1995) 'Small Business Networks and Local Ties in Turkey', *Entrepreneurship and Regional Development*, vol. 7, no. 3, pp. 265–82.

RECOMMENDED READING

Casson, M. (1990) *Enterprise and Competitiveness*, Clarendon Press, Oxford.

Global Entrepreneurship Monitor (2001) *GEM Executive Report*, GEM Project, Babson College/London Business School, Boston, USA.

Hisrich, R.D., McDougall, P.P. and Oviatt, B.M. (1997) *Cases in International Entrepreneurship*, Irwin, Chicago, USA.

Morrison, A. (ed.) (1998) *Entrepreneurship: An International Perspective*, Butterworth-Heinemann, Woburn, MA.

Scase, R. (1998) 'The Role of Small Businesses in the Economic Transformation in Eastern Europe', *International Small Business Journal*, vol. 16, no. 1, pp. 13–21.

12

PREPARATION FOR BUSINESS START-UP: RESEARCH, DESIGN AND IMPLEMENTATION OF BUSINESS PLANS

LEARNING OUTCOMES

At the end of this chapter you will be able to:

1. Describe different sources of information.
2. Discuss the potential of online databases for information gathering.
3. Evaluate the potential of primary and secondary sources of information for entrepreneurs.
4. Describe the importance of different sources of information for carrying out a feasibility study.
5. Describe the importance of qualitative research for the business plan.
6. Construct cash flow forecasts in the light of research undertaken.
7. Construct the main sections of a business plan.
8. Describe the importance of strategic planning for the successful development of a business.
9. Appreciate the importance of careful research for the accuracy of forecasts in the business plan.
10. Construct a cash flow forecast from some income and expense assumptions.
11. Discuss the advantages and limitations of (short) business plans for the adequate monitoring of business performance.
12. Discuss the wide variety and flexibility of business plans and the need for a coherent national standard.

INTRODUCTION

In this chapter, we examine the steps required for researching, developing and designing business plans in relation to the business start-up process. Designing and writing the business plan should be seen as the outcome of a careful research process and subsequent planning procedure, illustrated in Figure 12.1. We will discuss some of the stages of this research process in more detail, but the business plan should be regarded as part of that procedure, not as the end of that process.

The business plan is part of the ongoing process of strategic planning for the

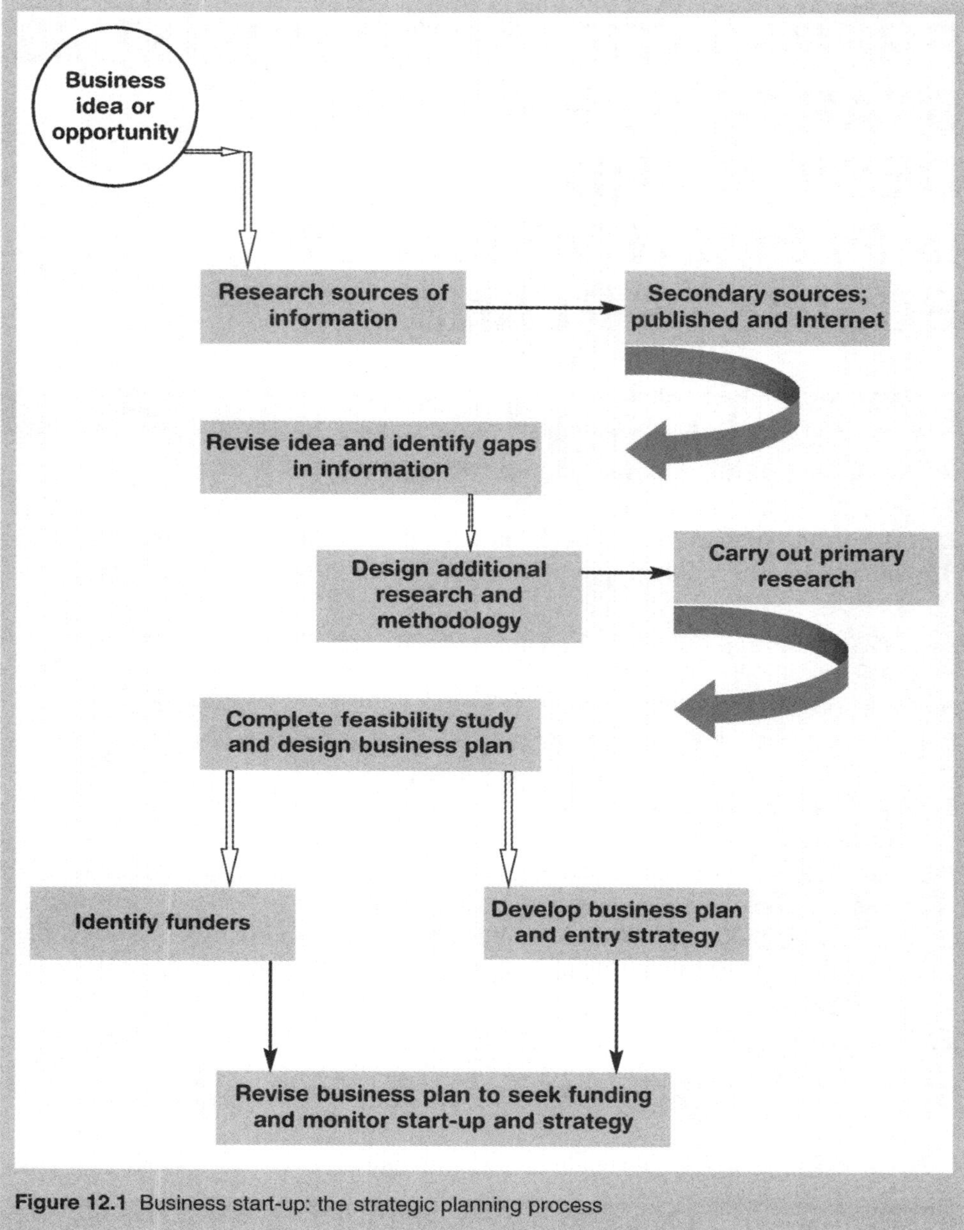

Figure 12.1 Business start-up: the strategic planning process

entrepreneur and small business, whether produced for a start-up business or for an existing business. The business plan can have several purposes:

PURPOSES OF A BUSINESS PLAN

- it may be produced to raise funding from banks, venture capitalists or perhaps it may be required to obtain grant funding from an agency such as a Business Link or a Local Enterprise Company;

- it may serve as a strategic planning document for the entrepreneurs, a plan to guide the business and serve as a basis for taking strategic decisisions;
- it may serve as a subsequent monitoring device.

Nowadays there are many guides produced by banks, enterprise agencies, accountants and published books on this ongoing planning process.[1] These are often also available in CD format with a 'skeleton' business plan format already provided. This chapter does not attempt to replicate these guides, which are often excellent summaries of the essential first steps in starting in business for new entrepreneurs. These guides are often a framework for organizing ideas and formulating a skeleton business plan. Many agencies and bankers would say that most new business start-ups are now required to produce an elementary business plan. This is a major advance on what might have existed only 10 years ago, when a person with a business idea could talk it over with a bank manager and produce some rough 'back of the envelope' calculations and walk out of the bank with a start-up overdraft. The majority of start-ups and even expansions of existing businesses are still planned on the basis of some cash flow forecasts with a few introductory pages of explanation. Although there have been major improvements, partly as a result of the expansion of the agency movement (discussed in Chapter 9), there remains tremendous variety in the standard of business plans that are produced with many that are severely limited in scope. There is, as yet, no research into the quality and effectiveness of many business plans that are produced. There is an often-quoted statement that a business plan is 'out of date as soon as it is produced'; yet, if a business plan is to be effective, this should not be the case. This chapter aims to explain how a business plan can be used effectively as an ongoing monitoring and strategic planning document which, although it may need revision, should be effective for several years. After all, if considerable effort has been expanded on research, as recommended in this chapter, then this should have some pay-off in the future planning and monitoring of the business.

One problem when designing and writing a business plan is that different funding bodies can have different requirements. We have seen in Chapter 5 that even among different bank managers there were considerably different opinions in terms of what was expected and required from entrepreneurs when producing a business plan for a start-up business.[2] In addition, venture capitalists will require a much more detailed business plan and perhaps more market analysis than a bank manager will, for the obvious reason that the venture capitalist will not be able to take security to safeguard his/her investment. An enterprise development agency will also vary in its requirements if a business plan is required to secure grant-aided funding. Thus, the advice to potential and existing entrepreneurs before writing the business plan is to seek to determine what format is preferred by the potential funder in terms of presentation and content. In the case of banks, this is usually obtainable from their own start-up guides and suggested formats on CDs. This will avoid unnecessary rewrites or changes to the presentation. It is best to have a full business plan that you are satisfied with and will serve you as the entrepreneur when taking strategic decisions for the business. Remember that the business plan should be produced for yourself, not for the potential funder, although it can be modified, shortened, summarized or extended for different potential funders (or users) and you should be prepared to make these changes. Some additional hints on the presentation of business plans are given at the end of this chapter.

Following the process illustrated in Figure 12.1, we discuss sources of information and research methods before discussing in more detail the design and implementation of business plans.

SOURCES OF INFORMATION

A business is often at its most vulnerable when launching because it will not have the same knowledge or information as its competitors. It will need to establish a range of contacts with suppliers and buyers, its credit rating will inevitably be low and it may not be aware of what credit it can take advantage of, or what are the best sources of advice. There may also be shortages of skilled labour and it will still have its reputation to establish. These problems can at least be reduced if a new business takes advantage of the wide range of sources of information that are now available.

Secondary Data Sources

Sources of information are conveniently classified as either primary or secondary information sources. All secondary information sources include officially published data, provided by the government or their agencies or by other institutions, such as banks, the CBI, trade unions, local authorities and Chambers of Commerce. In addition, most institutions have online web pages, which may provide access to sources of information. For example, the DTI provide information via the Internet through their 'businessonline' service, containing information on Business Links and their services.

It is likely that, in the future, printed sources of statistical data will become redundant as online access methods are further developed. However, at present these (official) sources are still being developed and reference to published sources is still necessary. The main sources of published data are illustrated in Table 12.1, with some comments provided on the relevance and value of each source.

Online and CD-ROM Databases

The development of online and CD-ROM databases has meant that it is possible to gain direct access to some databases, giving advantage in terms of direct access and downloading data. These can be powerful packages, providing additional graphical illustrations and analysis. Libraries have databases that store basic statistical data as a database on a CD disk. These may be databases of literature, journal articles or statistical and financial information. The development of these databases has made

Source	Type of data	Comment
National Income and Expenditure Year Book	Main components of national income and expenditure	Provides national or regional data on output, incomes, wages and prices
Annual Abstract of Statistics	Summary tables on population, national income and the labour force	More comprehensive than the Year Book
Census	Demographic and socio-economic data	Data analysis and trends often published separately
Monthly Digest of Statistics	Components of national income	
Economic Trends	Data on economic indicators	Useful indicator of major economic trends
Regional Trends	Regional economic indicators	
Population Trends	Demographic indicators	Useful predicator of future market trends
Financial Statistics	Data on financial indicators	Gives indications of credit activity
Bank of England Quarterly Bulletin	Gives detailed money supply and lending data	
New Earnings Survey	Income and hours worked of the labour force	Useful source on wage rates
Business Monitors	Data on specific industries	Useful indicator of trends in industry
Census of Production	National output data	
Labour Market Trends	Data on earnings and employment rates	Useful source of data with occasional articles
MINTEL	Market intelligence reports	Valuable source of intelligence and market data if available (fee-based)
Trade and industry journals	Qualitative data	Occasional articles can be useful
Patent Office	Information on existing patents	Provides a search facility
Euro-information centres	Various information on EU funding	Selected localities

Table 12.1 Secondary data: published sources of information

'literature searches' far easier and there is nowadays an increasing amount of information and basic data which is available on CD-ROM. Some examples are given in Table 12.2.

The Internet

Increasingly, an alternative approach to gathering information on competitors may exist through the Internet. Most, if not all, large firms have their own web page, and with the search engines that now exist, information on potential competitors can be obtained and downloaded. For suggestions of search engines in this area see the discussion on the use of the Internet for business in Chapter 8. Obviously, the importance of the Internet will increase in the future as more organizations develop their own web pages and an increasing range of secondary sources of information becomes available through the Internet. At present, however, printed versions of secondary sources are still in demand, because of the time taken to search the Internet and the variation in quality on web pages. For example, until a web address is accessed, at present the researcher is unlikely to know the extent of and quality of information that is made available. Table 12.3 gives some useful web addresses that can be valuable sources of secondary data and information.

Source	Type of data	Comment
EXSTAT	Micro-level data on companies	Brief summaries of trading records
FAME	Financial data on all companies	Powerful package including graphical illustration and financial ratios
DATASTREAM	Financial data	Financial analysis
KOMPASS	European database	Details on companies throughout Europe
Patent Office	Existing patents	Fee-based service
Local industrial directories (usually produced by local authorities)	Information on local companies	Quality of information and source varies

Table 12.2 Examples of online and CD-based databases

Web address	Type of information	Comment
www.statistics.gov.uk	Range of national data	The Office for National Statistics website. Variable quality of information. Summary articles
www.businessadviceonline.org	Broad range of business-related information	The Small Business Service website. Links to individual Business Links
www.newbusiness.org	Information on business start-up and advice provided by the Scottish Enterprise network	Updated information on the Business Birth Rate Strategy of Scottish Enterprise
www.dti.gov.uk	Range of industry information and government initiatives	Useful for links to other sites
www.scotent.co.uk	Information on support agencies in Scotland	Links to Local Enterprise Companies
www.cabinet-office.gov.uk	Up-to-date information on areas of government priority	Occasional reports available; employment reports, social inclusion reports
www.hm-treasury.gov.uk	Occasional reports. Tax information	Useful for updates on the Budget and taxation changes

Table 12.3 Sources of information on the web

Primary Data Sources

Although there are a vast range of secondary sources of information, it will be appreciated that they often do not provide the right combination of data or perhaps the data is incomplete. There are many situations when this is going to happen with the requirements of entrepreneurs for specific information regarding products and potential demand. As an entrepreneurial student, you may be preparing for entrepreneurship. As a potential entrepreneur who is considering launching a new product, the only way to find out information concerning potential demand is to carry out your own market research using survey techniques and questionnaires. For these reasons, we will concentrate on some of these survey techniques.

There are a number of ways that primary information can be obtained, the most obvious being through the use of questionnaires and a variety of methods, including postal surveys, telephone surveys and face-to-face interviews. However, data may also be obtained by observation: traffic surveys; by interview over a longer period of time (longitudianal research) to establish, say, whether there are changes in social attitudes; by records of respondents, e.g. purchases of families recorded by the Family Household Expenditure Survey, and so on. A brief survey of some of the methods that can be used to obtain primary data is given below.

Survey Methods

In a feasibility study and/or a subsequent business plan, you may wish to organize an analysis of potential customers using a survey method. There is a danger that these surveys will be done superficially, often containing questionnaires that only reveal the most basic information. You will need to aim for high-quality information and that can only be achieved if your questionnaire and survey is well designed. Since the information obtained from any survey is going to form the basis of conclusions and recommendations in the final business plan, the quality of this final business plan is going to depend crucially upon the research techniques used, and the design of your questionnaire. Past experience has found that student entrepreneurs that carry out their own research pay insufficient attention to the design of questions and the survey method to be used. Some careful consideration to the design of questions and survey method will improve the quality of analysis that can be subsequently carried out in either a feasibility study or a business plan.

The various methods include questionnaire-based surveys, normally postal, and telephone and interview-based surveys that may be more open-ended. Their main advantages and disadvantages are illustrated and summarized in Table 12.4.

Any survey method will depend, for accurate and coherent subsequent analysis, on the research design that will include the questionnaire design. It may be acceptable to combine these different survey methods, for example short interviews of a reasonable sample may be combined with more in-depth material with a small number of respondents. In-depth interviews are designed to obtain qualitative information, whereas larger surveys are designed to obtain quantitative information.

Method	Advantages	Disadvantages
Postal survey questionnaires	Sample size can be large if response is adequate	Low response rates unless incentives are used
	Relatively quick	Difficult to control for respondent
	Inexpensive	Responses may be unreliable
	Can provide useful basic data	Sample is self-selecting and may be biased
	May be the only option for some data	Only limited information can be obtained
	Responses can be completely confidential	Responses may be incomplete
	Structured questionnaires make for easy analysis	Questionnaire needs careful construction
Telephone survey questionnaires	Saves time over postal survey	Questions may be more limited
	Response rates are often much higher than postal survey	Respondent has little time to consider question
	Control over respondent and responses	Data may not be available easily
	Sample less likely to be biased	
Face-to-face interviews	Provide qualitative, in-depth information	Relatively expensive and time-consuming
	Complete control for researcher	May be difficult to analyse
	Flexible, allowing additional issues to be pursued	Subject to personal bias of researcher
	Most reliable method in terms of validity of response	
Focus groups	Group-based interviews to give synergy and encourage greater response	Requires a trained facilitator to get best results
	Can save time and expense	Group needs to be carefully balanced
	Well-tried method in market research	Difficult to record outcomes in a coherent manner

Table 12.4 Advantages and disadvantages of the main survey methods

THINK POINTS 12.1

Preparation for business start-up: research design and implementation of business plans

1. What are the different purposes for which we might need to develop a business plan?
2. What is the difference between primary and secondary sources of data?
3. You have been asked to advise a start-up entrepreneur on the most important sources of secondary data information; what advice would you give?
4. An entrepreneur wishes to research a new service; what advice could you give on different survey methods that might be used to identify customer needs?

Research Design

The research design and survey method used will depend on the aims and objectives of the research. For example, a full feasibility study undertaken in advance of a business plan will aim to provide both quantitative data and analysis and more in-depth qualitative information, so a combination of methods will be appropriate. Research design involves the selection of the appropriate survey method(s), the sample and the design of appropriate questions. The design involves matching the survey method or combination of methods to the aims of the study and research. Good research design and giving some thought to the survey method used will pay dividends later, in analysis and the production of the final business plan. This is shown in diagrammatic form in Figure 12.2.

Sampling Method

Some attention should be paid to how you are going to chose your sample. The sampling frame may be provided, such as the provision of a membership list of an association; you may then decide to survey the whole membership, the population, or choose a sample. How this sample is chosen will affect the interpretation that can be placed on the final results. The sample will be drawn from some sampling frame, such as *Yellow Pages*, a membership list, or perhaps the electoral roll in a local area. Samples may be of the following types:

1. Purely random. To select a true random sample, each member of the population must have the same chance of being selected. One way to choose a random sample is to generate random numbers using a computer programme. You use the numbers to select respondents from your sampling frame.

2. Representative sample. A representative sample contains a microcosm of the features of the population in their appropriate proportions. Thus, if you are surveying firms, you may wish to have representations of different firm sizes in

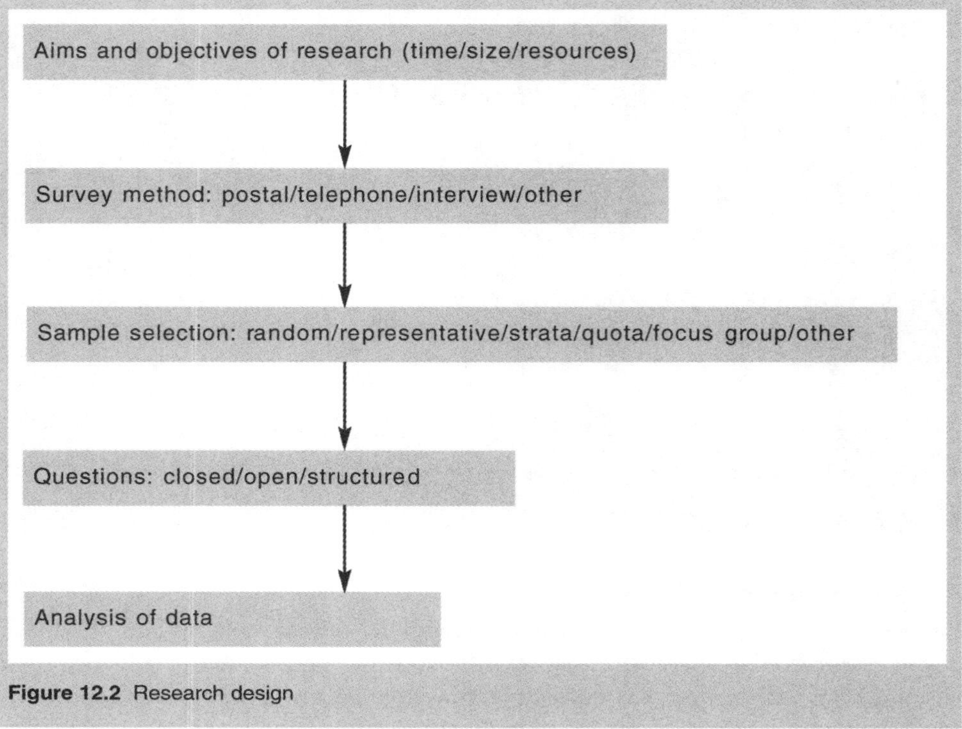

Figure 12.2 Research design

true proportions to their numbers in the population of all firms. That is, 97 per cent of your sample should employ less than 20 employees. The extent to which your sample can be representative will depend on having information about the population. Samples can only be representative if features of the full population are known, such as the proportion that earn less than 'X' per week, or the proportion that are male/female, married/not married and so on.

3. Stratified sample. A stratified sample attempts to breakdown the population in a coherent manner, using one or two criteria. One example might be the industrial sector of businesses that are respondents. The sample is not representative in having true proportions but you use the criteria of, say, industrial sector, as a way of ensuring some representation is included from each group or 'strata' of the population. Samples may be chosen randomly from each strata if the sampling frame permits this.

4. Quota sampling. Quota sampling is a commonly used technique in market research where a characteristic of the population (often age/gender) is used to provide quota numbers for interviewers to ensure a minimum number of respondents is identified in each category. In contrast to stratified sampling, this method is often used where no sampling frame is available.

Given limited resources and time, the potential entrepreneur may have little scientific basis for the selection of the sample. A small amount of research will pay dividends, however, and prevent the business plan appearing as though it has been 'thrown together'. A short methodology section in the business plan (or feasibility study) will indicate that some thought has gone into the research behind the plan and that assumptions are well founded, have a good basis and the strategic plans and projections are not haphazard or just 'dreamt up' by the potential entrepreneur. This can make a tremendous difference and also affects the confidence in which you can present a business plan to any potential funders. Good research will not leave any 'holes' that can be picked up on by potential backers of the proposition.

Question Design

As before, some care devoted to question design will pay dividends when analysing results of any research. There are some simple rules regarding good question design that are recommended and illustrated below (see box).

QUESTION DESIGN:

Some simple rules

Questions should be:

- unambiguous;
- relatively short;
- not be biased or leading in some way;
- designed to achieve the objectives of the research;
- structured, semi-structured or open-ended, but open-ended are generally best avoided in postal questionnaires.

New Developments

As well as extensive guides that can be purchased or are easily available, a modern PC will make a tremendous difference to the quality of the final printed version of the business plan, making it easy to produce forecasts on a spreadsheet, or to produce illustrations of market research through bar charts. In addition, there are software packages that provide a full business planning package. These will provide the essential sections and help you to produce financial forecasts. Of course, any amount of software cannot replace the basic planning process that requires adequate research. A business plan, however well produced and presented, will only be as good as the quality of data and information inputted into the software that is being used. Obtaining impressive software should not blind the entrepreneur or user to the need to provide good quality research and reliable data that will be processed by the software into a business plan that will serve the business as a valuable planning tool for a number of years.

THINK POINTS 12.2

Preparation for business start-up: research design and implementation of business plans

1. Why is research design important for the collection of primary data?
2. In conducting surveys, what would be wrong with just stopping people in the street to ask them questions?
3. What are the advantages of postal surveys (over other survey methods)?
4. What are the disadvantages of interview-based surveys?

DESIGNING THE BUSINESS PLAN

There are a number of standard sections that would normally be included in any business plan. These should include sections on aims and objectives, competitive analysis, marketing strategy and SWOT analysis. However, the sections required for the business plan will vary depending on the nature and sector of the business. A manufacturing business requires a different business plan from a service sector-based business. An exporting firm requires a different business plan from a components supplier who relies on large UK customers. A small start-up concern requires a different business plan from a medium-sized firm that is planning an expansion into different products. This is one of the problems faced by software packages that aim to provide a standard package that can be used by any business. A business plan has to be flexible and it is impossible to be prescriptive since every business plan will be different and will be produced for different requirements. Having said that it is impossible to be prescriptive, there are certain sections and guidelines that can be discussed, and we attempt to do this below. We attempt to discuss what might be expected from any business plan; you may not wish to include all of the sections – not everyone will have the time or resources to produce a full and detailed business plan. However, some thoughts given to the following suggestions will help to plan for possible different scenarios, competition and future changes that will be faced by the entrepreneur. Some thought at the research and design stage will improve the process of decision-making that is one of the main purposes of any business plan.

The following sections are recommended when designing the content of the business plan. As stressed above, these sections are not prescriptive and can be modified to suit the purposes of individual entrepreneurs and business plans.

1. Executive Summary

If your plan is carefully researched, constructed and written then an executive summary will be very useful to the users of the business plan, who may be potential funders or partner entrepreneurs in the business. Although the executive summary should be the first section, it is likely to be the last section to be written and it can be the most difficult because you have to summarize the main contents of the business plan. You will find it useful to build the executive summary around the competitive strategy.

2. Introduction

A short introduction should give some background to the business, the key people and an introduction to the nature of the business and the industrial sector. This section can be used to give the main aims and objectives of the business. In this section you will need to explain the purpose of the business plan. Is it to map out an expansion plan for the business? Or is it to provide a strategy for the launch of a new business? The aims and objectives could be placed in a separate section. You can also use this section to explain the rationale for the business and the business plan. Deciding how to differentiate between what are aims and what are objectives of your business can be difficult. A general guide is that aims can be considered to be quite broad and less specific than objectives. Objectives should be written in terms of specific outcomes. For example, an aim of, say, a five-year business plan would be to:

- **provide a strategic planning process to become a major competitor in the industry.**

Whereas an objective of the same business plan might be to:

- **achieve a fourfold growth in sales within five years.**

In the introduction you can provide additional information such as the nature of incorporation if a start-up, whether the company is registered, whether you have registered for VAT, in which case a VAT number should be quoted, starting employment levels, resources and whether there is a need for recruitment of staff and personnel.

3. Market Analysis and Research

In this section you can report the findings of market research that might have been undertaken, if primary research has been completed, along the lines suggested for this section. You should avoid the temptation to give too much information although, as suggested before, illustrations of the main findings can be quite useful for presentation purposes and for potential readers of the plan. However, those readers will not want to wade through a large amount of information and data. If the questionnaire that has been used as the basis for the research has been well designed then it should be possible to present the information and analysis in the form of summary tables, with brief comments on the significance and importance of market analysis and summaries of the potential total market and market share.

Some of the software packages that were mentioned above will give a market opportunity analysis. Additional analysis provided by such software can be a useful way of impressing any potential funder.

This section should be used to explain the assumptions behind income generation in the cash flow statements. Are the income levels based on the market research findings? Or perhaps they are based on other factors such as seasonality? State of economic levels of activity? Capacity levels if a manufacturing concern? Other factors should also be included, such as the basis of payment; income may be generated on the basis of commission, fees or sales. If sales of product and services are involved then some form of normal credit period will be assumed. Standard practice is, of course, 30-day credit periods between the sale taking place and income shown in the cash flow. If your business is subject to strong seasonal factors, such as high sales in the Christmas period, then this should be shown in the income statement of the cash flow, with allowance made for any credit period.

You may wish to consider outlining a brief marketing and distribution plan. This can be contained within the business plan, or if distribution is a major part of the firms' operations then it is recommended that a separate document is produced. The marketing plan effectively sets out how sales are to be achieved. It may include all aspects of the 'marketing mix' (see box).

THE MARKETING MIX

- Pricing policy.
- Promotion (advertising and other forms of promotion).
- Production. The outlets and marketing strategy should reflect the production capabilities of the business.
- Place (the location of the business and outlets used).

It is important to get these aspects of the business integrated, so that distribution channels and outlets do not overburden the production process and capabilities and that the outlets are appropriate to cope with production capacities. An example is given below to illustrate such concepts (see box).

EXAMPLE: MATCHING MARKETING WITH PRODUCTION

A small firm had produced a new form of hanging plant basket bracket that was produced to a new design and to a high quality. Yet the marketing strategy adopted bore no relation to production capabilities. The hanging bracket was marketed through a major gardening chain store and, as soon as one large order was placed, the firm could not cope with the production quantities required by a major multiple retailer. This problem of matching production to outlets and distribution channels cannot always be resolved, but planning for different outcomes in the business plan can help to resolve this problem if it does arise and a separate marketing plan can be a valuable planning tool for any business.

Access to retail outlets can be a problem for some businesses. You should demonstrate that you have given some thought to this and that you have secured retail outlets if the product is new.

4. Production Strategy

If your business is concerned with manufacturing and production, a separate section should be devoted to the planning of production. If the business is concerned merely with expanding, using existing production facilities, through perhaps obtaining new market outlets, then a separate production plan will not be necessary. However, you may need to plan for additional production facilities, new machinery and increased capacity. You will need to identify the additional resources and capabilities that will be required for new production levels. Additional skilled staff may be required and recruitment policies should be explained.

For a new start-up business that requires production facilities then obviously the business plan will need to describe how these are to be obtained and how staff are to be recruited.

The assumptions described in this section will form the basis for the projections in the expenses of the cash flow statements. There may be some research necessary in order to predict these figures accurately. You should not rely on your own estimates but obtain, as far as possible, quotations for supplies and equipment that is required.

Timing

An important element of any manufacturing business is timing production to co-ordinate with sales orders and to match supply of materials with production capabilities and sales orders. This is the importance of integrating market predictions and sales back through the production process and ensuring that the supply of materials and components is of the quality required to ensure that your customers are satisfied with the quality of the product. It must be stressed that orders can be lost if insufficient attention is paid to quality in the production process and obtaining quality from suppliers. This can be a particular problem for a new (producing) firm which can be vulnerable if certain specifications have been laid down to suppliers with no guarantee that these are going to be met. If possible, although this may use up some resources, it is worth trying to get some prototypes made to check quality. Of course, this will be a particular problem where new technology or new production techniques are being employed, which is one of the reasons why financing technology-based firms contains different and special issues from other types of start-ups.

Timing is important because resources and finance will be required before products are made, before sales are made and certainly well before income is received. This should be reflected in the cash flow statements. Any manufacturing and producing firm is certain to have a negative balance in the first part of the cash flow. It is better to plan properly for this, so that financial resources can either be set aside, if internal resources are available, or funding requirements can be made clear in the business plan.

Action plans

To aid the planning process it is worth providing an action plan. The purpose is to map actions against time and the production process. This will allow you to plan different requirements into the production and marketing stages as they are required over time.

An action plan can be produced for any type of business and modified to produce a Gantt Chart, which maps out the sequential timing of decisions against production/ sales levels and can serve as an action plan for the business.

5. SWOT Analysis

A section on SWOT analysis involves the identification of strengths, weaknesses, opportunities and threats for the business. There can be some dispute over how SWOT analysis can be presented and explained. To some extent, a SWOT analysis should consist of a series of short bullet points so that the reader can see quickly the main strengths and weaknesses of the business and the opportunity. However, the statements that comprise the bullet points should not be so short that they become perfunctory statements and the reader is left wishing for further explanation or elaboration. Again, a balance has to be struck between the need to keep the statements short (and preferably punchy) and the need to provide adequate information that the reader or user of the business plan can understand and comprehend.

A long list of strengths and weaknesses is not necessary; the list should be relatively short, perhaps half a dozen bullet points under each heading. It is also better to be honest. A long list of strengths followed by short list of weaknesses is more likely to raise suspicions from potential funders rather than impress them.

The SWOT analysis should 'fit' the business plan. If many strengths are shown but other aspects of the business plan are perhaps weak (such as limited analysis of market projections), then the SWOT analysis will look out of place in the context of the rest of the business plan.

There are few guidelines that can be given for the SWOT analysis. You as the entrepreneur(s) are the best person or people to write the SWOT analysis but, bearing in mind the points raised above, you should not be afraid to put down your strengths. These may include extensive experience in the industry, a reputation for quality, a high knowledge of working practices and employment conditions in the industry, existing contacts with potential customers and knowledge of new techniques/technologies that can be applied to existing production processes.

A SWOT analysis will always remain subject to personal preferences and views. The reader of the business plan should be aware of this and will make some allowances for this. A different individual could interpret strengths and weaknesses in different ways. Unless a business plan is put together by an independent consultant, a SWOT analysis will remain a personal statement by the entrepreneur(s) of their view of the strengths and weaknesses of the business and the opportunities provided by the business creation or development.

6. Competition

The competition and a section dealing with competitive analysis will follow from the identification of threats in the SWOT analysis. The extent of knowledge on competitors will probably vary, but it should be possible to identify the major competitors and what their relative strengths are. It is also useful to identify what strategies they have used to establish their market position. For example, have they used market nicheing strategies? Or perhaps more aggressive market penetration strategies? Or have they established their position merely by reputation and word of mouth?

In Chapter 2, we discussed some of the reasons for the success of small firms in the last 10 years. Often the reason for the start-up of a new firm by an entrepreneur is that they have recognized a market niche in an industry that is not being catered for by existing (large) firms. A small firm/entrepreneur will have the flexibility to respond to new market opportunities and market niches. While it is likely that the competition may consist of well-established firms, they may not have the flexibility to respond quickly to new market opportunities and challenges.

The analysis of competition should match the market analysis that is presented in the business plan as discussed above. If you are predicting a relatively large market share, this will not fit with a competitor analysis which suggests that the major competitors are strong, well established and that the market is difficult to penetrate. This analysis should also fit the marketing strategy. A market nicheing strategy will probably aim for high-quality services or products and likely outlets should have been identified that are willing to take your products or potential customers should have been identified if a service is being marketed.

You should also give some thought to potential competition. As opportunities develop, it could be that you may face competition either from additional entrepreneurs who start up or from retaliation from the existing competition. If the business plan is to be a valuable document over a three- or five-year planning period then some thought must be given to future competition and the likely sources of that competition.

It is possible to provide contingency plans. However, given that the number of different possible scenarios is infinite, you will not be able to provide a contingency plan to cope with all possible eventualities and possible reactions and strategies of the competition. All that can be done is to recognize that the outcomes that are predicted in the business plan can change and that the business plan should be used to monitor operations and then adjust predictions and/or strategy as circumstances change. As we will see later, it is desirable to conduct a limited amount of sensitivity analysis which will demonstrate to potential funders that you have thought about different outcomes and the reaction of existing and potential competitors.

7. Competitive Strategy

In some ways this is the most important section of the business plan, since it should map out the strategy for the survival, development and growth of your business. A strategy should be identified that will enable the business to meet the aims and objectives which will have been set out in the early part or sections of the business plan. The development of competitive strategy will be the natural outcome of the process of researching the market opportunity, the nature of the product or service, the SWOT analysis and the competitive analysis. Porter has provided a well-known taxonomy of generic market strategies, which are indicated below.[3] It is likely that your strategy will fall into one of these three categories. Porter shows that competitive strategies are a response to the environment in which the business operates; in other words, they are generic to the environment and the nature of competition faced by the business. Porter's three generic strategies are cost leadership, differentiation and focus.

Cost leadership

Under this strategy, the emphasis is on maintaining a competitive edge through a cost advantage over competitors. It may, but does not necessarily, involve undercutting competitors on price and maintaining a competitive edge on price. Undercutting through price does contain disadvantage: it may lead to some form of price war and even if competitors are at a cost disadvantage they may be better placed to sustain losses that might be incurred through any price-cutting war to gain customers. The advantage of cost leadership for entrepreneurs will lie in the generation of additional income that may result from cost reduction and which may be reinvested to provide new production techniques or new products.

Differentiation

This strategy may follow from a need to diversify production or services. It should not be confused with the third (focus) strategy. It is a strategy which is more likely to apply to existing and well-established producers where, perhaps, products have entered a maturity stage of their life cycle and there is a need to diversify production to maintain growth in the firm.

Focus

This third strategy is the one that is most likely to be adopted by new firm entrepreneurs. It recognizes that many market opportunities result from specialization. Small firms have the advantage that they can be flexible as well as specialized. The development of a focus strategy involves the identification of a market niche that has not been exploited by existing producers. The firm should be able to gain a reputation quickly for satisfying this market niche. Identifying the correct time to launch and exploit the market opportunity can be crucial. Thus there are market 'windows of opportunity' that appear at different times. Launching too early or too late can miss this opportunity.

Although Porter's categories have been very influential, they may be seen as a bit limiting. Kay has produced a useful alternative analysis of competitive strategy that focuses on the importance of value added that a firm can bring to the industry.[4] The extent to which a firm will produce value added to its costs of production will determine its success. For example, in an analysis of the retail food industry, Kay shows that the marketing strategies adopted by Sainsbury's and Tesco have been very successful at adding value to their operations. At the time of Kay's analysis, Kwik-Save was also identified as successful, with a very different marketing strategy aiming to capture the low-cost end of the market but still providing value added to its operations. The poor market performer (at the time) was Asda, which was considered to have a low value-added performance. However, since this analysis, Asda has responded with more aggressive marketing to increase its market share.

These analyses stress the importance of getting the strategy right for the type of market that you are in. There is no right or wrong strategy, but it must be appropriate for the business, the operation, the market and the business development plan.

8. Critical Success Factors

The identification of critical success factors is a useful section that should be included in the final business plan. It can serve as a useful summary and checklist of factors that have been identified in other sections of the business plan and is best placed towards the end of the business plan. Like the SWOT analysis, it will tend to be a personal reflection on the most important factors that are going to be critical to the success of the business. Thus, again, it is impossible to be at all prescriptive about this section, but you may like to think about the following factors:

1. What factors does the success of the business hinge upon? Are they factors concerned with gaining orders or are they concerned with securing quality from suppliers?

2. How important are the key personnel to the success of the business? If a key member of staff leaves, how will this affect the performance of the business? Can they be replaced?

3. How important is the recruitment strategy of the business; does the success of the business depend on obtaining appropriate skilled staff?

4. Does the success of the strategy adopted depend on how competitors react?

It is worth considering each section of the business plan and identifying just one or two key factors from each section that will be critical to the performance of your firm and to its success. As an entrepreneur, this will help you to identify key and critical success factors and, at later stages, to monitor performance. Having identified such factors, you can adopt strategies that can ensure success or lead to alternative arrangements. For example, if a supplier is identified as a critical factor, you may wish to investigate alternative arrangements of ensuring supply.

9. Cash Flow Statement

The cash flow statement contains the projected income from sales and other sources and all the expenses concerned with the launch and operation of the business. It is best prepared on a computer spreadsheet package, although business planning software, mentioned before, will have its own spreadsheet and financial analysis built in.

The importance of the cash flow statement is that it shows the timing of income and expenses and should show all these figures for 12 monthly periods of up to three or perhaps five years, depending on the potential users of the business plan. It shows the liquidity of the business at any one time and reflects the need or otherwise to raise funds and credit. If the business plan is being prepared for a bank manager then it is unlikely that cash flow forecasts will be required beyond three years. If, on the other hand, it is being prepared for a venture capitalist then it is more likely that five years' cash flow forecasts will be required.

A *pro forma* cash flow statement is shown as an example in Figure 12.3 but the detail of the cash flow will obviously depend on the individual business. The notes given in the *pro forma* are referred to below:

1. Income will consist of sales, fees and commission. It may include income from grants, or loans. The timing of the receipt of this income should be as accurate as possible. A small adjustment to the timing of the income can affect the extent of any negative or positive net cashflow.

2. Total income just calculates the total for each month. On a spreadsheet this is easily calculated by inserting the appropriate formula to sum cells and then copying across different cells.

3. Expenses can either be summarized under different headings or shown individually, but they should identify all expenses from the operations of the business. They will include equipment, materials, computing equipment, staffing, car leasing, insurance, and promotional expenses. Again timing is important and should be as accurate as possible since a small adjustment will affect the extent of the positive or negative cash flow.

4. Staffing should include national insurance contributions, although NI payments can be shown separately.

5. It is important to consider and include items such as insurance. If you are a producer you will need products' liability, public liability and employers'

HYPOTHETICAL COMPANY YEAR 1

	JAN	FEB	MARCH	APRIL	MAY	JUNE	JULY	AUGUST	SEPT	OCTOBER	NOV	DECEMBER	TOTAL (11)
INCOME (1)													
SALES		3500	4000	5000	5500	5000	6000	3000	6500	6500	7000	10000	62000
FEES	2025	2025	2700	2025	2700	2700		1350	3375	2700	3375	2025	27000
GRANT													0
ENTERPRISE AGENCY	7000												7000
													0
TOTAL INCOME (2)	9025	5525	6700	7025	8200	7700	6000	4350	9875	9200	10375	12025	96000
EXPENSES (3)													
MATERIALS	3500	3000	3000	3500	3000	3000	3500	3000	5000	4000	4000	3000	41500
EQUIPMENT													
MACHINERY	5000	5000	5000	5000									20000
COMPUTERS		3600											3600
PRINTER		1000											1000
VIDEO			750										750
TABLES			600										600
CHAIRS		600											600
BOOKCASES			300										300
WAGES (4)													
PRODUCTION	2893.75	2315	2893.75	2315	2315	2315	2893.75	2315	2893.75	2315	2325	2315	30095
OFFICE	607.5	607.5	810	607.5	810	810		405	1012.5	810	1012.5	607.5	8100
HEAT AND LIGHT			1000			1000			800			1200	4000
RATES				1000						1000			2000
INSURANCE (5)				1500						1500			3000
TELEPHONE			200			200			150			250	800
CONSUMABLES													0
PRODUCTION	200	200	200	200	200	200		200	200	200	200	200	2200
OFFICE STATIONERY	300	100	100	100	100	100		100	100	100	100	100	1300
VAT (REBATE) (6)						−1575			−1500			−1500	−4575
TOTAL EXPENSES (7)	12501.25	16422.5	14853.75	14222.5	6425	6050	6393.75	6020	8656.25	9925	7627.5	6172.5	115270
NET CASH FLOW (8)	−3476.25	−10897.5	−8153.75	−7197.5	1775	1650	−393.75	−1670	1218.75	−725	2747.5	5852.5	−19270
OPEENING BALANCE (9)	0	−3476.25	−14373.75	−22527.5	−29725	−27950	−26300	−26693.75	−28363.75	−27145	−27870	−25122.5	
CLOSING BALANCE (10)	−3476.25	−14373.75	−22527.5	−29725	−27950	−26300	−26693.75	−28393.75	−27145	−27870	−25122.5	−19270 (12)	

Figure 12.3 Cash flow forecast for a hypothetical company and pro forma

liability insurance. If insurance is a relatively small part of sales, perhaps only 2 per cent, it can be paid in just one annual premium.

6. If the business is registered for VAT then it will be entitled to a VAT rebate on VAT payments. These can be claimed every three months. Registering for VAT becomes mandatory over a threshold turnover of £52,000, but registration is advisable at levels below this to claim VAT rebates.

7. Total expenses merely add up the expenses in each column and this is easily done on a spreadsheet.

8. Subtracting the total expenses from the total income shows the net cash flow for each month. A general point to consider is that you will want to take advantage of any credit. This will be reflected in the liquidity of the business as shown in the net cash flow.

9. The opening balance for the first month is normally shown as zero, although it is possible to have reserves (from previous operations) shown in the opening balance.

10. The closing balance adds the opening balance to the net cash flow. The closing balance is automatically carried forward to become the opening balance in the next month (period).

11. The totals are added horizontally. They need not be shown, but they are a useful check on calculations and can show the total income and expenses for the year.

12. The last closing balance for the year will become the opening balance for the next year and should be carried forward as in previous months.

13. If drawings are made by the owner/entrepreneur, perhaps as a sole trader, then these are best shown as part of the expenses concerned with the operation of the business. These are likely to be regular withdrawals and they should be shown monthly rather than a total figure at the end of the year.

Note: The cashflow statement is not the same as profit and loss.

As stated before, the net cash flow reflects the liquidity of the business. The cash flow can show additional income, say borrowings, that are not part of the profit and loss account.

10. Forecasted Profit and Loss Account

It is advisable, but not essential, to forecast an end-of-year profit and loss account. This involves adding up all the trading income and subtracting the cost of goods sold to get the trading profit and loss. General expenses for the year can be totalled, including depreciation subtracted from the trading profit to get the net profit.

11. Forecasted Balance Sheet

A forecasted balance sheet is sometimes required, particularly by bank managers and this can be relatively easily calculated from the projections for the end of year.

The balance sheet is a statement of assets and liabilities at any particular time. As a planning tool it is not very useful since it only provides a snapshot at any one time, but it may be required by bank managers.[5]

A number of financial ratios can be calculated and included in terms of profitability and liquidity. It is not necessary to go into detail on the calculation and usefulness of these but standard business planning software will calculate these automatically.

12. Sensitivity Analysis

The purpose of the sensitivity analysis is to provide a test of the susceptibility of the business to changes, or a test of the robustness of the business proposition to cope with unforeseen changes. We can assume that most of the expense forecasts will be accurate. Despite careful research, income forecasts will still contain some uncertainty and the purpose of sensitivity analysis is to examine the consequences of changing some of the income forecasts on the net cash flow.

There is little point in developing any sensitivity analysis beyond the first year of operation, but it is worth formulating for the first year with what may be called an optimistic and a pessimistic scenario.

The optimistic scenario might increase sales and other income by 10 per cent. Expenses will need to be adjusted to allow for this, for example through increased cost of materials and perhaps through increased salary costs. The pessimistic scenario might decrease sales and other income by 10 per cent, with appropriate adjustments of expenses.

WRITING THE BUSINESS PLAN

As indicated before, the business plan is best prepared on a computer using a standard word-processing package, such as WordPerfect or Word, combined with a spreadsheet package, such as Excel or Lotus, for preparing the cashflow. Alternatively, business planning software that is now available will integrate a spreadsheet with a word-processing package that contains the main sections of the business plan.

Some hints and guidelines on the actual writing and presentation of the final business plan are given below.

1. The construction of the cash flow statement should be undertaken at a relatively early stage, perhaps after the analysis of the market research. This has the advantage of deciding what information and forecasts need to be justified and

explained in the written parts of the business plan. It also allows you to consider whether you have done sufficient research and whether there are any additional expenses that need to be calculated.

2. It helps presentation if you use relatively wide margins, for example we would recommend at least 1-inch-wide margins on either side and generous top and bottom margins. This avoids presenting too much information on one page and allows the potential user or funder to make notes.

3. Start each section on a fresh page. Again this improves presentation and enables the user to find sections quickly.

4. Avoid appendices where possible. If appendices are used to provide market research data, it can be difficult for the reader/user to refer to data while reading the appropriate section in the business plan. Appendices may be used sparingly, for example to give CVs. These may be left out of some versions of the same business plan.

5. Do use illustrations, although do not overdo this. Illustrations are useful and can help the user assimilate data quickly. Ability to do this, however, may depend on the sophistication of the software being used.

6. Do include a contents page at the beginning. This will enable the reader to locate different sections and navigate around the business plan quickly.

7. Most word-processing packages provide for the inclusion of headers and footers. Generous top and bottom margins will allow a header and/or footer to be inserted on each page of the business plan. This could be the name of the business.

8. Do include some notes to the accounts, whether you are providing a cash flow statement only or a more detailed set of accounts that may include profit and loss and a forecasted balance sheet. Even though assumptions will have been given in different section in the business plan, it will still be necessary to provide some notes on certain figures in the cash flow to explain what additional assumptions have been made or the basis of calculation.

9. Do put contact names on the front or inside page of the business plan.

10. The business plan should not be too long, perhaps 30 pages including appendices is a rough maximum (or 10,000 words). There is no ideal length, although there is little point in producing a very detailed plan if the only aim is to raise a small overdraft at the bank.

11. Bind the business plan securely (not stapled) and provide a cover that will stand up to some wear and tear. If you wish to, you can go the expense of getting the

business plan properly bound by a printer. However, we do not recommend this since you may want to change certain sections or add pages. Generally this will provide you with less flexibility than a loosely ring-bound document, which will allow you to modify and produce different versions of the same business plan for different users and funders.

12. Finally, an overused phrase is that the business plan should 'stack up.' We would defy anyone to explain exactly what this phrase means but it is best expressed by saying, in principle, that different sections should integrate and support the findings. Assumptions should underpin the forecasts. If different sections are out of line, this will be transmitted as an unbalanced plan. A strategy section that emphasizes small scale and quality should match other sections such as the market research, marketing strategy and cash flow forecasts.

THINK POINTS 12.3

Preparation for business start-up: research design and implementation of business plans

1. What different competitive strategies could be adopted by a start-up entrepreneur?

2. What is the difference between a cash flow forecast and a forecast profit and loss account?

3. How would a business plan differ from a feasibility study?

4. Assuming that the business plan has been completed, you have raised funding and you have started the business, what should you do now with the business plan:
   (a) Throw it away?
   (b) File it in case the funder needs to see it?
   (c) Continue to use it?

   Explain your answer.

IMPLEMENTATION

As stressed above, the business plan should not become out of date as soon as the business begins operations. Before operation and trading the business plan is a document that can be read and used by a number of different people – perhaps other partners in the business and perhaps analysed by potential funders. It should enable planning of the launch and operation of the first stage of the business.

After start-up or launch of the new product/diversification, the business plan can be used to monitor performance against the projections. It can be used to signal better (or worse) performance, dangers and critical success factors. Timings can be crucial and, if properly planned for, production and marketing plans can be matched against business plan forecasts to give some guide to the performance of the business. Income and expense forecasts can be matched against real outcomes to give an indicator of performance. During the first year any change in performance can be matched against the sensitivity analysis carried out in the business plan and this will give some indication of the extent to which the business is outperforming or underperforming forecasts in the business plan.

It must be remembered that the business plan is a strategy document as much as anything else. It is not there merely to provide a financial forecast, but to provide the strategy for the survival, development and growth of the business. If forecasts do prove to be substantially different from real outcomes then the strategy will need to be reviewed and possibly changed and adapted to different circumstances.

Assuming that the business plan has been produced for at least three years, it will need to be reviewed at the end of the first year. If there has been substantially different outcomes, it will be worth revising the business plan, perhaps by revising cash flow outcomes. Assuming that a spreadsheet has been used, this should be achieved relatively easily. The strategy and details provided in the business plan should still be appropriate and be used (perhaps with some modifications) for the remainder of the planning period. Forecasts should now be more accurate and more reliable. As the business plan is reviewed in subsequent years, the advantages of forward planning should become apparent. The business plan should serve to guide planning throughout the life of the business.

BUSINESS PLANNING: FURTHER HINTS

1. *Be confident in the presentation of the business plan.* Careful research should increase confidence. Potential funders will still need to be impressed by your own confidence and knowledge behind the forecasts that are in the business plan. No matter how well the business plan is prepared, potential backers are still influenced by presentation.

2. *Prepare for questions on the business plan.* Is there anything missed out? If profit and loss is not presented, some rough calculations will give a potential backer an indication and may prepare you for questions on this.

3. *Talk to different people.* Take the business plan to different agencies and backers and get their opinion on how it 'stacks up'.

4. *Don't give up if you can't raise funding at the first attempt*. For example, our own research has shown that different bank managers can have quite different interpretations of the same business plan, despite the advent of expert systems and credit-scoring.[2]

5. *If you can afford it, get the comments of a qualified accountant to verify the contents of the business plan*. Again, research has shown that bank managers are more (positively) influenced by business plans that have been authorized by accountants.

6. *Be patient*. Be prepared to accept a long process of vetting if you are seeking funding from a venture capitalist. The due diligence procedure of a venture capitalist can take six months or more before a decision is made on whether to back a proposition.

7. *Be prepared*. A venture capitalist will also be looking for exit routes. If you are seeking this form of funding, you will need to be prepared for the eventual initial public offering (IPO) (share issue) of the business, which is the normal exit route for a venture capitalist.

8. *Investigate*. Try to find out what potential funders are looking for. Many agencies that might provide funding have very specific criteria, for example that you attend enterprise training sessions (if a new entrepreneur). Whether you need these or not, you will have to attend to qualify for the funding. There can be an assumption on the part of existing managers (in large firms) that they do not need enterprise training, yet the management of a start-up small firm concern needs different management skills from that of a large firm.

CONCLUSIONS

The research, design and implementation of the business plan is part of the ongoing planning process within any firm. If, as a start-up entrepreneur, you adopt planning policies that are based on sound research and careful consideration of strategy, this will have benefits throughout the life of the business. We have already indicated that, during the 1980s, there were high birth rates of new small firms and entrepreneurs but, at the same time, these were accompanied by high death rates. One of the reasons for these high death rates has been insufficient thought and time given to planning properly the strategy of the new firm.

We started this chapter by commenting that nowadays business plans are much more common and much more detailed than they used to be; only 10 years ago, properly researched business plans were quite rare. One of the reasons for the growth in the use of business plans has been the spread of the agency movement and the requirement of banks (sometimes working in co-operation with agencies) for business plans if any funding is required. However, another reason is that it has become accepted that a carefully constructed business plan is important to the survival and successful performance of any business, whether large or small.

Business plans are very flexible. They can be used for both large and small firms, for start-ups or for expansion, for private or public sector organizations, they can be a few pages or a substantial document running to 10,000 words or more supported by appendices. Yet there is still no overall standard format by which any one individual business plan can be measured. It is because they are so varied and that they are relatively new (in evolution and use) that it is unlikely that there will be any standard produced in the near future. So how do we measure whether a business plan is of good quality? We are left with that overused phrase mentioned before, that a good business plan should 'stack up', or it should 'hang together'. We have indicated that what this really means is that the different sections should be interconnected, that it should be underpinned by careful research, by knowledge of the market opportunity and that the assumptions and research should underpin the financial forecasts.

SUGGESTED ASSIGNMENTS

1. Feasibility study

Students are allocated into groups to research and produce a feasibility study for an existing firm/enterpreneur. The feasibility study may involve a new market opportunity or a change of strategy, perhaps involving diversification from existing markets. The firm will be local and identified as a potential client by the university/college. Students work as consultants to the client enterpreneur and are required to:

(a) Negotiate and agree terms of reference with the enterpreneur.
(b) Use appropriate research methods including market research with an appropriate questionnaire.
(c) Identify and analyse existing and potential competition.
(d) Identify the additional costs/resources that will be required to exploit the opportunity.
(e) Examine the local labour market as appropriate if additional staff are required.
(f) Produce a feasibility study as a written report with sections that include: introduction/terms of reference, research methods, findings, conclusions and recommendations.
(g) Present the findings to the enterpreneur and obtain feedback.

2. Business plan

Students are required to complete a business plan through the development of research work carried out for the feasibility study. The business plan should follow the guidelines given in this chapter and include sections on:

- Executive summary
- Introduction
- Market analysis and assumptions for cash flow
- SWOT analysis
- Competition analysis
- Competitive strategy
- Required resources with budget
- Cash flow forecast
- Profit and loss forecast, if required by client
- Notes to the accounts
- Conclusions
- Appendices if required

The business plan will be produced by the students working in small groups and working as consultants for a client enterpreneur/firm. The completed written business plan will need to be of high quality, word-processed and produced with a hard cover. Students should complete a final presentation to the entrepreneur/ client.

REFERENCES

1. For example, Barrow, C. (1995) *The Small Business Guide,* Kogan Page, London, or any of the commercial banks' own guides.

2. Deakins, D. and Hussain, G. (1991) *Risk Assessment by Bank Managers,* Birmingham Polytechnic Business School, Birmingham.

3. Porter, M. (1980) *Competitive Strategy: Techniques for Analysing Industries and Competitors,* Collier MacMillan.

4. Kay, J. (1993) *Foundations of Corporate Success: How business strategies add value,* OUP, Oxford.

5. Fletcher, M. (1994) *Bank Managers' Lending Decisions to Small Firms,* Department of Entrepreneurship, University of Stirling, Stirling.

RECOMMENDED READING

Williams, S. (2000) *The Business Start-up Guide*, Lloyds/TSB Bank, Bristol.

Butler, D. (2000) *Business Planning: A Guide to Business Start-up*, Butterworth-Heinemann, Oxford.

INDEX